THE
MIRAGE MAN

THE
MIRAGE MAN

BRUCE IVINS, THE ANTHRAX ATTACKS,
AND AMERICA'S RUSH TO WAR

DAVID WILLMAN

BANTAM BOOKS I NEW YORK

Published in the United States by Bantam Books,
an imprint of The Random House Publishing Group,
a division of Random House, Inc., New York.

BANTAM BOOKS and the rooster colophon
are registered trademarks of Random House, Inc.

LIBRARY OF CONGRESS CATALOGING-IN-PUBLICATION DATA

Willman, David.
The mirage man : Bruce Ivins, the anthrax attacks,
and America's rush to war / David Willman.
p.   cm.
Includes index.
ISBN 978-0-553-80775-2
eBook ISBN 978-0-345-53021-9
1. Bioterrorism—United States—Prevention.
2. Terrorism—United States—Prevention.   3. Anthrax—War use.
4. Anthrax—United States—Prevention.   5. Ivins, Bruce E.
I. Title.
HV6433.35.W55   2011
363.325'3092—dc22   2011006232

Printed in the United States of America on acid-free paper

www.bantamdell.com

2   4   6   8   9   7   5   3   1

FIRST EDITION

Book design by Casey Hampton

For Joan, Alison, and Joseph

CONTENTS

PROLOGUE

The first of the mysterious infections emerged in South Florida, three weeks after the terrorist attacks of September 11, 2001. Robert Stevens, a sixty-three-year-old photo editor who worked at offices housing the *National Enquirer* and other tabloids, was diagnosed as having inhaled spores of anthrax.

President George W. Bush directed a member of his cabinet, Health and Human Services secretary Tommy Thompson, to hold a news conference on the case. Thompson played down its significance, saying there was no reason to believe Stevens's illness resulted from anything other than a natural exposure to anthrax. "It appears that this is just an isolated case," Thompson said. "There is no evidence of terrorism." When pressed by a reporter to explain how Stevens became infected, Thompson said health officials were unsure, but they knew he had hiked in the woods of North Carolina and drunk from a stream before falling ill.

Stevens died the day after the news conference, bringing Americans face-to-face with an unfamiliar menace. The anthrax bacterium is well known to veterinarians, much less so to physicians. Cattle and deer die every year in the United States from anthrax.

But people? Almost never. (And never by drinking from a stream.) Meanwhile, a colleague of Stevens, seventy-three-year-old Ernesto Blanco, lay gravely ill in another Florida hospital. Blanco, whose job entailed sorting the piles of U.S. mail sent to the *National Enquirer* and other publications of American Media Inc., had been diagnosed with pneumonia. Soon after Stevens's death, further analysis revealed that Blanco, too, was infected with anthrax.

The cases were not confined to Florida. In New York, blackish sores appeared on several people who worked at or had visited the offices of the three major television networks. They had been infected when spores came in contact with their skin. The source of the anthrax at the tabloid offices in Florida remained a mystery. But in New York, two anonymous, anthrax-laced letters eventually were found—one addressed to NBC News anchor Tom Brokaw, the other to "Editor" of the *New York Post*. A similar letter landed in the epicenter of the national government in Washington, addressed to Tom Daschle, the majority leader of the United States Senate. Another letter containing anthrax was addressed to Democrat Patrick Leahy, chairman of the Senate Judiciary Committee. Each letter came within a thirty-four-cent, pre-stamped envelope that bore the image of an eagle in the upper right-hand corner. Each 3½-inch-by-6¼-inch envelope was postmarked Trenton, New Jersey.

The notion that there was only a single, isolated case gave way to confusion and fear: The largest Senate office building was closed for decontamination. The House of Representatives was shut down. Delivery of mail was stopped at the White House. At the Supreme Court, the justices vacated the building for the first time since the structure opened in 1935.

Besides Robert Stevens, four others would eventually die of inhalational anthrax because of spores that had leaked out of letters and contaminated an untold volume of mail. Thomas L. Morris Jr. and Joseph P. Curseen Jr., postal workers in Washington, D.C., were exposed on the job. Kathy Nguyen, a hospital worker in New York City, and Ottilie Lundgren, a ninety-four-year-old woman in rural Oxford, Connecticut, were most likely infected by "cross-contaminated" mail. The anthrax attacks left seventeen others with nonfatal infections. Some ten thousand people at risk of infection were treated with antibiotics.

A benign portal of American life, the mailbox, had become an instrument of terror. The nation, it seemed, was in the throes of a biological attack. But by whom? The anonymous letters all contained photocopied messages with the date "09-11-01" and these three lines:

> DEATH TO AMERICA
> DEATH TO ISRAEL
> ALLAH IS GREAT

The letters gave impetus to profound shifts in federal policy set in motion by September 11: Overwhelming majorities of Congress voted to enact the USA Patriot Act, which, among other things, eased prohibitions against electronic eavesdropping. Speculation about who sponsored the anthrax attacks outpaced verified information. President Bush spoke of a "possible link" to Osama bin Laden. Hawks in the administration and elsewhere suggested that Saddam Hussein might be responsible. Their remarks, coupled with the president's emphatic statements that Saddam possessed biological and chemical weapons and might even be developing nuclear ones, intensified the clamor for war. Wildly inaccurate media accounts stoked the hysteria. In March 2003, the United States invaded Iraq.

The letter attacks gave rise to Bush's signature domestic policy response, Project BioShield, which provided billions of dollars to develop vaccines or antidotes against anthrax and other "threat agents." The government also began bankrolling construction of dozens of laboratories equipped to conduct experiments with deadly biological pathogens. Each facility promised to expand the nation's research capacity—but created new security risks by granting thousands of scientists unprecedented access to the tools of biowarfare.

Within days of the first anthrax death, the FBI launched what would become one of the most far-reaching investigations in the annals of law enforcement. Together with the U.S. Postal Inspection Service, the FBI conducted thousands of interviews and scores of searches. The investigators traveled to six continents to question potential witnesses. The case soon focused on one suspect above all others—Dr. Steven Hatfill, a scientist who had worked for two years at the U.S. Army's biowarfare research center at Fort Detrick, Maryland.

In numerous leaks to the news media, officials with access to investigative details made clear their belief that Hatfill was the anthrax killer. Investigators delivered the same message privately to congressional leaders and to those at the highest levels of the Bush administration. Yet the FBI never formally accused Hatfill of a crime. His reputation in tatters, Hatfill sued the FBI and the Justice Department.

Another scientist at Fort Detrick remained far less visible, although he was well known to investigators. The FBI had in fact called upon this scientist, Bruce Ivins, for early assistance with the investigation. When it came to the poorly understood complexities of *Bacillus anthracis*, the investigators, who had never before tried to solve an anthrax killing, could not have found a better-qualified expert at Fort Detrick. Ivins was an accomplished microbiologist who had established himself as an important anthrax researcher for the Army during the run-up to the 1991 Persian Gulf War, when military leaders feared that Saddam Hussein would unleash the bacterium on the battlefield.

Patent applications filed after the war listed Ivins and several Army colleagues as co-inventors of a "next-generation" anthrax vaccine. There was interest in a new vaccine because some service personnel blamed the old one for serious side effects, including immune system disorders. Yet the Pentagon's support for the new product ebbed and flowed with the politics of yearly budget cycles. Ivins could see that the perception of progress in the laboratory—and opportunistic speed—were crucial if the new vaccine was ever to be developed.

On October 22, 1997, Ivins had reason to exult over the arrival of a precious shipment: 1,000 milliliters of purified anthrax bacteria, suspended in liquid at the Army's Dugway Proving

Ground in Utah and delivered to him in seven sealed, shatter-resistant jars. As he examined the anthrax in the light of his lab's phase-contrast microscope, particles of the material glistened, a sign of purity. When he judged that one of the jars was not sufficiently pristine, he replaced it with anthrax spores that he and a lab technician had grown and purified at Fort Detrick. Ivins then combined the highest-quality material into two flasks and, ultimately, into one. All of it had been derived from what was named the "Ames strain" of anthrax—material shown to be more virulent than other strains used for laboratory research.

Ivins was a master of the delicate art of growing, harvesting, and purifying spores of anthrax. He now had a single, large batch to ensure consistency in his upcoming experiments on rodents, rabbits, and monkeys. Some of the animals would be injected with the new vaccine and then forced to breathe a spray of live anthrax. Success could lead to the crowning achievement of his career: a safer, more effective vaccine. Ivins stored the spores in his lab and accounted for them on an Army form called a Reference Material Receipt Record. He listed this batch as "RMR-1029."

THE
MIRAGE MAN

ONE

SHE WOULD *KILL* YOU

For most of the twentieth century, Lebanon, Ohio, embodied the small-town America of Norman Rockwell. It was a place where doors were left unlocked, where kids roamed without fear. The shops in the well-scrubbed downtown were family-owned. Malts and burgers were served at the soda fountains on Broadway. On the same street, Ohio's oldest inn and restaurant, the Golden Lamb, boasted of having entertained ten U.S. presidents, not to mention Henry Clay and Charles Dickens.

Founded as a stagecoach stop in the state's southwest corner, midway between Cincinnati and Dayton, the town of Lebanon ("LEBB-in-in") grew into a bedroom community of several thousand. Farm kids mixed with classmates whose parents worked for National Cash Register, General Motors, and Frigidaire in Dayton, for General Electric or the German-family breweries in Cincinnati, the Armco Steel plant in Middletown, and the paper mills in Franklin.

Lebanon's nicest neighborhoods were just south of downtown, across the double-arch Turtle Creek Bridge, built in 1897. The first cross street up the hill from the bridge was Orchard Avenue, home to prominent families, including doctors and for a number of years the town's only municipal court judge.

The second-generation proprietor of Ivins-Jameson Drugs, a Lebanon fixture with roots in the nineteenth century, also landed on Orchard Avenue. T. Randall Ivins—the T. stood for Thomas but most everyone called him Randall—had been in no particular hurry to take on the mantle of the family business. Born in 1905 in Lebanon, Randall was raised on the high ground above Turtle Creek, known as South Broadway Hill. His was a childhood that could have been scripted by Mark Twain. He and his pals filled summer days with baseball in an open lot; they rode the trolley to the outskirts of Cincinnati to see Buffalo Bill's Wild West Show. Their favorite swimming hole was a clear-water stream within walking distance of their homes, in the woods of McBurney Hills. There they fished and made use of an aptly shaped tree stump to stash their corncob pipes and tobacco.

Randall left Ohio after the seventh grade to attend Princeton Preparatory School in New Jersey; he later majored in journalism at Wilmington College of Ohio and psychology at Princeton University. After graduating he worked as a cub reporter at the *Commercial Tribune* in Cincinnati, and as a public school teacher, eventually serving as principal of Lebanon's elementary school. It was said that his time as an educator had not been entirely successful—he was simply too nice, incapable of imposing or maintaining discipline.[1]

In December 1933, Randall married twenty-six-year-old Mary Johnson Knight, a petite brunette who had earned a four-year degree in home economics from Florida Women's State College. Family lore held that the Knights were original settlers at Jamestown, that their genes were the stronger for having survived its hardships. Mary grew up in Brandon, Florida, near Tampa. She and Randall had met while he was vacationing in the North Florida Panhandle.[2] Shortly after marrying, the new couple set about planning a family, and they hired an architect to build a home, at 26 Orchard Avenue, just around the corner from where Randall had grown up. The structure was single story with European flourishes, notably an ornamental turret that rose to the right of the front door.

With his marriage to Mary, Randall decided on a career in pharmacy. He enrolled in classes at the University of Cincinnati to get his state license and he began working at Ivins-Jameson Drugs, the family store founded in 1893 and still operated by his father, C. Wilbur Ivins, a charter member of the Lebanon Rotary Club. Randall had arrived none too soon. In January 1938, C. Wilbur died from a stroke while wintering with his wife in Sarasota, Florida. The store was left in the hands of his son and Clarence Jameson, whom the elder Ivins had trained and had taken on as his partner nineteen years earlier.

On April 22, 1946, Mary gave birth to the couple's third and final child, Bruce Edwards Ivins. His older siblings were Thomas, eleven, and Charles, "C.W.," seven. Bruce would learn how to avoid Tom, who C.W. later suspected had grown to prefer the status of only child.[3]

Their brother, however, was not their biggest concern. Mary Ivins was prim, and comfortable using force to get her way. She was more than willing to impose whatever discipline the kindly Randall might shy away from. Her eruptions were frequent and could not always be predicted, though Bruce could see that C.W. made it a top priority to try to anticipate what was most likely to set her off.[4]

The Ivinses were well off by local standards and lived comfortably, while buying nothing on credit. The parents drove what C.W. called "ocean liners," the heavy, smooth-riding sedans that defined the golden age of Detroit's Big Four. Color photographs captured some of the family's early moments together, including Christmas Eve 1947. Bruce, one year, eight months, is seen pressing keys on the family grand piano while his brothers watched. A snapshot from a year later shows C.W., Tom, and, to the right, Bruce, tightly clutching his brown teddy bear.[5] By first grade, Bruce had devised an unusual way to play with it and other stuffed animals. He put blindfolds on them.[6]

Mary hovered over her youngest son, closely monitoring his academic progress and his interactions with other children. During his elementary school years, she always served as a room mother to Bruce's class. She and Randall also hosted elaborate, well-attended Halloween parties for Bruce and his classmates.

Apart from the gaiety of those parties, Mary Ivins ran the household like a boot camp. Her maxim for child rearing: "Idle hands are the devil's workshop." C.W. later explained, "Mom was one of these people that you had to justify your actions. So we learned always to have a reason for doing anything. If you acted on impulse you were gambling that you were going to get hit by lightning by impulse, too." [7]

Piano lessons were mandatory, and so was worship. Although Mary had been raised in the Southern Baptist church, she disliked the local Baptist preacher, so she and her sons attended Lebanon Presbyterian, where Pastor J. Taylor McHendry, "Little Mac," presided. After church each Sunday, the boys were required to wear their suits and ties for a midday meal in the family's formal dining room, outfitted with mahogany furnishings, a Czech chandelier, and French wallpaper with velvetlike flocking. "If Mom ever caught you feeling it, she would *kill* you," C.W. recalled. "Mom could explode. She didn't know about the sliding switch that could adjust the illumination. It was either on or off. She inflicted terror on all of us." [8]

During summers Mary Ivins would load Bruce and C.W. into the family sedan and set out on weeks-long excursions while Randall stayed behind in Lebanon. She designed the trips to educate her two youngest sons about American history and geography. Mary's snapshots document some of the places they visited: the Grand Canyon, the Painted Desert, Yellowstone National Park, the Colorado Rockies, the Badlands in South Dakota, Valley Forge, Pennsylvania. [9] There also was a trip, in 1956, in which the family traveled through Princeton, New Jersey. [10]

C.W. was a partial buffer between Bruce and their mother. "She just made him feel on edge, like she did everybody else," recalled Martha Leuzinger, who worked at the drugstore and saw a lot of Mary Ivins.[11] When C.W. went to college, by which time Tom had been out of the house for several years, Bruce was left behind in a household thoroughly dominated by his mother, his home life grimmer than ever as he prepared to enter the sixth grade.

When her husband's older business partner, Clarence Jameson, died in 1959, Mary, who had been working part-time at the pharmacy, consolidated her influence at the renamed Ivins Drugs. She fired anyone she felt didn't meet her standards. While Randall continued to mix and fill the prescriptions, Mary took control of everything else. Always formally dressed, her hair set in a wave, she built up what was, for small-town Lebanon, a lavish line of high-end cosmetics, including Chanel No. 5. She made sure that the other products, including the cigars, the refrigerated display of Whitman's Samplers, and the horehound candy drops, kept up front in a wooden barrel, remained in ample supply.

"When she came in, everybody was on their toes," said Jacqueline Sams, a student Mary had recruited as a part-time employee and whose brother was Bruce's friend. "You didn't know what was going to set her off."[12]

One day she spotted a rumpled man sitting outside on the concrete steps and, obviously, down on his luck. As the store clerks watched, Mrs. Ivins filled a bucket with water, calmly strode out to the steps, pretended to stumble, and thoroughly drenched the man.[13] On another occasion, suspecting that a couple of boys had done some minor vandalism to the Ivins residence, she waited until nightfall and, dressed in a disguise, splashed paint onto the side of the house where one of them lived.[14]

Bruce was a physically and socially awkward child, "Bruce the Goose," as his irreverent classmate Larry Buchanan nicknamed him. A story from his grade school years recounts the time he was playing softball and got thwacked in the head by the ball, batted not by anyone resembling slugger Ted "Big Klu" Kluszewski of the hometown Cincinnati Reds, but by a bookish and bespectacled girl, fellow fourth grader Elaine Kraus.[15]

While Randall Ivins had wandered freely as a boy, his youngest son was more comfortable with a chemistry set. Bruce took to wearing a plastic pocket protector, and he talked in rapid-fire bursts. He treasured the expensive microscope his parents bought him and he featured it in his ninth-grade science project. The instrument elevated Bruce from the crowd—enabling him to see things that his classmates could not with their hobby-grade microscopes. When he walked he leaned forward from the waist, as if propelled by an inner purpose. He was a teenager so preoccupied that he didn't seem to notice what some classmates remember to this day—the persistent knots of mucus suspended in his nostrils. With rare exception, he moved about Lebanon alone.[16]

Many of his peers at Lebanon High School found Bruce to be uncommonly high-strung, a boy who craved approval, yet struggled to fit in. Bob Edens passed by the Ivins residence every weekday afternoon and on weekends, delivering the *Dayton Daily News* on his sturdy Schwinn. Edens, a good enough student himself, thought Bruce was uniquely strange. "He was very intelligent and made sure that everyone around him knew it," Edens recalled. "He was a pain in the ass. He had an inability to become a part of the group in a natural way. So he would act out to get attention in weird ways. It was, 'I'm here. Notice me.' . . . He had no sense of normalcy. He was just a highly wound individual."[17]

Another classmate, Lana Neeley, a neighbor on Orchard Avenue, described what happened one day when her mother asked her to deliver something to the Ivins home. Lana was invited in, and as she waited for Mrs. Ivins, "Bruce asked me if I wanted to come down to the basement and see the gunpowder he'd just made." Lana, then fourteen, declined. She told her mother she would never set foot in the Ivins house again.[18]

One of Bruce's warmest relationships at Lebanon High was with a teacher, Dean Deerhake, a rail-thin man with a flattop haircut who crackled with enthusiasm. Deerhake taught junior year chemistry, and Bruce, who had excelled in biology the year before, was one of his top students. Ivins did not join the crowd easily, if at all, Deerhake recalled. "Some of the questions he would ask would cause some of the other students to turn their heads. He was different. A little bit out in left field."

Deerhake himself was a bit different. He wouldn't hesitate to stand on a desk if he thought it might strike a chord with his charges. It was Deerhake who persuaded Bruce to try the cross-country team, which he coached after school. Cross-country provided a team framework for a solitary activity: training regularly over long distances and running two miles on race day through the Ohio countryside. Bruce Ivins wasn't fast enough to race with the varsity, but in the fall of 1963, his senior season, he once finished with a time of 13:47, placing him thirteenth among forty or more "reserve," or junior varsity, runners.[19]

As Bruce's teacher and coach, Deerhake got to know his parents. He found Mary immediately intimidating, Randall just the opposite. The summer before Bruce's senior year, Randall approached Deerhake with a proposition, no doubt made possible by one of the pharmaceutical salesmen who regularly called upon Ivins Drugs: Would Mr. Deerhake be interested in driving Bruce up to the drug company's manufacturing plant in Michigan, for an insider's tour? It would be about a four-hour drive each way, entailing an overnight stay. The payoff would be a scientific opportunity for student and teacher—a chance to observe firsthand the conversion of raw materials to finished medical products.

Deerhake said yes, and he and his wife drove Bruce to the plant in their blue Ford Custom sedan. They saw a movie (*West Side Story*), and Bruce seemed to relax on the road with the cheerful Deerhakes. He fit in as if he was their son.[20]

Bruce's isolation as a teenager was magnified by his struggle to communicate with the opposite sex. "He was just a loner. He was so backward with women," said classmate Patricia McDaniel.[21] His plight wasn't made any easier by his self-consciousness about his looks. Gaunt, with a forehead that rose tall and flat, his profile was unmistakable. He was not considered a handsome young man. "His nose wouldn't be taken care of. He was just a duckling," said Ellen Leuzinger, who was a year younger.[22]

In his pained social interactions at Lebanon High, Bruce was operating, as in most aspects of his life, in the long shadow of his mother. One of the few schoolgirls with whom he was friendly was Elaine Kraus, the same Elaine whose batted ball had hit Bruce in the head in the fourth grade. Whip-smart and toughened by life on her parents' hundred-acre farm, Elaine was on a college-prep track, like Bruce. Both were members of the Current Events Club and the school newspaper staff, and they took part in campus stage productions.

Elaine, like so many others, viewed Bruce as nervous, hyper, "almost socially backward." She noticed that sweat would bead on his forehead and he would become so stressed he could hardly sit still. To his "Bruce the Goose," she was "Elaine the Brain." Proud nerds before the term had currency, they were buddies of a sort, though Elaine felt no romantic attraction to him. And Bruce never hinted at such to her. None of which deterred Mary Ivins. "*I don't know why you and Bruce aren't going out. You know, the two of you ought to get married.*" Elaine heard this from Mrs. Ivins whenever she saw her.[23]

In his four years at Lebanon High, Bruce was known to have had one date. It was with Ellen Leuzinger, one of three sisters Mary Ivins had recruited to work at the family drugstore, where Bruce also worked, on Saturdays. Ellen, hardworking and attractive, knew that Mrs. Ivins "was looking over every little piece of his life." Her date with Bruce, centered on that fall's homecoming dance, would be no exception.

Mrs. Ivins drove Bruce to Ellen's house in the family's Chrysler New Yorker. A lot of the kids at the dance were planning to bowl afterward. Chauffeured by Mrs. Ivins, Ellen and Bruce were perhaps the first couple to leave the dance, and they were definitely the first to arrive at the lanes. They bowled quickly and left—before any of their classmates arrived. Then it was time for Mrs. Ivins to drive Ellen home. "Everything was very, very planned." Ellen recalled Bruce as "tender-hearted, sensitive, a gentleman. . . . I don't remember if we held hands. We surely didn't have a kiss."[24]

It was clear to most of his acquaintances that Bruce was destined to be a scientist. He earned As in biology (he was selected for the biology honors club) and chemistry, and was strong in physics. In the summer of 1963, he was among a group of high-performing high school students who participated in a science program at Ohio State University. He was also invited to exhibit his special project, "Antibiotics," at the 1963 state fair in Columbus.[25]

Bruce had other talents. He was gifted at the family's Baldwin piano, and he sang in the school chorus.[26] He was the ubiquitous photographer of the school newspaper and the yearbook, the *Trilobite*. If there was a basketball game or other notable extracurricular event, Bruce more than likely was there, weighty camera and flash strapped around his neck.[27]

And yet it was because of Bruce's reticence that an English teacher, Joe Haven, decided to cast him in a stage role that might draw him out. He selected Ivins for this particular senior class play, Haven said, "thinking that this would be good for him. Give him a little more personality."[28] In *The People vs. Maxine Lowe,* a woman was on trial for the murder of her husband. In the climactic scene, the lawyer points directly into the courtroom audience at Vincent Barclay, who has been sitting silently while Maxine's fate swung in the balance.

Played by Bruce Ivins, the suddenly exposed villain tries to bolt but is forced to the witness stand. There, in a swift denouement worthy of Perry Mason, Ivins's character breaks down. "Yes, I shot him!" Bruce shouted, nearly sobbing as he turned to the judge. "Yes—I killed him—and I wanted to see her burn for it." His performance impressed cast and audience alike. "He had some real believable emotion," recalled Nick Nelson, who played the prosecutor.[29]

Throughout his struggle to fit in with peers, Bruce endured unrelenting dysfunction within his family. There were two ways to cope with Mary Ivins: Behave at all times in a way that might please her, or learn to hide from her those forbidden activities that were just too pleasurable to forfeit. Bruce, C.W., their father, and the employees at Ivins Drugs developed sensitive radar for the approaching storm. Usually by mid-morning, Mary Ivins would arrive in heels, a cyclonic force. Her tight smile, wielded with condescension, was not to be trusted. It cloaked her penchant for withering insults or worse. "The woman was a little touched," recalled Jacqueline Sams.[30]

By the spring of 1964, when Bruce reached his final semester of high school, Randall Ivins was fifty-nine years old, gray at the temples and almost bald, a weathered five-foot-eleven with tobacco-stained teeth and a paunch. From nine in the morning until at least nine o'clock at night he could be found at Ivins Drugs, dressed always with a professional formality, white coat, white shirt, tie.

Using a mortar and pestle, he still mixed and "compounded" some of what he dispensed. He made one of his medicines by percolating grain alcohol over dried herbs, yielding a tincture whose effectiveness he swore by. He also touted the benefits of his father's concoctions, including a product called "Snivi" (Ivins spelled backward), sold as a liver stimulant.

Randall was a generous man who tended to see the best in people. In 1956, when Don Hawke, one of his employees, asked Randall whether he would object if he, his longtime apprentice, bought a competing pharmacy directly across the street, the older man encouraged him to do it. Over the ensuing years, the two helped each other almost daily, exchanging materials, products, whatever either pharmacy might need. "Really nice man," Hawke recalled emphatically. "Helped me in some tough times."[31]

Little that Randall did appeared to please Mary. "I had seen her give him some tongue-lashings," said Jackie Sams. "So I was very careful. My thinking was, 'If she talks to her husband this way, no telling what she might do with me.' She was a little woman, but she had a very sharp tongue." Said Ellen Leuzinger, "She was very cruel to him, all the time. . . . Mr. Ivins was scared of her."[32]

Evening at Ivins Drugs was when Randall could be most at ease, with Mary at home. Jackie Sams would walk across the street to the Best Café to fetch dinner for Randall, which was always the same: chopped steak, smothered in A-1 sauce; cottage cheese, with more A-1 sauce; and a glass of tomato juice. At any time of the day Randall might also send her over for a slice of pie, usually apple. This was an indulgence absolutely forbidden by Mary Ivins. Hence a workaround: The pie was to be left inside a drawer of the store's back office. If Mrs. Ivins showed up, the slice became Jackie's. If he *knew* Mary wasn't coming, he'd fill his pipe and light up. At home he was forbidden to smoke indoors, except within his own bedroom and then only with a window fully opened—no matter the temperature in winter. Did Randall ever violate the rule? "No," C. W. Ivins recalled softly, "because he was living the next day."

For most of their marriage Randall and Mary maintained separate bedrooms. Her room adjoined her all-pink bathroom, off-limits to the other members of the household. Randall shared a bathroom with his sons. Despite their separate quarters, Randall found it difficult to elude the wrath of Mary. When the amiable proprietor of Ivins Drugs arrived at work with gashes on his arms, neck, or head, employees came to understand why. It was an ugly and poorly kept secret in Lebanon: At home, the volcanic Mary Ivins, standing only five feet tall, did not express her displeasure with words alone.

"Different little lady," said Don Hawke. "One day he came in and he had a black eye. Of course, she hit him with a broom. He said, 'She missed me the first time.' He was scared to death of her." Several years later Rick Sams saw Randall in the pharmacy with bandaging on his head. "Skillet," Randall said. Another time it was a fork to his hand. Things could and did get more extreme, as happened the night the phone rang at 2 A.M. at the home of Dr. Ralph Young, a neighbor on Orchard Avenue.

"Ralph, come down here. I've killed Randall."

Dr. Young raced out, expecting the worst. It was 320 yards from his home to the Ivinses' front door. To his surprise it was answered by Randall—alive but pressing a garment to his blood-splattered head. Dr. Young bandaged Randall up and, neighbors or not, sent along his bill. This house call, he told his wife, had exceeded the bounds of professional courtesy.[33]

The sustained abuse inflicted a lasting trauma on an unwilling witness—the couple's youngest son. Years later he would recall seeing his father bloodied by Mary Ivins.[34] More than a few of Bruce's acquaintances from Lebanon, among them Ellen Leuzinger, were certain that his mother's behavior damaged him. As Leuzinger saw it, "Bruce was programmed by her."[35] Don Hawke agreed. "I don't think Randall had a whole lot of influence on Bruce," he said. "All the influence on Bruce was from Mary."[36]

After graduating from Lebanon High, Bruce left Orchard Avenue for the University of Cincinnati, but he remained within his mother's reach. After living in a dormitory his freshman year, he rented an apartment with several other students, until Mary Ivins showed up. She declared the quarters unfit for her son and demanded that he move out, prompting all of the roommates, including Bruce, to relocate to a different apartment.

Bruce led a regimented existence as an undergrad, studying diligently, exercising on schedule, always taking vitamins. He was generally liked by his roommates, but he chafed at sharing his food with others and was said to have once made a veiled threat if more of it went missing: "I can drop something in your water."[37]

Some who saw him in Lebanon during school breaks thought that Bruce was progressing emotionally. "He was so much better," said Ellen Leuzinger. "Not so geekish. Smiled a lot more. Talked a lot more." He even took Ellen's younger sister, Martha, on a date to see the Monkees at Cincinnati Gardens.[38]

But despite these intimations of normality, something happened to Bruce at the University of Cincinnati—something that would consume him for the rest of his life. He noticed a young woman, a fellow undergraduate, whom he found appealing. She declined his request for a date, and with the passage of time, she forgot about his overture. Ivins, however, never stopped dwelling on her rejection. He attributed it to her membership in a Greek letter sorority, Kappa Kappa Gamma. From her lack of interest in him, an obsession would fester.[39]

TWO

YOU WILL ACCEPT ME

While Bruce entered graduate school at the university, his mother was rebuffing suggestions that she consult a doctor about her persistent abdominal pain. When she finally did, the diagnosis offered no hope. On June 23, 1970, Mary Ivins died of metastatic liver cancer in a Cincinnati hospital. She was sixty-three years old.[1] Although she had lived in Lebanon for nearly four decades, the local weekly, *The Western Star*, published no obituary. There was no memorial service.

Fierce in life, Mary was no less ornery about her death. "My mom, she never stopped fighting the Civil War," recalled C. W. Ivins. "She made it very clear in her will and her last wishes that she was not going to be buried in 'Yankee territory.'"[2] Consistent with her wishes, Mary Ivins's cremated remains were returned to Florida.

For the sixty-five-year-old Randall Ivins it was the end of a nightmare. Randall chose not to attend the interment of his wife's ashes. Freed at last from her abuse, he sold the pharmacy building at the corner of Mulberry and Broadway within a few months. After a run that had begun in the 1890s, Ivins Drugs was no more. Randall began traveling again, flying out to visit

C.W., who had moved to California and delighted in introducing his father to the Sierra Nevada mountains.

Bruce, meanwhile, had proven to be a strong college student, twice making the dean's list while majoring in chemistry and bacteriology. His strong performance as a bacteriology major won him induction to Phi Beta Kappa, the national honor society.[3] In addition to his core science curriculum, he had completed eighteen units of psychology.[4] After earning his undergraduate degree he remained to study for a master's in microbiology, which he received in late 1971. The university then accepted him as a candidate for a Ph.D. His doctoral advisor, Professor Peter Bonventre, remembered him as introspective, someone who would "happily sit in a dark room for an hour or two on his own. He was a little different."[5]

That didn't mean he was always silent. In countless conversations over breakfast or lunch with a fellow doctoral student, Robert Baughn, Ivins held forth on "a whole gamut of subjects" and was equipped to support his positions on matters both philosophical and scientific. "Bruce was one of the smartest people, book-wise, that I've ever known," Baughn remembered. "Common-sense-wise? He was the kind of guy that didn't have the sense to come in out of the rain."

Baughn recalled that Ivins was never without a black leather notebook in which he plotted out his daily movements in fine detail. Once when Ivins left it out on his desk, Baughn and another student leafed through the book. "It was, '7:15—brush teeth. 7:20—comb hair. 7:30—finish dress.'" Baughn considered Ivins quirky, not crazy, and he had seen a warm side to him. Baughn was touched by how, when he occasionally brought his young daughter to the university, Ivins would excitedly rush out into a corridor to play with her.[6]

Bruce, who with his brothers had been led by Mary Ivins each Sunday to the Presbyterian church in Lebanon, reassessed his faith after her passing, and in the spring of 1972 he converted to Catholicism. If she were alive and knew, he wrote in a personal letter, "my mother would have had a STROKE."[7]

Bruce became a regular at Newman Hall, a place for campus

Catholics to socialize and worship. He attended mass and prayer group meetings and played piano and other instruments there. His entrée to Catholicism was the result of his friendship with a fellow microbiology student, Bill Hirt, who, along with his wife, Ann, was impressed by Ivins's intellect and gentle nature. The Hirts also were struck by their friend's gift for music. Ivins would hear a song on the radio and say, "That sounds like B-flat." And then he would play it on the piano.

Ivins talked to the Hirts at length about his upbringing. His mother, he said, was severe and harassing. He regarded his father as contemptibly indifferent. Ivins said he felt so disconnected from his family that "I think I must have been adopted because I'm so different from my two brothers and my parents."[8] Even his conception, he told the Hirts, was devoid of tenderness. He later claimed in a note to them that he was born "a 'Positive Pap Smear Baby,'" adding: "Back in the mid 1940s, if a woman came up with a positive pap smear, she was told to get pregnant, and that the hormonal changes would correct the medical condition. Soooo . . . my parents couldn't stand each other at that time . . . and I became a medical necessity!"[9]

The bizarre tale about his conception was not as sad as the truth. Randall and Mary Ivins had planned the arrivals of their first two children, but by late 1945, when Thomas was eleven and C.W. was six and a half, the couple had no desire to add to the family. Hence Mary Ivins's fury when she learned that she was pregnant. In conversations with a sister-in-law, Ellen "Nell" Knight, Mary described how she tried to abort the pregnancy: Over and over, she descended a series of steps by bouncing with a thud on her buttocks. When he was an adult, his Aunt Nell shared this information with Bruce Ivins and other family members.[10]

Bill and Ann Hirt grew so fond of him that they chose Bruce Ivins to be godfather of their firstborn, a daughter. And they arranged a date for him with one of Ann's sisters, Mary Westendorf, a teacher at a Catholic school in Dayton, Ohio.[11]

Although they went out only once—Bruce took her to dinner

at the venerable Golden Lamb in Lebanon—Mary remembered enjoying their conversation. Bruce alluded to his unhappy childhood, telling Mary she was lucky to have loving siblings and a family that got along. Bruce struck her as a gentle soul, but also a loner in search of acceptance.[12]

Not long afterward Bruce went on a church-sponsored retreat, where he met Mary Diane Betsch, a nursing student from Cincinnati who was eight years his junior. Raised a strict Catholic in a German American family, Diane, as she was known, was almost as tall as Bruce at five-foot-ten. Unlike him, the strong and sturdily framed Diane was an impressive athlete, excelling at basketball, swimming, and softball. The couple did share musical talents: Bruce was a facile keyboardist, guitarist, and composer, Diane a strong violinist and vocalist. On August 22, 1975, they married in Cincinnati. Bill Hirt served as best man.

Bruce submitted his Ph.D. thesis ("Binding, Uptake, and Expression of Diphtheria Toxin in Cultured Mammalian Cells") in December 1975, and he and Diane headed to the University of North Carolina at Chapel Hill, where he took a position as a postdoctoral researcher and Diane worked as a registered nurse. A few months after the move, Bruce was awarded his doctorate in microbiology from the University of Cincinnati. It was mid-1976 and he was now thirty years old.

Bruce's boss, Priscilla "Pris" Wyrick, was a microbiologist brimming with passion for the work at hand. Though Wyrick occasionally played pickup basketball with Diane and found her "very charming and pleasant," Ivins was nonetheless apologetic about his wife, who he said felt intimidated in the company of academics. This, he explained, was why the couple didn't have people over for dinner and why Diane was not seen at social events with his colleagues.

Nearly every afternoon Ivins would excuse himself for an hour to clear his head with yoga or meditation in a campus library. He also could be spotted riding his bike around campus, carrying a sack with his juggling gear. He juggled four or five items at a time, anywhere someone might notice him. "He was very aware of other people's opinions of him. Very sensitive to other people's opinions of him," Wyrick recalled. Ivins was also curious and concerned about others' day-to-day woes. "He was enthusiastic and vivacious, just wanted to know about you and make you feel good." But Wyrick sensed a subtext: "If I'm this way to you, you will accept me." [13]

Solicitude aside, Ivins saw himself as a person of superior intellect and wanted badly to win admission to Mensa, the society of the brainiest.[14] On the other hand, he perpetually lamented his lack of "athletic looks" and skills—deficits he blamed for his inability to gain easy social acceptance. He wanted to be liked, but was always struggling to fit in, a man transparently convinced of both his gifts and his shortcomings.

The once reluctant teenager was nonetheless eager to strike up conversations, even when they distracted his colleagues from their work. And while his inquiries were never viewed as obviously sexual, he began prying into the backgrounds and the personal lives of female colleagues in ways that made them uncomfortable.

One of the women was Elizabeth Brownridge, a lab technician whose desk adjoined his. She saw Ivins as pleasant but an "odd bird." He was immune to nonverbal cues and either couldn't or wouldn't respect social boundaries. "He was very interested in people's personal lives. And sort of wanted to know more about you, personally, than sometimes you were willing to tell," Brownridge recalled. "Sometimes he would go too far and you'd just say, 'Knock it off.' He wanted to be accepted and wanted to be part of the gang, but he was just a little off the beam." [15]

Both Wyrick and Brownridge viewed him as a religious straight arrow. "Sort of a Mr. Goody Two-shoes," as Wyrick put it. "A good churchgoing man, good Christian, good religious sort of life." In fact, Ivins struck acquaintances as a man who would look down on them for any moral transgression.[16] Based on the side of him that they saw, Ivins was not someone people would have suspected of any form of wrongdoing, let alone criminality.

They would have been shocked, then, to know what Ivins was

up to one night in Chapel Hill. He had been keeping watch on the campus chapter of Kappa Kappa Gamma, the sorority he still blamed for his rejection by a coed years earlier. And now he was ready to do something about it.

As he approached the sorority house on this particular night he noticed that several lights were on, but based on his past observations he was confident that no one was inside. Ivins entered through a bathroom window. With the help of a penlight, he climbed a staircase and prowled the next level. When he found a locked hallway closet, he forced it open with a piece of metal.

Inside the closet, he found a few loose papers related to Kappa Kappa Gamma rituals. And something else, something of far more value to him: It was the "cipher," a glass-enclosed sheaf of documents used to decode the sorority's most closely held secrets. After roaming the chapter house for about an hour, he left with the prized cipher and other papers that interested him.[17]

Ivins was determined to learn as much as he could about the customs of KKG and other sororities. After he discovered that a doctoral student working across the hall from him had been active in Kappa Kappa Gamma, Ivins startled her one night with a spot-on recitation of the group's secret initiation rituals. Then he pressed for details. *"Why did you do that?"* Ivins asked her. *"What was the meaning of that?"* The doctoral student, Lori Babcock, tried not to let Ivins see how shocked she was at what he knew. "Bruce, I don't know what you're talking about." Babcock thereafter tried to steer clear of Ivins, but she would never forget the encounter. "The hair on the back of my neck went right up when he started toying with me," she recalled. "I just thought it was real creepy and bizarre."[18]

When Ivins questioned Priscilla Wyrick about her own student-days sorority, Chi Omega, she cut him off. Referring to his daily yoga and meditation regimen, she asked, " 'Okay, what's your mantra?' And he said, 'Oh, I can't tell you that.' And I said, 'Well get off the secret handshakes and secret passwords. That has nothing to do with your science. It's none of your business.' "

Yet Wyrick was pleased that Ivins had come to Chapel Hill. She found him to be conscientious, bright, a very good scientist.

He was meticulous about his experiments. "He was very careful at the bench. I never had to question the authenticity of his data. Ever." Wyrick also noticed that Ivins was "extremely careful" while handling cultures of bacteria.[19]

When it came to shutting off Ivins's unwanted personal inquiries, Wyrick had a distinct advantage: She was the boss. The lab tech Elizabeth Brownridge was not; nor was Lori Babcock; nor was another doctoral student who worked in a separate lab but in the same building, twenty-four-year-old Nancy Haigwood.

The daughter of a Marine Corps officer, Haigwood had moved frequently as a child and was accustomed to meeting new people. She sensed that the newly arrived Bruce Ivins "was clearly looking for people he could befriend and hang out with." She welcomed him to UNC and also met his wife, Diane. When Bruce learned that Haigwood and her husband were relocating to a new house, he and Diane joined ten or so other people who helped them move.

Haigwood, preoccupied with her scientific work, soon found Bruce Ivins to be "cloyingly nice" and "annoyingly intrusive." He had noticed a T-shirt she wore, identifying her former sorority, Kappa Kappa Gamma, and began pressing for details. What were KKG's practices, its customs, its rituals? As a graduate student, to what extent did she remain involved with KKG? Haigwood let Ivins know that she no longer had interest in these things—and even less in discussing them. "Most people, if you tell them to back off or change the subject, they would never come back to that. Bruce came back to it at least once a month— maybe more frequently. He was always doing it in a very kind of *friendly* way."

Ivins wrote a note to Haigwood, lamenting that she was not reciprocating his overtures of friendship. The episodes struck her as strange, yet harmless. Haigwood concluded that Ivins was in need of constant approval and attention, but she had no inkling what he was really up to.[20] Ivins tried to learn everything he could about her. He would drive past her home at any hour, just to gaze in.[21]

As Ivins would later confide to a psychiatrist, he envied Haigwood's self-confidence. He imagined her as both the ideal mother he never had and as his wife. He experienced Haigwood's distancing of herself from him as a replay of his mother laughing at him. Though in fall 1978 Bruce and Diane Ivins moved some three hundred miles from Chapel Hill to the suburbs of Maryland, where Bruce took a research position at the U.S. Defense Department's health sciences university in Bethesda, he continued to obsess about Haigwood. When he felt bothersome gastrointestinal symptoms, along with sadness and insomnia, he attributed all of it to her absence from his life. He confided to the psychiatrist that he had thought through various plans to kill Haigwood, including with poison.[22]

By the spring of 1979, everything that Nancy Haigwood had worked so hard for, all of her aspirations, hinged on converting the data in her lab notebook into her doctoral dissertation. The notebook was filled with hand-recorded hypotheses, results of experiments, notes, pictures, all the records that captured her scientific work over the previous several years. There was no duplicate. She kept the notebook in a locked room on the seventh floor of a laboratory building at UNC.

One day, it was gone.

She alerted her professors, UNC scientists Clyde A. Hutchison III and Marshall Edgell. Pris Wyrick got word, too. Eventually, after fruitless searching, the police were brought in. After a couple of days of sheer agony, Haigwood received an anonymous note. The writer said that the notebook could be found at a certain street mailbox in Chapel Hill, near the campus. The authorities found Haigwood's irreplaceable notebook there—inside the blue United States Postal Service mailbox. The case was closed without an arrest. Haigwood was left with her suspicions, which she would not voice to Ivins until a year or more later. "I put a little mark in my head thinking, 'The only person who's sneaky enough to do something like that is Bruce.'"[23]

It was preposterous to think that he would go to such trouble to steal the notebook. Right? Wrong. Ivins had executed a carefully planned scheme to punish Haigwood, the self-assured "Kappa," for her indifference toward him.[24]

With his furtive retaliations against Kappa Kappa Gamma and now Nancy Haigwood, Ivins was settling into a recognizable pattern: One-on-one, he was the smiling, devout colleague who exuded empathy. Behind people's backs, he was prone to bizarre, secretive acts of vengeance, for the most obscure of slights.[25]

THREE

SECRETS AVAILABLE

The value of biological warfare will be a debatable question until it has been clearly proven or disproven by experience. The wide assumption is that any method which appears to offer advantages to a nation at war will be vigorously employed by that nation.

—U.S. Secretary of War Henry L. Stimson, reporting
to President Franklin D. Roosevelt, April 29, 1942

I t was at a bleak moment during World War II—amid fear that the Germans were preparing to drop bombs filled with botulinum toxin on Britain—that the U.S. biological warfare program was born. Intelligence reports suggested that Japan also could launch a biological attack. Secretary of War Henry Stimson's emotionless note to FDR belied the terror evoked by such weaponry.

Needing a place for testing that was isolated but not too far from the Pentagon, officials converted a landing strip known as Detrick Field, outside Frederick, Maryland, into the center of the nation's infant biological program. The weapons of biological

SECRETS AVAILABLE25

warfare could be bacteria, viruses, or toxins that cause disease—and the targets could be humans, animals, or plants. Though no such weapons were deployed against the British or the Americans, the victorious Western Allies continued to work toward developing the munitions.[1]

After World War II, anthrax became a staple of the fledgling U.S. arsenal. It is a hardy organism that can lie dormant for many decades, if not centuries.[2] The disease it causes is not contagious, but anthrax had for centuries been a scourge to sheepherders and, later, cattlemen in temperate climates. Indeed, the pioneers of microbiology, Louis Pasteur and Robert Koch, had worked on anthrax because in their time, the late 1800s, it was a major killer of domestic grazing animals in Europe.[3] If ingested by an animal grazing on plant shoots in contaminated soil, anthrax spores can penetrate the lining of the gastrointestinal tract and swarm through the blood, attacking the spleen, the brain, and virtually every organ. As recently as 1945, an outbreak of anthrax in Iran was reported to have killed a million sheep. The advent of veterinary vaccines eventually reduced the toll, though anthrax deaths among livestock and deer have persisted in the United States and elsewhere.

As has been understood since the work of Pasteur and Koch in the nineteenth century, anthrax exists in two distinct states, as actively growing bacteria and as dormant spores. In the active state, it grows readily to high concentration within animal (or human) tissue, releasing toxins that can kill its host within a few days. And if the blood of a carcass is exposed to air, an abundance of newly formed anthrax cells can be deposited into the dirt, waiting in the dormant state, as spores, for the right conditions to infect and kill again.[4] The spores are inert, within a shell-like coating. But when moved to a favorable environment—as within a living animal—the spores revert to the active state, undergo rapid cell division, and unleash their deadly toxins. In the laboratory, anthrax is grown readily, either within a liquid broth or on the surface of an agar-based, gelatinous material in a Petri dish.

The bacterium's scientific name, *Bacillus anthracis*, derives from the Greek word for coal, *anthraki*. This alludes to the black scabs that appear on the skin of a person who develops cutaneous anthrax after exposure to an infected animal or its hide or fur.[5] Among humans, cutaneous anthrax is the most common form of the disease, accounting for 95 percent of reported U.S. cases. It is rarely deadly if treated promptly. Another form, gastrointestinal anthrax, is seldom seen, but is highly lethal. Infection by this second form results from eating the undercooked meat of a stricken animal.

The third form of the disease, inhalational anthrax, is also highly lethal and extremely rare. If treated promptly with an antibiotic, it can be cured. But because the initial symptoms of exposure—cough, painful tightness of the chest—can be confused with a bad cold or a range of other maladies, treatment may come too late to prevent death.

As the world's two superpowers vied for supremacy, anthrax appealed to both U.S. and Soviet military planners as a possible weapon because of its lethality and because it would remain stable during prolonged storage. And since it was theorized that, under ideal weather conditions, anthrax could be disseminated over a wide area, it was also thought capable of inflicting mass casualties. In 1950 and 1951, when military researchers sprayed two nonlethal simulants of anthrax from ships in the Pacific, two miles from San Francisco, the simulants dispersed with the wind and were detected at monitoring stations up to thirty miles away. The results convinced the biowarfare scientists at Fort Detrick that, had anthrax spores been sprayed instead of the simulants, many thousands of people could have been infected and killed.[6]

Yet the totality of U.S. laboratory work and field testing, from the 1940s to 1969, suggested that even the most carefully designed biological weapon remained undependable for use in combat: A change of wind direction, for example, might sweep anthrax back onto the attacking force. Compared to nuclear armaments that could be delivered from land-based cruise missiles, high-altitude bombers, or submarines, no biological agent seemed as reliable for killing on such a large scale.

And so on November 25, 1969, President Richard M. Nixon

announced that the United States would unilaterally end its biological weapons program immediately and "confine its biological research to defensive measures." Nixon's move proved catalytic: In April 1972, the Soviet Union agreed to the newly negotiated Biological Weapons Convention, providing the president a peacemaking boost at a time of upheaval over the Vietnam War. By 1975, more than one hundred countries had signed the treaty, which described use of the weapons as "repugnant to the conscience of mankind." There was, however, a glaring loophole: The treaty provided no means for verifying compliance.

Nixon was aware of the pitfalls inherent to deploying biological weapons—and he was no ingenue when it came to dealing with the Soviets. He had made a realpolitik calculation: With its nuclear arsenal, the United States possessed an overwhelming deterrent against any country that might consider waging biological warfare.

The shrewdness of Nixon's calculation could be questioned after an event several years later in the USSR. By signing the 1972 treaty, the Soviets had promised to abandon the development of biological weapons. Having come aboard in response to Nixon's first move, they assessed their options under the agreement. And then they cheated.[7]

Dramatic evidence of their betrayal emerged in early April 1979, when an explosion rocked a military research complex, 1,200 miles southeast of Moscow, in the low-slung Ural Mountains. The complex, officially known as the Military and Virology Institute, housed anthrax—and the blast loosed a plume of it on the city of Sverdlovsk, home to some 300,000 people.

As much as 10 kilograms of anthrax might have been released, some of it floating on the wind. The blast may have been caused by a missing air filter, which, because of a lapse in communication between workers, was not replaced before the beginning of a new shift.[8]

The first sickened patients were military and civilian employees of the research institute. Soon many others sought treatment, including employees from a ceramics factory nearby. The initial symptoms suggested pneumonia. However, the patients soon de-

veloped high fever, followed quickly by serious breathing difficulties, choking attacks, and even death. The bacterium killed at
least sixty-four people and caused more than one thousand others to be hospitalized. It was the worst biowarfare accident ever
recorded. Autopsies revealed advanced accumulation of fluid in
the lungs and other symptoms that clearly pointed to inhalational anthrax as the cause of death.[9]

The first media report of the incident was published six
months later, in October 1979, by a Russian-language newspaper
in Frankfurt. U.S. intelligence agencies sought more details—but
the Soviets denied that the institute was used for bioweaponry or
that there had been an accident. The deaths and hospitalizations,
the Soviets said, were caused by an outbreak of anthrax among
animals whose meat was then eaten by certain unfortunate residents of Sverdlovsk. American officials remained unconvinced. In
March 1980, during the first review conference for signatories to
the bioweapons treaty, the U.S. ambassador pointedly raised
questions about Sverdlovsk with his Soviet counterpart.[10]

The Americans made no move to withdraw from the treaty.
But the reports about the incident at Sverdlovsk resonated at
Fort Detrick, where years before Army scientists had worked in
secrecy to develop germ weapons. Nixon's decree in 1969 had
sent many of the old bioweaponeers packing, and also led to the
increased staffing of a newly formed scientific unit at the sprawling base: the United States Army Medical Research Institute of
Infectious Diseases. The microbiologists, physicians, and other
specialists at USAMRIID would also handle anthrax and other
deadly biological agents. Their stated mission, however, was
purely defensive: developing medical countermeasures, like vaccines, to protect U.S. forces in the event of a biological attack.

Sverdlovsk galvanized thinking in certain quarters of the U.S.
defense and intelligence establishments. If the Soviets were still
producing anthrax munitions, what else might they be doing to
gain an advantage? Was the biological weapons treaty sowing a
dangerous complacency? The best available answers were not
comforting. But other than renouncing the treaty and seeking a

resumption of the offensive program, what could U.S. defense planners do?

Compared to multibillion-dollar aircraft or missile defense programs with powerful political sponsors, USAMRIID was an orphan. Its budgets were unfailingly tight, its mission confined to developing the medicines to protect American forces. While the intelligence agencies continued to investigate the Soviets, USAMRIID formed a three-member committee with a modest goal: hire at least one new microbiologist, whose first assignment would be to test supplies of anthrax vaccine to see if the product would actually work.

The committee identified two candidates as best suited for the job. Both worked at the Defense Department's Uniformed Services University of the Health Sciences in Bethesda, Maryland, about forty miles south of Fort Detrick. "Almost a flip of the coin which one we went with first," recalled one of the committee members, senior microbiologist John W. Ezzell Jr.[12]

The Army offered the job to Susan Welkos, a microbiologist whose scientific qualifications were rated slightly stronger than the other candidate's. The interviews had been held during the first half of 1980. But by the time the offer was made, Welkos had accepted a position elsewhere. Army officials did not want to wait. The number-two-ranked applicant—Bruce Edwards Ivins— had solid references. He was co-author of a handful of published scientific articles, an indicator of promise.

Ivins had studied the genetic building blocks of a variety of pathogens: His doctoral thesis in Cincinnati was on diphtheria, the childhood killer of the early twentieth century. As an academic researcher in North Carolina, he was part of a team that had focused on chlamydia, the sexually transmitted disease. Most recently, at the Defense Department university in Bethesda, Ivins had studied cholera, a bacterial infection prevalent where drinking water is not protected from sewage. The hiring committee members saw something else that they liked—a self-effacing deference to authority.[13]

On December 2, 1980, the Army hired Ivins as a civilian microbiologist in USAMRIID's Bacteriology Division. His salary jumped from $16,000 a year to about $27,000. As was routine for microbiologists at Fort Detrick, the Army granted him a "secret" level security clearance—without any evaluation of his psychiatric fitness.[14] The Army knew very little about this man it had entrusted with one of the planet's most dangerous microorganisms. It did not know, for instance, that over the previous year or so he had been under the steady care of a psychiatrist, Dr. Naomi B. Heller in Washington. It was to Heller that Ivins had confided his burglary of the Kappa Kappa Gamma house and his frightening thoughts about Nancy Haigwood.[15]

Landing the new job provided the thirty-three-year-old Ivins with an abiding lesson: Fear—this time it was the Russians—could create opportunity for him.

———

Ivins got off to a solid start at USAMRIID. He was an able scientist, and colleagues found him likable. He entertained co-workers by juggling fruit, sometimes while lying on his back. At occasional after-hours gatherings, he played the piano and sang, reeling off clever lyrics about his colleagues. John Ezzell, who had had a role in hiring him, shared an office with Ivins in the Bacteriology Division and later remembered him as having "a really great personality. Always asked about your family."[16]

Again, his colleagues had no inkling that there was another side to Ivins. He was a master at affecting the vocabulary, ideas, and opinions he thought others wanted to hear. He observed their preferences closely, and tailored his behavior and conversation accordingly. To some, like his brother C.W., he was a no-nonsense conservative. To others, like Bill and Ann Hirt of Cincinnati, he was a big-hearted liberal. To Nancy Haigwood, Ivins could be a caricature of gender-neutral orthodoxy, once telling her, "If you're giving a public talk—I detest male-centric terms like 'seminar'—I'd love to come hear it."[17]

Unknown to his colleagues, Ivins remained obsessed with retaliating against Kappa Kappa Gamma. He had compiled a list of East Coast campuses with Kappa chapters, and had visited the Library of Congress to search telephone directories for the chapter addresses.[18] Apparently it was not enough that he had stolen the sorority's cipher several years before. One night soon after he had started his job at Fort Detrick, he drove for about three hours from his home in Maryland to West Virginia University, where he knew that KKG had an active chapter. He was careful to go there during a break in the academic calendar, when fewer people would be around.

This time no lights were on at the chapter house. Ivins again entered through a ground-floor window. Finding nothing of interest upstairs, he returned to the first floor of the chapter house, where, as before, he forced open a locked cabinet. Inside it he found Kappa's Book of Ritual, the complete compendium of its passwords and secrets. To Ivins, this was the Holy Grail. Since he already had the cipher, he would now be able to decode all the rituals. He slipped in and out of the house in less than half an hour. His round-trip was a manageable six hours. Now he held a sense of power over the sorority—and he liked it.[19]

When they moved from North Carolina to Maryland, Bruce and Diane had first rented a townhouse on Ridgeline Drive, in a densely built section of Gaithersburg, about midway between Washington and Frederick, home of Fort Detrick. The area was becoming a favored location for biotech companies, attracted by the relatively cheap real estate and proximity to agencies dispensing lucrative federal research grants.

By coincidence, Nancy Haigwood, now a Ph.D. virologist, had also moved to Gaithersburg, to take a high-level position at one of these fledgling companies. Haigwood didn't know it, but the condominium she and her fiancé, Carl Scandella, moved into was on the same street where Bruce and Diane Ivins had lived until just a few months before. The Ivinses had then bought a home directly across the street from Fort Detrick, but Haigwood's arrival on Ridgeline Drive did not escape Bruce's notice. After a mutual acquaintance mentioned that Haigwood was living in Maryland with Scandella, he had found their address in a public phone directory.

By this time Ivins, thirty-five, had grown openly critical of sororities and fraternities, venting his grievances against them in a signed February 19, 1982, letter to the local *Frederick News-Post*:

> [V]andalism, theft, maiming, and killing are a deeply rooted tradition with college Greeks. . . . College fraternity and sorority members invariably ignore, rationalize, or gloss over a myriad of detracting facts when discussing their organizations. They never talk about the cruelty; they never talk about the arrogance, the superficiality, the immaturity; they never talk about members having to abdicate the personal, individual decision-making process with respect to dressing, dating, and even thinking; they never talk about the subversion of truth, reason and honesty for the singular purpose of loyalty to a narrow group. . . . The one conclusion that can be drawn after rigorous examination of the pertinent facts is that college fraternities and sororities as they exist today are morally indefensible.[20]

Some months later, on a summer morning in 1982, Haigwood and Scandella were leaving their home when they noticed the letters "KKG"—the insignia of Kappa Kappa Gamma, her old sorority—spray-painted in red on an adjoining wooden fence. The letters were also sprayed on the sidewalk and on the back window of Scandella's 1981 Honda Accord hatchback. *"That's Bruce Ivins!"* Haigwood exclaimed on the spot. She and Scandella reported the vandalism to local police; no arrest was made.[21]

This was not the end of the vicious mischief that Ivins directed at Haigwood. One day the following year, a colleague mentioned to Haigwood that she had noticed her letter to the editor, published in the *Frederick News-Post*. The comment startled Haigwood; she had never written a letter to the newspaper. But there it was, in the May 9, 1983, issue of the paper—a six-paragraph letter defending hazing rituals conducted by KKG and other campus Greek organizations—signed by Nancy L. Haigwood, from her exact address on Ridgeline Drive:

> As a member of Kappa Kappa Gamma, one of our nation's oldest and most prestigious college sororities, I am continually dismayed by attempts of the media and other outsiders to disparage the Greek System. I am especially incensed at vitriolic attacks on our practices of "hazing," which non-Greeks fail to realize serve numerous valuable functions. . . . No one ever hears non-Greeks laud the accomplishments of those within their ranks, yet the proud Halls of American History are lined with men and women who were members of college fraternities and sororities. No matter what the press may say about us, I'm still proud to be in a sorority, proud to be counted among our country's very best.[22]

Unbeknownst to Haigwood, Ivins took the deception a perverse step further.[23] Three weeks later he mailed a photocopy of the letter published in Haigwood's name to a mother whose twenty-year-old son had died in a fraternity hazing incident. "Because of the nature of its subject matter, I thought that you would want to see it," Ivins said in an accompanying handwritten note to the mother, Eileen Stevens, of Sayville, New York, who had come to his attention through media coverage of her efforts to stop hazing abuses.

In the same letter, Ivins lauded Stevens's leadership while pressing her for copies of any personal accounts of "sorority hazing events" that she may have received. Ivins, who from May 1982 through May 1986 sent Stevens a total of five notes or letters, told her he wanted the testimonials for a book he was researching about the "codes, value systems and the verbal and physical abuse" of college sororities. He pressed her to pass along any testimonials of abuse involving members of Kappa Kappa Gamma or three other sororities. Ivins described himself as a distinguished civilian microbiologist working for the U.S.

Army. Several sorority members, he said, were cooperating with his efforts, including one woman who gave him a photocopy of "her organization's ritual book." His research had slowed, Ivins told Stevens, "due to some very exciting scientific developments which recently took place at Fort Detrick. (I'm working on the anthrax project.)"[24]

Stevens presumed that Ivins was sincerely concerned about sorority hazing, and she provided him with some of the research materials she had gathered. Three years later, in May 1986, Ivins sent her another photocopy of his counterfeit letter to the editor of the Frederick newspaper. He included a typed, single-spaced missive filling two pages, which expressed renewed outrage about Nancy Haigwood's supposed position. "I have personally gotten into several arguments about hazing with fraternity and sorority members, who have privately said that since I was not 'Greek' I had no right to criticize hazing," Ivins wrote, adding, "I wonder if only murderers have the right to criticize murderers, only Communists have the right to criticize Communists, only terrorists have the right to criticize terrorists."[25]

Throughout the four years that she received correspondence from him, Stevens felt no reason to question Ivins's motives. "What a nice man," she thought. "*He really gets it. He cares.*" The reality was that Ivins had constructed a web of falsehoods to malign a former colleague and to manipulate a bereaved mother who, out of despair at losing her firstborn, in 1978, was trying to help others. More than three decades later, her living room displays two large photographs of her son, Chuck Stenzel. She was saddened to learn about the lies that Ivins had told her. "It was cruel. How shrewd and how sly this man must have been that he could connive to this degree."[26]

———

Nancy Haigwood knew nothing about Ivins's letters to Eileen Stevens. But she did call the *Frederick News-Post,* and the newspaper published her one-sentence note disavowing the counterfeit letter.[27] She also called Ivins to confront him with her suspicions. "You're the only person who would have written this letter," Haigwood told him. "I know you did it and I don't appreciate it and you have to stop." Ivins stonewalled, conceding nothing, just as he had done years earlier, when she asked directly if he had stolen her lab notebook and then placed it in a mailbox.[28]

Haigwood had no way to pierce his denials. Nor did she realize the extent of his nefariousness. Ivins had begun assuming the name of Haigwood's fiancé, Carl Scandella, and a female derivative, Carla Sander, to send more counterfeit letters and to receive mail, some of it pornography. Now that he had both the cipher and the Book of Ritual, Ivins placed a classified advertisement in *Mother Jones* in May 1984:

> **Attention "non-Greeks!"** Receive a
> free copy of the secrets and initia-
> tion ritual of Kappa Kappa Gamma
> college sorority from an ex-
> member by sending SASE to:
> Carla Sander, P.O. Box 3536,
> Gaithersburg, MD 20878.[29]

Ivins was a close observer of his target audience and his choice of *Mother Jones* was no accident. Viewing the magazine as far to the left, he figured its readers would be likely to oppose sororities and other exclusive groups.[30]

Continuing to write in the name of Carla Sander, Ivins took out a similar ad in *Rolling Stone*. And he submitted another letter to the *Frederick News-Post*, also in that name, which was published under the headline " 'Secrets' available." The letter writer purported to be a past member of Kappa Kappa Gamma and praised a West Virginia University member of the sorority who had been mentioned in an earlier item in the newspaper. The letter continued:

> Speaking of the common "sisterhood" which we share, the Bible (Luke VIII, 17) tells all of us, "For nothing is hid that shall not be known and come to light." Several months ago, after much soul searching, I came to an important decision in my life: I decided that all of my sorority's secrets should be

made manifest, that her rituals should be known and come to light. If any *News-Post* readers wish to know the Kappa secrets and initiation ritual, I will be happy to share the information with them. All they need to do is send a self-addressed, stamped envelope to: Carla Sander, P.O. Box 3536, Gaithersburg, Md. 20878.[31]

(Including Gaithersburg, Ivins simultaneously maintained post office boxes in no fewer than four cities.)[32]

Ivins again got someone to bite on his deception. A writer for the *Chicago Sun-Times*, Jeffrey Zaslow, responded by mail to Carla Sander's ad in *Rolling Stone*. Sure enough, Zaslow received from the PO box in Gaithersburg two pages, single-spaced, about Kappa Kappa Gamma, including the sorority's password, pledge, handshake, and motto. Zaslow devoted a column to his long-distance transaction with Carla, calling what she did "a calculated act of revenge."[33]

Possessing the secrets of Kappa Kappa Gamma emboldened Ivins to seek gratification in more direct ways, too. At one point, he arranged to perform music for the KKG chapter at the University of Tennessee in Knoxville. The scientist who could delight Army colleagues with his improvised ditties made a different impression on the Tennessee coeds. As he sang the words from the secret rituals of Kappa Kappa Gamma, sorority members called the police, who escorted Ivins out.[34]

And so Ivins continued living a double life, his public face that of the playful Ph.D. microbiologist. After moving to Maryland, he had entered a local talent show and won with his juggling routine. Among other tricks, he could juggle several balls while riding a unicycle. Ivins sought out other enthusiasts, too, teaching an adult education course in juggling at a high school and forming the Gaithersburg Jugglers, later the Frederick Jugglers.[35] Through the 1980s, his name and picture appeared regularly in local news articles about his or the group's activities.

Ivins's differentness took many forms, some of them quite public. The 1986 explosion of the space shuttle *Challenger* and, with it, the death of teacher-astronaut Christa McAuliffe, animated him to an extreme. He promptly sought to copyright an instrumental he wrote in her honor, "Christa's Song (Reach for the Stars)." A year later, Ivins wrote a letter about McAuliffe to NBC television, in which he pitched an idea for creating a miniseries focused on her life story. Ivins addressed his letter to 30 Rockefeller Plaza in New York City; NBC rejected his proposal.[36] In 1988, when he learned that an elementary school about twenty miles from Frederick was going to be dedicated in McAuliffe's honor, Ivins contacted the school principal, Eugene Haines, saying he wanted to perform the instrumental he had written. Haines found Ivins to be "kind of kooky," but after a face-to-face meeting at the school in Germantown, Maryland, the principal allowed him to participate in the school's dedication, which was attended by McAuliffe's parents.[37] (The same year that McAuliffe died, Ivins was drawn to another famous female astronaut, Sally Ride. He drove fifty miles to see her speak that fall at Goucher College, in Baltimore. Two decades later, he would post under a pseudonym a dozen or more messages about Ride on the Internet, alternately praising her and soliciting information about what college sorority she may have belonged to.)[38]

Oddities aside, Ivins was establishing himself as a skilled scientist with anthrax. In August 1984, he and five colleagues won second-place honors at that year's Army Science Conference for their research paper, "A Molecular Approach Toward the Development of a Human Anthrax Vaccine." He received positive performance evaluations and steady raises in pay.

Bruce and Diane Ivins appeared to have a stable future in Frederick. Although she was no longer working as a nurse, she brought in steady income from a day-care business she ran at the couple's modest home. The timing seemed right for starting a family. Bruce, however, could not beget children. The couple registered with a state agency, and in the fall of 1984 they adopted one-year-old twins, Amanda and Andy. The children had been living with foster parents in rural Flintstone, Maryland. After the adoption, Bruce and Diane decided to preserve the twins' connection to their first caregivers—foster parents Kay and Jerry Andrick. The families would share Thanksgiving and other occasions, almost always at the Andricks'.

As parents, Diane and Bruce had starkly different styles: Diane, not unlike Bruce's mother, doled out the discipline. Bruce, mirroring his father, hewed to a pick-your-battles approach that never seemed to find one. Yet whatever the parenting differences between Diane and Bruce, they took steps to fortify the twins against any stigma they might feel about being adopted. "I just always remember them telling us," Amanda recalled, " 'We got to pick you. Not all parents get to. But we were lucky enough to pick you.' "

Amanda didn't know why her parents were unable to have children of their own, but she knew that the problem had to do with her father. Her only knowledge of what the difficulty might have been stemmed from a spare comment her mother had made. "She said, 'Your dad couldn't.' " [39]

Even before he became an adoptive father, Bruce Ivins had been at ease with young children, and once Amanda and Andy entered his life he delighted in entertaining them. Whether he was juggling walnuts for the twins or shocking them with his zany eating choices, he had a knack for making them laugh. On summer vacations, typically at state parks in Ohio like Shawnee or Burr Oak, Bruce was the twins' constant companion. A snapshot from one of the trips shows a grinning five-year-old Andy clinging to an inner tube and Bruce, with boxy sunglasses and soaked white T-shirt, smiling waist-deep to his left.

Ivins's involvement in family life was made more convenient by the proximity of his job. Door-to-door it took only a couple of minutes to ride his bike from home to the two-story complex of labs and offices that housed USAMRIID. At night, before the twins went upstairs to bed, Bruce sat at the family's Baldwin piano, the same one he'd used as a child. There, night after night, he played "Christa's Song."

Diane was raised a Catholic and she made the religion a strong presence in their home. Both parents were committed to raising Amanda and Andy within the Church and its teachings.

The twins were sent to parochial schools and took their places each weekend at St. John the Evangelist, the Roman Catholic church in downtown Frederick, where both of their parents sang and Bruce led alternative folk masses.[40]

In the years after his mother's death, Bruce Ivins did not grow closer to his father, who had continued to live on Orchard Avenue. Bruce, concerned that his father was squandering money on a younger woman, arranged to sell the house and moved him to a house in Frederick, just a block away. Within a couple of years, on March 6, 1985, Randall Ivins, the beleaguered husband who had been a meek figure in the upbringing of his youngest son, died. Bruce arranged for and attended a memorial and burial in Lebanon—but he would not let go of his resentment toward Randall for bowing to Mary Ivins's tyranny.[41]

FOUR

BRUCE BEING BRUCE

By mid-1986 Bruce Ivins and several of his colleagues were publishing the results of their tests on hundreds of rodents—work that could be leading to something big: a safer and more effective human vaccine against anthrax.[1]

One article, of which Ivins was lead co-author, described the cloning of a key anthrax protein, a step toward patenting a new vaccine.[2] And in February 1990, Ivins and a co-author asserted that the existing vaccine had "undesirable characteristics," including a "reduced ability to protect laboratory animals against certain virulent strains of [anthrax], such as the Ames strain."[3]

Developing a pharmaceutical product is typically fraught with obstacles, and the new anthrax vaccine was no exception. The USAMRIID researchers had to scrape just to get rats and guinea pigs for their experiments. But as the Persian Gulf War loomed in late 1990, Ivins learned anew how a perceived biowarfare threat could create opportunity.

When Iraqi forces rolled into the neighboring oil-rich state of Kuwait on August 2, 1990, the commander at USAMRIID, Colonel Charles L. Bailey, conferred with his contacts at the Defense Intelligence Agency, the Pentagon's intelligence arm. What

Bailey learned alarmed him: Analysts throughout the intelligence community suspected that Saddam Hussein possessed biological weapons, in particular, botulinum toxin and anthrax.

If President George H. W. Bush sought to dislodge the Iraqis from Kuwait, a U.S. ally, American troops could be vulnerable. The United States had some anthrax vaccine, but not much, and the amount might not even matter. War could break out within months or even weeks, and the best evidence at hand, data gathered in the 1950s from New England textile mill workers, showed that no fewer than six shots of the vaccine over an eighteen-month span were needed to immunize a person against inhaled anthrax. The vaccine was produced at a dilapidated plant owned and operated by the Michigan state health department. As for protection against botulinum toxin, the Army had no useful medical product at all.

Bailey summoned to his office Deputy Commander C. J. Peters and Colonel Arthur M. Friedlander, the Bacteriology Division chief under whom Bruce Ivins worked. Anthrax was the highest priority, Bailey told them. The slow-acting vaccine could not be relied upon to counter an imminent threat of anthrax. What about an antibiotic? The thinking was that several—including penicillin—might be effective. But if soldiers were exposed to aerosolized anthrax, for how long would they need to take an antibiotic to overcome the otherwise high risk of death?[4] And what if Iraq had succeeded in preparing anthrax in a way that made it resistant to an antibiotic? Bailey pressed Peters and Friedlander, both physicians and accomplished researchers, for answers.

Peters first had to acknowledge that he himself didn't have enough of the answers. Anthrax is a bacterium—and Peters was trained in the study of viruses. He would have to turn to Friedlander and Bruce Ivins in USAMRIID's "bac-t" division for help. Friedlander was widely recognized as an expert in the field; by late summer 1990 Ivins had been working with anthrax for nearly a decade and he was well skilled at preparing the spores for experiments. His work soon entailed growing the bacterium in Petri dishes and suspending the anthrax organisms in liquid. The mixture was then aerosolized as a mist to be inhaled by rodents, rabbits, and monkeys at lethal dosages and beyond. These studies were aimed at testing antibiotics and vaccine formulations to see if they could be relied on to protect service personnel against anthrax.

As the scientists conferred about the urgent challenge at hand, Peters saw that Ivins was literally bouncing up and down during discussions. He seemed to relish a crisis atmosphere in which he could showcase his skills. Though Peters viewed him as a solid rather than a brilliant scientist, he appreciated Ivins's "Boy Scout" spirit.[5]

Commander Charles Bailey also took note of Ivins's zest, but he regarded the microbiologist as "squirrelly," a misfit too inscrutable to be entirely trusted. An incident from a couple of years earlier gnawed at Bailey: One day Ivins visited him in a lather of excitement, telling Bailey that a younger woman at a local swimming pool had asked for blueprints of all offices, labs, and animal pens at USAMRIID. At the time, publicity-seeking activists elsewhere had been making a splash with nighttime break-ins to liberate animals used in medical experiments.[6]

USAMRIID was a big consumer of such animals for its own tests, so Ivins's account gave grounds for concern. Bailey was struck by Ivins's solicitous manner in conveying the tip; he seemed almost too eager to win kudos as the protector of USAMRIID. Yet Bailey had wasted no time in relaying the information to the FBI. Not long afterward, agents told him that they were unable to corroborate any of it.

The incident did, however, have a lasting consequence: Bailey pushed for the swift installation of electronic access cards—a security system capable of thwarting trespassers and, with its later expansion to the interior labs, tracking the comings and goings of every USAMRIID scientist.[7] This system would someday provide invaluable information about the lab hours kept by Bruce Ivins.

As Saddam Hussein continued to rebuff the United Nations and the White House, war grew imminent. Thousands of U.S. troops were being deployed, many to Saudi Arabia. Given the circumstances, the USAMRIID specialists knew that waiting eighteen months for each GI to achieve immunity with injections of the anthrax vaccine was out of the question. Commander Bailey needed an answer to the original question: For how long would a soldier need to take an antibiotic to overcome exposure to inhaled anthrax? And which antibiotic would be best?

Friedlander, Ivins, and others at USAMRIID quickly launched a study in which rhesus monkeys of both sexes would be forced to breathe a concentrated mist of anthrax. Beginning the next day, most of the monkeys, twenty-eight, would then be injected with an antibiotic every twelve hours for thirty days. Nine other monkeys would be treated with both an antibiotic and, at two intervals, the anthrax vaccine. The experiment showed that each of the antibiotics provided significant long-term protection against anthrax infection.[8]

Based on all the scientific information available, the Pentagon ordered precautionary vaccinations, but only for Special Forces personnel, those most apt to engage first in battle. Although the affected troops would not get a full course of anthrax vaccine, the hope was that one to three injections would impart some immunity. Vaccinations for other personnel would depend upon supply, which remained paltry. Prompt treatment with an antibiotic would be imperative for anyone exposed to anthrax.

But which antibiotic would be best? One product, erythromycin, could cause harmful side effects if used by persons exposed to prolonged direct sunlight. This war would be fought in open desert—erythromycin was out. Two low-cost options, doxycycline and penicillin, along with Cipro, a drug patented more recently, were found to be effective in the just completed experiment with the monkeys. Deputy Commander Peters had a related question for Ivins. Pondering it would allow the eager microbiologist to think like an intelligence agency analyst—or to put himself in the shoes of Saddam Hussein's military scientists:

"Bruce, how hard would it be for them to make penicillin-resistant anthrax?"

Ivins replied, "High school science fair project."

If Saddam's scientists could pull this off, the U.S. military would be left with no proven effective medical countermeasure. Peters and Friedlander thought that Cipro was the best choice because the Iraqis would have had the least amount of time to produce anthrax that resisted this newer drug. But though Cipro had been marketed for certain infections in the United States since 1987, it had not been proven effective against anthrax.

"At that time Cipro had just been shown to work against anthrax in Petri dishes," Peters said. "So we cranked up animal testing—and Bruce was very important in running the samples and pulling everything together."[9]

Charles Bailey took a different approach to countering the threat of botulinum toxin, the poisonous substance that causes botulism, the most dangerous form of food poisoning. Bailey and others worried that the Iraqis might be able to deliver "bot" with low-range Scud missiles or perhaps a crude spraying device mounted on a land vehicle. Under Bailey's leadership, Army veterinarians developed a botulinum antitoxin and stockpiled it for potential use in the Persian Gulf.[10]

Ivins, who in early 1990 had told a high school classmate that his work with the Army was "really interesting, even exciting at times," now saw himself as being center stage as the armed services prepared for war.[11] In a handwritten Christmas card to her, Ivins described the sense of urgency: "Since August, everyone in the Bacteriology Division at USAMRIID has been very busy in support of Operation Desert Shield. There is a real fear that Iraq has biological weapons. I hope we don't go to war. Have a fine holiday season and a great 1991."[12]

As U.S. forces deployed to the Mideast, physician-colonel Robert P. Kadlec paid an urgent visit to USAMRIID, to stock up on doses of both the standard anthrax vaccine and a vaccine against botulinum. Kadlec left USAMRIID toting two Styrofoam chests, loaded with vials of the two vaccines, which he delivered to Fort Bragg, North Carolina. Kadlec, a flight surgeon destined for a high-level career in biowarfare preparedness, personally injected both vaccines into about eight hundred of the war-bound service personnel attached to the military's Special Operations Command. As he pushed it into the service members' triceps, Kadlec learned firsthand that the anthrax vaccine caused pain. The shot typically left a nodule—indicating the body's "take" of the vaccine.[13]

On January 16, 1991, a U.S.-led international coalition began driving Iraqi forces out of Kuwait and back to Baghdad. No botulism, anthrax, or other biological or chemical weapon was unleashed during the forty-two-day war. But lessons had been learned and new approaches developed that could conceivably be useful against future threats. And the effort had required months, not years. The results: A preexisting anthrax vaccine, never before used by the military, had been administered to some service personnel. A relatively new antibiotic, Cipro, had been shown in the recent animal tests to be effective against anthrax. A botulinum antitoxin had been developed under the supervision of Colonel Bailey.

Before the war ended, USAMRIID was taking more steps to develop a next-generation anthrax vaccine—one that planners hoped would confer immunity faster than the existing product. Patent documents would later list Ivins as a co-inventor.[14] His efforts won him a letter of commendation from the Army surgeon general. "If Bruce hadn't been on the team, they probably wouldn't have progressed with the next-phase vaccine," C. J. Peters recalled. "Nobody else had the insight to carry out all the angles on the animal testing."[15]

At the time of the first patent application, Ivins's yearly salary from the Army was $59,103. The family lived modestly, and in a holiday card to a classmate from Ohio several years before, Ivins had lamented the circumstances that kept them in a smallish Cape Cod, a couple of hundred yards from Fort Detrick's main gate. "Unfortunately for us, real estate is really expensive this close to Washington, D.C., so our house sometimes seems a little cramped."[16]

The year-to-year uncertainty over funding for his vaccine work also unsettled him. "Federal budget cuts in the military have a number of us worried at Fort Detrick," he wrote in the same holiday card, adding, "there haven't been any large scale 'reductions in force' . . . yet." [17]

Military careers are made in times of war. And Ivins, although a civilian employee, stood to benefit, too. He had first observed the power of fear when the Army hired him in response to what the Russians were doing in Sverdlovsk. The events surrounding the Gulf War reinforced for him the lesson that fear, or better yet full-blown panic, was a guaranteed motivator of government bureaucracy.

Unlike some self-important Ph.D.'s, Ivins showed unswerving obeisance to his superiors, notably the uniformed officers at Fort Detrick who usually lacked his expertise but were nevertheless above him. His style won over senior officers. One of them was Major Gerard "Gerry" Andrews, who encountered Ivins in a corridor the first day he reported for duty at USAMRIID, in late 1992. "He introduced himself. And I said, 'I know who you are, Dr. Ivins.' And he said, 'Don't call me Dr. Ivins. I'm Bruce.' And he welcomed me to the [Bacteriology] Division." Ivins's demeanor put Andrews immediately at ease. [18]

Ivins developed a similarly cordial relationship with Dr. W. Russell Byrne, an Army colonel who in the late 1990s would serve as chief of the Bacteriology Division. Byrne was an experienced researcher, but he did not regard himself as Ivins's peer scientifically. Yet Ivins invariably addressed him as "Colonel Byrne" when "Russ" would have sufficed. "He took direction from people who were not his equals," Byrne recalled. "When I needed him to do stuff—he just did it. He was agreeable. He took me more seriously than he should have, to tell you the truth. I'm an M.D. I'm *not* a Ph.D." [19]

The continuity and closeness of the relationships between civilian scientists such as Ivins and officers who held leadership positions at Fort Detrick was unusual. At a typical Army installation, officers remain only eighteen to thirty-six months before moving on. To do otherwise could hamper their ability to climb in rank. But at Fort Detrick and other installations within the

Army Medical Corps, high-ranking officers make as few as two or three moves during their service careers.

The officers and civilian staffers at Fort Detrick sometimes spend decades together—shopping at the same stores, worshipping at the same churches, attending the same school functions for their children. Combined with the relative remoteness of Frederick, this "homesteading" fosters an uncommonly tight community. Colonel Byrne, for instance, met Ivins at USAMRIID in 1993 but also got to know him as a fellow parishioner at St. John the Evangelist.

With his plastic pocket protector and penchant for scraggly clothes, Ivins was recognized in Frederick as an endearing character, a team player, a nice guy. He was the one who rode his bike to work, his floppy pant legs clamped with clothespins. On weekends he might show up at a neighbor's, chain saw in hand, to thin an overgrown tree. And he merrily staked out provocative positions on hot-button topics of the day. If he happened to stretch a social boundary, acquaintances were likely to say it was just "Bruce being Bruce."

FIVE

DARK FAMILY MATERIAL

To hear Ivins tell it, his own family had treated him as an unwanted outsider. He had been ignored by his father, cruelly micromanaged by his mother. He had no relationship with his oldest sibling and for twenty years did not communicate with their other brother. Beneath a surface amiability, he was in fact a man of simmering resentments, dating to those childhood years.[1]

He seethed particularly over the way he had been treated by his domineering mother. His middle brother, C.W., learned this in the mid-1990s when, after the two brothers had reconciled, he broached a memory of Mary Ivins. *"I don't want you to ever bring that up again or talk about her again,"* Bruce said.[2]

Bruce Ivins had always sought to form his closest social bonds not with adult family members but with female colleagues. To them and not to Diane, he poured out his inner tumult—his insecurities, his fears, his longing for acceptance. As of the mid- to late 1990s, his most intimate conversations were with two laboratory technicians who assisted his work with anthrax: Mara Linscott, who would soon enter medical school, and Patricia Fellows, who specialized in growing and harvesting anthrax spores used for animal experiments. Linscott was twenty-nine years his junior; Fellows, fifteen. Ivins openly dreaded their eventual departure—and fantasized about what it would take to lure them back. He wrote a joking tribute in the departing Linscott's honor: "Allah smiles on all your accomplishments. After your degree please come to my country and talk to us about your work at Fort Detrick. Please bring your anthrax strains with you when you come. Most sincerely, Saddam."[3]

Of the two, he grew especially attached to the athletic and youthful Linscott, sending her hundreds of e-mails in a few short years about work and personal matters, including complaints about his wife. "I've never been able to confide in Diane because she basically dismisses, belittles, or criticizes what I say, so I say nothing to her and keep it all inside," Ivins wrote.[4]

Complicating the situation was the fact that Mara Linscott's older sister, Cheryl Linscott, was the best friend of Ivins's wife.[5] Bruce complained repeatedly to family members and friends about what he described as Diane's inflexible ways, which he ascribed to her "Prussian" upbringing. Yet he appeared to care enough about his wife to begrudge the amount of time she spent with Cheryl, with whom she coached youth swim teams.[6]

His dealings with Linscott and Patricia Fellows also left Ivins resentful at times. The women were close friends, and this grated on Ivins, who fretted that he was being excluded. They lent him a sympathetic ear, but they also traded notes about his manic ways. Once when Linscott was away from her desk, Ivins made a copy of the key to her apartment. He also filched Fellows's computer password, enabling him to spy on her e-mails and read what the women were saying to each other about him. On October 27, 1999, he referred indirectly to what he had learned—and to his feelings of isolation—in an e-mail to Linscott, who in July had left USAMRIID and moved to Buffalo, New York, to attend medical school:

> It's getting to be lately that I've felt there's nobody in the world I can confide in. You're gone now, and one of the reasons I was so sorry to see you go was a very selfish one— I could talk to you openly and honestly, and that was in itself

a great lifter of my spirits. Losing Pat [Fellows] as someone I can spill my guts to is crushing—it would mean that I am truly alone—completely alone. I know that you and Pat are such great friends—when you two are together, I've frequently felt like I totally don't belong. . . . I have come to learn, much to my surprise and disappointment, that Pat has been saying some very negative things behind my back. Apparently I am being made to appear mentally ill or just plain mean. It's hard to understand, especially since I've never spoken about her in other than glowing terms. It seems that whatever I say or do can get twisted, exaggerated or misconstrued by her, and now the bond of trust that I thought I had with her is gone. . . . Also, I know that the two of you are great friends, but please don't tell her that I told you about this. The whole thing is very disheartening.

Ivins told a psychiatrist that Linscott's absence had plunged him into a state of misery. The physical symptoms he'd suffered two decades earlier, after his departure from Chapel Hill and Nancy Haigwood, had returned. He had thought about ways to kill Haigwood—and now he was having homicidal ideas about Linscott, too. He said that he had access to deadly materials in the labs at USAMRIID and that he had obtained cyanide, perhaps to poison a neighbor's dog, and ammonium nitrate, to make a bomb.[7] On November 1, 1999, Ivins, while keeping his worst thoughts to himself, suggested to Linscott and Fellows that his torment stemmed from a twisted family background. He sent this e-mail to both of them:

There is something we should probably talk about. . . . It deals with some perceived interpersonal problems and some special "sensitivities" of mine. I'm including both of you on my emails. I can give you the information in one of three forms—you decide which one you would rather have, and email back: (1) A brief synopsis, probably no more than a paragraph, talking about the problem. (2) A longer explanation, going somewhat into the family historical background of the problem, but not getting into the historical specifics. (3) The full exposition, including some VERY dark family material, and possibly a few pages long. (This would be the sort of stuff that would be talked about in a clinical psych class.) If you choose this, I would need you to agree to keep it to yourselves. There's nothing in it about any unsolved crimes or something bad about to happen to something, but it's not the sort of thing I would like to spread around to others.

That there was a dark side to Ivins was apparent not just from his e-mails to these women—or his inappropriate attachment to them. His many letters to newspapers, including the *Baltimore Sun*, the *Washington Post*, and the local *Frederick News-Post*, showed Ivins to be capable of rage and possessed of a strange compulsion to draw attention to himself. The provocateur in Ivins came into view once again when he wrote a signed letter, published by the *News-Post* on September 17, 1993, which discussed the subject of pedophilia—declaring it to be a matter of "sexual orientation" and expressing concern about "discrimination" against pedophiles.

In a clear case of discrimination on the basis of sexual orientation, this past week the University of the District of Columbia denied the North American Man-Boy Love Association (NAMBLA) the use of its campus facilities for the purpose of holding a conference. NAMBLA is an organization which asserts that children are sexual human beings who have a right to sexually love other human beings, including adults.

Ivins concluded,

I would like to ask *News-Post* readers, especially members of the gay/lesbian-bisexual community . . . to contribute their opinions to this page on the question of whether individuals whose sexual orientation is children should be protected from discrimination in employment, housing, adoption rights and other areas. I look forward to reading the responses.

Ivins succeeded in eliciting outrage from local readers. "This is the most disgusting, perverted letter I have ever read in this paper, and the organization is the most ridiculous one I have ever heard of," wrote a woman from Frederick.[8] "To the author, Bruce Ivins, it sounds to me like he is one of these NAMBLA members who seeks pleasure from innocent children," wrote a man from Emmitsburg, Maryland, adding: "It will take a determined effort from the good citizens of this area to stand against pedophiles. Don't be convinced that these sexual practices are normal or acceptable. It's time to put a stop to the deterioration of this country's moral values."[9] Wrote another: "I'd give the boys from NAMBLA extra special protection, until such time that an arena is built, a very special arena indeed. One large enough to hold the crowds that will stone these lizards to dust."[10]

Having baited people into a fury—the newspaper published no fewer than ten letters in response to him—Ivins stepped away from the fire he'd lit. His original letter, Ivins now wrote, had been misunderstood. "Several persons have pointed out to me that I neglected to present my opinion on the subject of [sex acts between boys and men] and, realizing my oversight, I would now like to do so. I am totally opposed to NAMBLA and its goals." He went on: "In our nation's season of 'tolerance' it is wise to remember that it is not morally wrong to be intolerant of pedophilia, and it is not a sin to discriminate against people who seek to legalize the sexual abuse of our children."[11]

From his duplicitous letter that started it all to his backpedaling clarification, the entire episode is one that most people in sensitive positions—let alone a government microbiologist entrusted with protecting the nation against biological attack—would have avoided. Not Ivins. In an earlier, January 1992 letter to *Newsweek,* he had grotesquely impugned the values of those who opposed biodefense research: "To some, apparently, protecting soldiers from disease is more morally repugnant than molesting children."[12] He even offered commentary on the O. J. Simpson case. During Simpson's first-degree-murder trial in 1995, Ivins wrote to the *Baltimore Sun* to cast aspersions on the character and parenting of the lead prosecutor, Marcia Clark.[13]

While Ivins played his morality games in letters to news organizations, there was plenty about himself that he kept out of sight. He opened another post office box, where he received under Carl Scandella's name *Bondage Life* magazine along with glossy photographs of blindfolded and bound women. He kept editions of *Censored Shots*, and *Panty and Stocking Digest* magazines, as well as *Hustler*. He would eventually say he was a cross-dresser.[14]

His private pursuits notwithstanding, Ivins and his wife subscribed to a magazine published by the American Family Association, a Christian advocacy group that opposes abortion and encourages followers to "reform our culture to reflect Biblical truth."[15] Both husband and wife made clear their opposition to abortion, and Diane even became the leader of Frederick Right to Life, an organization that staged public demonstrations. Bruce and Diane gave money to the Family Association for several years but stopped in 1997. They resumed donating in November 1999—a month after *American Family Association Journal* reported on AFA's filing of a federal lawsuit focusing on a controversy surrounding the disciplining of a fourth grader at a school in Wisconsin: the Greendale Baptist Academy.[16]

SIX

THIS WAS HIS BABY

Anthrax was not used on the battlefield during the Gulf War, yet it became a source of increased dread for military planners, refocusing responsibility on USAMRIID to protect U.S. troops against future attack. In December 1997, about the same time that Russian researchers claimed they had altered the genetic structure of anthrax, Defense Secretary William Cohen announced that injection with the established vaccine would become mandatory for most U.S. service personnel.[1]

Cohen's decree and concern about the Russian research—if, as claimed, the altered anthrax defeated the Russians' vaccine, how would the U.S. vaccine fare?—energized Ivins. For the first time since the Gulf War, there was a clear demand for vaccinations against anthrax, as well as an interest in ensuring that the vaccine was effective and safe. In a letter to a former classmate in his hometown of Lebanon, Ohio, Ivins described what he saw as the central role he was playing in helping the nation gird against possible biological attack.

"Iraq, North Korea and other similarly swell nations keep me busy working on anthrax vaccines," he wrote in December 1997. "The military will start vaccinating soldiers, sailors, marines and airmen (airpersons?) against anthrax in a few months to protect them from a bio-warfare attack of anthrax spores." [2]

Cohen had committed the military to a product that was far from ideal. Though the existing anthrax vaccine provided immunity, it was a crude preparation with residual, unpurified bacterial proteins that might also cause undesirable side effects. The vaccine proved fiercely controversial. Thousands of military personnel, including some veterans of the Gulf War, complained of adverse reactions ranging from painfully swollen muscles and joints, to headaches, to more serious immune system disorders. More than one hundred service members risked courts-martial or other disciplinary consequences by refusing to be vaccinated. [3]

Critics began to ask whether an unauthorized ingredient, an oily substance called squalene, had been added to some anthrax vaccine stock, speculating that this could have caused the generalized symptoms referred to as Gulf War Syndrome. The criticism would hit home for Ivins because he had experimented with adding squalene to some vaccine formulations to see if it would increase the capacity of the vaccine to protect lab animals from anthrax. "Since I've done a lot of work (not in humans) with experimental vaccines containing squalene, there are some Congressional fingers pointing at me and my experiments," he wrote the same former schoolmate from Lebanon. [4]

Pentagon officials and representatives of the manufacturer acknowledged some problems—while insisting the vaccine was generally safe and effective. In 1999 and 2000, inspectors from the U.S. Food and Drug Administration found problems with the vaccine's purity and potency, raising concerns about how effective it would remain after up to three years of storage. By this time BioPort Corp., a privately owned company, had bought the rights to the vaccine from the original manufacturer, the Michigan public health department. Nonetheless, the aged manufacturing plant in Lansing verged on dysfunctional. Production was halted. Army officials assigned Ivins and others at USAMRIID to help BioPort resolve the deficiencies. After making a trip to its manufacturing plant, Ivins reported that all of the vats used to grow anthrax "leak to different degrees." [5]

Ivins and his Army colleagues were well qualified to diagnose the problems. "They were the world experts on anthrax vaccine," recalled scientist David L. Danley, then a colonel at Fort Detrick. "And it wasn't like the United States had a huge number of experts in this area." Ivins soon came to view the BioPort staff as inept. Danley recalled that both he and Ivins were "very, very frustrated" with BioPort's shortcomings in testing its vaccine.[6]

For Ivins the stakes went beyond just the problems with the existing BioPort vaccine, known as AVA: Even as he was trying to correct those problems, he was continuing his work, begun before the Gulf War, on what he hoped would be an improved, next-generation anthrax vaccine. This would be a genetically engineered and much purer vaccine, a product that might provide immunity with fewer injections, cause fewer side effects, and have a longer shelf life.

Danley suspected that Ivins's excited claims about the new vaccine outpaced the results of his tests with mice and guinea pigs: Too often the new vaccine was failing to protect the animals after they were exposed to concentrated mists of anthrax.

"I had not been happy with some of the animal data," Danley recalled. "And I let him know that. And he would defend it. . . . You know, this was his baby. And he was proud of it, as well he should have been."[7]

Ivins would eventually hold the new vaccine's birth papers: He was named as a co-inventor on applications for the two patents that supported future licensing of the vaccine, one filed in November 1994, the other in March 2000. As a co-inventor of this new vaccine, called rPA, for recombinant Protective Antigen, Ivins would be in line to collect patent royalties if the vaccine ever progressed from the lab. The unknown for Ivins was whether the U.S. government would maintain an interest in buying *any* variety of anthrax vaccine—and whether his services as an anthrax expert would continue to be needed.[8]

By the year 2000, Ivins's expertise had enabled him to make significant contributions to the design of the new vaccine: He and his co-inventors had identified the genes responsible for the expression of three proteins that the bacterium secretes to become lethal. They then separated out the gene responsible for expression of one of the proteins, Protective Antigen, and inserted it into a special strain of anthrax bacteria made safe to humans. This new production strain secreted only Protective Antigen, which is the one used in the injectable vaccine to trick its host—be it animal or human being—into making anthrax-fighting antibodies. Moreover, Ivins had succeeded in amassing the large batch of anthrax, RMR-1029, for the ongoing and future experiments with the next-generation vaccine. But the Pentagon's commitment to this work was still small compared with its spending for any number of gold-plated defense contracts.

Researchers at USAMRIID who had visions of creating new vaccines or antidotes faced challenges not present at more elite institutions. In addition to the difficulties with securing lab animals, they labored in worn facilities that more reflected the mid-twentieth century than the dawn of the new millennium. They had to compete for federal research grants as if they were untenured university instructors. Senior federal scientists who worked less than an hour's drive away at the National Institutes of Health drew higher salaries. Yet when a national need arose, such as training hazardous material specialists for the 1996 Olympics in Atlanta, or identifying which species of mosquito could spread the deadly West Nile virus, or checking out innumerable biological threat hoaxes, USAMRIID got the call. More than a few present and former USAMRIID scientists nursed a sense of neglect, of disrespect. Bruce Ivins was attuned to this mind-set and quick to play to it.

The shortage of resources upset Ivins—who also blamed some disappointing research results on his inability to purchase the lab animals he needed. "In this last experiment which we just concluded, we strangely got no protection at all, in terms of either survival or increased time-to-death," Ivins said in an e-mail to a colleague on October 7, 1999. "I believe that the main problem is that the mouse is such a generally poor and unpredictable model for anthrax. The guinea pig is a MUCH better model for anthrax infection/protection." In an e-mail the next month Ivins put his predicament in sharper relief: "We are going into guinea pigs next, and we most certainly will when we finally get some funds. Right now, we don't have enough money to pay for housing the animals, much less for purchasing them." [9]

As of the spring of 2000, Ivins was juggling two important responsibilities: During the week of April 10, he helped carry out an aerosol "challenge" with 110 rabbits that had been inoculated with his experimental rPA vaccine. The next week Ivins traveled to BioPort's plant in Lansing to confer with company representatives about AVA, their troubled anthrax vaccine, which still had not been returned to production. [10]

Ivins was also monitoring how national politics might affect his work. At one point, he voiced trepidation about the likely presidential nominees of both major parties, while bemoaning the problems with the old vaccine. "Apparently Gore (and maybe even Bush) is considering making the anthrax vaccine for the military voluntary, or even stopping the program," Ivins e-mailed on June 28, 2000. "Unfortunately, since the BioPort people aren't scientists, the task of solving their problem has fallen on us." [11]

Although Ivins derided BioPort, he and his fellow researchers were dependent on the company's vaccine for their own annual booster shots. With BioPort's persistent manufacturing problems having brought production to a prolonged halt, the supply of its vaccine was dwindling. Once it was gone, there would be no booster shots—and Ivins and the other scientists would have to stop handling anthrax. Of even greater concern to Ivins was the prospect that the problems at BioPort could cause a shutdown of all anthrax-related research. [12]

By July 4, 2000, Ivins saw the troubles with BioPort's product deepening. "If lot 22 does not pass the potency test, then everything hits the fan—no more vaccine for anyone, including people here at RIID. I'm sure Congress will not be pleased." [13]

He voiced particular bitterness at how the Pentagon's funding priorities and BioPort's troubled vaccine were affecting progress on his co-invention, the next-generation rPA vaccine. If the Pentagon had invested in rPA over the previous five years, Ivins wrote Mara Linscott, the product would probably have been brought on line. "Now we're confined to working on the old

AVA vaccine. I don't know what's going to happen with any of our future proposed studies on OUR recombinant PA vaccine. They may get totally canned."[14] Ivins also voiced frustration about the lack of support for his co-invention in e-mails to a classmate from Lebanon High, Rick Sams.[15]

In the first paragraph of a belated holiday card that he sent to another Lebanon High classmate in early 2001, Ivins discussed his wife, their children—and his professional plight. "It was a zoo for me at work this year. We're working on improving the old anthrax vaccine, working on making a new anthrax vaccine, getting ready for an international Anthrax Conference in Annapolis in June of this year, and answering Freedom of Information Act requests and Congressional Inquiries. Whew!"[16]

Ivins was emphatic about his concerns when speaking to colleagues at USAMRIID. The source of his discomfort with the Freedom of Information Act requests and congressional inquiries was a journalist, Gary Matsumoto, who was questioning the safety of the anthrax vaccine administered to U.S. troops for the 1991 Gulf War. In a lengthy article in *Vanity Fair* in May 1999, Matsumoto gave voice to the criticisms that had been percolating for years and suggested that the military may have surreptitiously added squalene to the vaccine in an attempt to boost its effectiveness against anthrax.[17] The article called into question whether the controversial additive caused various Gulf War–related illnesses among service personnel. But Matsumoto's article conceded, "There are no documents available proving that the army used a squalene adjuvant . . . and the army has specifically denied it."[18] (Indeed, no credible evidence has emerged to show that squalene was added to the anthrax vaccine administered to U.S. service personnel.)

The article did not name Bruce Ivins. Yet those who had been at USAMRIID since the Gulf War knew that Ivins had been integral to the rushed efforts to validate what the original vaccine could do. Matsumoto had described those efforts as part of a secret Pentagon program, Project Badger. After reading the article, Ivins wrote to his boss, Russell Byrne: "[T]hanks for passing these along to me. I wonder when the National Enquirer will come out with its headlines on 'Guinea Pig Soldiers Get Killer Vaccine.'"[19]

Matsumoto continued to seek internal documents regarding experiments that Ivins had helped lead, magnifying Ivins's anxiety over how his work might be portrayed. Ivins and several colleagues had added squalene to versions of the anthrax vaccine given to some guinea pigs and rhesus monkeys, research that they had documented in two scientific articles. And the two patent applications for the next-generation vaccine, on which Ivins was named as a co-inventor, both allowed for the possibility of utilizing squalene as an adjuvant to increase potency.[20]

In an e-mail to his colleague Arthur Friedlander, Ivins vented about a pending Freedom of Information Act request from Matsumoto: "Tell Matsumoto to kiss my ass. We've got better things to do than shine his shoes and pee on command. He's gotten everything from me he will get."[21]

SEVEN

AVENGING ANGEL

Since childhood, Bruce Ivins had been tormented by resentments toward those he believed had rejected him. Beneath his persona of "Bruce being Bruce," the quirky, happy-go-lucky colleague, the good neighbor who cared deeply about others and just wanted to help, he boiled. Ivins eventually expressed a deepening awareness of how troubled he was.

"Occasionally I get this tingling that goes down both arms," he told Mara Linscott, on April 3, 2000, a year after she had left USAMRIID to attend medical school. "At the same time I get a bit dizzy and get this unidentifiable 'metallic' taste in my mouth. (I'm not trying to be funny, Mara. It actually scares me a bit.) Other times it's like I'm not only sitting at my desk doing work, I'm also a few feet away watching me do it. There's nothing like living in both the first person singular AND the third person singular!"[1]

Ivins fretted that he may have inherited whatever abnormality had driven his mother to be such a violent, haunting force. He confided that he was depressed and anxious, that he had impulses to seek revenge, and that he had an alternate personality. Psychiatrists had prescribed various drugs, including an antidepressant, Celexa, for his routine use. But by the spring of 2000, Ivins said he was worried he would not be able to resist the urge to do harm.[2]

As part of his care, in June 2000 Ivins submitted to weekly one-on-one talk therapy with a clinical counselor, Judith M. McLean, based at Comprehensive Counseling Associates in Frederick, an organization headed by Dr. Allan L. Levy, who had recently become Ivins's psychiatrist.

McLean learned from Ivins that he was an accomplished scientist and had access to dangerous substances, but she did not know anthrax was among them. Ivins began opening up to her about his life outside science: He had harsh things to say about his deceased mother and described a painful childhood, during which he never fit in with other kids and felt as if he had no friends. He said he had sometimes committed acts of anonymous vandalism against those who wronged him. Ivins had earlier told a psychiatrist that he carried a loaded gun at college. Imagining stationary objects inside of buildings as his enemies, he said he fired at them, once destroying a wall clock. He told McLean about people from his childhood against whom he wanted to exact revenge.[3] Ivins bared similar thoughts to Mara Linscott in an e-mail on June 27, 2000:

Even with the Celexa and the counseling, the depression episodes still come and go. That's unpleasant enough. What is REALLY scary is the paranoia—you saw a brief flash of it last Tuesday night when, for no reason, I acted as I did. The reason it's so scary is that I remember my mother becoming more and more paranoid from her mid-forties until she died at 63. The psychiatrists I've spoken to personally and professionally say she sounds very much like a paranoid psychotic or paranoid schizophrenic. She could seem perfectly normal one moment, and then in another moment she was a totally different, quite terrifying individual. Remember when I told you about the "metallic" taste in my mouth that I got periodically? It's when I get these "paranoid" episodes. Of course I regret them thoroughly when they are over, but when I'm going through them, it's as if I'm a passenger on a ride. . . . Depression, as long as I can somewhat control it with medication and some counseling, I can handle. Psychosis or schizophrenia—that's a whole different story. . . . Ominously, a lot of the feelings of isolation—and desolation—that I went through before college are returning. I don't want to relive those years again.[4]

Ivins informed Judith McLean that he first sought psychiatric treatment in the late 1970s, soon after he worked as a lab researcher at the University of North Carolina in Chapel Hill. At that time, Ivins said, he had impulses to harm those who had offended him. He acknowledged breaking into a sorority house and another building in Chapel Hill. Without naming her, he cited a particular sorority member as an object of his enmity. He said he had used the Internet to buy the ingredients for making a bomb and had studied how to assemble one. His impulses to inflict harm were getting stronger, he told McLean, and he wasn't sure he could contain them.[5]

Again, Ivins reported his mental state to Mara Linscott:

The thinking now by the psychiatrist and counselor is that my symptoms may not be those of depression or bipolar disorder, they may be that of "Paranoid Personality Disorder." It's seen frequently in blood relatives of schizophrenics, and it can be [a] preliminary sign of the onset of schizophrenia. I can't tell you how terrifying that is, Mara,—it scares the H*** out of me, actually, and it's that reason that I depend on connecting with you and Pat [Fellows]. I wish I could talk to Diane about it, but it's just no use. She's very judgemental, and she's very dismissive of deep personal problems. I've talked to you about the genetic component of mental problems in our family, and my getting the symptoms fits. I just absolutely don't want to turn into the kind of person my mother was.[6]

Ivins added two days later, on July 6, 2000:

I always thought my mom was not all there, but I never really wanted to consider the possibility of paranoid schizophrenia in her. Looking back now, it's not all that far-fetched but, as I told you, the terrifying thing is what may happen to me. At least I'm going for help. When I see the terrible things that some paranoid schizophrenics have done, it honestly makes me want to cry. I don't want to be like that, and to think that I may be heading toward becoming that kind of person that is the exact antithesis of who I want to be, I can't begin to tell you how much it hurts and scares me.

Ivins offered through Comprehensive Counseling to be interviewed as part of a mental health case study, provided, he told Linscott, he remained anonymous. "I certainly don't want to see any headlines in the National Enquirer, 'PARANOID MAN WORKS WITH DEADLY ANTHRAX!!!'"[7]

Judith McLean found that Ivins harbored pronounced resentment toward various women—but that he also was more willing to bare his soul to them. Ivins seemed to develop a favorable view of McLean. "Things went well with the counselor today," he wrote Linscott on June 29. "Next session she would like me to bring in some pictures of me as a kid, and in the meantime read a book called, 'Breaking the Chains of Low Self Esteem.'"[8]

When McLean met with Ivins again in early July, she asked him about his current fixation with a former co-worker—whom he referred to only as "Mara." When Ivins told McLean that Mara was about thirty years his junior and single, the counselor encouraged him to reconsider whether his strong interest in her was appropriate. (Years later McLean would learn Mara's last name.)[9]

Ivins's preoccupation with Linscott had included his sending her packages under false names. Once he mailed her a soccer jersey in the name of Mia Hamm, the U.S. Olympic team star. Ivins on another occasion used the name of the shortstop Derek Jeter to send Linscott paraphernalia of the New York Yankees, which he knew was her favorite baseball team. He posed as "Laundry Boy" to send her detergent, postmarked from Virginia. He did these things in part to test whether Linscott could "decode" the identity of the sender.[10]

On the afternoon of July 18, 2000, Ivins arrived for his fourth session with McLean. They began discussing anew his obsession with Mara. He said he felt deeply attached to her, but she did not show the same interest in him. She was not responding regularly to his e-mails, and this angered him.

In a matter-of-fact manner, Ivins described how he had driven recently to upstate New York to watch Mara play in a soccer match, and how he had brought along a jug of wine that he had spiked with poison. If Mara had not been injured during the match, he would have offered her the wine when they met for a casual visit afterward. He had the ability, he told McLean, to create "lethal poisons" and the expertise to use them for revenge. He said he saw himself as an "avenging angel of death."[11]

McLean informed Ivins that she was duty bound to report to the authorities any homicidal threat. Given what she regarded as Ivins's compulsive, vengeful state, McLean asked if he would be willing to submit to an evaluation by a psychiatrist. Ivins agreed to do so as soon as it could be arranged. Before he left that day, McLean persuaded him to sign a statement pledging not to harm anyone and to contact her immediately if he had further "homicidal thoughts."

McLean was trying to stay outwardly calm and nonjudgmental, yet she was afraid of what Ivins might do—to her or to someone else. She found him "creepy, scary, spooky," and was determined to sound a warning. On the day Ivins revealed his poisoning plot, McLean's supervisor, Dr. Allan Levy, who was Ivins's psychiatrist, was on vacation, so she called the psychiatrist who was covering for him, Dr. Orrin Palmer, who in turn phoned Ivins. McLean also called the Frederick police that night and spoke to an officer who said it sounded as if no crime had been committed. She got a similar response when she called a lawyer who represented the practice she worked for, Comprehensive Counseling.

The next day, July 19, 2000, McLean reached Dr. David Irwin, who had once been Ivins's psychiatrist, about performing the mental evaluation to which Ivins had agreed. Irwin said that Ivins had been like an "overstretched rubber band"—the "scariest" patient he had ever treated. But after talking to Ivins, the psychiatrist relayed a mixed conclusion to McLean: He said that Ivins was no longer exhibiting homicidal thoughts, though he had clear "sociopathic intentions." Irwin was unsure whether adding a new, antipsychotic drug to his current regimen of Celexa and Valium would help. The other psychiatrist McLean had enlisted, Dr. Palmer, said that any decision about adjusting Ivins's medications should wait until Dr. Levy returned from vacation.

Ivins, in his back-to-back conversations with Irwin and Palmer, seemed amenable to the whirlwind efforts to assess his mental state. When Dr. Levy returned, Ivins agreed to begin taking Zyprexa, an antipsychotic drug for treating schizophrenia or episodes associated with bipolar disorder. But in his ongoing e-mails to Mara Linscott, he made clear that he had soured on his counselor, Judith McLean.

On July 23, 2000, only five days after he revealed to McLean his plan to poison Linscott, Ivins told Linscott: "It's been a real stressful week, from all stand points. Home, work, and it's not going well with the counselor I'm going to. (She said she thinks I went up to see you to have an affair.) I'm going to have to ask to get put with another counselor or into a group therapy session. . . . Sometimes I think that it's all just too much." [12]

On July 25, Ivins arrived at Comprehensive Counseling for his fifth weekly session with McLean. He again spoke to her in an expressionless monotone. "You betrayed my trust," he told her. The two conversed briefly and agreed that it would be best for him to switch to another counselor or to enter group therapy. The next day Ivins wrote to Linscott, "I had my last visit with my counselor yesterday, and I told her why I wanted to make a fresh start with someone else."

A few days later, he wrote Linscott: "You and Pat [Fellows] are the only ones I've talked to concerning my mental/emotional medical adventures, and you alone are the only one I've talked to with respect to taking Zyprexa," Ivins wrote. [13] The next day, Fellows told Linscott that Ivins's junior lab tech had said that of late, "Bruce was Dr. Jeckyl and Mr. Hyde. . . . Too bad Bruce wasn't there to help!" [14]

In early August 2000, Ivins began participating in group therapy sessions at Comprehensive Counseling, and he continued to share with Mara Linscott the mental problems besetting him—without ever mentioning that he had planned to poison her. He wrote Linscott on August 12:

This has been a week of extreme ups and downs. Last Saturday, as you probably guessed from my email, was one of my worst days in months. I wish I could control the thoughts in my mind. It's hard enough sometimes controlling my behavior. When I'm being eaten alive inside, I always try to put on a good front here at work and at home, so I don't spread the pestilence. Unfortunately, I have to talk about it to someone, so you become my "secret sharer." I get incredible paranoid, delusional thoughts at times, and there's nothing I can do until they go away, either by themselves or with drugs. [15]

Two days later, Ivins elaborated:

I told Pat [Fellows] again today that even though I know it's not logical or rational to think that everyone is going around disliking (or worse) me, saying bad things about me, trying to destroy me personally and/or professionally, the thoughts are still there and still demand attention. When I talk to you about paranoia, depression, etc., how it really surfaced within the last 5 years, it's not just some abstract, detached thoughts I'm giving you. They're things which come from the darkest recesses and which are both sad and scary to me. [16]

At times over the ensuing weeks and months he said the prescription drugs he was taking were making a difference. For instance, on August 23, 2000, Ivins wrote that "suicidal thoughts were a part of my life for the past few years until I got put on the medication." [17]

Yet he was soon back to belaboring his difficulties. "The people in my group [therapy sessions] just don't pick up on what I
try to say," he wrote Linscott on March 4, 2001.

> They are not into the kinds of problems I bring up, so it's
> hard for them to deal with them. The psychiatrist is helpful
> only because he prescribes the Celexa. He's not that easy to
> talk to, and he doesn't really pick up on my problems. The
> woman [counselor Judith McLean] I saw before I went into
> group wanted to put me in jail. That wasn't very helpful ei-
> ther. I'm down to a point where there are some things that are
> eating away that I feel I can't tell ANYONE. You are proba-
> bly the easiest for me to talk to, but it is difficult for me to ask
> that you not tell anyone else what I say. That is a lot to ask
> for, and you may feel that you need to share it with others.
> (Obviously if someone says that he or she is about to commit
> a crime, you should share it with the right people.) Confiden-
> tiality is too much to ask of you, so perhaps I should just take
> the Celexa and let whatever happens take its course. . . . I've
> already said too much.[18]

Soon afterward, psychiatrist Allan Levy doubled his dose of
Celexa.[19]

As Ivins struggled through the years with his psychiatric problems, he occupied one of the nation's most sensitive biodefense
positions: He routinely handled deadly and highly portable anthrax spores, and he had around-the-clock access to Fort Detrick's specially equipped biocontainment labs. Yet at no point
did Ivins's employer, the U.S. Army, review his mental health.
"Dr. Ivins was never evaluated by USAMRIID for mental fitness," an Army official wrote, in response to a Freedom of Information Act request filed by the author.[20]

This was all the more surprising given that some colleagues
knew generally of his ongoing psychiatric care. Ivins, along with
all other employees who were vaccinated against anthrax or
other pathogens, was quizzed each year by Army physicians
about his health. On February 18, 1987, he had completed a fed-

eral medical form by placing question marks next to these items regarding his psychiatric history: Memory Change, Trouble with Decisions, Hallucinations, Improbable Beliefs, and Anxiety. He routinely acknowledged that he had received outpatient psychiatric treatment, for what he described as job-related stress. It was no different in the spring of 2001, when Ivins again reported to Ward 200, home of the Special Immunizations Program, SIP, for a complete physical and the usual questions.

If Ivins had held a similarly sensitive position with the Army's nuclear or chemical warfare programs, his use of the antidepressant Celexa and the antipsychotic Zyprexa—not to mention his admission by e-mail of paranoid or delusional thoughts—would have subjected him to immediate scrutiny and suspension from sensitive duties.[21] Still, Ivins's complete medical records were within reach of the Army officials responsible for renewing his security clearance. But at USAMRIID any potential concerns about Ivins's mental health were trumped by deference to his privacy and his status as a respected senior scientist.[22]

EIGHT

I AM AN ANTHRAX
RESEARCHER!

n spring 2001, Army Major General Stephen Reeves took charge of research, development, and acquisition of all chemical and biological defense equipment and medical countermeasures for the U.S. armed forces. Reeves's predecessor had been relieved of command after he was unable to overcome the problems with the original AVA anthrax vaccine manufactured by BioPort.

This heavily influenced the approach of the two-star general, who dressed in desert-brown fatigues and spoke with an easy directness. He was also spurred by an internal memo in April in which President Bush's political strategist, Karl Rove, told Deputy Defense Secretary Paul Wolfowitz that the unresolved controversy surrounding Gulf War Syndrome and the anthrax vaccine posed "political problems for us."[1] Wolfowitz questioned whether the vaccine's health risks to U.S. military personnel were acceptable in light of what he viewed to be the "unlikely contingency" of a major anthrax attack. His staff pressed General Reeves as to whether the anthrax vaccine program was worth continuing. The pressure radiated throughout the chain of command, all the way to USAMRIID.[2]

Determined to satisfy Wolfowitz's concerns and to get the BioPort anthrax vaccine back on line, Reeves met with Bruce Ivins and David Danley to bring himself up to speed. He also arranged for regular meetings between the FDA officials who were considering whether to allow BioPort to resume production and the people who were pushing for that outcome. The meetings were typically attended by ten to fifteen Army officials, and BioPort executives brought dozens of their employees and consultants.[3] The vaccine had been the company's only revenue-generating product, and it was no exaggeration to say that Bio-Port's survival hinged on rescuing it. Company representatives contended that the FDA was using too stringent a standard for evaluating the effectiveness of the vaccine. The FDA stood firm. As the days of summer faded, production of BioPort's vaccine remained halted.

Ivins, for reasons that he kept to himself in mid- to late August of 2001, began working in his USAMRIID hot suite late at night and on weekends—alone. The hot suites are lab complexes with reverse airflow and powerful venting, designed to keep potentially deadly germs from escaping. The windowless suites are not the most comfortable of workplaces: To enter them, scientists must completely disrobe and don protective gear, which can range from scrub suits to hooded outfits resembling space suits. A thorough shower is required before leaving the suite.

None of these labs was equipped with video cameras that could have recorded what Ivins was doing. But electronic keycard records would later show that he spent more nighttime hours in the suite in August than during the previous seven months. For instance, on August 13, a Monday, Ivins was in the hot suite from 9:25 P.M. to 12:41 A.M. His nocturnal activity grew more intense with another three-hour-plus stint on August 31—the first of what would be twelve consecutive nights that he was there by himself. At no other juncture was he known to have spent so many consecutive nights in the suite.[4]

In the midst of this string of late nights, Ivins wrote to Linscott, whose return he longed for: "Oh, Mara, Mara, Mara! You don't have any idea how much we miss you!!!! I know that you are on to bigger and better things, but I don't think I'll ever stop secretly wishing that you were back here once again. You were superb, and I never, ever regretted having you in the lab. Maybe you'd like to be one of the physicians here working [clinical] trials of the new anthrax vaccine!!!!" [5]

In conversations with others, Ivins appeared to be increasingly worried about the status of the Army's overall anthrax vaccine program. On September 6, 2001, he lamented in an e-mail to Lebanon High School classmate Rick Sams the lack of support for his work. Ivins also took note of news reports about a secret Pentagon proposal to test whether the existing BioPort vaccine would be effective against more potent, genetically engineered anthrax. [6]

"Things never cease to be chaotic around here, largely because of the political nature of the entire military anthrax vaccine program," Ivins wrote. "We just learned that the Pentagon has a secret project to develop anthrax bacteria with augmented virulence and the possible ability to defeat the anthrax vaccine. I'm opposed to this kind of research, but my voice doesn't count." [7]

And Ivins again expressed concern about what would happen to the prospects for a new vaccine if the BioPort vaccine were kept out of production. "We are currently finishing up the last of the AVA, and when that is gone, there's nothing to replace it with," Ivins wrote in an e-mail to Linscott on September 7, 2001. [8]

Adding to his concern about the future of his project was the knowledge that Pentagon officials already had been prodding managers at USAMRIID to shift personnel and resources away from anthrax vaccine research to the development of products to be used against other biological warfare pathogens, such as glanders, tularemia, and plague. [9] In the summer of 2001, Army management approached Ivins about studying glanders, a bacterium that kills both livestock and humans. One Army officer at USAMRIID later told the FBI that Ivins had reacted vehemently to the idea. "I am an anthrax researcher! This is what I do." [10]

The officer, microbiologist Lieutenant Colonel Jeffrey Adamovicz, who was then Ivins's direct supervisor, also knew that Ivins wanted to continue working on anthrax. But they both believed that funding for anthrax vaccine research would be decreased.

On August 29, 2001, Ivins traveled to the Pentagon to discuss the plight of the next-generation vaccine at a meeting called by Anna Johnson-Winegar, deputy assistant secretary of defense for chemical and biological readiness. Some three decades earlier, Johnson-Winegar had been the first researcher to work with anthrax at the then newly formed USAMRIID. Now she had a major say in funding priorities for all of the Pentagon's medical research programs—and she had doubts about the effectiveness of the new anthrax vaccine. It was Johnson-Winegar who had written the letter that resulted in the overtures to transition Ivins from anthrax to glanders.[11]

Ivins saw another threat to his co-invention: With funding from the National Institutes of Health, a government contractor had manufactured a modest quantity of rPA in what was intended to be the first use of the vaccine in human beings. If rPA performed well in the study, its chances would improve for displacing AVA as the military's anthrax vaccine. But the contractor that had produced the small lot of rPA was demanding more money to hedge against potential lawsuits.

"They were paid and they produced it," Ivins said in a lengthy e-mail on September 7, 2001. "Now they are refusing to release it unless the Army pays some incredible sum of money for lawsuit indemnification (about $200,000 per year for the next 50 years). The Army refuses to do that of course, and everything is in Limbo."[12]

Meanwhile, officials at the FDA weren't budging on the oldline vaccine, AVA. The regulators insisted that bringing AVA back on line hinged on satisfactory data, not yet provided by BioPort. General Reeves made it clear that the Army's top priority was getting AVA back into production. In his mind, the development of rPA "was beyond the back burner."[13]

It galled Ivins that while rPA remained blocked, the Army was expending so much effort to help the BioPort scientists, who were, in Ivins's view, incompetent. "I think he was frustrated because he was one of the inventors of that rPA. That was his baby," recalled Colonel David Danley, who worked closely with Ivins at Fort Detrick and conferred with him at church at St. John's, where the two friends had sung together for more than fifteen years.[14]

As far as Bruce Ivins could see, the anthrax vaccine program— the apex of his life's work—was stalemated. And there was no looming crisis, no Soviet accident with anthrax, no anxiety of a Gulf War to shatter the inertia.

Nothing was more likely to invigorate Ivins than a dramatic news story. In addition to the O. J. Simpson case, he closely followed the Oklahoma City bombing and the JonBenet Ramsey murder.[15] One of the many letters he wrote to *Newsweek* referenced an article the magazine published about the arrest of Ted Kaczynski, the Unabomber.[16] Those who worked around Ivins grew inured to his excited, even extreme reactions to the headlines of the day.

At some point between 8:30 and 9 A.M. on September 11, however, Jeffrey Adamovicz, Ivins's boss and the deputy division chief, realized that this time Ivins was bursting with information that could not be ignored. On that still, blue-skied Tuesday morning, when Ivins bolted out of Room 19 and across the hall, Adamovicz could see that he had something urgent to share. "Bruce Ivins came running into my office and said, 'They've just slammed a plane into the World Trade Center!'"[17]

The attacks in New York and on the Pentagon immediately became personal for Ivins and his family. Their two-story house on Military Road was within sight of the main gate into Fort Detrick. By noon on September 11 barricades were posted, diverting all vehicle traffic. The Ivins children, the twins Amanda and Andy, were seniors at Prospect Hall, a Catholic high school on the southwest side of Frederick. Parents of some of the students worked at the Pentagon or in downtown Washington, and school administrators halted classes early.

By the time the family reassembled on the evening of September 11, the shocking events were still sinking in. Ivins had brimmed with alarm that morning. Only a few paces from his own driveway lay Fort Detrick's fenced perimeter, and Ivins had worried aloud to colleagues about the prospect that one of the hijacked planes would ditch into the biowarfare facility. Around his children, however, Ivins had always avoided discussing the dangers of living so near all those deadly microorganisms. It was no different now, several hours after the hijackings.

Yet there was no avoiding the day's horrific images when he and Amanda sat down that night to watch the news. The footage evoked a response in him that she had not seen before.

"I remember he and I watching people jumping out of the towers. He just started crying. I'd never seen my dad cry before. He was sensitive, but he didn't cry." His reaction so unsettled Amanda that she left the room.[18]

By Saturday, September 15, 2001, Ivins's focus appeared to have shifted toward the hijackers—and their unspecified enablers. "I am incredibly sad and angry at what happened, now that it has sunk in," he wrote a friend by e-mail. "Sad for all of the victims, their families, their friends. And angry. Very angry. Angry at those who did this, who support them, who coddle them, and who excuse them."[19]

A few days later he told Mara Linscott, "Things are still on edge here" at USAMRIID. He favored a fighting response to September 11 and he noted that he told his therapy group about how he had carried a gun "for years," hoping that a mugger would approach him. "I used to walk in a bad part of town hoping someone would try something so I could use it." In the same e-mail, he raised his still simmering anger at his mother. "There are several people in our group who belong to the 'bad mothers club.' We all had mothers from hell, who physically or mentally or verbally abused their kids, were never satisfied with their performance, etc."[20]

NINE

THIS IS NEXT

Bruce Edwards Ivins, the prodigy of the dysfunctional family from small-town Ohio, the postdoc who saw himself so smart as to be Mensa material, the career Army microbiologist, was now fifty-five years old and at a crossroads: The anthrax vaccine program—and with it his stature as a scientist—was at risk. From his formative experience with the Gulf War and before that the accident in Sverdlovsk, Ivins knew that one thing could rescue the program: the transformative power of fear. The events of September 11 had outraged him. But they might also present an opportunity.

After having spent parts of twelve consecutive nights in the hot suite, including nearly an hour on the night of September 11, Ivins was at USAMRIID only during regular hours for the next couple of days. And then he resumed piling up nighttime hours in the specially equipped laboratory:

Beginning on Friday, September 14, and continuing on Saturday and Sunday, Ivins was at USAMRIID on three consecutive nights. For a total of more than seven hours he was again alone in the hot suite. He left USAMRIID those nights at 12:22 A.M., 11:59 P.M., and, on Sunday, September 16, at 9:52 P.M.

On Monday, September 17, Ivins worked four hours outside the hot suite in the morning, and then drew from his annual leave time to take the afternoon off. After attending a group therapy session at Comprehensive Counseling late in the day, he returned to USAMRIID's main building at 7 P.M. and stayed for just thirteen minutes without entering a lab. For nearly twelve hours, until he arrived at USAMRIID the next day at 7:02 A.M., Ivins's whereabouts were known only to him.

Sometime between 5 P.M. on Monday, September 17, and noon the next day, envelopes addressed by hand to Tom Brokaw, the NBC News anchor, and to "Editor" of the *New York Post* were dropped into a street-level mailbox in leafy downtown Princeton, New Jersey, 197 miles from Fort Detrick. The Princeton mailbox was far from Fort Detrick—yet close enough for a calculating perpetrator: Even if a slightly circuitous route were followed so as to avoid the fixed cameras at toll plazas, the round-trip could be driven in less than eight hours.

The letter to Brokaw was addressed to 30 Rockefeller Plaza in New York City, the same address, it turned out, where Bruce Ivins had sent his letter in 1987, pitching a miniseries about Christa McAuliffe.[1] Neither of the two anthrax-laced envelopes bore a return address, but the mailbox, at 10 Nassau Street, Princeton, was adjacent to an office of another institution with which Ivins was well familiar, the sorority Kappa Kappa Gamma. On September 18, the envelopes were collected from the mailbox and postmarked at a mail-handling facility in nearby Trenton. Each envelope contained a photocopy of the same hand-printed six-line letter:

09-11-01
THIS IS NEXT
TAKE PENACILIN NOW
DEATH TO AMERICA
DEATH TO ISRAEL
ALLAH IS GREAT

The sender seemed to know that penicillin, the antibiotic, was effective against something else that was tucked into each envelope: a pinch of visibly coarse powder, its granules flecked off-black, tan, and white. "THIS IS NEXT" was anthrax.[2]

Three days later, on September 21, 2001, while the existence of the anthrax-laced letters remained unknown to the public, Bruce Ivins prophesied more trouble. He did so in an e-mail to Nancy Haigwood that came "out of the blue" as far as she was concerned. For decades, Ivins had maintained his fixation with her and her sorority, tracking her moves from North Carolina to Maryland to the San Francisco Bay Area and then to the Pacific Northwest. He had stayed in touch with sporadic calls and notes.

Haigwood had long regarded Ivins as peculiar, yet she also pitied him. Although she had made no effort to keep in touch, she had also not insisted that he stop contacting her. Ivins was annoyingly strange, but he seemed desperately in need of a friendly ear. And besides, Haigwood during these years was living and working a continent away, as a scientific researcher in Seattle, then in Portland. She did not see him as an imminent danger to herself. She was willing to remain a mostly passive recipient of his messages.[3]

In his September 21 e-mail, Ivins suggested that he and his colleagues were at center stage in what he expected to be an ongoing crisis for America. "Here at USAMRIID we are constantly getting security updates, and since we are the primary BW [biological warfare] research center in this country, we are all more than a bit on edge. It's believed that Fort Detrick may have been one of the possible targets for the plane that crashed in Pennsylvania." (Ivins was referring to United Airlines Flight 93, which crashed in Shanksville, Pennsylvania, on September 11, 2001.)[4]

Ivins then drew upon his exhilarating experiences from a decade earlier to speculate about the future. "During the Gulf War we worked very long days and were on call 24 hours a day, 7 days a week. I won't be surprised if that becomes the case again. The Diagnostic Division of the institute is on full alert and ready to process environmental samples when they come in. In a related matter, I've decided to take Red Cross training to become a disaster volunteer."[5] (His application to the Red Cross cited his expertise in "anthrax research.")[6]

Ivins would later say that he decided to e-mail Haigwood on September 21 in order to refresh their acquaintanceship.[7] He talked in the same e-mail about developing an unspecified product. "The bureaucratic paperwork and red tape have increased exponentially, and the lab work has plummeted. I hope one day to actually see a product for our labors."[8] This product was, of course, the next-generation anthrax vaccine.

One day earlier, on September 20, Ivins had touted in an e-mail his expertise with anthrax to a scientist whose employer was also involved in helping to develop the new vaccine:

> I would be willing to come up to Battelle [Memorial Institute] to offer advice or suggestions with respect to spore production, purification, storage, etc. When we first started working on it years ago, it took us quite awhile to learn the 'art' and techniques involved in getting spores which were stable, pure, unclumped, etc. Honestly, in 1 day to no more than a week, I might be able to save more than several weeks to several months worth of work on your part. Although spore production and purification sounds, on the surface, very easy and cookbook, there are some little nuances in methodology which are important, yet hard to write down.[9]

It was just two days before Ivins had written this e-mail—boasting of his ability to shave weeks or months off the time it would take to prepare "stable, pure, unclumped" spores—that the anthrax-laced letters addressed to Tom Brokaw and the *New York Post* were postmarked in Trenton.

On September 26, Ivins described to Mara Linscott the post-9/11 reactions of the people in his group therapy sessions and his own quite different state of mind: "Of the people in my 'group,' everyone but me is in the depression/sadness/flight mode for stress. I'm really the only scary one in the group. Others are talking about how sad they are or scared they are, but my reaction to the WTC/Pentagon events is far different."

In the same e-mail, Ivins linked the perpetrators of September 11 to anthrax:

I just heard tonight that the Bin Laden terrorists for sure have anthrax and sarin gas. . . . The news media has been saying that some members of Congress and members of the ACLU oppose many of the Justice Department proposals for combating terrorism, saying that they are unconstitutional and infringe too much on civil liberties. . . . Osama Bin Laden has just decreed death to all Jews and all Americans. But I guess that doesn't mean a lot to the ACLU.[10]

At the time he wrote, the existence of the anthrax-laced letters with their "DEATH TO AMERICA," "DEATH TO ISRAEL" message had still not been discovered by the authorities or the news media.[11]

From September 17 to 24, Ivins spent no time in the hot suite at night. On the night of Wednesday, September 25, one week after the first letters had been postmarked in New Jersey, he stayed nearly two hours in the suite, leaving at 9:27 P.M. And he was alone there every night from September 28 through October 5, totaling 15 hours and 17 minutes. During those eight nights he left USAMRIID at 10:59 P.M., 11:18 P.M., 12:04 A.M., 10:43 P.M., 9:39 P.M., 10:55 P.M., 10:12 P.M., and 12:43 A.M. His longest nights in the suite were Wednesday, October 3, for 2 hours, 59 minutes; Thursday, October 4, for 3 hours, 33 minutes; and Friday, October 5, for 3 hours, 42 minutes.[12]

In the midst of his second round of late nights in the hot suite, for which his lab notebooks provided no plausible explanation, Ivins had hinted anew to Linscott about a biological attack. He wrote on October 3:

You should feel good about having received anthrax [vaccine] shots. I remember mentioning to you the possibility that after you got your degree you might be interested in being an "on call" physician for any suspected BW attacks in this country. With your experience (and the fact that you've been immunized against different agents) and with people in high places talking about BW terrorism being likely, your knowledge, skills and abilities could be a real asset. I'm hoping such an attack doesn't happen, of course. On a more humorous note, if a BW "crop duster" ever does buzz through your city, you can just look up in the sky, knowing your immune system is ready, and give him the finger.[13]

It was now the Columbus Day weekend, a three-day holiday for federal workers, including those at USAMRIID. At some time between 3 P.M. on Saturday, October 6, and noon on Tuesday, October 9, two more envelopes laced with anthrax were slipped into the same mailbox in Princeton as used for the first letters. These mailings were near-duplicates of those sent in September: the same model of prestamped envelopes, addressed by hand and sealed with transparent tape; a photocopied note, also with hand-printed lettering; and a pinch of powdered anthrax placed inside the note itself, which was folded twice horizontally and twice vertically, a style once common among pharmacists.

TEN

ON THE WRONG TRAIL

O n the afternoon of October 3, 2001—the same day on which Ivins had written to Linscott about possible "BW" attacks—sixty-three-year-old Robert Stevens lay gravely ill at JFK Medical Center in Palm Beach County, Florida. He had arrived early the morning before, confused and with a 102.5-degree fever. Now he was unconscious, his lymph nodes swollen, his organs failing.[1]

Physicians at JFK considered the range of possibilities. They questioned his wife, Maureen, for clues about his recent activities. Stevens, who edited photographs for American Media Inc., publisher of supermarket tabloids such as the *National Enquirer* and the *Sun*, did much of his work at his desk, making calls to arrange for photos, examining and sorting prints delivered by U.S. mail.

The couple met in Maureen's native England when Robert worked there as a freelance photographer. On Friday, September 28, they and their twenty-one-year-old daughter had driven the last leg of a two-day journey from the parents' home in Lantana, Florida, to Lake Lure, a resort in North Carolina. On the way the three stretched their legs with a short hike and a commercial tour of a mountain cave. Maureen recalled that Bob at one point drank by hand from a waterfall. He started feeling ill on Sunday, September 30, complaining of numbness and chills. Although he was sick, Bob stayed at the wheel the next day for the nearly seven-hundred-mile drive home.

That night his condition worsened. Now noticeably disoriented and still feverish, he arose from bed vomiting. Shortly after 2 A.M. on October 2, Maureen drove him to the emergency room at JFK. Although still confused, Bob Stevens was able to walk into the hospital. Yet by 8 A.M., when Maureen returned, he had suffered a seizure and lost consciousness. What would make a patient so sick so fast? An infectious disease specialist, Dr. Larry M. Bush, was summoned to develop a diagnosis and a strategy for treatment. Bush reviewed CT scans and radiographs of the patient's chest. The X-ray images showed the middle section of Stevens's chest compartment, or mediastinum, was abnormally widened, suggesting extreme inflammation.

Several vials of cerebrospinal fluid were drawn. Ordinarily the fluid, which surrounds the brain and spinal cord, would be clear, but Bush could see that Stevens's looked cloudy. What Bush saw when he examined it under a microscope was even more ominous: rod-shaped bacteria that were lined up like boxcars.

Bush realized that those rod shapes resembled something extraordinarily rare and frightening: *Bacillus anthracis*—anthrax— the hardy germ that can long lie dormant before infecting livestock or other grazing animals. Stevens's widened mediastinum was another sign of inhalational anthrax—usually fatal unless caught promptly and treated with an antibiotic. Still, these signs did not yet amount to proof.

Bush quickly relayed his concerns to Dr. Jean Malecki, the Palm Beach County health director. More testing of the cerebrospinal fluid would be done overnight at a state lab in Jacksonville, Bush explained. A sample was also being flown to the federal Centers for Disease Control and Prevention in Atlanta.

Yet Dr. Bush wanted Dr. Malecki to know right then: He was convinced this was inhalational anthrax—perhaps the first such case ever seen in Florida.[2]

No inhalational anthrax had been reported in the entire United States in more than two decades. And only eighteen cases were reported from 1900 to 1978. Most of the victims were exposed through their occupations, such as mill workers handling goat hair or hides.[3] Bob Stevens was a photo editor, not a wool sorter. But by the night of Wednesday, October 3, the state lab confirmed that he was, indeed, infected with *Bacillus anthracis*. The diagnosis would remain confidential for only a few more hours.

On the morning of Thursday, October 4, President George W. Bush traveled by motorcade from the White House to the State Department for a speech to career staffers. Bush wanted to rally the employees after the events of September 11. He told them how vital their craft of diplomacy was to countering the seeds of terrorism. As he voiced his confidence and faith in them, the president's eyes welled with tears. The emotion startled his press secretary, Ari Fleischer, who observed Bush every day and could anticipate his spoken words along with his more visceral reactions.

As they returned to the White House, the president gestured for him. Inside the Oval Office, Bush told Fleischer that he had learned earlier that morning about a confirmed case of anthrax in Florida. It was twenty-three days after September 11. The country had been bracing for a second wave of terrorism—and the president thought the moment had come. "You could just see a distressed, saddened man," Fleischer recalled. "Because he thought it was happening again. . . . I've never seen him so low." Fleischer remained in the Oval Office when, a few minutes later, Bush was visited by Vicente Fox, the president of Mexico. The two leaders conversed briefly about matters related to the September 11 attacks. Bush, without revealing what he had just told Fleischer, remarked to his Mexican counterpart: "If there's another incident—we'll have to dig way down within our souls to rally the world."[4]

Health and Human Services secretary Tommy Thompson had gotten his own briefings, chiefly from the Centers for Disease Control, one of the agencies he oversaw. That afternoon Thompson went to the White House, where Bush designated him to make the administration's first public comments about the case in Florida. Thompson's reflex reaction, like that of other elected figures in the aftermath of the September 11 attacks, was to emulate Mayor Rudy Giuliani, who amid public panic demonstrated defiant calm, showing the world that New York would not be intimidated.

Thompson was a lawyer with a down-home style that had helped get him elected governor of Wisconsin four times, and, like Giuliani, he had presidential aspirations. At 3:43 P.M., he strode before the bright lights of the White House briefing room, accompanied by Fleischer. Thompson had been advised that Robert Stevens had inhalational anthrax, but that it was unclear how he had contracted it. Suggesting that Stevens's infection was probably unrelated to terrorism, Thompson told the assembled members of the press that "sporadic cases of anthrax do occur in the United States," although the most recent reported case was in 1976.[5] The anthrax diagnosis in Florida, Thompson said, "may be a result of the heightened level of disease monitoring being done by the public health and medical community."

This was supposed to be good news. "The system works," Thompson said, three times. This was an "isolated case," he said, six times. A physician just recruited from the Centers for Disease Control, Scott Lillibridge, stepped to the microphone and reiterated this message. Cases of anthrax, Lillibridge said, "are sporadic, episodic things that happen from time to time." These infections "may occur from contact with wool, animal products, hides, that sort of thing."

Thompson was asked, "[I]s there any reason to believe this is a result of terrorism?" He replied: "It appears that this is just an isolated case. There is no evidence of terrorism." The fact was that neither Thompson nor anyone other than the perpetrator was then in a position to know whether the Florida case was caused by terrorism or by stray spores from a sheep's hide.

A reporter with CBS, John Roberts, kept pressing: "Did [the patient] happen to work around wool?"

Thompson interrupted: "We don't know at this point in time. That's entirely possible. We do know that he drank water out of a stream when he was traveling through North Carolina last week." [6]

Could this mean that Stevens contracted anthrax by, of all things, swallowing water? If this checked out, it would be the first such case recorded in U.S. history.[7] The president's number one health official, who had no formal scientific training and almost no knowledge of *Bacillus anthracis*, was out of his lane. Whether or not Stevens drank from the stream could have nothing to do with how he contracted inhalational anthrax.

At the hospital where Stevens lay comatose, federal, state, and local health officials took notice of the White House news conference. Larry Bush, the infectious disease specialist who had first suggested the diagnosis of inhalational anthrax, was astonished by Thompson's mention of the mountain stream. It made no sense to him.

At the Pentagon, Colonel Robert Kadlec, the flight surgeon who in the preparations for the Gulf War had injected hundreds of Special Forces personnel with anthrax vaccine, looked at colleagues in disbelief. Inhalational anthrax—from a stream? "You gotta be shittin' me!" [8]

Away from public view, tension was flaring between senior CDC officials and the FBI, which after September 11 had been on the alert for more terrorism. As exemplified by Dr. Lillibridge in the White House briefing room, the CDC's impulse was to regard the Florida case as an isolated event, a one-off that most likely had a natural cause. An axiom of public health seemed to be in effect: When you hear hoofbeats, think horses, not zebras.

This was a sound way to approach most natural outbreaks of infectious disease, to rule out the ordinary before considering the extraordinary. Yet it was also true that the CDC had virtually no experience responding to an act of biological terrorism. How could it? The only such event known to have occurred in the United States was in 1984, when members of the Rajneesh religious cult, founded by an Indian mystic, sprinkled salmonella bacteria on salad bars at ten restaurants in the area of The Dalles, a city in Oregon, sickening 751 or more customers. The crime had been perpetrated in a failed attempt to influence the results of a local election by incapacitating potential voters.[9]

Thompson's remarks about the diagnosis of anthrax in Florida were reported that night by each of the major television news networks. While the health authorities tried to make better sense of the case, at 9:57 on the night of October 4—the next to last of eight consecutive nights he would be working alone in a hot suite at USAMRIID—Bruce Ivins e-mailed an epidemiologist at the CDC, seeking details and offering to help. "I just heard this evening (and read over internet news) that a case of pulmonary anthrax may have been identified in Florida," Ivins wrote. "Is this true, or is this just hysteria? . . . If there's anything I can help with here (if you or your coworkers are involved) please let me know." [10]

The CDC epidemiologist, Arnold F. Kaufmann, was well acquainted with Ivins. The two had first met at an anthrax conference in Britain in the 1980s and had stayed in touch intermittently. But Kaufmann could not recall another occasion when Ivins contacted him with questions about a pending matter. He decided to call Ivins the next day.

Moments after Ivins answered, on the morning of Friday, October 5, it appeared that he was highly agitated about the Florida case. Kaufmann confirmed that the patient had inhalational anthrax. Ivins then let fly his opinions. The CDC and its collection of fools were "missing the boat," he said. "Why are they wasting their time in North Carolina?" The CDC was "on the wrong trail." He pressed Kaufmann for details about what else was being done. Kaufmann explained that the CDC had "to cover all bases" and that teams were working in both North Carolina, where Stevens had gone hiking, and in Palm Beach County, Florida, where Stevens had lived and worked.

The conversation lasted no more than fifteen minutes, but it left an impression on Kaufmann: Bruce Ivins seemed to be taking this case personally.[11]

———

How did Robert Stevens contract such a spectacularly rare infection? The FBI turned for help to Paul S. Keim, a geneticist in Flagstaff, Arizona. On October 4 at about 1:30 P.M., Keim received a call from Douglas J. Beecher, one of only two microbiologists then employed by the bureau. Beecher said that a sample of Stevens's cerebrospinal fluid had been drawn so that Keim's lab could help to identify the strain of anthrax that was killing Stevens.[12]

At six-foot-five, Keim looms over most people. Whether discussing the lab work he oversees at Northern Arizona University in Flagstaff or his latest raft trip through the nearby Grand Canyon, he exudes enthusiasm. Yet his unhurried voice is rarely the loudest in a room. It needn't be. Keim's success at untangling the genetic code of organisms from soybeans to snails to anthrax speaks for itself.

He was born in Twin Falls, Idaho, a high-desert town where his father, Bob, served as a preacher for the Church of the Brethren, one of three Protestant denominations in North America that espouse pacifism. Paul Keim's paternal grandfather was also a Brethren preacher in Idaho. The family soon moved to Sacramento, California, and then to McPherson, Kansas, a winter wheat and oil field town about fifty miles northwest of Wichita. There Paul and his younger brother for a time attended a two-room schoolhouse. Many of their buddies were the sons of farmers or parents otherwise involved with agriculture. Paul thought he wanted to be a lawyer—until an outspoken high school science teacher lit a fire under him to pursue a career as an evolutionary biologist.

In 1972, when Paul started his senior year of high school, the Vietnam War was winding down but combat continued. As did the draft. School officials across the country warned young males to register—or else. Consistent with his religion and the example set by his grandfather and father, Paul registered—not for the draft, but as a conscientious objector. If his draft number were called, he would go to prison instead of basic training. Within months President Nixon announced a peace agreement. Keim's abhorrence of war would remain a part of him.

He enrolled at tiny McPherson College, and, after cracking its starting basketball lineup his sophomore season, he transferred to Northern Arizona University, where he continued to build a foundation for a scientific career by majoring in both biology and chemistry. After graduating in 1977, he broadened his expertise, earning a Ph.D. in plant biochemistry from the University of Kansas, and then training as a microbiologist during six years as a postdoctoral associate and research assistant at the University of Utah. There, under the tutelage of an acclaimed mentor, Karl Lark, Keim's eyes were opened to an emerging frontier: applying molecular biology to the study of genetics. Keim learned how to clone DNA along with the technique for locating its information-carrying components. Just as important, Lark instilled in Keim "a scattered and chaotic approach" that freed him to think more creatively. (One of Keim's senior colleagues, Mario R. Capecchi, would win a Nobel Prize.)

In 1987, Keim and his wife, Jenny, left Utah for Iowa State, where for two years Paul studied the genome of the soybean, research that had the practical goal of increasing yields of the multipurpose food source. He wound up constructing the first molecular genetic map of the soybean.

Keim had left other comfortable situations to stretch himself— to pursue the challenge of applying lessons learned from one field to another. The trade-off was that, nearly two decades after getting his undergraduate degree, he still lacked the sheaf of published papers that university hiring and tenure committees wanted to see. He returned to Northern Arizona University, the only place to offer him a full-time faculty job. He looked forward to studying the genetics of a wide range of plant and animal life, some of it near Flagstaff, elevation seven thousand feet.

By the spring of 1994 Paul and Jenny were the parents of two young children and Paul, then thirty-eight, had at last gained tenure—but his position paid the grand sum of $30,000. Keim discussed his situation with a biologist friend, Paul J. Jackson at the Los Alamos National Laboratory in New Mexico. Jackson invited Keim to work the summer in Los Alamos, where Jackson and his staff were involved with a sensitive government project. "We're doing this genetic analysis," Jackson said. "But it's secret stuff, confidential. I can't tell you about it yet. I've got some money; I'll pay you for the summer if you come over. We'll get you a security clearance so we can talk about this project. I think you could really contribute to it."

Keim drove his pickup the four hundred miles to Los Alamos, where he slept weeknights in his camper, in nearby woods. Jackson's project, Keim learned, concerned anthrax. The client was the Central Intelligence Agency. The agency was trying to figure out which potential adversaries possessed anthrax and, if so, where it may have originated. Of particular interest was whether North Korea had sent anthrax to Libya, Iraq, or elsewhere. "They needed to tell one type of *Bacillus anthracis* from another type of *Bacillus anthracis*. And I looked at their problem and I said, 'Wow, this is really approachable by the ecological methods that we're using for plants and animals and birds.'"

The opportunity was a perfect fit with Keim's years of experience. A high-level security clearance was granted. One of the projects he was assigned entailed analyzing material that United Nations inspectors had found in hundreds of large paper sacks at Al Hakam, a facility about forty miles southwest of Baghdad. French scientists said it was anthrax—a worrisome conclusion. In 1996, Keim accompanied Jackson for a spirited meeting with officials at CIA headquarters in Langley, Virginia, where the two scientists explained their contrary conclusion. "Our result said that it was not anthrax. But it was damn close," Keim said. Jackson and Keim said it appeared to be a derivative of *Bacillus thuringiensis*, Bt, an anthrax simulant that is not lethal to humans but can be used for pest control. Only this material didn't kill insects. Aside from using it as a simulant for biowarfare testing, it remained unclear what the Iraqis could have been doing with the material, which they had treated with a claylike drying agent called bentonite.

Keim was excited about the scientific challenges posed by anthrax. Compared to most organisms, anthrax (invariably *Bacillus anthracis* in Keim's vocabulary) is uncommonly homogenous; no matter where it is found around the world, the bacterium has very little genetic variation, and what variation there is can be hard to detect. Scientists must examine precise regions of the genome to distinguish one strain of anthrax from another. The parsing of the strains can be helped greatly by maintaining a repository of as many samples as possible, allowing for efficient comparisons.

Local political sensitivities prevented Paul Jackson from housing such a collection at Los Alamos. Keim and his staff in Flagstaff filled the void, quickly assembling some two hundred anthrax isolates from around the world and, eventually, more than two thousand. Keim and one of his most skilled assistants, microbiologist James Schupp, began peering into the DNA of the myriad samples. Some of the strains were barely distinguishable; others were obviously different. His lab's reputation for discretion and competence was further enhanced when Keim was called upon to analyze remnants of anthrax spores that a religious cult, Aum Shinrikyo, had sprayed over Kameido, Japan, a suburb of Tokyo, in 1993. No casualties were reported. Using a DNA fingerprinting technique that Keim invented, the lab found that the material was the nonlethal Sterne strain of anthrax, used to vaccinate animals.[13] (In 1995, followers of Aum Shinrikyo mounted a different attack, dispensing a chemical weapon, sarin gas, in the Tokyo subway. This time, at least a dozen people were killed.)

———

Anthrax research was ongoing worldwide, conducted by a relatively few top experts who met occasionally to discuss their findings. In September 1998, Paul Keim and Bruce Ivins got acquainted at one such gathering, a meeting of the International Conference on *Bacillus anthracis*, in Plymouth, England. Keim presented details of his team's progress in distinguishing the differing strains of anthrax. The dean of British anthrax researchers, Harry Smith, stood amid the 130 or so scientists who attended and called Keim's work the most significant development to be aired at the conference.

Without question the most sensational issue to be discussed at the Plymouth meeting was a recently published paper in which Russian scientists claimed to have genetically engineered a strain of anthrax capable of withstanding their country's protective vaccine.[14] Western scientists had been unable to verify the reported results, and more than a few were skeptical. But concern persisted among U.S. officials—and biowarfare experts, including Bruce Ivins.

In a letter to one of his high school classmates, Ivins spotlighted his role in countering the newly revealed menace. "FLASH!! Stop the presses! Russian scientists have just announced that they have developed (using recombinant DNA techniques) a virulent strain of anthrax bacteria RESISTANT to the vaccine. Thanks, guys. (Next stop with their strain is . . . Tehran? . . . Baghdad?) Oh well, back to the lab." [15]

Even before publication of the Russians' article, rumors of a new super-strain of Russian anthrax had been taken seriously by U.S. intelligence and defense officials, triggering fresh interest in the next-generation anthrax vaccine that Ivins and his USAMRIID colleagues had been working on. (It was the publication of this Russian research that had coincided with Defense Secretary William Cohen's decision to require anthrax vaccine injections for most service personnel.)

Ivins himself was accomplished at growing and purifying anthrax spores for experiments on animals. Now, in an attempt to speed along the many experiments that would be necessary to test the new vaccine, he arranged for the transfer of 1,000 milliliters of highly concentrated Ames anthrax spores, suspended in liquid form, from the Army's Dugway Proving Ground to USAMRIID. Ivins washed some of the spores to purify them of dead anthrax cells and other debris. Then he mixed in other spores that he and a colleague had grown and prepared at USAMRIID.

Ivins wrote in his notebook that the newly assembled batch (he referred to it in conversation as "the Dugway spores") contained at least 99 percent pure spores with no clumping. He accounted for it on the Army's Reference Material Receipt Record form, and assigned the spores inventory number 1029. The batch would become known as RMR-1029.[16]

What the Russians might be up to was a focal point for both Ivins and Keim. Ivins and others at USAMRIID were interested in whether certain virulent strains of anthrax were more deadly than others. A related concern was whether the existing U.S. anthrax vaccine could be relied upon to protect against any strain of anthrax in the world. Keim, with his far-reaching collection of strains, and Ivins, with his ability to conduct virulent-anthrax tests on animals at USAMRIID, were in a position to help each other. Their meeting in the fall of 1998 set in motion a scientific relationship that endured.

U.S. officials were bedeviled by this latest Russian riddle. The breakup of the Soviet Union had called into question the security of the former superpower's arsenal of all types of weapons. Although public attention in the United States was focused on the chilling prospect of poorly guarded or loose nuclear material, another possibility was that Russian anthrax could find its way to a rogue state or to a terrorist organization. And there was little doubt that the Russians had made lots of anthrax, as was strongly suggested by the deadly 1979 accident at Sverdlovsk.

The cause of the deaths was covered up for years by the Soviet regime but was finally acknowledged in 1992 by newly elected president Boris Yeltsin, who had earlier represented Sverdlovsk as a member of the Communist Party. Keim, through his work with Paul Jackson at Los Alamos, helped examine samples of brain matter and other tissue recovered from a few of the Sverdlovsk victims and smuggled to the United States. Their initial findings suggested that the plume at Sverdlovsk carried multiple strains of virulent anthrax. This did nothing to quell concern over whether the existing U.S. vaccine conferred sufficiently broad protection.

Even before FBI microbiologist Douglas Beecher's call on the afternoon of October 4, 2001, alerting him that the Florida patient's cerebrospinal fluid was on a plane to Flagstaff, Keim had been involved with plenty of sensitive work. He had done the special analyses for the CIA, and he had advised criminal defense lawyers on DNA evidence. Yet most of that was aimed at bringing greater understanding to events of the past. He had seen no need to carry a cell phone or a pager. Now he could sense his life changing. He was being brought into the heart of investigating what could be a national security crisis.

Around 5 P.M., Keim began the eight-minute drive from his campus lab through Ponderosa pines to Flagstaff Pulliam Airport. The two staffers on duty at the airport manager's office were tracking the flight from Atlanta. One of them asked Keim if he'd like to drive out onto the tarmac when the plane landed. About thirty minutes later, Keim did just that, pulling his Toyota 4Runner to about sixty feet from the starboard wing. The jet's side hatch opened and a woman descended the steps, carrying a cardboard box with a vial inside, on ice.

When Keim returned to the lab, two of his assistants were waiting. The three worked through the night, using high-speed computing along with the lab's repository of DNA fingerprints, called profiles, of the most likely anthrax strains. By about 7 A.M., they had concluded that it appeared to be the Ames strain, a virulent anthrax used by some biodefense researchers—the first were Bruce Ivins and his Army colleagues at Fort Detrick, Maryland—since the 1980s. Keim conferred by phone with officials at both the FBI and the CDC, heretofore the lead federal agency looking into what had at first seemed a matter of public health, not criminality. The CDC officials had conducted their own overnight analysis of Stevens's fluid, using technology transferred to the agency earlier by Keim. They agreed: It was indeed the Ames strain.

What had come to be known as the Ames strain originated on a sprawling Texas cattle ranch in Hebbronville, Jim Hogg County, about a hundred miles southwest of Corpus Christi. In 1981, a burly local veterinarian, Mike Vickers, scraped anthrax-infected tissue from the brain and other organs of a dead Texas Beefmaster Hereford, packed the material on ice within a zip-locked bag, and sent it by bus to veterinary officials at Texas A&M University for a diagnosis. Vickers wrote in his postmortem report that when he had found the cow in the morning she was "unable to rise," adding: "By noon she was dead." (Anthrax kills livestock and deer with some regularity in this part of South Texas.)[17]

By coincidence, the officials at Texas A&M had recently gotten a letter from an Army biologist at Fort Detrick, who said he was seeking new anthrax strains to challenge the military's existing vaccine. When testing by the Texas officials confirmed that Vickers's cow was killed by anthrax, albeit not a strain they were familiar with, they sent samples to the Fort Detrick biologist, Gregory B. Knudson—using a prepaid mailing label displaying the return address as the National Veterinary Services Laboratories in Ames, Iowa.[18] Hence the Ames strain, a misnomer that years later would cause some confusion.

In early 1981, after the package arrived at Fort Detrick, Bruce Ivins and others began using Ames to infect animals as part of their efforts to develop new vaccines and other biowarfare countermeasures. It was through this work that Ivins became a master at producing highly purified spores of Ames anthrax. He knew what growth medium worked best and when to raise or lower the temperature of an incubator to produce the highest concentration of pure spores. He would examine the material with a microscope and if the spores looked shiny, "refractile" in the argot of anthrax, he knew he was on the way to success. Ivins cultured and grew ample quantities of the spores—eventually sharing them with researchers at other labs in the United States and abroad. Keim's lab in Arizona was among the recipients of Ames strain anthrax (although apparently not RMR-1029, the unique batch of Ames that Ivins prepared in 1997).

Keim knew that, aside from the original dead cow, Ames was not a strain that had been observed in the wild. He called the FBI's Douglas Beecher to share the news. Both knew what it meant to have discovered Ames within the Florida patient: "The implications were that this was a bioterrorism event," Keim recalled. "It came out of a laboratory." [19]

Robert Stevens died on October 5, 2001, the day after Keim received the sample of his cerebrospinal fluid. The FBI and the U.S.

Postal Service formed an investigative task force, which would be called Amerithrax. Beecher was disappointed to learn that trash from American Media's offices in Boca Raton, where Stevens had worked, was routinely incinerated instead of going to a local landfill. This would make more difficult the investigation into how Stevens might have come in contact with anthrax.

Meanwhile, Ernesto Blanco, a seventy-three-year-old man who sorted and distributed the mail at American Media, had fallen gravely ill and was hospitalized at Cedars Medical Center in Miami. Blanco, too, was diagnosed with inhalational anthrax, caused by exposure to the Ames strain.[20] Two days after Stevens died, testing confirmed the presence of anthrax spores on the photo editor's computer keyboard at work and in the mailroom. But how anthrax got into the American Media building remained a mystery. No accompanying note or letter was ever found.

Unknown to those trying to solve the puzzle, on September 18, 2001, postal sorting machines in Trenton, New Jersey, had processed the hand-inscribed envelopes, addressed to Tom Brokaw and to the New York Post, which contained spores from the same batch that had infected the American Media employees in Florida. The letter addressed to Brokaw had been opened two weeks earlier, on September 25, by one of his aides, Erin O'Connor. That same day she had complained of redness on her neck. Over the next several days she developed a softball-size wound on her shoulder, along with a low-grade fever. A dermatologist and an infectious disease specialist in New York had said that they could not rule out a skin, or cutaneous anthrax, infection and O'Connor began taking Cipro on October 1. Also in New York, a seven-month-old boy developed a bright red sore on the back of his left arm on September 29, the day after a babysitter brought him to visit the offices of ABC News, where his mother was a producer for World News Tonight. At CBS News, Claire Fletcher, an aide whose job included opening mail addressed to anchor Dan Rather, noticed on October 1 that she had a mark on her face, which she assumed was related to an insect bite. It, too, turned out to be anthrax.[21]

Considerable confusion had surrounded the envelope received at NBC. Initially, representatives of both the New York public health department and USAMRIID told Brokaw that his aide, Erin O'Connor, had most likely been bitten by a spider. Although a prescient dermatologist had prescribed Cipro to O'Connor as a precaution against anthrax, Brokaw pushed for a definitive diagnosis.[22] O'Connor ultimately was found to have cutaneous anthrax by the Centers for Disease Control, after a specialist there examined a tissue sample from her wound.[23] No suspicious envelope or note turned up at either CBS or ABC, but analyses by the CDC of samples from both patients exposed in those offices confirmed that they, too, had cutaneous anthrax.[24]

Paul Keim and Douglas Beecher had quickly recognized the Florida anthrax infections as a bioterrorism event. But on October 11—one week after Keim and the CDC determined that Robert Stevens was killed by the Ames strain—the FBI's J. T. Caruso told a congressional panel, "It is important to emphasize that, despite media suggestions to the contrary, there is no evidence that the presence of anthrax in the American Media building is a terrorist act." The anthrax detected there, Caruso said, "appears to be an isolated event."[25]

ELEVEN

IN CIPRO WE TRUST

E ven before September 11, Vice President Dick Cheney had begun pressing the Bush administration to consider biological terrorism, above all smallpox, as a significant danger. Cheney had been stirred up by a controversial mock exercise, "Dark Winter," carried out three months earlier by academics and former government officials, who warned that a domestic biological attack could result in "massive civilian casualties," along with "reduced U.S. strategic flexibility." [1]

Unlike anthrax, smallpox was contagious. But thanks to the World Health Organization, whose efforts were led by a physician and epidemiologist named Donald A. "D.A." Henderson, smallpox had been eradicated globally as a disease. As of 1972, U.S. health authorities had stopped vaccinating school-age children against the scourge. Cheney, however, believed that Iraq or another hostile entity might have acquired smallpox, perhaps from profiteering Russian scientists. Now, on the heels of September 11, the elimination of the virus as a public health threat was invoked as a new reason to fear it: Because of the cessation of vaccinations in the schools, tens of millions of Americans had grown up with no immunity to the disease.

The Bush administration had no verified information that Iraq or any other rogue regime or terrorist had gotten hold of smallpox—and some experts openly ridiculed Dark Winter's dire assumptions about how fast an outbreak could spread.[2] Nonetheless, Health and Human Services secretary Tommy Thompson announced in October 2001 that he intended to assemble 300 million doses of smallpox vaccine, enough to inoculate the entire U.S. population if necessary.[3] Dr. Philip K. Russell, a physician and retired Army general whose command had included USAMRIID, was brought on as an aide to Thompson and assigned to stockpile the vaccine quickly. "It was panic time," Russell recalled.[4]

Trepidation about a second-wave terrorist attack was no less acute on Capitol Hill. Even before learning of the letters discovered in Florida and New York, aides to Senate majority leader Tom Daschle had brainstormed about biological attack scenarios—and they anticipated that Daschle could be a high-priority target.

He was. On Tuesday, October 9, envelopes addressed by hand to Daschle and another prominent senator, Judiciary Committee chairman Patrick Leahy, were picked up from the same mailbox in Princeton where the earlier letters to Brokaw and the *New York Post* had been dropped. That same day the new envelopes were sent through high-speed postal machinery in Trenton, where they were postmarked. Three days later, a Friday, one of the letters reached the office of the Senate majority leader. Several aides to Daschle noticed the envelope, sitting atop a bundle of unopened mail on the sixth floor of the Hart Senate Office Building. Based on the return address—"4TH GRADE GREENDALE SCHOOL"—it appeared to be a letter from schoolchildren.[5]

That same day, October 12, a contingent of senior Senate staffers had gathered in a large room elsewhere on the sixth floor to meet with Al Lenhardt, the Senate's sergeant at arms, to discuss the threat of anthrax-laced mail, which had become a matter of concern since the death of Robert Stevens in Florida. Clara Kircher, office manager for Senator Leahy, a Democrat from Vermont, appeared to surprise the gathering when she said Leahy's office was no longer accepting deliveries of *any* U.S. mail. Lenhardt insisted that the screening of incoming mail to the Senate offices provided adequate protection.[6]

Later that afternoon, a contingent of indigenous Alaskans inadvertently frightened an intern in Daschle's office, Grant Leslie. To express their appreciation of Daschle's opposition to drilling in the Arctic National Wildlife Refuge, the Alaskans handed Leslie some fur from an Alaskan musk ox. Having just learned that anthrax can occasionally be found on animal hides, Leslie alerted colleagues, who called in the Capitol Police to field-test the material. It was harmless. But because of all the day's commotion, the entire bundle of mail in the office was left unopened through the weekend.

When Leslie returned to work on Monday, October 15, the letter from the "4TH GRADE GREENDALE SCHOOL" was still atop the bundle, bound tightly with plastic strips. Leslie cut the strips—and, before sorting any of the other mail, opened by hand the envelope from the schoolchildren, which, based on the office's experience, might contain cute self-portraits or other items that the automated letter opener could damage. The entire top and the side flaps of the prestamped envelope were sealed with transparent tape. As Leslie used scissors to cut no more than an inch of one of the envelope's corners, a puff of light tan powder burst out. Some of it landed on her lap, on her shoes, and on the pant leg of Bret Wincup, an intern standing next to her. Leslie instantly feared that what had looked like innocent mail from a class of fourth graders could be something sinister.

Daschle's office manager, Kelly Fado, was summoned by intercom by a staffer who asked her, calmly, "What's the number we're supposed to call to report white powder?" After rushing up a short flight of stairs to the sixth floor, Fado entered a room that now had a muddy, moldy odor. She could see residue suspended in the air, like talcum powder. Grant Leslie sat frozen at a table, holding the envelope closed, as another colleague called the Capitol Police.

The officers who responded told Leslie to remain as still as possible so as not to fan any of the powder that had spilled from the envelope. But instead of bagging it for evidence right then, the officers, who wore no protective gear, finished what Leslie had begun: They unsealed the right-hand vertical seam of the envelope to examine the contents. While Leslie was taken into an adjoining room as a precaution, one of the officers began reading aloud from a photocopied, handwritten letter:

> 09-11-01
> YOU CAN NOT STOP US.
> WE HAVE THIS ANTHRAX.
> YOU DIE NOW.
> ARE YOU AFRAID?
> DEATH TO AMERICA.
> DEATH TO ISRAEL.
> ALLAH IS GREAT.

Several blocks away, at the FBI's Washington Field Office, Scott Stanley's pager went off, telling him that something suspicious—perhaps dangerous biological material—had been found at the Hart Building. Stanley, in addition to being a gun-carrying agent, held a Ph.D. in biomedical sciences, and he had trained extensively to handle bioterrorism events. He rushed to the scene to find moon-suited Capitol Police working to secure in a hard-plastic "overpack" the envelope addressed to Senator Daschle. Stanley spoke with Leslie, who seemed remarkably calm under the circumstances, and he sought out the building's sergeant at arms in order to turn off the air-conditioning, which could otherwise disperse the loose powder throughout the structure. Stanley also saw that handheld devices used by the Capitol Police, similar in appearance to home pregnancy test kits, registered quickly with the color red. This was the most preliminary of data—but the first verification that the powder was anthrax.

By the time the air handling was shut down, it was too late.[7] Some of the fine, dusty material had been sucked into the ventilation ducts and spewed into the atmosphere of the nine-story Hart Building, the everyday workplace for half the members of the Senate and hundreds of staffers. If more sophisticated analysis confirmed the powder to be anthrax, there was no telling how many people in the building might be at risk of death.

Grant Leslie, Kelly Fado, and a handful of other Senate staffers were given prophylactic doses of the antibiotic Cipro by congressional physicians. So was Agent Stanley, even though he had already received a full battery of anthrax vaccine shots. The more daunting task was to determine how many others passing within the Hart Building's one million square feet of interior space had been exposed. Physicians and technicians began collecting nasal swabs from staff members who had been on both the sixth and fifth floors.[8] If not treated quickly with an antibiotic, inhalational anthrax is apt to cause death in most cases. And coming so quickly on the heels of September 11, and the death of Robert Stevens, there was no way to know just how potent this anthrax might be.

The Daschle letter drew immediate media attention, which was in fact initiated by President Bush, who, when asked at the White House if there were any new developments with anthrax, alerted reporters to what was unfolding on Capitol Hill. Asked whether bin Laden was responsible, Bush said, "There may be some possible link. We have no hard data yet. But it's clear that Mr. bin Laden is a man who is an evil man."[9]

That evening the Daschle letter led all three major television networks' newscasts. But it was not the day's only anthrax-related story: Television anchor Peter Jennings interrupted ABC's prime-time programming to tell viewers that another anthrax case had been confirmed. This was the infant son of one of the network's own producers. Jennings's counterpart at NBC News, Tom Brokaw, referred again to his own network's brush with anthrax infection, which NBC had first announced three days earlier.

Brokaw, who had said near the outset of his evening newscast on October 15, "This is a terrifying new time," closed with a personal reflection. "Finally, tonight, how those of us at NBC News have been changed by the confirmation of the anthrax in a letter sent here. First, obviously, we're still away from our normal working quarters, and after our editorial meeting this morning we had a course in anthrax 101 from top officials of the CDC. . . . In the meantime, not all of the anxiety or the anger has worn off, but in Cipro we trust."

News of the death of Robert Stevens in Florida, the hospitalization of his colleague Ernesto Blanco, and the Daschle letter in Washington coincided with a change in Bruce Ivins's behavior. To Patricia Fellows, his close colleague at USAMRIID, it was unmistakable. "Bruce has been an absolute manic basket case the last few days," she wrote in an e-mail to their mutual friend, Mara Linscott.[10]

TWELVE

BENTONITE?

Afternoon, October 15, 2001

A handful of federal agents transported the Daschle letter from the Hart Building, driving some fifty miles northwest to Frederick, Maryland. Just ahead stood the gates of Fort Detrick, home of the United States Army Medical Research Institute of Infectious Diseases.

By 2 P.M. the mysterious cargo had been delivered inside for safekeeping and analysis. It was in the sealed overpack, a yellow-orange plastic tub the size of a painter's bucket. John Ezzell, one of Fort Detrick's senior scientists, had prepared extensively for a moment such as this.

Beginning in 1997, Ezzell and FBI officials had developed a formal procedure, a protocol, for examining materials suspected of bearing anthrax or other lethal pathogens. The FBI laboratory was not equipped for such work, but USAMRIID, with its biocontainment hot suites, was. Wherever the items were handled, the FBI's goal was to establish a well-documented chain of custody. In order to help ensure the conviction of a perpetrator, the bureau would need to show at a trial that the evidence was handled in a way that prevented it from being contaminated or otherwise altered.[1]

Ezzell, the son of a dentist, was a Ph.D. microbiologist with almost two decades of experience handling anthrax. Before that, he had studied Legionnaires' Disease. He took special notice of what he encountered within the Daschle letter: tan-tinted powder that, while still within both its original envelope and a ziplock plastic bag, undulated when the bag was touched by a hand, as if propelled by static electricity. Ezzell at one point held the hand-scrawled letter as Darin Steele, an FBI agent standing outside the glass-enclosed containment lab, used a digital camera to take pictures of the killer's message.

Ezzell, while handling the powder within an enclosed biological safety cabinet, also noticed that the material had an acrid smell. He mentioned this to another FBI agent on hand, Scott Stanley, along with his suspicion that the odor was caused by the broth, or growth medium, in which the spores had been grown. More alarmingly, the lab's powerful ventilation hood lifted some of the powder from the surface. Ezzell, who was chief of USAMRIID's Special Pathogens Branch, had been vaccinated against anthrax, but he was concerned enough that, after finishing his work that day, he began a two-week regimen of Cipro.

Ezzell by this point had overseen the testing of perhaps thousands of suspicious items that had been brought to USAMRIID—all of which turned out to be hoaxes or false alarms. This appeared to be different, and the immediate tests at the Army institute would confirm it. Later that day Ezzell told two of his superiors, Colonel Erik Henchal and Edward Eitzen, a physician who had served as commander of USAMRIID since 1999: "This is like seeing the face of Satan. This is the closest thing I've seen to weaponized anthrax."

Ezzell did not say that the anthrax *was* "weaponized." As he explained later in his native North Carolina drawl, he'd never before handled or seen weaponized anthrax—a term that was inherently ambiguous. But this much was clear to him: The

Daschle letter in a sense was a copycat of all the hoaxes that had preceded it. Except that this time, instead of salt or talcum powder, it was real anthrax.

No one could rightfully fault Ezzell for speaking without precision after such an unsettling experience. But his private remark to Commander Eitzen rose out of the building like a skyrocket. Officials at the Pentagon, the Department of Health and Human Services, and the White House were riveted by what Ezzell now had in his custody at USAMRIID. Those who were briefed at the White House immediately notified National Security Advisor Condoleezza Rice and the Secret Service.[2] And the scope of the attacks remained unknown. Three days later, on October 18, testing confirmed another anthrax infection of the skin, this one blackening the right middle finger of a newsroom assistant at the *New York Post,* Johanna Huden.[3]

For those eager for war against Iraq, Ezzell's use of the word "weaponized" was manna—muscular vocabulary that could be inserted into talking points and saber-rattling op-ed pieces. At a technical level this meant that the spores may have been coated with a chemical additive to prevent clumping and to ease their dispersal into the air, where they could more readily penetrate a victim's lungs. If the spores in the Daschle letter were coated, this would signal a sophisticated process that, in the minds of policy hawks, likely implicated the regime of Saddam Hussein, possibly in partnership with al Qaeda.

Oddly enough, the notion that the mailed material had been treated to make it more deadly provided some comfort to the community of present and former USAMRIID scientists: If the anthrax had been altered with such a sophisticated chemical additive, they reasoned, there was little chance that the letter attacks could have originated in Frederick. After all, anthrax spores had not been chemically treated at USAMRIID since the long-ago days of the offensive bioweapons program.

It could come as no great surprise, then, that among the USAMRIID scientists there existed a willingness, even an eagerness, to believe that the anthrax letter attacks were perpetrated by a foreign menace, perhaps Iraq. Some of the military scientists had formed their opinions years earlier. They knew that in 1988 Saddam Hussein had used chemical weapons to kill thousands of Kurds in northern Iraq. They recalled the intelligence reports preceding the Gulf War, warning of Saddam's capacity to use anthrax or botulinum toxin. In fact, Saddam had not used a biological or chemical weapon during the Gulf War. And, under the watch of inspectors organized by the United Nations during the mid- to late 1990s, remnants of his biowarfare programs had supposedly been dismantled. Yet many of the scientists within the intermingled defense, intelligence, and scientific communities suspected that Saddam still controlled secret stockpiles of such weaponry, including anthrax.

After the war, some U.S. military scientists had assisted the United Nations or the CIA in hunting for Saddam's supposed caches of these weapons. A few of those scientists had come from or returned to work at USAMRIID, but they were constrained from speaking publicly about their speculations. Those who had retired and were unbound by service controls over contact with the media were, however, free to speak their minds. Among the most vocal theorists that the letter attacks were generated from abroad was Richard O. Spertzel, a retired Army colonel and former deputy USAMRIID commander. Spertzel, trained as a veterinarian and as a microbiologist, was respected by his peers as a solid, if stubborn, scientist. He had served from 1994 to 1999 as a supervising inspector for the United Nations, hunting for biological weapons in Iraq, and was known among his fellow inspectors as a bulldog, a man convinced that Saddam Hussein was concealing an active biowarfare program. Spertzel told PBS's *NewsHour with Jim Lehrer* that he believed both the anthrax mailings and contemporaneous hoaxes were perpetrated as a sequel to the September 11 attacks, perhaps by Iraq and Osama bin Laden working together.

"I'm one of those individuals who think there is a very definite connection," Spertzel said on October 17, 2001, adding: "I find it far too coincidental that a series of letters, both fake ones ... and actual letters would go out, that is actual letters containing anthrax spores, in a very narrow time frame in mid, late September. That's coincidence far too much."[4]

Appearing a few weeks later before the House Committee on International Relations, Spertzel declared: "I believe that it had to be an overseas connection, state sponsorship. I could name several possible sources, but clearly No. 1 on my list would be Iraq."[5]

A former commander of USAMRIID, retired Colonel David R. Franz, a biologist who had been chief inspector on three U.N. biowarfare search missions in Iraq, also insisted that the mailings were of foreign parentage. "I have always felt that it would require state sponsorship, that another country, some proliferant nation in this world, would have to help the terrorists," Franz told MSNBC's Chris Matthews.[6] By pointing their fingers abroad, Spertzel and Franz, neither of whom had examined the powder, were all but ruling out anyone at USAMRIID.

Such was the furor over Iraq's possible complicity that, at a news conference on October 19, President Bush was asked, "Mr. President, do you know yet whether there is a definite link between the anthrax attacks and any foreign interests, particularly al Qaeda or Iraq?" Bush replied, "I don't have knowledge of a direct link of the anthrax incidents to the enemy. But I wouldn't put it past them. These are evil people, and the deeds that have been conducted on the American people are evil deeds. And anybody who would mail anthrax letters, trying to affect the lives of innocent people, is evil."[7]

Officials throughout the government were clamoring to know what the scientists at Fort Detrick were learning about the exact properties of the anthrax mailed to Daschle. In line with the protocol he had drafted with the FBI to secure any evidence from a bioterrorism event, John Ezzell arranged for the Daschle envelope to be kept in a designated holding area, protected by an electronic keycard access point and by a separate, coded lock. Ezzell had wasted no time examining the envelope's contents, confirming for the FBI that the powdery material was lethal anthrax. Test results gathered by a colleague also showed that infection from the anthrax appeared to be treatable with any of ten antibiotics, including penicillin.[8]

When the FBI had brought Ezzell the envelope addressed to Brokaw, it was virtually devoid of visible powder, a result of mishandling by the New York City Department of Health, whose lab personnel had spilled almost all of the contents.[9] This did not bode well for Ezzell. His challenge at USAMRIID was to begin analyzing what little anthrax remained. Yet by swabbing the inside of the envelope, and using a tiny instrument resembling a spatula to dislodge a granular speck of anthrax, Ezzell was able to retrieve enough of it to grow new material, enabling him to verify that Brokaw, too, had been sent the Ames strain.

Not all of his colleagues, however, were content to let Ezzell take the lead. Another senior official, without consulting either Ezzell or his boss, Colonel Erik Henchal, arranged for the Daschle envelope and its contents to be handed over to a different scientist: Bruce Ivins.[10]

The carefully planned security arranged by Ezzell and the FBI was subverted. Some of the details of how this occurred would remain forever unclear to Ezzell, but Army e-mails and personal recollections showed that the impetus for getting the Daschle anthrax into Bruce Ivins's hands came from a virologist at USAMRIID named Peter B. Jahrling. Although he did not supervise either Ezzell or Ivins, Jahrling held the title of senior scientist at USAMRIID and he was a prominent figure in biowarfare research.

Jahrling had gained notice within the pages of Richard Preston's 1994 bestseller, *The Hot Zone,* for his work with the deadly Ebola virus. Jahrling's career accolades included the Secretary of Defense Medal for Meritorious Civilian Service. Gregarious and excitable, the retired Army captain, now working at USAMRIID as a civilian, was apt to voice thoughts unfiltered, as fast as they came to him.

The FBI had assigned Jahrling no role in the unfolding criminal investigation. Yet within two days of the Daschle envelope's arrival at Fort Detrick, Jahrling contacted Ivins with this assignment: Determine the density of spores per gram of the anthrax—

and let me know what you find.[11] On the afternoon of October 17, an aide to Ezzell, Stephanie Redus, unlocked the refrigerator where the envelope was stored. Ivins signed for it and carried it in two zip-lock plastic bags to a hot suite where he performed the requested analysis.[12]

Meanwhile, in Washington, Ivins was now on the mind of another acquaintance. Psychiatrist Naomi Heller was taking notice of the anthrax-laced letters that were frightening the nation. She remembered the peculiar scientist she had treated some two decades earlier, the man who had confided his burglary of the sorority, his familiarity with poisons, his homicidal thoughts. He had actually sought an appointment as recently as a couple of years ago, after she had retired. Heller had nothing to go on except her intuition. She worried that Ivins might be the mailer.[13]

Ezzell was furious when he learned that the Daschle envelope was opened in the same hot suite where Ivins had worked on a daily basis with anthrax spores. This was precisely the scenario that the protocol was intended to prevent. The room, known as B3, was an unkempt mess, with dirty countertops and floors. B3 housed five laboratories, where Ivins and the other researchers kept hundreds of containers of all sizes, with no particular labeling scheme. There was not even an inventory of the many tubes and flasks that contained anthrax. Refrigerators and freezers holding anthrax and other pathogens carried no labeling describing the contents.[14] Ezzell had once told his boss, Colonel Erik Henchal, that the suite was a "pigsty."

Now Ezzell feared that Ivins could have inadvertently contaminated the evidence with other, stray spores. It also galled Ezzell that Ivins was provided the envelope itself; all that was needed for him to calculate the density of spores per gram was a tiny sample of the anthrax. Ezzell, averse to internecine wrangling, never confronted Jahrling, Ivins, or anyone else. His only solace was that some of the powder, that which fell earlier from the Daschle letter into the paint-bucket-like overpack, had remained stored in a secure location.[15]

Ivins gushed over the powder he had been given to analyze. "I've never seen anything like this before," Ivins told his supervisor, Jeffrey Adamovicz, as he worked with the material in the hot suite.[16] Ivins spoke similarly to Gerry Andrews, chief of the Bacteriology Division. "He said the stuff was incredible. I mean, he wouldn't, couldn't, stop talking about it," Andrews recalled. "He said he'd never seen anything like that before. . . . It was like smoke. That's what he said it looked like. That's exactly how Bruce described it. He said it was just hovering in the air." [17]

Ivins told his former faculty mentor, Priscilla Wyrick, "It scared the shit out of me. . . . I've never seen anything with such quality, high grade in all my life. I've been working up here for twenty years and I've never seen anything that pure. It's the first time I've ever been scared up here."

Ivins volunteered to Wyrick that he couldn't produce anthrax of such quality. "I'm good but not that good." [18]

Peter Jahrling, who had promptly received Ivins's data characterizing the anthrax, also detailed one of his own aides to prepare some of the Daschle material for examination under an electron microscope. What Jahrling saw convinced him that the anthrax had been treated with a chemical additive. Such an artificial enhancing or weaponizing of anthrax could suggest the involvement of a foreign state.

Jahrling, believing that national security was at stake, raced across the Fort Detrick grounds to deliver news of his apparent discovery to Major General John S. Parker, a physician who oversaw USAMRIID as head of the Army's Medical Research and Materiel Command.[19] Within days Jahrling was briefing an array of officials throughout the government by phone and in person: *This is the highest grade material I have ever seen. This is amazing. . . . It's floating. There's very few people in the world who could do this.*[20]

Jahrling's excitement underscored the crucial, unanswered questions about the anthrax powder: Who was sending it? Were the letter attacks the dreaded "second wave" of Islamic terrorism?

At the Pentagon, an atmosphere of crisis had prevailed since the morning of September 11, when the hijackers slammed

American Airlines Flight 77 into the westernmost facade and, in so doing, breached the symbolic heart of U.S. national security. Some walls remained darkened by the soot. It was against this backdrop, on October 24, 2001, that Jahrling, accompanied by General Parker, drove from Fort Detrick to Washington for a series of high-level briefings. Jahrling carried with him the electron microscope photographs to make his point that the Daschle letter material had likely been artificially treated to increase its lethality. His opinion was shared by General Parker, who had examined the photographs.

After meeting in the morning with Tommy Thompson at the Hubert H. Humphrey Building, Jahrling and the general drove across the Potomac River to the Pentagon.[21] There they were met in a conference room by Deputy Defense Secretary Paul Wolfowitz and several of his aides.

Parker provided an overview of the analyses that had been done on the anthrax powder by the scientists at USAMRIID. The general then handed over the briefing to Jahrling, who—echoing the language Bruce Ivins had used—said the anthrax was very pure and, with only the slightest disturbance, "appeared like smoke." The powder flowed easily, Jahrling said, and did not clump.

It was one thing to suspect that the Daschle powder had been weaponized with a special coating. But Jahrling, as he circulated the photographs, suggested something even more sinister: The spores appeared to have been treated with a particular chemical additive, bentonite. Wolfowitz, a foreign policy theorist who also held a degree in chemistry, tilted his head slightly. "Bentonite?"

Jahrling informed him that bentonite was the claylike material known to have been used by the Iraqis in their suspicious work with a spore-forming but nonlethal cousin of anthrax. If the supposed additive observed by Jahrling was, indeed, bentonite, it was a red arrow implicating Iraq in a biological attack upon the United States.

"Everyone grabbed on to that," recalled Dr. Robert Kadlec, a Pentagon advisor on biological warfare who attended the briefing. "The presumption as these guys are briefing Paul Wolfowitz was that this stuff had bentonite and therefore was linked to Iraq. It was 'Holy shit.' We already knew we were going to war—it was just a matter of with whom. If this is it, it's casus belli." [22]

Coincidentally that same day, the president's newly arrived homeland security advisor, former Pennsylvania governor Tom Ridge, had scheduled a meeting at the White House to try to halt the inconsistent comments about anthrax coming from various administration officials. Ridge wanted the administration to "speak with one voice." He planned to deliver this message simultaneously to Attorney General John D. Ashcroft, FBI director Robert S. Mueller III, and Health and Human Services secretary Tommy Thompson. [23]

General Parker and Jahrling were fifty miles away, just returning to Fort Detrick, when they were summoned to the 7:30 P.M. meeting at the White House. Still in the general's SUV, they made a U-turn and headed back to Washington. [24] Inside the Roosevelt Room, Jahrling was called upon for another presentation regarding his analysis of the anthrax. All of the top-level officials summoned by Ridge were there: Ashcroft, Mueller, Thompson, and various aides. [25]

The explosive assertions about anthrax, made more deadly with an additive, leaked with the news cycle. The next day, on October 25, 2001, a front-page article in the *Washington Post*, "Additive Made Spores Deadlier," publicly planted the idea that the anthrax had been weaponized, treated with what the *Post* described as a "high-grade additive." The additive's presence in the Daschle spore powder, said the *Post*, "was confirmed for the first time yesterday by a government source familiar with the ongoing studies, which are being conducted by scientists at the Army Medical Research Institute of Infectious Diseases in Frederick." The additive was said to be "so sophisticated that only three nations"—the United States, Russia, and Iraq—could have made it.

The *Post* article attributed the information to anonymous sources without mentioning Jahrling, Wolfowitz, or the just concluded private briefings. [26] The *New York Times* on the same day published on an inside page a similar article, attributed to three named scientists who said they had learned about aspects of the federal investigation. One of those quoted was Richard Spertzel, the former deputy USAMRIID commander and United Nations weapons inspector for Iraq.[27]

Also on October 25, the Senate prepared to take a final vote on the USA Patriot Act, legislation promoted by the Bush administration as a way to eavesdrop on the communications of would-be terrorists. The Patriot Act was opposed by civil libertarians as an overreach, and though some, notably Senate Judiciary Committee chairman Patrick Leahy, had insisted on methodical consideration of the legislation, the furor over the anthrax attacks made further delay untenable. On October 24, the House had voted 357–66 for passage, following floor statements that noted the plight of postal workers victimized in Washington.

In urging their Senate colleagues to follow suit, Republicans Kit Bond of Missouri and Arlen Specter of Pennsylvania also invoked the anthrax attacks. "We know," Bond said, "that as a result of the tragedy of September 11 and the continuing problems we are having with anthrax and other threats from abroad, we need to do a better job of seeing who comes into this country to make sure people who wish to do us harm are, if possible, screened out before they get here." Said Specter, among the most seasoned members of the Senate: "There is a very heavy overhang over Washington, D.C., today with what is happening here with our efforts to respond in so many ways to September 11. Now with the anthrax, we are all concerned about what may happen in the future."

The Senate approved the Patriot Act by a vote of 98–1. President Bush signed it into law the next day.[28]

Peter Jahrling had not come close to proving that the anthrax was artificially altered with bentonite, or with anything else. But his presentations lent his scientist's imprimatur to the growing suspicion that a foreign adversary—most likely Iraq—was behind the anthrax mailings. Though there is no indication that Jahrling acted with less than good intentions, he was not, in fact, an expert on the subject about which he was speaking. He had no experience handling anthrax, let alone interpreting microscopic images of it. He was a Ph.D. virologist, well versed in scourges such as Ebola or smallpox. Anthrax is a bacterium, not a virus.[29]

With war at stake, Robert Kadlec thought of the one scientist he considered best qualified to evaluate the supposed discovery of bentonite. On the topics of Iraqi anthrax and bentonite, few if any people in the United States government were better informed than James Burans. A Navy microbiologist, Burans had developed methods for rapidly identifying biological warfare agents, including anthrax, in the field as well as the lab. He had experience worldwide, having worked, starting in 1985, at Navy research labs in Egypt, the Philippines, Indonesia, and Lima, Peru, his current posting. His work had taken him to many other countries in Africa, Asia, and the Mideast, too—including Iraq. In 1996, he won the Navy's Legion of Merit medal.

Burans, who fittingly enough had received essential training in how to handle anthrax from Bruce Ivins and two other scientists at USAMRIID, had then gone on to lead the Navy Forward Laboratory in Saudi Arabia during the first Gulf War. After the war, Burans participated with teams of United Nations inspectors in the search for biological and chemical weapons. He knew from that work that although Iraq had possessed anthrax before the war, the material was markedly different from the Ames strain used in the 2001 letter attacks.

Testing that Burans oversaw in the 1990s had found that the Iraqis had acquired the Vollum strain of anthrax, the same substance used in the U.S. offensive biowarfare program until President Nixon's decree stopped that work in 1969. Burans and his colleagues had recovered samples of Vollum from soil at the Al Hakam production facility, within an hour's drive from Baghdad, where the Iraqis dumped liquid stocks of the anthrax and set it afire with diesel fuel. Burans and the U.N. inspectors had also retrieved from Al Hakam samples of the nonlethal anthrax simulant made by the Iraqis, *Bacillus thuringiensis*. The Bt was said by the Iraqis to be strictly for use as an agricultural insecticide. They had grown it in fermentors and sprayed the material into bentonite, which coated and dried the spores. Burans had seen large quantities of Bt stored in hundreds of 2-kilo paper sacks at Al Hakam and had brought samples back to the United States, where Paul Keim, among others, had analyzed the material and concluded that it was not anthrax.

When Kadlec called him in late October 2001 to discuss Jahrling's claims, Burans was puzzled by the frenzy over bentonite and the suggestions of Iraq's involvement with the letter attacks. After all, scientists had already established that the anthrax mailed to Senator Daschle was the Ames strain, and Burans, who maintained close contact with U.S. intelligence agencies, knew of no evidence to suggest that Iraq had ever obtained Ames. He questioned the basis upon which people were implicating Iraq. Burans suspected a version of the game of telephone: Scientists at USAMRIID who examined the Daschle powder had discussed their work with former colleagues and other outsiders, who in turn told others. Somewhere in the sequence, exaggeration outpaced verification. The result was hysteria that threatened to mislead the United States toward war.

After his conversations with Kadlec, Burans contacted a scientist friend at the FBI, Agent Scott Decker, and offered to help clear up the confusion. Burans noted that he had firsthand information regarding the Iraqi Bt, the product that had been treated with bentonite. Decker accepted Burans's offer of help.[30] Burans hoped that he could improve USAMRIID officials' understanding by sharing with them his photographs or even his test tube samples of the Iraqi material. If Burans's photographs of Iraqi bentonite matched what Peter Jahrling had shown, Iraq might indeed be complicit in the anthrax mailings. If not, those eager to link Saddam Hussein to the attacks would have to look elsewhere for valid supporting evidence. Burans proposed to meet with Jahrling and others at USAMRIID who had examined the Daschle letter. That meeting would take place about a week later—but not before news organizations had further fueled the anti-Iraq hysteria.

THIRTEEN

SERIOUS PEOPLE

The newspaper accounts reporting that the anthrax had been enhanced with a lethality-boosting additive had not mentioned bentonite, let alone its traceability to Iraq. That connection would be emphatically asserted a day later by ABC News, which on the evening of October 26, 2001, led *World News Tonight* with a blockbuster, introduced by anchor Peter Jennings: "ABC News has learned what made the anthrax so dangerous in the letter to Senator Tom Daschle was a particular additive which only one country, as far as we know, that's a very important caveat, only one country, as far as we know, has used to produce biological weapons."

Jennings then cued ABC's Brian Ross, whose no-nonsense style defined him as the most formidable investigative reporter in the network news business. Ross wasted no time citing the basis for his sensational report: "Peter, from three well-placed but separate sources tonight, ABC News has been told that initial tests on the anthrax sent to Senator Daschle have found a telltale chemical additive whose name means a lot to weapons experts. It is called bentonite." Ross continued, as footage rolled on screen: "The discovery of bentonite came in an urgent series of tests conducted at Fort Detrick, Maryland, and elsewhere. This is what bentonite looks like under a microscope, a substance which helps keep the tiny anthrax particles floating in the air by preventing them from sticking together." The presence of bentonite in anthrax, Ross said, was "a trademark of Saddam Hussein's biological weapons program."

Jennings introduced another correspondent's succinct paraphrase of White House press secretary Ari Fleischer, who was said to have denied that bentonite was found in the anthrax sent to Senator Daschle.[1]

Ross was undeterred by Fleischer's statement. On October 28, he offered more details to support his contention that the anthrax mailed to Senator Daschle contained bentonite. Appearing on *This Week*, ABC's Sunday morning public affairs show, Ross said that "despite continued White House denials, now four well-placed and separate sources have told ABC News that initial tests on the anthrax by the U.S. Army at Fort Detrick, Maryland, have detected trace amounts" of bentonite and another supposed additive, silica. Ross juxtaposed his exclusive about the anthrax mailings with another dubious indicator of Iraqi malevolence. "[A]t the same time those results were coming in, officials in the Czech Republic confirmed that hijack ringleader, Mohamed Atta, had met at least once with a senior Iraqi intelligence agent in Prague, raising what authorities consider some extremely provocative questions."[2] (No credible information ever emerged to verify that such a meeting actually occurred.)[3]

One of the ABC show's hosts, Cokie Roberts, soon segued to that day's star guest of *This Week*, Defense Secretary Donald H. Rumsfeld, while remarking on the "perception, certainly here in Washington," that the Bush administration was hesitant to accuse Iraq of involvement in the anthrax mailings or the September 11 attacks. The perception, Roberts said, boiled down to: "[T]his administration doesn't want to say the word 'Iraq' for fear of having to go in, and that then the Arab world could blow apart."

Referring to the details just supplied by Brian Ross, Roberts asked Rumsfeld about both the hijacker Atta's alleged meeting in

Prague and the mailed anthrax, which "could have been tampered with by this bentonite, that is Iraqi based." The defense secretary responded that he had no direct knowledge on either point but added: "I know that serious people are looking at both of those matters seriously." Rumsfeld's words helped buoy Ross's report because they differed from White House spokesman Ari Fleischer's unqualified denial regarding bentonite.

Hours later on the network's nightly news, Ross pushed his anthrax story beyond just the "initial" tests. "The White House says it's still too early to rule in or rule out any foreign or domestic terror group in the anthrax attacks. But federal investigators tell ABC News that now a second set of tests on the anthrax sent to Senator Daschle has also indicated the presence of bentonite, as well as another compound called silica." Ross then characterized Rumsfeld's noncommittal response on *This Week* as buttressing his original exclusive. "The White House had initially denied any bentonite was found in the anthrax, but Secretary of Defense Rumsfeld backed off on that today when asked about both the Atta meetings and the reports of bentonite."[4]

On October 29, Ross dug in even deeper on the network show *Good Morning America*. This time he invoked the assessment of the Daschle material by former United Nations weapons inspectors, who in the 1990s had searched Iraq for anthrax and other biological weaponry. Ross reported: "Former U.N. weapons inspectors say the anthrax found in a letter to Senator Daschle is nearly identical to samples they recovered in Iraq in 1994. . . . And under an electron microscope, trace amounts of telltale additives are matching up, according to at least four well-placed sources, although the White House denies it." In response to a question by co-host George Stephanopoulos during the same broadcast, Ross qualified his attribution: "Former U.N. weapons inspectors have told ABC News they've been told the anthrax spores found in the letter to Senator Daschle are almost identical in appearance to those they recovered in Iraq in 1994 when viewed under an electron microscope." Ross was conceding that he was relying on hearsay, and not on firsthand sources who actually examined the material mailed to Daschle. But he reiterated his earlier report: "ABC News has also learned that at least two labs have now concluded the anthrax was coated with additives of the kind linked to Iraq's biological weapons program, bentonite and silica."

Near the conclusion of Ross's appearance on the show, Stephanopoulos said, pointedly: "Brian, I spoke to a senior White House official this morning, and they are standing by their story that no test has concluded that there was bentonite in this anthrax. What is this about?" Ross responded, "It's hard to understand. They've been saying that since Friday [the day of Ross's first exclusive on bentonite]. We've been going back to four separate well-placed sources who say there was bentonite detected in the tests at Fort Detrick, Maryland . . . and they can't understand what the White House is talking about." [5]

Given his stature, Ross's string of reports raised the prospect that Saddam Hussein was complicit in the anthrax mailings. But did Ross and ABC News have the story right?

The network forcefully defended his reporting. "We have four separate well-placed sources who told us that initial tests showed bentonite," ABC News spokesman Jeffrey Schneider told *USA Today*, adding: "Our sources continue to tell us that under an electron microscope, the Daschle sample is indistinguishable from samples taken out of Iraq in the early '90s." The network, Schneider said, was "confident" in its reporting. [6]

Questions were surrounding that reporting. On November 1, *World News Tonight* anchor Peter Jennings asked Ross, "Brian, what's the latest we know about the additive called bentonite in the anthrax, which made it so allegedly dangerous?" Ross responded: "Well, Peter, today the White House said that despite initial test results which we reported suggesting the presence of a chemical called bentonite, a trademark of the Iraqi weapons program, a further chemical analysis has ruled that out." [7]

Ross did not describe the nature of this "further chemical analysis," when it was performed, or whether he found it credible. After having dismissed in his earlier reports Ari Fleischer's consistent denials of bentonite, Ross left viewers on November 1 to wonder what the truth was about an essential scientific detail that carried implications for war.

Ross also glided past the details of his trumpeted exclusives: In his first report on October 26, Ross had said that bentonite was identified by "an urgent series of tests conducted at Fort Detrick" and elsewhere. On October 28, Ross said that the bentonite discovery had been bolstered by a "second set of tests." Had the results of the urgent tests and the second set of tests been misstated? And what about the "well-placed" sources cited by Ross—three of them on October 26, four on October 28 and 29? He had at no point identified them. Nor did Ross say which "former U.N. weapons inspectors" told the network that the anthrax spores sent to Daschle matched the material they recovered from Iraq.

Ross had, however, invited onto the October 26 broadcast two men he introduced as former U.N. weapons inspectors. Their on-camera comments gave weight to Ross's claim that bentonite was detected in the anthrax sent to Senator Daschle. Tim Trevan, the first of those former officials to be shown, strongly buttressed Ross's conclusion that tests had found bentonite, the supposed Iraqi trademark. After a segment in which Ross spoke against the backdrop of spliced-together videotape showing bentonite under a microscope, soldiers guarding Fort Detrick, and Saddam Hussein in fatigues, overseeing his high-stepping Iraqi troops, Trevan came on the air.

"It does mean for me that Iraq becomes the prime suspect as the source for the anthrax used in these letters," Trevan said.

Few viewers could have known that, in fact, Trevan was never a weapons inspector and that he never touched the ground at Al Hakam or any other suspected munitions site in Iraq. He had served from 1992 to 1995 as a political advisor and spokesman for the chairman of the United Nations Special Commission (UNSCOM) on Iraq. Trevan also wrote a 1998 book, *Saddam's Secrets: The Hunt for Iraq's Hidden Weapons.* Viewers might have been surprised as well to learn that Trevan, by his own acknowledgment, knew nothing beyond hearsay about what was, or was not, in the anthrax mailed to Daschle or anyone else.

"I didn't have any firsthand knowledge of what material was in those letters," Trevan acknowledged years later. "I was getting this second- or third-hand from people who were at Fort Detrick." [8]

The second ex-official quoted by ABC News was Richard Spertzel, the former deputy commander of USAMRIID and U.N. weapons inspector who had been among the first to publicly assert a link between the September 11 attacks, al Qaeda, Iraq, and the anthrax mailings.[9] After Ross narrated file footage showing Al Hakam, the Iraqi facility the inspectors had visited in the 1990s, Spertzel appeared on camera, saying: "That basically became proof positive that bentonite was a valuable asset in doing this."

Spertzel's intimations of an Iraqi link to the anthrax attacks also took him to Capitol Hill. On December 5, 2001, he told the House International Relations Committee that bentonite was not Iraq's only additive of choice for weaponizing anthrax. Iraq "also sought a supply of pharmaceutical grade silica in 1988 and 1989," he said, adding that "suggestive evidence indicates Iraq was able to obtain such material. . . . Iraq was also interested in obtaining other materials that would make a good additive for weapons-grade material." [10] In Spertzel, ABC News had found a scientist with unswerving suspicions about Iraq's role in the letter attacks: He would persist for years in fingering the Iraqi regime.[11]

Yet while Spertzel strongly suspected Iraq's complicity in the anthrax letter attacks, he at no point examined the Daschle powder and he never saw any data showing the presence of bentonite. Nor, Spertzel said later, was he told by anyone at Fort Detrick or elsewhere that any testing had found bentonite.[12]

ABC News never disavowed any aspect of Ross's reports, and the network's official biography of Ross has continued to tout the work: After September 11, 2001, says the bio, posted on the network's Web site, "Ross and the Investigative Unit broke numerous stories about the investigation into the terrorist attacks and anthrax letters." [13] White House press secretary Ari Fleischer would later call ABC's bentonite exclusive "the single worst media story I've ever seen."[14]

There was no bentonite or any other discernible additive in the anthrax sent through the mail. Yet the media accounts that fed the perception of weaponized spores, perhaps linked to Iraq, stood. The fact also remained that although he had denied the presence of bentonite, the supposed Iraqi signature, Ari Fleischer was not the Bush administration's only or its most prominent voice. When Defense Secretary Rumsfeld was given the opportunity by Cokie Roberts of ABC News to renounce the mistaken claims of bentonite, he had temporized, saying only that it was a matter for ongoing study by "serious people."[15]

Official Washington's reflex to the anthrax attacks was to safeguard the centerpieces of the national government. From October 17 to October 23, Speaker Dennis Hastert shut down official business of the House of Representatives while all buildings used by members and staff were checked for anthrax. The Senate's Hart Building was completely closed, effective October 17. Eventually operations of the Supreme Court were also disrupted. At the White House, mail delivery was halted.

Another likely site of contamination, the Brentwood postal facility in Northeast Washington—through which all mail to the congressional offices had been processed—was overlooked. Only a few minutes' drive from the U.S. Capitol, Brentwood's high-speed mail-handling machinery, exerting thousands of pounds of pressure per square inch, had apparently squeezed powdered anthrax spores from at least one envelope. Brentwood's sorting machines, which process up to thirty thousand envelopes an hour, were cleaned daily with highly pressurized air, which probably propelled even more anthrax into the open. Spores rose as an invisible plume, some thirty feet above the men and women processing the mail.[16]

The spores at Brentwood went undetected until it was too late. On October 21 and October 22, mail handlers Thomas L. Morris Jr., fifty-five, and Joseph P. Curseen Jr., forty-seven, died from inhalational anthrax. Both were popular. Morris, a twenty-eight-year postal employee, headed a bowling league in Forestville, Maryland. Curseen, a graduate of Marquette University, attended St. John the Evangelist, a Catholic church in Clinton, Maryland, where he fainted from his infection before returning to work one final time.[17] Two other postal employees, fifty-six-year-old Leroy Richmond and another man, also fifty-six, who asked the authorities to withhold his name, were hospitalized in late October with inhalational anthrax but survived. Unlike the staffers on Capitol Hill, the four men at Brentwood had not gotten the benefit of urgent nasal swabs and preemptive doses of Cipro. Nor had any of their postal colleagues.[18]

Three people were now dead from the letter attacks. Other anthrax infections were suspected from Florida to Washington to New York.

As FBI officials managed the fledgling efforts to decipher the makeup of the anthrax, the Bush administration's hawks were watching. They viewed Saddam Hussein as a menace, a sponsor of global terrorism who should have been toppled during the 1991 Gulf War. Several current administration figures—Defense Secretary Rumsfeld, Undersecretary of State for Arms Control John R. Bolton, and Deputy Defense Secretary Wolfowitz—were among those who had signed a 1998 letter to President Bill Clinton saying the removal of Saddam was America's "only acceptable strategy."

The war proponents were now bolstered not only by Brian Ross's reports but also by the editorial pages of *The Wall Street Journal*. The expertly prepared "weapons-grade" anthrax, "with electrostatic charges eliminated to facilitate aerial spread," was but the latest outrage to place at Saddam's doorstep, wrote Robert L. Bartley, the newspaper's editorial page editor. "There is plenty of reason to presume he's behind the current attacks, with bin Laden and his al Qaeda network as a front or ally." Bartley closed by underlining his point: "It's fatuous not to regard Saddam as the chief anthrax suspect."[19]

Nor was the drumbeat for military action confined to one

party or backbenchers. Senator Joseph Lieberman of Connecticut, the Democratic nominee for vice president in 2000, called for taking out Saddam—citing the anthrax mailings and his pursuit of "weapons of mass destruction, chemical and biological." [20] Senator John McCain of Arizona, who the year before had sought the Republican nomination for president, also suggested that Saddam might be responsible for the anthrax mailings. [21]

The misguided claims and conjecture appeared to make an impact. By late October 2001, 74 percent of respondents to a nationwide poll said the just-launched war on terrorism should be expanded to target the Iraqi regime. [22] Concern only deepened on November 16, 2001, when an FBI team sorting through 280 barrels of quarantined mail intended for Capitol Hill found more anthrax—this time in the letter addressed to Senate Judiciary Committee chairman Patrick Leahy. [23] Although the Leahy letter was postmarked in New Jersey on October 9 and addressed to his Capitol Hill office, it had been mistakenly diverted to a State Department mail facility in Sterling, Virginia. The misdelivery would provide a plausible explanation for a near-fatal case of inhalational anthrax that struck fifty-nine-year-old David Hose, a State Department mail worker. [24]

Around November 1, both James Burans and Robert Kadlec arrived at Fort Detrick to sit down with Peter Jahrling, John Ezzell, and others who had examined the anthrax mailed to Daschle. "The whole goal of that meeting was to make the folks who had the Daschle sample and were analyzing it . . . aware that reference materials from Iraq were available," Burans said. "As news reports were discussing that the Daschle material may have been produced in Iraq, or may contain bentonite, we were merely informing them that there were samples of material that were available for analysis that came from [the] Al Hakam facility, the Iraqi production facility."

Burans brought photographs taken with an electron microscope, vividly showing the bentonite-coated spores of Iraqi Bt. The scanning technology provided pictures of flat surfaces, as well as the three-dimensional contours of the material. After reviewing the electron micrographs, Jahrling acknowledged, "This doesn't look like the material that we have." As Kadlec recalled, "You could tell these were markedly different." [25]

Amid all the public speculation about bentonite and Iraq, Burans kept a profile as low as his basso profundo voice. The "aha" moment he had provided was not reported in any news accounts. In November 2001 the FBI's Scott Decker quietly brought Burans aboard as a scientific consultant to the investigation. Burans helped the bureau standardize its approach for further analyzing powder recovered from the letters, and he became a reliable resource for investigators trying to sort fact from fiction.

Burans soon got to see for himself electron micrographs of the material from the Daschle letter, the magnified images that had been the subject of so much theorizing. There was no evidence of bentonite-covered spores. "It didn't look anything like the material that was harvested in Iraq," he recalled. [26]

By early 2002, FBI laboratory director Dwight E. Adams and other bureau officials had conferred with several outside experts to determine the most reliable means of analyzing the anthrax retrieved from the letters. The FBI lab was well practiced at analyzing human DNA, drugs, guns, and other forensic evidence common in criminal cases. Yet when it came to identifying and quantifying whatever might exist in the anthrax powders, the lab was not ideally equipped. Although an FBI technician had measured what appeared to be a high amount of silicon in the anthrax sent to the *New York Post*, Adams knew that the bureau's instrumentation and technique could not provide the most precise data. In consultation with the outside scientists and those within government, the FBI enlisted the Sandia National Laboratories in New Mexico, where engineers routinely examine materials with the highest-power microscopes. "This was bigger than the FBI laboratory, plain and simple," Adams recalled. "We needed help. This was a whole new ball game." [27]

In February 2002, the engineers at Sandia began a more intensive examination of the spores, using specialized software and powerful electron microscopes to search for any additive. On Tuesday, March 12, 2002, the Sandia team informed the FBI that its initial, "bulk" analysis showed that silicon, which next to oxygen, is the second most common element in the earth's crust, was present in the spores. This identified *what* was in the spores, but not exactly *where*. Within a week, Sandia completed a more thorough study: By examining thin slices of spores, the engineers were able to see what was inside. They reported to the FBI that the silicon was actually under the surface, or exosporium.[28]

The data from the Sandia team, led by materials engineer Joseph R. Michael, supported two pivotal conclusions: Because the silicon was under the outermost covering of the spores, it did not make the anthrax more dispersible and lethal. Second, the silicon appeared to have been incorporated naturally during growth of the spores—not as a result of artificial coating.[29]

Sandia's work provided further proof that the anthrax in the letter attacks had not been enhanced with an additive. Yet as with the initial revelation by James Burans, this, too, would fail to defuse the hysteria over a purported connection between Iraq and the anthrax attacks. And for one of the same reasons: It was never reported in the media.

The presence of silicon in *Bacillus* spores as part of a natural growth process had been documented years earlier in the scientific literature.[30] And the distinction between an additive that appears on the surface of the spores as opposed to inside them was crucial: The coating of spores with a silicon-containing additive would be a signature of an offensive biological weapons program—not peaceful research aimed at developing vaccines.

Sandia's findings, buttressed by its enlarged electron micrographs, were shared immediately with the FBI, whose officials quickly passed the information to the White House. Yet from the halls of Congress to the mass media and even within the scientific literature, the myth persisted that additive-enhanced or otherwise *weaponized* spores had been sent through the U.S. mail, perhaps by Islamic terrorists or Saddam Hussein.

The very next month, on April 7, 2002, *Newsweek*, citing an unspecified scientific analysis sent to top government officials, announced that the anthrax addressed to Senator Leahy "was coated with a chemical compound unknown to experts who have worked in the field for years."[31] Two days later a *Washington Post* article said that unspecified lab tests had identified "a chemical used to coat the trillions of spores to keep them from clumping together."[32]

On May 1, 2002, *JAMA,* the influential journal of the American Medical Association, published an article describing the anthrax in the letters as "weapons grade."[33] The authors elaborated on this vague term by saying the powdered anthrax had been "treated to reduce clumping." The article was presented as a "consensus statement" about managing cases of anthrax, but remarkably, it provided no footnote or any other factual support for claiming that the mailed spores had been treated.[34] Its lead authors were two Baltimore-based bioterrorism researchers, physicians Thomas V. Inglesby and Tara O'Toole, who just a few weeks earlier had promoted their belief that one of the September 11 hijackers, Ahmad al Haznawi, had had a skin-related anthrax infection in June 2001 while living in Florida. In a memo that reportedly reached the director of the CIA, Inglesby and O'Toole had said the surmise of this infection "of course raises the possibility that the hijackers were handling anthrax and were the perpetrators of the anthrax letter attacks."[35] Although it generated attention from print and broadcast media, no corroboration for their speculation ever emerged. (Inglesby and O'Toole also were lead designers of Dark Winter, the controversial bioterrorism exercise carried out in June 2001.)[36]

On June 11, 2002, Congressman Mike Pence, a Republican from Indiana, asserted in a letter to Attorney General John Ashcroft that the anthrax in the letters was "weapons grade" and "genetically modified to increase its virulence." Pence, saying he was troubled by the FBI's "apparent lack of progress," claimed the anthrax spores "were coated with a chemical not used by scientists in the United States." He asked Ashcroft, "Why has the FBI apparently concluded that the source of these anthrax attacks was domestic when there is significant evidence to suggest an international source for these materials?" Pence provided no evidence for his scientific claims.[37]

On October 28, 2002, a front-page article in the *Washington Post* described the material that had been sent through the mail as a "weaponized aerosol" with "coated spores." The same article tied the letters and their supposedly weaponized contents to the question of whether to launch war against Iraq: "Bush administration officials have acknowledged that the anthrax attacks were an important motivator in the U.S. decision to confront Iraq, and several senior administration officials say today that they still strongly suspect a foreign source—perhaps Iraq—even though no one has publicly said so." [38]

The director of the FBI laboratory, Dwight Adams, tried to convey the verified scientific details during closed-door briefings on Capitol Hill and with executive branch officials. Adams, who was both an agent and a Ph.D. scientist, made clear that the spores contained no additive.[39] Among those whom he briefed in mid-2002 was an aide to Congressman Rush Holt, a New Jersey Democrat whose district encompasses Princeton.[40] Adams relied on the data generated by the team at Sandia and on other laboratory testing that had found the anthrax was *not* resistant to antibiotics.[41] Yet while Adams tried to set the facts straight, officials at the highest levels of the Bush administration were privately dismissing the Sandia results as just one of many pieces of a scientific conundrum.[42]

Joseph Michael, the team leader at Sandia, is a Ph.D. engineer from Lehigh University who specializes in using electron microscopy. As an authority in his field, he was bewildered by the continuing reports that the anthrax used in the attacks was enhanced with an additive. Michael wanted to set the record straight by publishing his team's data. But going public was not his choice to make: He and the dozens of other outside scientists assisting Amerithrax had signed contracts prohibiting the unauthorized release of any investigative information.

When Michael asked his contacts at the FBI about publishing the techniques used to gather the data, he was turned down.[43]

Unlike USAMRIID's Peter Jahrling, who had warned that the anthrax appeared to have been treated with an additive, Michael was never invited to the White House or the Pentagon. He had no way to amplify his voice outside the investigation. Yet while the details from Sandia were blocked from publication, the contrary conclusions of another lab found their way into print.

The Armed Forces Institute of Pathology in Washington, D.C., had been asked by Jahrling to analyze a sample of the anthrax addressed to Senator Daschle. Unknown to the FBI, an aide to Jahrling provided the institute with the sample in late October 2001.[44] Within a couple of days, the institute relayed its findings to USAMRIID—and described them publicly a year later in its own quarterly newsletter, published in October 2002. The newsletter quoted scientist Florabel G. Mullick, who said the institute found silica, a compound of silicon and oxygen. Silica, she said, "prevents the anthrax from aggregating, making it easier to aerosolize." Mullick did not specify whether the material appeared to have been added artificially, but her quoted remarks bolstered those who alleged weaponization.[45] If silicon-containing material were located on the surface of the spores, Mullick's statement might have been accurate. But the data generated by her institute—unlike the more thorough analysis conducted at Sandia—suggested only *what* was present, not *where*.[46]

Without authoritative data demonstrating that the spores were *not* treated with an additive, the spurious claims—coming from such respected sources as *JAMA*—became accepted as fact. The FBI, by keeping the Sandia data confidential, succeeded in safeguarding the secrecy of certain investigative details. Yet by doing so, and sharing the data only with senior government officials, the bureau let stand unfounded statements that were contributing to the clamor for war.

FOURTEEN

OUR OLD FRIEND SADDAM

Bruce Ivins no longer needed long-distance consultations with the Centers for Disease Control to track the latest with the investigation. Even before the discovery of the letter addressed to Tom Daschle, the FBI had begun coming straight to USAMRIID for guidance on the most basic question: Who had access to this anthrax?

Ivins showed himself to the investigators to be a can-do scientist, eager to help. With his Army colleagues, however, he made a point of appearing otherwise, playing to the sense of resentment prevalent at USAMRIID. On October 12, 2001, when the FBI had circulated a written request for information about how widely the Ames strain might be disseminated among U.S. or foreign research labs, Ivins bristled: "[I]f we are the only recipients of this 'tasker,' it is transparently evident that we are being harassed by our regular detractors simply because we are DOD researchers. It is not within the purview of USAMRIID researchers to ascertain where the USDA has sent its strains of *Bacillus anthracis* or any other organism." [1]

Besides, Ivins told fellow microbiologist Jeffrey Adamovicz and others, the anthrax attacks most likely came from a foreign source.[2] On Saturday, October 13, Ivins elaborated in an e-mail to a British researcher: "By the way . . . do you think (as I have my suspicions) that our old friend Saddam may have something to do with the anthrax 'problems' currently occurring in the US? It would certainly be a sneaky sort of 'payback' for the Gulf War."[3]

As he promoted the likelihood that Iraq was the perpetrator, Ivins also offered reasons why no one at USAMRIID should be suspected as a culprit. At USAMRIID, Ivins stressed, scientists worked with anthrax only in a wet formulation, never handling it as a dry powder. "Nobody but an idiot or a truly crazy fool would work with 'anthrax spore powder,'" Ivins wrote on November 23, 2001.[4] No one at the institute, he said, had the equipment or skills to produce the powder found in the Daschle letter. He pointed to another Army installation, Dugway Proving Ground in Utah, as the only facility that worked with dry powder anthrax.

Ivins elaborated in an e-mail to Martin Hugh-Jones, a Louisiana State University anthrax researcher. "The only place that I know of that makes the anthrax spore powder is Dugway Proving Ground. They also made Ames spores (liquid suspensions) for us in 1997 in several fermentor runs. We work with anthrax spore suspensions here and have neither the expertise nor the equipment for generating 'spore powder.'" Four hours earlier, in an e-mail to Hugh-Jones that otherwise had nothing to do with discussing wet or dry anthrax, Ivins concluded: "Regards, Bruce (We don't make anthrax spore powder at USAMRIID) Ivins."[5]

In private conversations with investigators, Ivins told a different story. Beginning with his first formal interview with the FBI, on November 19, 2001, Ivins implicated a departed colleague, biochemist Joseph Farchaus. Along with Ivins, Farchaus was one of several co-inventors of the next-generation anthrax vaccine. Ivins pointed out that his ex-colleague lived not far from Trenton, New Jersey, where the anthrax-laced letters were postmarked.[6] To hear Ivins tell it, Farchaus had bullied him while at USAMRIID, once giving him "noogies." Ivins's statements prompted the investigators to thoroughly scrutinize Farchaus and they found no evidence of wrongdoing. Farchaus also told them that he could not recall ever having sharp words with Ivins, let alone a physical clash.[7]

On January 23, 2002, the day after authorities reopened the formerly anthrax-contaminated Hart Senate Office Building, Ivins called FBI agent Darin Steele, who was now at USAMRIID nearly every day. Along with sharing historical insights about the Ames strain, Ivins offered the names of several more present or former colleagues who he said could have committed the attacks. He would ultimately allege that no fewer than seven present or former USAMRIID colleagues might have been culpable.[8]

About a week later, Agent Steele arranged to have a lengthier conversation with Ivins. The interview proceeded chronologically, beginning with Ivins's college years and fast-forwarding to his career with anthrax. Ivins said that it would have taken great technical expertise to have dried the spores loaded into the letters. He passed along a rumor that Iraq had tried to obtain the Ames strain from Britain's Porton Down biowarfare research facility and said he feared that the letters were a test run for a more devastating biological attack—perhaps with smallpox. As for himself, Ivins said that he had no training in making powders and was not involved in the attacks.[9]

Although few outsiders could have known it, Ivins's protests by e-mail that no one at USAMRIID could make anthrax spore powder were squarely at odds with the facts. John Ezzell, his longtime colleague, had for several years during the late 1990s produced it at USAMRIID. This project was funded by the Defense Advanced Research Projects Agency, a Pentagon unit responsible for developing new technology for use by the military. DARPA needed Ezzell's services because the agency was backing development of a portable high-tech device, a mass spectrometer, which could be used to detect anthrax and other biological or chemical agents on the battlefield or in civilian settings, such as high-rise office buildings.

In order to test the machine's reliability, powdered anthrax, the type that a terrorist or a hostile foreign government might wield, was needed. Ezzell was asked to provide highly concentrated anthrax—pure spores. After culturing and harvesting the material, he and other USAMRIID scientists used repeated cycles of distilled water to wash away any contaminants. They irradiated the spores, rendering them harmless to humans. Ezzell then dried the material, using a standard lab machine called a lyophilizer.

The result was highly purified anthrax powder—snow white, fine and fluffy. Ezzell and his staff used the powder and other biological agents, including a simulant for plague, in the tests of the mass spectrometer. After about five years of trial and error, DARPA stopped funding the project because the device, designed to function much like a smoke detector, could not distinguish between substances in the natural environment and potential biological weapons. Ezzell's work proved that the spectrometer was useless for its intended purpose; he had also demonstrated that a skilled microbiologist at USAMRIID could indeed make powderform anthrax.

Ezzell's years-long production of the powdered material was well known within the tightly knit circle of scientists who handled anthrax at USAMRIID. "We never hid the fact that we did it," Ezzell recalled. Ivins did not help with the project, but he was in a position to know about it. Ezzell said later he would be surprised if he hadn't mentioned the project to him.[10]

It had been Ivins himself who pushed for the purchase of a lyophilizer. In 1996, he attended a two-day course on how to operate the equipment, and he later taught others how to use it. A lyophilizer was inventoried at USAMRIID under his custody.

When investigators asked him about the lyophilizer in April 2003, Ivins said that he had not used it since the mid-1990s. But Ivins had in fact used the machine more recently than that, on at least one occasion that could be documented. On August 21, 2001, a colleague asked Ivins by e-mail: "Bruce, [a colleague] told me you are the one to see about using a lyophilizer in B-5. Can you show me how to use it or tell me who else knows." Ivins replied the next day, "Absolutely . . . anytime is fine. Come by in the morning and we'll get it set up."[11]

Using a lyophilizer was not the only way that powdered anthrax could be produced at USAMRIID. The anthrax could also be dried in centrifuges commonly used there. The first step would be to use a floor-mounted centrifuge, the size of a kitchen stove, to separate the spores from the liquid in which they were suspended. This machine, a Sorvall model RC-2B, would spin the spores, held within glass tubes, into pastelike clumps. After the liquid was drained, the clumps would be transferred to a smaller, tabletop centrifuge outfitted with a strong vacuum to suck away any remaining moisture. This "speed-vac" centrifuge would convert the pasty clumps to dry pellets of anthrax. The pellets could then be ground into fine powder with tools as basic as a razor blade and a mortar and pestle.

The new work related to the anthrax attacks gave USAMRIID an importance it had not had since the first Gulf War, thrusting the often overlooked institute into the forefront of protecting America against biological attack. As many as seventy staffers worked one of the three daily shifts in support of the Amerithrax investigation.[12]

Ivins reveled in the moment. On November 14, 2001, he sent an e-mail to seventeen family members and acquaintances under the subject line "In the lab," describing his hands-on work with one of those germs. "Hi, all . . . We were taking some photos today of blood agar cultures of the now infamous 'Ames' strain of Bacillus anthracis." Ivins attached three photos; the first showed him in a hot suite handling with his bare hands at least eight Petri dishes containing what appeared to be the live cultures.

Among the seventeen addressees of the e-mail were Nancy Haigwood and Priscilla Wyrick. Haigwood, a microbiologist herself, found the photos odd in two respects: handling anthrax without gloves was bad laboratory practice, and circulating such photos seemed a kind of grandstanding that was inappropriate.[13]

Ivins didn't mention it in his e-mail, but in late 2001, FBI agents were starting to approach scientists at USAMRIID about submitting to lie detector tests. The first to be scheduled for polygraphs were those directly assisting the investigation, including

Ivins. Neither Ivins nor his colleagues were identified as suspects, but the FBI intended the tests as a precaution—to help ensure that the anthrax mailer was not freewheeling among the investigators.

Given the limited number of researchers who worked with Ames strain anthrax, "We knew right out of the gate we could have an offender working on our evidence," recalled Agent Scott Stanley.[14]

As the date of his polygraph approached, in late February 2002, Ivins became demonstrably agitated. "He was bouncing off the walls," recalled his colleague John Ezzell. "I said, 'You need to calm down, buddy.' Everybody was trying to get him to calm down." In his colleagues, Ivins had a sympathetic audience because they, too, were displeased at having to submit to the polygraphs.[15] Nonetheless, he appeared to pass his test, which enabled him to remain among the USAMRIID scientists assisting the investigation.[16]

The scientists were examining not only the actual anthrax letters but also the many hoaxes and items from buildings that might be contaminated, plus air samples drawn from locations in Washington. Amid the upheaval a seasoned USAMRIID lab technician named Terry Abshire was culturing and studying the material that had thrust America into a new state of siege.

Using a thin wire tool with a tiny loop at its end, Abshire streaked onto a dozen or so Petri dishes some specks of the powder mailed to Senator Daschle. She put the dishes in a laboratory incubator set to about 37 degrees Celsius, the body temperature of a human being. Within just a few hours, the microscopic anthrax cells would grow into colonies visible to the naked eye. In about a day, she would check the colonies for any clues.

For two decades, Abshire had been John Ezzell's go-to aide at USAMRIID. Ezzell relied on her both for her technical skill and her eye for detail. In addition to her hands-on work in the lab, Abshire had helped Ezzell develop the protocol with the FBI for securing incoming materials that might serve as evidence in a courtroom.

Abshire was well trained in microbiology and ordinarily she would have checked the Petri dishes in less than twenty hours, because incubating anthrax for longer periods ran the risk that the cells would form spores, making the material more danger-ous to handle. But in a most uncharacteristic lapse, Abshire al-lowed the anthrax cells to incubate for at least forty-eight hours. The letter attacks in Washington, New York, and Florida had placed enormous strains on many of the USAMRIID scientists, and it was showing. By the time she opened the incubator and saw the Petri dishes, Abshire realized her slipup.[17]

As she looked them over, Abshire noticed plenty of growth on the dishes, also known as blood agar plates. There were multiple colonies of new anthrax cells, but the overwhelming majority of the colonies appeared to be normal for *Bacillus anthracis*—flat with rounded contours. However, to her great surprise, not all of the colonies looked that way.

Abshire was working alone, in a twenty-five-foot-by-twenty-five-foot hot suite on the second floor of USAMRIID's Building 1412. Ezzell was in his office in the nearby headquarters build-ing. It was midday when he answered her call beckoning him. Once inside Building 1412, he removed his street clothes and donned surgical scrubs to enter where Abshire was working. The final doorways whistled as he opened and passed through, the negative air pressure intended to suction away any contami-nants. Once he'd put on the necessary protective gear, he and the similarly outfitted Abshire walked over to the incubator. She withdrew the Petri dishes, each about the diameter of a compact disc, and she and Ezzell examined them. He, too, saw the irregu-lar colonies, which were rough, wrinkled, and yellowish gray, unlike the rest of the colonies, which looked something like ground glass.

Ezzell's initial skepticism over what this could be disappeared. He asked Abshire to repeat the procedure to see if the same structures emerged. If so, it might provide a genetic clue about the source of this apparently unique batch of anthrax. He also wanted the experiment performed on some of the spore powder recovered from the letter sent to the *New York Post*.

The next round of testing of the material mailed to Daschle verified Abshire's initial results: The irregular-shaped colonies again appeared, in about the same proportion. Out of every fifty or so colonies, one or two looked irregular. The results were the same for the anthrax incubated from the *New York Post* letter. This strongly suggested that the spores sent separately to New York and Washington hailed from the same batch. Abshire's lapse—the delay in examining the Petri dishes—had created an investigative opportunity by inadvertently allowing time for some of the colonies to change into this unusual form. It was a long shot, but the discovery of these strange colonies—deemed morphologic variants, or "morphs"—might even provide a trail to the killer.

Ezzell quickly relayed word about the morphs to FBI agents Darin Steele and Scott Stanley. As Abshire continued to culture samples of anthrax that had been drawn from various batches kept by researchers at USAMRIID, she noticed another pattern: Some of what she was growing appeared to resemble the irregular colonies from the Daschle material.

Abshire shared this observation with Bruce Ivins, whom she considered an expert regarding Ames strain anthrax.[18] On January 10, 2002, Abshire e-mailed Ivins pictures of fresh colonies she had grown from samples of Ames anthrax that had been delivered to USAMRIID direct from the Texas cow in 1981. Samples of this original material had gone to two scientists at USAMRIID: Gregory Knudson, long since retired, and Ivins. Beneath the e-mailed picture of the colonies Abshire had just grown from Knudson's sample, Ivins wrote: "Ames strain—from Greg Knudson's culture collection at USAMRIID. Similar in appearance to Bacillus anthracis colonies from mail."

On January 23, 2002, Ivins handed the photo with his caption—along with a separate photo of what Abshire had ostensibly grown from his own original Ames material—to FBI agents in Frederick. He was now directing investigative attention toward Knudson.

Ivins knew that lessons learned from the mapping of the human genome were making it possible to differentiate among three com-

monly known strains of anthrax: Sterne, ideal for vaccinating livestock and not harmful to humans; Vollum 1B, stockpiled in
weaponry when the United States maintained an offensive biowarfare program; and Ames, the use of which Ivins and his colleagues
had pioneered at USAMRIID. Yet in the initial aftermath of the letter attacks, he was among many who doubted that even the best-
equipped geneticist could distinguish between various batches of
Ames spores.

If Ivins was correct, finding the anthrax killer would be more
than a long shot, perhaps impossible. Absent an advance in microbial forensics, the emerging field of using biochemical clues to
track a germ weapon to its source, investigators would be in the
same position they had faced with cold cases of rape and other
crimes before the advent of DNA fingerprinting. Ivins discussed
the situation with his supervisor, Jeffrey Adamovicz, then deputy
chief of USAMRIID's Bacteriology Division.

"He was, just like the rest of us, thinking to himself, and
thinking out loud, too: 'You catch somebody you think did it—
how can you prove it? You can't really tell one strain of Ames
from another. How are you going to prove that the guy took that
strain and put it in letters and mailed it, as opposed to any other
strain that might be out there?'"[19]

On January 31, 2002, regulators at the FDA did what they had
refused to do before the anthrax letter attacks: They capitulated
to the manufacturer of the old-line anthrax vaccine by lowering
the standard for proof of potency that the agency had insisted
upon.[20] Health and Human Services secretary Tommy Thompson
trumpeted the FDA action, calling the reapproved vaccine "a
critical component in our arsenal against bioterrorism." Just as
important, Thompson said, federal health officials now were
"moving rapidly in developing a possible new generation anthrax vaccine."[21] This was a reference to the vaccine co-invented
by Bruce Ivins.

What a difference the shocking events had made for Ivins.
Only a few months earlier he had feared, and with ample reason,
that his life's work with anthrax was descending into irrelevancy.

The delivery through the mail of just a tiny bit of the bacterium had changed everything. In 1990, he had been the can-do team player, making his mark during the frenzied run-up to the Gulf War. Now he was again at the epicenter—ostensibly helping the investigators deconstruct a frightening bioterrorism event—and he was back at work on his baby, the next-generation vaccine.

General Stephen Reeves, who had struggled since early 2001 to save the anthrax vaccine program in the face of Karl Rove's and Paul Wolfowitz's pointed skepticism, had no doubt about what prompted the turnabout. "If not for 9/11 and the anthrax letters, this thing was in a death spiral," Reeves said. "I think that, if given a choice, the White House would have killed this program." [22]

FIFTEEN

OH MY GOD, I KNOW HIM!

The consensus among scientists remained that it was not possible to distinguish between one lab's batch of Ames strain anthrax and another's. If this assumption stood, investigators would have to rely on other means of tracing the bacterium sent through the mail. One official with a federal checkbook, however, was willing to challenge the prevailing thinking.

As director of the U.S. National Science Foundation, Rita Colwell had the luxury of shaping the future of discovery. At the time of the anthrax mailings, her agency was funding research aimed at unlocking the genetic code of *Bacillus anthracis*. The work was being performed about halfway between Capitol Hill and Fort Detrick, at TIGR, the Institute for Genomic Research, in Rockville, Maryland. The privately held institute was founded by J. Craig Venter, the scientist-impresario who had famously raced the United States government to unravel the human genome.

Colwell was also familiar with the groundbreaking work on anthrax done by Paul Keim's lab in Arizona. As early as October 2001, Colwell, herself a microbiologist, saw an opportunity: Why not pair the world-class skills of TIGR and Keim to examine the genetics of the anthrax from the letters? And why not jump-start the collaboration with a grant from the National Science Foundation?

In consultation with the FBI's Scott Decker, Colwell put out the word through her contacts in academia and in the intelligence, biodefense, and medical research communities: "If *any* reasonable proposal comes in, we will fast-track it." Decker, who had earned a Ph.D. in human genetics at the University of Michigan before completing additional study at Harvard Medical School, was focused on analyzing the then available evidence with the goal of developing a lead, something that would point toward a perpetrator. He greatly welcomed Colwell's interest.[1]

When researchers at TIGR proposed to sequence the DNA of anthrax found within the cerebrospinal fluid of the first letter-attack victim, the Florida photo editor Robert Stevens, Colwell approved it in less than two days. She was confident that significantly more federal funding would follow from the FBI and from other agencies, namely the Office of Naval Research, the Department of Energy, and the National Institutes of Health.

In Rockville and in Flagstaff, members of Colwell's newly formed team set out to sequence the DNA of the lethal material sent to Florida—and then to compare those results with TIGR's already completed analysis of a different batch of Ames anthrax used at Porton Down, Britain's biowarfare research center. Colwell had no doubts about the importance of the work. "The only way we'll nail the perpetrator is through molecular genetics and gene sequencing," she told colleagues.[2]

In New York, Washington, and elsewhere along the East Coast, the September 11 attacks and the anthrax mailings created an atmosphere of siege. Bringing to justice whoever was responsible for the mailings presented the FBI with one of its biggest challenges ever. The bureau's main laboratory, in Quantico, Virginia, was not outfitted to analyze a live bacterial pathogen such as anthrax. Hence the value of Rita Colwell and her network of expert biologists and geneticists.

The events of the fall had put a severe strain on the FBI. Along with investigating the unanswered questions of the September 11 attacks, the bureau was burdened with examining thousands of hoaxes, pranks, and random threats related to anthrax or other dangerous substances. Hundreds of agents, often accompanied by local law enforcement officers, chased tips in the area of Trenton, where each of the recovered anthrax letters had been postmarked. From suspicious-looking mail to everyday cleanser left in a hotel room sink, it seemed as if the entire East Coast was in a panic over white powder.[3]

Perhaps no one felt the pressure more than FBI director Robert Mueller. He worked assiduously to bolster confidence in the bureau's ability to solve the case, meeting almost daily with the president at the White House and with cabinet members, notably Vice President Cheney, Attorney General Ashcroft, and Health and Human Services secretary Thompson, plus Bush's new homeland security advisor, Tom Ridge. Only recently, on August 3, had the Senate confirmed Bush's nomination of Mueller as FBI director. The 98–0 vote reflected the Senate's wide bipartisan respect for his commitment to public service.

Robert Swan Mueller III was reared in the affluent Main Line suburbs west of Philadelphia. He attended boarding school in Concord, New Hampshire, and earned an undergraduate degree at Princeton before getting a master's at New York University. Others of his background could and did find ways to evade military service. Mueller enlisted—and served with distinction as the leader of a Marine rifle platoon in Vietnam. He won the Bronze Star and two Navy Commendation Medals, among other honors.

In the decades after his graduation from law school at the University of Virginia, Mueller chose positions in government over the white-shoe firms doing the corporate world's work. By 1982, he rose to become Criminal Division chief in the San Francisco U.S. Attorney's Office. He later served in the Justice Department under President George H. W. Bush. After a stint with a private law firm in Boston, he returned to Washington in 1995 to prosecute murder cases. President Bill Clinton then appointed Mueller, a Republican, as United States attorney in San Francisco, a post he held from 1998 to early 2001. Colleagues who have worked with or under him described Mueller as uncommonly hardworking—but also impatient and too often unwilling to abandon ill-considered decisions.

The year had been a momentous one for him professionally and personally. Almost immediately after the Senate confirmed his nomination, he underwent surgery for prostate cancer. On September 4, the fifty-seven-year-old Mueller took over as FBI director. Just over a week later, serious questions were being raised about whether it could have disrupted the carefully planned September 11 hijackings.

Pieces of alarming information had been within the bureau's grasp. The arrival of young Saudi men at various flight schools in the United States had drawn the attention of some local FBI agents in Arizona, where a supervisor warned headquarters on July 10, 2001: "The purpose of this communication is to advise the Bureau and New York of the possibility of a coordinated effort by USAMA BIN LADEN (UBL) to send students to the United States to attend civil aviation universities and colleges." [4]

Evidence would later connect three Saudis who got flight training in Arizona to the hijacking of the jetliner that was crashed into the Pentagon. For the FBI, it got worse: On August 23, 2001, the Central Intelligence Agency had alerted bureau headquarters to be on the lookout for two of those hijackers, Khalid al Mihdhar and Nawaf al Hazmi, who the spy agency said were linked to bin Laden. Officials at FBI Headquarters had failed to relay their names to agents in the San Diego area, where the men had lived temporarily.

"They had their full names, they had all the information, but they didn't disseminate shit to the field," recalled Steven Butler, who at the time was an FBI agent in San Diego. "Two days after the World Trade Center came down is when San Diego received that intelligence information," said Jeff Thurman, another FBI agent in San Diego. [5]

As September 11 demonstrated, there were ample grounds to doubt the bureau's skills in recruiting informants—and in gathering, analyzing, and acting upon intelligence about potential threats.

Now some critics suggested that it was time to strip the FBI of responsibility for investigating domestic terrorism. There was talk in Washington policy circles of shifting those duties to a newly envisioned Department of Homeland Security, to a version of Britain's MI5 service (responsible for protecting against threats to its national security), or to the CIA, which since its creation in 1947 had been restricted to spying abroad.

Mueller fought to keep the FBI's responsibilities intact. He assured the White House and members of Congress that the bureau was up to the challenge. Not only would it track down the terrorists and find the evidence needed to convict them in a court of law; Mueller said repeatedly that *preventing* terrorism would be the top priority. As part of that effort, he directed his agents to be more preemptive, to deviate from conventional investigative procedures when necessary. Instead of monitoring from a distance someone suspected of plotting a terrorist attack, the FBI could supplement its electronic monitoring and discreet observation with overt surveillance. This could also tie up dozens of agents, to the possible detriment of pursuing other suspects or leads.

Meanwhile, Mueller chose as the leader of the anthrax investigation Van A. Harp, a thickly built native of Toledo, Ohio, whose career spanned generations of crime fighting: When he joined the FBI in 1970, J. Edgar Hoover was still director and Jimmy Hoffa was still in prison. Harp had worked cases in Buffalo, Detroit, and Lansing, Michigan, and he led the FBI's office in Cleveland for several years. Some of the investigations he oversaw focused on organized crime and public corruption.[6] In July of 2001, Mueller's predecessor had installed Harp as head of the Washington, D.C., Field Office. Harp, however, was not an ideal choice to lead the closely watched anthrax case. At fifty-five, he had reached the FBI's standard retirement age. And a protracted imbroglio in his past should have stirred doubts about his judgment.

Harp had played a much disputed role in the FBI's internal review of the disastrous standoff at Ruby Ridge, a mountain hamlet in northern Idaho. The events in August 1992 left two dead by gunshot: a deputy U.S. marshal and, days later, the wife of a man named Randy Weaver, who was facing federal weapons charges. In September 1993, officials at FBI Headquarters brought in Harp to assist a review of the incident being undertaken by Justice Department lawyers. Four months later, Harp and an FBI colleague beat the lawyers to the punch by circulating their own review first. It offered a sweeping justification for all the actions of bureau personnel, notably the sharpshooter who wounded a rifle-toting Randy Weaver and then fired into the family cabin, killing Weaver's unarmed wife, Vicki.

The Justice Department's Office of Professional Responsibility criticized Harp and several other FBI officials, saying they tried to conceal potential wrongdoing by the bureau. One senior FBI official ultimately was sentenced to eighteen months in prison for destroying an internal critique of the bureau's performance at Ruby Ridge. The federal prosecutor in that case referred several additional issues to the Justice Department for administrative review, including Harp's conduct. Justice's Office of Professional Responsibility determined that Harp had tried to "cleanse" another FBI agent's written description of the rules of engagement, drafted by headquarters, under which the sharpshooter had fired. In June 1999, the office accused Harp of misconduct and recommended discipline ranging from censure to suspension for thirty days. The FBI's Office of Professional Responsibility rejected the Justice office's conclusions, saying it saw no evidence that Harp had acted with bad intent.

His fate remained in limbo until the waning days of the Clinton administration. On January 3, 2001, Assistant Attorney General Stephen Colgate cleared Harp of misconduct. Six months later, Harp won the last of his promotions, to assistant FBI director, in charge of the Washington Field Office.[7]

By the fall of 2001, Harp was a battle-scarred survivor on his last lap with the FBI. Solving the anthrax case would be the crowning achievement of his career. But Harp initially seemed surprisingly detached from the details: Robert Roth and Dave Dawson, the two men he designated as his top supervisors on the case, had scant contact with him as they launched one of the most important and scientifically daunting investigations in the bureau's history.

Agent Roth later recalled under oath, "I'm not sure we met with Van in the first 90 days of the case." Asked by a plaintiff's lawyer whether his FBI bosses' interest in the anthrax case was "more or less intense than typical criminal investigations," Roth testified: "I thought initially, for the first 60–90 days, it was less intense than I would have expected."[8]

Roth and his co–case agent, Dawson, shared responsibility for the daily operations of the investigation. The two were friends and worked well together—yet it was much more common for the FBI to have a single case agent. (Roth was working on a violent-crime squad on the day the letter to Senator Daschle was discovered. Dawson was chosen from the FBI's National Security Section.)

Harp was soon facing strong pressure from members of Congress and others to quicken the pace. In November, the FBI released a profile, or "behavioral assessment," of the perpetrator. Among other traits, the mailer was said to be "comfortable working with extremely hazardous material." The person "has access to a source of Anthrax and possesses knowledge and expertise to refine it." In a mass mailing on January 29, 2002, Harp asked for help from all thirty thousand members of the American Society for Microbiology, the largest professional organization for scientists working with bacteria, viruses, and other aspects of microbiology. After pointing out that five innocent people had been killed by the anthrax letter attacks, Harp made his plea:

> It is very likely that one or more of you know this individual. A review of the information-to-date in this matter leads investigators to believe that a single person is most likely responsible for these mailings. This person is experienced working in a laboratory. Based on his or her selection of the Ames strain of Bacillus anthracis one would expect that this individual has or had legitimate access to select biological agents at some time. This person has the technical knowledge and/or expertise to

produce a highly refined and deadly product. This person has
exhibited a clear, rational thought process and appears to be
very organized in the production and mailing of these letters.
The person might be described as "stand-offish" and likely
prefers to work in isolation as opposed to a group/team setting.

Harp also said it was "possible this person used off-hours in
a laboratory," and he pointed out that the FBI was offering a
substantial cash reward for information leading to an arrest and
conviction.

When she read the FBI letter in Seattle, Nancy Haigwood instantly flashed back on her encounters over the previous twenty-
five years with Bruce Ivins: His unrelenting obsession with her
former sorority. The stolen lab book, along with the anonymous
note leading to the book's reappearance inside a nearby U.S.
mailbox. The graffiti. The fabricated letter to the Frederick
newspaper signed in her name. The recent, unsolicited e-mails.
He had foretold trouble that would affect USAMRIID just three
days after the first anthrax-laced letters were postmarked, and
this was well before the existence of the letters was known to the
public. In November he had proudly sent pictures of himself
doing hands-on work with the "now infamous 'Ames' strain of
Bacillus anthracis."

She couldn't prove it, but Haigwood had a strong gut feeling
about the identity of the anthrax killer: "Oh my God, I know
him!" She called the number provided by the FBI. The mailer, she
said, might be Bruce Ivins.[9] The bureau filed away her tip.

The team of genetic experts that Rita Colwell had assembled
drew notice in the narrow realm of anthrax research. The efforts
at Northern Arizona University and at TIGR were tracked by
Martin Enserink, a writer for *Science* magazine. His November
30, 2001, article about Keim's highly specialized work provided
readers this succinct summary: "Armed with a vast collection of
strains and a refined DNA fingerprinting system, a research team

in Arizona may help solve who's behind the anthrax attacks—
and nail other bioterrorists in the future." Citing Keim as his
source, Enserink wrote that if the perpetrator used a "very rare"
batch of anthrax, "DNA evidence might clinch the case." [10]

Keim had already established that all the anthrax mailed in the
fall of 2001 was the Ames strain—which, investigators would
learn, was used at USAMRIID and seventeen other laboratories
worldwide. (Fifteen of the labs were in the United States, and one
each in Canada, Sweden, and Great Britain.) Investigators had interviewed dozens of researchers and examined more than four
hundred documents to identify transfers from one lab to another
of the Ames strain.[11] But could the Amerithrax scientists succeed
in identifying a unique batch of Ames, potentially narrowing the
field of suspects?

If the perpetrator had, indeed, tapped a "very rare" batch of
Ames anthrax, investigators might be chasing a killer neither as
cunning nor as lucky as Ted Kaczynski, the infamous Unabomber. Kaczynski had also struck anonymously through the
mail, sending rigged packages that killed three people and injured twenty-three others before the FBI caught him—eighteen
years after delivery of his first package.

While some of the experts continued to examine the anthrax
used in the letter attacks for characteristics that might provide a
unique DNA profile, the FBI set about trying to collect samples
from each of the eighteen labs that had used the Ames strain for
research purposes. If Keim and the others could find something
distinct within the attack material's DNA that matched the anthrax from one of those labs, investigators would lock on to that
facility as the most probable source of the mailings.

On February 15, 2002, the FBI began distributing subpoenas
to all the labs in the United States thought to be working with the
Ames strain. The subpoenas, which were drawn up with a protocol designed to prevent tampering or accidental contamination, required each scientist with a batch of the anthrax to
submit a sample. On February 27, Ivins did so, having drawn the
material from the large flask of spores he had logged as RMR-
1029 in October 1997. Indeed, Ivins handwrote the labeling he

affixed to two test tubes he filled with his sample: "Ames strain
RMR 1029 from Dugway (1997) Bruce Ivins, 2/27/02." However, those responsible for collecting the samples at USAMRIID
noticed that Ivins had not entirely complied with the protocol:
He had placed his anthrax in the wrong type of test tubes, called
slants, and John Ezzell, who was assisting the FBI's effort,
agreed, in consultation with the bureau, to reject Ivins's sample.[12]

Ivins, speaking privately with fellow microbiologist Jeff
Adamovicz, the deputy chief of his division, lamented the FBI's decision. "I remember him just kind of shaking his head, because they
had rejected his first sample. I said, 'Well, Bruce, just submit another sample.'" Ezzell was similarly blunt: "Bruce, the sample is
not done correctly. Resubmit it. Follow the protocol this time."[13]

SIXTEEN

I DIDN'T KEEP RECORDS

vins did not submit another sample until early April, by which time something else was on his mind. It involved a troubling secret he had kept for several months from the entire Army chain of command, a secret that might be exposed amid the FBI's glare.

In late 2001, Ivins had detected what appeared to be anthrax spores in Room 19, the personal office he shared with two other scientists. More worrisome, the office was a place where outsiders who would not have been vaccinated against anthrax might occasionally visit.[1] Household bleach diluted with water can kill anthrax spores, and Ivins sprayed this solution onto all the surfaces where he'd found the suspected anthrax. He used paper towels to wipe it away. But he did not document any of his work, nor did he record whether he rechecked the hot spots to see if he'd succeeded. What he did was at odds with official safety policies and procedures at USAMRIID, as he well knew.[2] He also had to know that if his secret ever got out, the FBI would ask how this anthrax got into his office, and why he behaved so furtively.

In April 2002, word of a mishap with anthrax involving two

junior colleagues gave Ivins a chance to reveal his secret on his terms, obscured by the confusion that he would create. The two younger scientists, working in the B3 hot suite on the morning of April 8, noticed that liquid-form anthrax had sloshed out and over the top edges of a flask and crusted as it dried, posing a risk that spores were released into the air. Worried they might have inhaled anthrax, the pair sought evaluations at the Fort Detrick infirmary. Though they were already vaccinated, Army doctors gave them booster shots and doses of Cipro as a precaution.[3]

Neither of the scientists became infected and, if not for Ivins, the incident would likely soon have been forgotten. But on Monday, April 15, 2002, he took steps that would transform their mishap into a spectacle. He roamed alone through various "cold" areas at USAMRIID, places, like his personal office, that were supposed to be free of any contamination. He swabbed from fifty-six surface points for more loose spores and placed the swabbings into Petri dishes to see if any colonies of anthrax would grow. When he checked the next day, Ivins saw that the roundish, ground-glass-like colonies indicative of anthrax had grown from fourteen, or 25 percent, of the swabbings.[4] This time Ivins did document where he swabbed—including surfaces within the men's change room and, again, his personal office space. And this time he did not bleach away the suspected spores until he had meticulously confirmed, and recorded, the presence of the live bacteria.

Ivins's motive for conducting his latest round of secretive swabbing was the more indefensible because it defied the advice he had been given by his new supervisor, microbiologist Patricia Worsham. When Ivins had proposed conducting his wide-ranging hunt for anthrax outside the biocontainment areas—where spores are never supposed to be—Worsham told him she saw no basis for it. She advised him not to proceed without the permission of the Bacteriology Division chief, Gerry Andrews.[5]

Ivins did share his findings with Worsham, with whom he had worked closely for years on—among other things—the next-generation anthrax vaccine. According to Worsham, Ivins had also confided his original secretive round of swabbing and bleaching to her around the first week of April 2002. (She said that Ivins told her in April 2002 that he had bleached his office in "November or December 2001." Ivins would say he did so in December.) She deferred to his judgment that the apparent discovery of anthrax in Room 19 was of low importance.[6]

However, on April 16, after Ivins informed Worsham that 25 percent of the spots he checked with his most recent swabbings appeared to be positive for anthrax, they decided it was time to alert the chain of command. It was two days later, according to Andrews, chief of the Bacteriology Division, that Ivins and Worsham told him about the secretive bleaching Ivins had performed several months earlier, as well as his more recent hunt for contamination.[7]

The lab mishap made the local news as of April 20, and operations at USAMRIID were interrupted amid the testing, bleaching—and official assurances of safety. Employees thought to be at potential risk were evaluated. Ivins told USAMRIID officials that his April swabbings were in response to the mishap involving his two junior colleagues. He said he "personally and privately decided to check non-biocontainment areas to see if containment may have possibly been breached. Without approval or consultation with anyone in the chain of command, I swabbed a number of locations."

An immediate building-wide survey confirmed contamination with live anthrax spores in three cold locations, apart from the B3 hot suite: the men's clean-change room, where scientists change from street to laboratory clothing; molding around the outside of a pass box, through which documents or other items can be irradiated with spore-killing ultraviolet light and then passed from the containment suite to the outside; and in only one office—Room 19. All three areas were cordoned off or locked until they could be scrubbed with bleach. Further testing found more anthrax spores within Room 19—on the top shelf of Ivins's desk, on his lab tech's computer, and under a corner air vent. Army officials told staffers and the Frederick community that the amount of loose bacteria found at USAMRIID was relatively low and therefore posed no serious health risk.[8]

But how did anthrax escape a supposedly airtight biocontainment lab and wind up in, among other places, the office of Bruce Ivins?

The mystery deepened when Army officials realized that the anthrax that had spilled in the hot suite mishap on April 8 was tagged with a distinct research marker—a marker that was not to be found in any of the loose spores outside the hot suites. This meant that the April 8 event and any other contamination at USAMRIID were, in the opinion of Gerry Andrews, *de-linked*.[9]

Army officials moved to cauterize what might otherwise become a public relations nightmare—played out under the scrutiny of both Congress and the news media. On April 23, the Army assigned a colonel from outside Fort Detrick, Dr. David L. Hoover, to conduct "an informal investigation of bio-hazardous contamination that came to the attention of authorities" that month.[10] Hoover, a physician at the Walter Reed Army Institute of Research in Silver Spring, Maryland, was instructed to

> reach detailed findings and recommendations that address the following issues:
>
> a. Whether USAMRIID personnel have safely handled, stored, or accounted for hazardous material within the Institute;
> b. Whether USAMRIID has an appropriate system of procedures to protect all personnel from exposure to hazardous material;
> c. Whether USAMRIID personnel responded appropriately once notified of suspected contamination within the Institute;
> d. Identify the source of contamination within the Institute, specifically *Bacillus anthracis* contamination found in three separate locations in Building 1425.

Hoover was told to collect statements under oath from witnesses, and he was given three weeks to investigate and submit a final report.[11] He was not told to investigate why a senior USAMRIID scientist—Bruce Ivins, who first discovered what appeared to be loose anthrax spores in late 2001—had failed for several months to report it to the chain of command. The investigation would be conducted under Army Regulation 15-6, which called for maximum speed. The tight deadline would deny Hoover the ability to reconcile conflicting statements from witnesses or to pursue in depth new information gained along the way.

Even before Hoover's appointment, Ivins had begun trying to explain his actions. In a one-and-a-half-page summary that he provided to USAMRIID officials, Ivins blamed the loose spores in Room 19 on his lab technician, Kristie Friend, whose desk he said was "covered with an enormous amount of dust." Friend had been spending most of her days assisting John Ezzell in the Diagnostic Systems Division—which was responsible for handling the anthrax-laced letters on behalf of the FBI. Ivins said he suspected that Friend may have inadvertently tracked spores from Ezzell's division into their office space.

"In casual conversations with me, Ms. [Friend] had suggested that she might have come in contact with or been contaminated with material from one of the pieces of evidence being investigated," Ivins said in his written statement.

Army investigative documents do not reflect whether Friend was ever asked about Ivins's claim that she had described having possibly been "contaminated." Friend told Colonel Hoover she had "no idea" how anthrax spores could have wound up in the office that she shared with Ivins.

Ivins, meanwhile, suggested that keeping his earliest bleaching and surveillance measures unknown to his superiors was an act of patriotism: To have told them sooner about any loose spores would have risked disrupting USAMRIID's efforts to assist the FBI-led criminal investigation of the anthrax mailings.[12] Ivins did, however, apologize for his secretive actions—while maintaining that he had acted with good intentions. "In retrospect," Ivins said in a written summary on April 18, "although my concern for biosafety was honest and my desire to refrain from crying 'Wolf!' unnecessarily was sincere, I should have notified my supervisor ahead of time of my worries about a possible breach in biocontainment. I thought that quietly and diligently cleaning the dirty desk area would both eliminate any possible B. anthracis contamination as well as prevent unintended anxiety and alarm at the institute." Until his junior colleagues' lab mishap in April 2002, Ivins said, he gave "little thought" to his off-the-books bleaching of his office area in late 2001.[13]

After collecting sworn statements from at least twenty staffers, Colonel Hoover submitted his report to the Army. He documented laxity and sloppiness that may have led to the release of spores outside the biocontainment areas. He said that in addition to the Ames strain, the Vollum and Sterne strains had been found in Ivins's office area. He noted that both Ames and Vollum were found in the men's change room, too. No contamination, however, was found in the Diagnostic Systems Division labs where Ezzell and Kristie Friend had done most of their work.

The documents assembled for Colonel Hoover revealed that, of twenty-two offices that outside technicians scoured for spores, only Ivins's contained Ames strain anthrax. And while Ivins said he had found spores in 25 percent of the locations he searched in April 2002, the outside technicians found them at a minuscule rate of 0.18 percent. Either he was uncannily lucky—or Ivins knew where to look for loose spores of anthrax, and had eliminated nearly all of them with his bleaching.[14] There was another possibility: Ivins, a master of ruses, had actually generated all of the positive cultures in his own lab—but claimed that he had obtained them by swabbing in supposedly safe areas.

Hoover did not recommend any disciplinary action against Ivins or anyone else. He did call for updating the USAMRIID biosafety manual and better training of personnel, along with more frequent safety inspections.[15] With the filing of Hoover's report, the breach of containment at USAMRIID could be dismissed as a minor blip, biowarfare research's version of no harm, no foul. No Army personnel were held to account on Capitol Hill. The news media, after reporting the bare details of the April 8 mishap and the Army's steady assurances of safety, moved on.

Ivins could not have wished for a better outcome. His account of the stealth swabbing and bleaching he had done in his personal office in late 2001 went unchallenged and all but unnoticed. Hoover, based on his initial Army instructions, had been empowered to explore whether Ivins or any of the others at USAMRIID responded "appropriately" when notified of suspected contamination. Was it *appropriate* for Ivins to have concealed from the chain of command for several months his bleaching of his office to counter the apparent presence of anthrax spores? Hoover's report offered no judgment.

Nor did Hoover explore the inconsistencies and implausibilities in what Ivins had said. On April 18, Ivins had written in his summary of events that faulty memory prevented him from saying whether he had sought to verify the effectiveness of his cleanup of any loose anthrax in his office area in late 2001. "I honestly do not recall if follow-up swabs were taken of the area. I may have done so, but I do not now remember reswabbing," he wrote.

Reswabbing—and documenting his efforts—would have indicated a safety-minded approach. Failing to do so would suggest that Ivins's highest priority was secrecy. It would strain credulity under any circumstance for a highly experienced anthrax researcher to say that he could not recall verifying that he had eliminated potentially lethal spores from his own office. Room 19, after all, was open to janitors and any number of visitors—including his own family members—none of whom was vaccinated against anthrax.

Ivins's professed forgetfulness was even more suspicious because by late 2001 it appeared that even a negligible amount of Ames strain anthrax could be deadly.

On October 31, 2001, Kathy Nguyen, a sixty-one-year-old New York City hospital stockroom worker, had died of inhalational anthrax, yet not a trace of the bacterium was ever found in the hospital or in her apartment building.[16] Nguyen's fate evoked immediate expressions of fear from health authorities that even the most minuscule amount of anthrax could kill.[17] On November 21, 2001, also close to when Ivins secretly bleached his office, the fifth victim of the letter attacks, ninety-four-year-old

Ottilie Lundgren, a resident of rural Oxford, Connecticut, died of inhalational anthrax—and nothing suspicious was found in any of her belongings or home. However, testing of samples taken from a postal facility in Connecticut showed that four sorting machines were contaminated with anthrax. One of the contaminated machines processed bulk mail for Lundgren's carrier route—raising the likelihood that she, as with Nguyen, was killed by a minute amount of anthrax, carried by a cross-contaminated piece of mail.[18]

In a May 6 statement to Colonel Hoover, Ivins gave this depiction of a proper response to suspected contamination: "When conducting [safety] surveillance in the past, we would sometimes find a few hot spots of contamination and clean them up, then re-check to make sure they were OK." Asked what procedures he would follow "if you have a potential exposure" to anthrax, Ivins responded: "That depends on seriousness. If there is a small spill, wipe up area with bleach, cleanup verified by swabs. Individual reports to supervisor."[19]

Before invoking once again his supposed concern about not disrupting USAMRIID's efforts on behalf of the FBI investigation, Ivins provided yet another rationale for having kept what he did secret: "I didn't keep records or verify the cultures because I was concerned that records might be obtained under the Freedom of Information Act."

Like his earlier excuses, this one did not square with Ivins's expressed concern about the safety risk supposedly created by his lab tech, Kristie Friend. Not only was Ivins unable to say whether he had followed up with swabbing to confirm that he had eliminated all the suspected spores from his office space—at no point had he surveyed what he ostensibly believed was the source of the contamination: Friend's work environment in the Diagnostic Systems Division. And while Ivins had swabbed for and found anthrax in the men's clean-change room in April, it was curious, considering he suspected Friend was the source of contamination, that he never swabbed the women's change room. The Army did swab the women's change room for anthrax—and found none.

Perhaps most revealing of all, Ivins never warned Friend about anthrax he had apparently found on her desk in their shared personal office space.[20]

The Army had instructed Hoover to identify "the source of contamination within the Institute." His 361-page report, completed on May 10, 2002, concluded that the available information yielded no clear answer.

At about the same time in April 2002 that Ivins admitted his earlier covert cleanup, he prepared a second sample of Ames strain anthrax in response to the federal subpoena. This was from the same batch he had tapped for his sample in February: RMR-1029. On April 10, he personally handed over the new sample, which he labeled "Dugway spores—1997." And this time he used the correct test tubes.[21]

Several Army officials at Fort Detrick thought it entirely appropriate that no disciplinary action was taken against Ivins related to his furtive swabbing and bleaching. Said one of Ivins's supervisors, Jeffrey Adamovicz: "He wasn't being secretive about it, he wasn't being evasive. He was being Bruce."[22] Gerry Andrews, who was chief of the Bacteriology Division and also a stalwart defender of Ivins, said he found it "pretty offensive" that the Army had even opened the Regulation 15-6 investigation.

Andrews, a career Army officer with a Ph.D. in microbiology, had arrived at USAMRIID a decade earlier. He had counted Ivins a friend and viewed him as "probably one of the most affable guys that I've ever known." Andrews accepted without reservation Ivins's explanations. "This whole business about 'Bruce is hiding the contamination.' That's a bunch of bullshit."[23]

The general who had had authority over USAMRIID and the Army's other medical research labs would later come to a contrary view of Ivins's conduct. Dr. John Parker retired from his command as of April 1, 2002, several months after Ivins's furtive bleaching of suspected anthrax spores. Asked what he thought of Ivins's secretive behavior and his failure to alert the chain of command, the genial Parker, a physician, stiffened. "To not have elevated it is *criminal*. It's inappropriate—because you may be endangering other people's lives." [24]

Whatever the limitations of Colonel Hoover's rushed three-week investigation, he had taken a snapshot of the circumstances surrounding the anthrax contamination at USAMRIID. The sworn statements that he collected could be evaluated by the FBI or presented to a federal grand jury.

By the end of May the Army had handed over to the bureau Hoover's entire report. Its many unanswered questions invited deeper scrutiny. Three months earlier, the Army had provided the FBI with electronic access card records, documenting when anyone—including Ivins—entered and left the biocontainment hot suites and other lab facilities. In response to the bureau's letter to members of the American Society for Microbiology, Nancy Haigwood had called in her suspicion that Ivins was the anthrax killer. If they needed further grounds to look closely at him, the Amerithrax investigators could have sought prompt access to his e-mails from 2000 and 2001, which would have revealed his concern that federal support for anthrax research was waning, jeopardizing the next-generation vaccine, his co-invention.

Yet as the spring of 2002 yielded to summer, Bruce Ivins was not a suspect. The FBI had its sights set on someone else.

SEVENTEEN

THEIR SECRET WEAPON

The FBI's Robert Roth thought that he had done all he could to design a quiet search. He wanted the ground rules conveyed to the participating investigators: No raid jackets, badges, or openly displayed guns. No overt law enforcement symbols. Roth preferred to move discreetly with what might be the breakthrough search for an investigation known inside the FBI as Major Case 184.[1]

The evening before the search was to unfold, Roth telephoned the object of all this attention, Dr. Steven J. Hatfill, a physician-researcher who had worked at USAMRIID from 1997 to 1999. As in their other conversations in recent months, Hatfill appeared friendly and said he would cooperate. He lived in the Detrick Plaza apartments, just across the street from the main gate to Fort Detrick. He agreed to meet the next day with Roth and other investigators.

On the morning of June 25, 2002, Hatfill drove to the FBI's RA, or residence agency, office in Frederick. Roth was waiting there, with his co–case agent, Dave Dawson, and Thomas Dellafera, a senior investigator from the U.S. Postal Inspection Service. Dellafera, a third-generation postal employee, felt a special commitment to the investigation. When the letter attacks unfolded, his office was located inside the Brentwood station in Northeast Washington—where Joseph Curseen Jr. and Thomas Morris Jr. inhaled the anthrax that killed them.

Roth had also recruited for the job FBI agent Brad Garrett, whose patient approach helped him to connect with victims, witnesses, and criminals alike. The fifty-three-year-old Garrett was known for his skill at eliciting confessions. As they escorted Hatfill to a private room, Garrett was struck by his good spirits. Hatfill had come to the RA alone, without a defense attorney.

Hatfill struck many as a swashbuckler, inclined to exaggerate. Raised in central Illinois, he earned his undergraduate degree in biology from Southwestern College, a school affiliated with the United Methodist Church and located thirty-five miles south of Wichita, Kansas. After enlisting and pulling a hitch in the U.S. Army, Hatfill spent most of the next decade in southern Africa. He earned his medical degree at the University of Zimbabwe— and later told acquaintances that he had worked with military forces of the formerly white-ruled Rhodesian government. Hatfill claimed to have earned a Ph.D. in microbiology—a fiction. He further puffed up his résumé by claiming a phantom membership in a British medical society.

When he returned to the United States, Hatfill focused at first on research into HIV, Lyme disease, and cancer. After a two-year stint at the National Institutes of Health, he worked from 1997 to 1999 under a federal grant as a virologist at USAMRIID, where he researched medicines to counter such lethal pathogens as the Ebola, Marburg, and monkeypox viruses.

Hatfill had taken a position in September 1999 at Science Applications International Corp., a firm that specializes in contract work with military and intelligence agencies, notably the CIA. In 2000, Hatfill and his boss at SAIC commissioned William C. Patrick III, a microbiologist who decades earlier had helped build the Army's offensive biological weapons program at Fort Detrick, to compose a brief report: Patrick the ex-bioweaponeer analyzed the extent to which a letter, laced with anthrax, could contaminate an office building.[2] Although Patrick's topic would later raise some eyebrows, the fact was that, since the late 1990s, authorities had investigated hundreds of hoax letters purporting to contain anthrax or other pathogens. The safety issues surrounding a potential biological attack were of high interest to the Centers for Disease Control and other public agencies.[3] Hatfill provided Patrick's report to the CDC and the pair also instructed military personnel, firefighters, and other first responders how to manage the scene of a biological attack or hoax.[4]

As the FBI agents sat down with Hatfill at the RA in Frederick, they sought to preserve his goodwill: The FBI did not know, Roth said, if Hatfill had anything to do with the mailings. But the only way to solve the case was, first, to eliminate as a suspect anyone who may have had motive or opportunity.

Roth, his hopes for a quiet day notwithstanding, had gotten an inkling of unwanted company an hour or so earlier. "I saw a helicopter going right down toward Steve's house. I was surprised Steve didn't see it."[5]

It was late morning, and Roth at last got to what he wanted from Hatfill: permission to search his apartment and swab it for anthrax. Roth said the operation would be low-key and unobtrusive. Hatfill agreed and signed the typewritten forms granting his consent.

Unknown to Hatfill, the search he had just approved was being watched by a phalanx of broadcast and print journalists who had made the trip to Frederick by land and by air. Hatfill soon got a hint of what was unfolding when he, Roth, and Garrett returned to the RA after eating lunch at a nearby shopping center. Garrett and Hatfill were first out of Garrett's sedan, at which point an SUV they had just passed pulled alongside. Its windows were down, and the driver trained a video camera on Hatfill and Garrett. Roth, still in the car, shouted at them to get back in, after which Garrett sped away.

Garrett and Roth were displeased at how events had deteriorated. They told Hatfill he had the right to withdraw his just signed consent. Visibly distraught, Hatfill said he was no longer consenting. Roth turned apologetically to Hatfill: He would have to get a judge's signature for a search warrant. And this could create the impression that Hatfill was uncooperative—that he had something to hide. Within a few minutes Hatfill relented and said he would continue to cooperate.

The agents drove Hatfill to a local hotel, where he could stay while the search unfolded. At Hatfill's apartment, search team members outfitted in moon suits to protect against anthrax roamed in and out accompanied by dozens of other investigators. Until now, Hatfill's name had not surfaced publicly in connection with the anthrax attacks. But that night ABC News, reporting what anchor Peter Jennings called "major news," identified Hatfill as the target of the search and a man the FBI had been scrutinizing for months.[6]

Neither Roth nor Garrett had tipped off the press, and it was hard to say who did because so many law enforcement and other public officials—probably several hundred, according to Roth—had been briefed about the impending search. "I've been to a lot of searches with media," Garrett said. "But nothing to this extent. It was just incredible."[7]

The frenzy spawned by the search—the helicopters and the many camera crews on the ground—snarled traffic for those who worked or lived nearby. This included Bruce Ivins, who was driving with his eighteen-year-old daughter. "We were coming home from somewhere," recalled Amanda Ivins, "and we saw all the satellite dishes and the vans. My dad said, 'I wonder what's going on there?' "[8]

To be sure, Hatfill's prominence as a suspect early in the investigation could be justified. He claimed on his résumé to have "working knowledge" of bacterial and viral biowarfare agents, in both wet and dry form. Although he was a virologist and not a bacteriologist, Hatfill had suggested to co-workers at USAMRIID that he knew how to deploy anthrax. In their June 2002 search of his apartment, investigators found a nonlethal anthrax simulant and protocols for producing spores that resembled those used by the Army's defunct offensive biowarfare program. And there was Hatfill's use of Cipro. On five occasions in 2001, including dates close to when the anthrax-laced letters were mailed, he filled or refilled prescriptions for the antibiotic.[9]

Along with other researchers, Hatfill wanted the government to do more to prepare for a biological attack. He had delivered PowerPoint presentations to local public safety officials that included warnings about an anthrax letter attack. One of his slides, titled "Multiple Hoax Mailing Trends," described this scenario: "Single letter containing WMD threat sent to multiple targets. Letters similar in content and point of origin. Letters delivered to . . . Government Agencies . . . News Agencies."[10]

In the summer of 2001, Hatfill, while working with SAIC, the private defense and intelligence contractor, had unsuccessfully sought a higher security clearance from the CIA. After the anthrax mailings, a polygrapher who had examined Hatfill for the agency told contacts at the FBI they should look into him.[11] There was also Hatfill's unpublished novel, "Emergence," in which a wheelchair-bound man attacks Congress using plague bacteria. His occasional liberties with the truth, not least his bogus doctorate, deepened suspicions about him. Within the first several months of the investigation, a total of four people, citing different suspicions, told the FBI they thought Hatfill was capable of having perpetrated the letter attacks.[12]

Yet no evidence emerged that Hatfill, the virus researcher, had ever handled anthrax, a bacterium. By the time the letters were dropped into the mail, he had been out of USAMRIID for more than two years—leaving him without access to a laboratory properly equipped for handling anthrax. Investigators promptly searched Hatfill's apartment, car, and storage spaces, along with his girlfriend's apartment and car. No anthrax was found.[13]

Hatfill would explain that he used the simulant in demonstrations he led to show public safety personnel what anthrax might look like. Similarly, Hatfill said he used the protocols—including photos of large fermentors that could be used for growing great quantities of anthrax—to assist his instruction of personnel who might be called on to search for bioweaponry overseas. As for his use of Cipro, Hatfill had a deviated septum and experienced per-

sistent sinus and bronchial infections, for which he had persuaded a medical doctor friend to write him the prescriptions.
On the morning of September 11, Hatfill underwent sinus surgery and again was prescribed Cipro.[14]

Although Hatfill's imagined hoax letter, duplicated and sent
to government and media offices, appeared to be prophetic, such
scenarios were floated among biodefense specialists. Moreover,
how likely was it that a killer would publicly predict his own
crimes? Bill Patrick, Hatfill's friend and colleague who was the
former product development chief for the offensive bioweapons
program, spent days explaining to investigators that Hatfill had
never asked for help obtaining or preparing anthrax spores.
Patrick at no point hired a lawyer.[15]

The intense investigative interest in Steven Hatfill could also be
traced to a confluence of gossip and sophistry. One of those most
responsible for focusing public attention on Hatfill was an activist
college professor, Barbara Hatch Rosenberg. A former cancer researcher who was trained as a molecular biologist, Dr. Rosenberg
had never worked with anthrax, yet she was well read and pas-
sionate on the subject of biological weaponry. Rosenberg was
teaching environmental science and health at the State University
of New York in Purchase, a community about thirty miles northeast of Manhattan.

News articles often cited Rosenberg's leadership role with the
Federation of American Scientists, which sought to prevent the
use or proliferation of biological weapons. She was among those
who questioned whether the United States was honoring its
promise to abandon its offensive program, as pledged in 1969 by
President Richard Nixon and required six years later by an international treaty.

On November 21, 2001, Rosenberg began to lay a foundation for her theory that the anthrax mailings were an inside job
countenanced by the federal government. Appearing on behalf of
the Federation of American Scientists, she told an international
gathering in Geneva, Switzerland, that the anthrax used in the

attacks "was derived, almost certainly, from a U.S. defense laboratory."

In a Web posting dated December 10, 2001, Rosenberg opined that the perpetrator was "probably an American microbiologist who has access to weaponized anthrax or to the expertise and materials for making it, in a U.S. government or contractor lab." More alarming, Rosenberg alleged in the same Web posting, "The US government has undoubtedly known for some time that the anthrax terrorism was an inside job."

In a lecture at Princeton University on February 18, 2002, Rosenberg said "government insider" contacts had told her that the main suspect was "a former Fort Detrick scientist who is now working for a contractor in the Washington D.C. area." She said that the FBI might be "dragging its feet" in charging the suspect because he was familiar with "secret activities that the government would not like to see disclosed." She said that she was determined to promote press coverage that would put "pressure on the FBI to follow up and publicly prosecute the perpetrator." [16] In comments aired several weeks later by the BBC, Rosenberg asserted that the letter attacks may have resulted from a secret CIA project "gone badly awry." [17]

Rosenberg's narrative steadily gained traction. On Capitol Hill, where some officials fumed over the FBI's performance, congressional aides conferred at length with her. She also found ready interest among journalists, notably Nicholas D. Kristof, a columnist for the *New York Times*. Rosenberg later recalled that she had first learned about Steven Hatfill, by name, from "probably a reporter," in February or March of 2002, after which she identified Hatfill and relayed what she believed about him to Kristof, who wrote six columns for the *Times* about the anthrax investigation. [18]

Kristof, a graduate of Harvard and later a Rhodes Scholar, had begun his newspaper career in 1984 at the *Times*. In 1990 he shared with a colleague the Pulitzer Prize for international reporting. He was later named an associate managing editor, a title he relinquished in October 2001 to write a weekly column, focused initially on terrorism. In his 2002 columns touching upon the Amerithrax case, Kristof disparaged the FBI and described Hatfill, at first anonymously, as among a handful of individuals "who had the ability, access and motive to send the anthrax."[19]

Rosenberg, wary of a defamation lawsuit, prided herself on describing Hatfill without actually uttering his name. But after a phone conversation with Kristof on May 22, 2002, she wrote a revealing note, saying of the columnist, "He got me to tell all about SH."[20] Two days later, Kristof's column framed the stakes as he saw them: The U.S. government's "failure to capture the anthrax killer" was "suggesting to Iraq and other potential perpetrators that they might get away with an attack." He warned of an ongoing "biological threat that requires much more vigorous and urgent countermeasures."

Kristof continued, "One of the first steps we can take to reduce our vulnerability is to light a fire under the FBI in its investigation of the anthrax case." Citing "experts in the bioterror field," Kristof sketched his first, still anonymous portrait of Steven Hatfill as the would-be perpetrator: "These experts point, for example, to one middle-aged American who has worked for the United States military biodefense program and had access to the labs at Fort Detrick, Md. His anthrax vaccinations are up to date, he unquestionably had the ability to make first-rate anthrax, and he was upset at the United States government in the period preceding the anthrax attack. I say all this to prod the authorities."[21]

In fact, Army records and the sworn testimony of Hatfill's boss at USAMRIID would show that Hatfill did not have an "up to date" anthrax vaccination as the fall 2001 mailings unfolded. And to say that Hatfill "unquestionably had the ability to make first-rate anthrax" was a stretch: Although Hatfill's résumé claimed "working knowledge" of biowarfare agents, there was no evidence that he possessed the skill to prepare spores as pure and lethal as those loaded into the anthrax letters.[22]

Rosenberg continued to supply Kristof with suggestions and sources to contact regarding Hatfill, and on June 13, 2002, she e-mailed him an update of her still evolving theory of an inside job:

Will the Suspect gradually fade from sight? Has a deal been made? Or will he be rehabilitated and rewarded for his service? Will there be no prosecution, no public notice, no deterrence of similar acts by others in the future?

Either the FBI is under pressure from DOD or CIA not to proceed because the Suspect knows too much and must be controlled forever from the moment of arrest; [For the good of the country, is it really more important to hide what he knows than to let justice be served?][23]

—or the FBI is sympathetic to the views of the biodefense clique;

—or the FBI really is as incompetent as it seems.

Rosenberg's ability to command attention was helped by the fact that aides to Senators Daschle and Leahy were unimpressed by the investigators. One of Daschle's senior assistants, Laura Petrou, described Roth as "a caricature of an FBI agent."[24] The tensions were on display on June 18, 2002, when Van Harp and three other FBI officials were summoned to a meeting in Leahy's office—to which the Judiciary Committee chairman had also invited Rosenberg. The meeting was handed over to Rosenberg, who had complained to Senate staffers that the FBI would not listen to her. For the better part of an hour she presented her views about the letter attacks and the culpability of Hatfill, without ever naming him. When Harp tried to press Rosenberg for concrete details, Leahy's staff cut him off.[25]

Kristof, in his column on July 2, 2002, continued his railing against the FBI, complaining that it had not placed the still unnamed suspect under surveillance, and stating that the "bureau's lackadaisical ineptitude in pursuing the anthrax killer continues to threaten America's national security by permitting him to strike again or, more likely, to flee to Iran or North Korea." In this column, for the first time, Kristof referred to Hatfill by a code name, "Mr. Z," and said he was the "likely culprit" in the eyes of "some in the biodefense community."[26]

Kristof wrote in the same column that Mr. Z had access in the fall of 2001 to an "isolated residence," which might be among "safe houses operated by American intelligence." The FBI, Kristof alleged, "knows that Mr. Z gave Cipro" to people who accompanied him to the house. And then there was the matter of his sex life: Mr. Z, according to Kristof, "was once caught with a girlfriend in a biohazard 'hot suite' at Fort Detrick, surrounded only by blushing germs."[27]

Next Kristof floated a staggering suggestion—which had been relayed to him by Rosenberg: During his years in Southern Africa, Mr. Z might have wielded anthrax against thousands of defenseless blacks in Zimbabwe.[28] "Have you examined," Kristof baited the FBI, "whether Mr. Z has connections to the biggest anthrax outbreak among humans ever recorded, the one that sickened 10,000 black farmers in Zimbabwe in 1978–80? There is evidence that the anthrax was released by the white Rhodesian Army fighting against black guerrillas, and Mr. Z has claimed that he participated in the white army's much-feared Selous Scouts. Could rogue elements of the American military have backed the Rhodesian Army in anthrax and cholera attacks against blacks?"[29]

Kristof's scenario was shocking, yet its central assumption was unsubstantiated: No research has established that the harm to the farmers resulted from an intentional anthrax release, as opposed to a natural occurrence. Nor had the FBI collected any first-person account that Hatfill distributed Cipro to guests.[30]

Rosenberg was thrilled with the column, telling Kristof by e-mail: "Even better than I had hoped." But a safe house operated by American intelligence? This perplexed her. "May I ask if you have a source for the 'safe house' idea or was it just speculation?"

Kristof replied, "Barbara, I'm on vacation in Oregon, watching all this from afar. As for safe houses, that is partly guesswork."[31] Kristof had nonetheless suggested Hatfill's complicity in a U.S. intelligence link to the anthrax mailings.[32]

On August 13, Kristof finally dispensed with Mr. Z. He acknowledged that, beginning in May, the suspect he had been referring to in his columns was Steven Hatfill.[33]

Inside the FBI, Kristof was a source of distraction and derision. His claims set off inquiries from elected officials that filtered down to the agents working the case. They resented the time required to prepare responses, which drained energy from real investigative work. On a wall inside the FBI's Washington Field Office, Roth began posting in large letters some of Kristof's statements. Alongside, Roth penned a comment to buck up his beleaguered colleagues: "One of the best things that can happen to you is to have this type of person criticize you." [34]

For his part, Kristof later conceded under oath that there was "uncertainty" about whether the anthrax that harmed the farmers was even a "manmade" event—let alone an attack perpetrated by Hatfill. [35] As for his statement that Hatfill had handed out Cipro, Kristof testified that this came from "some suggestion" by Rosenberg, although he was "fuzzy" on the point. Kristof's basis for writing that Hatfill and a girlfriend had a tryst in the hot suite, with "blushing germs" as witnesses? "I'm a little hazy," Kristof testified, adding that the anecdote had been conveyed to him as hearsay by both a confidential source and by Rosenberg, who would later say she doubted that she had done so. [36]

———

Kristof had not been alone in pummeling Hatfill. After a second search of Hatfill's apartment in Frederick, leaks to others in the media spotlighted a new turn in the case—the FBI's use of three bloodhounds, supposedly capable of following the scent of the anthrax used in the letter attacks. On August 1, 2002, just as the search began, investigators had invited Hatfill to meet with them downstairs, in an activity room at the three-story Detrick Plaza complex. At that point handlers entered and unleashed the bloodhounds, named Knight, Lucy, and TinkerBelle, which had been brought in from Southern California. Hatfill was sitting in a chair and TinkerBelle approached him excitedly, putting her front paws on his legs. Hatfill smiled and petted her, apparently unaware of the "evidence" that had just been generated against him. [37]

On August 12, *Newsweek* revealed the role of the dogs—the upshot of which was damning new conjecture about Hatfill as the suspected anthrax killer. The magazine named Hatfill and quoted one anonymous law enforcement source as saying that even as the hounds approached his apartment building, "They went crazy." Another investigator was quoted as saying, "When you see how the dogs go to everything that connected him, you say, 'Damn!'"[38]

On August 13, Nicholas Kristof also referred to the bloodhounds, writing in his column that they "responded strongly to Dr. Hatfill, to his apartment, to his girlfriend's apartment and even to his former girlfriend's apartment, as well as to restaurants that he had recently entered." Kristof added, "The dogs did not respond to other people, apartments or restaurants."[39]

Another boosterish depiction of the evidence from the bloodhounds was presented by the top investigative correspondent for ABC News, Brian Ross. On October 22, 2002, ABC's *World News Tonight* anchor, Peter Jennings, summoned Ross to announce his latest exclusive, saying matter-of-factly, "The FBI tells ABC News it is very confident that it has found the person responsible. ABC's Brian Ross is here. Brian? Same case—same individual." Ross: "That's right, Peter—Steven Hatfill. And while there's no direct evidence, authorities say they are building what they describe as a growing case of circumstantial evidence. And their secret weapon has been a three-member team of bloodhounds." One of the bloodhounds, Ross said, "actually led its handler directly to Hatfill."[40]

The reactions of the dogs would ultimately prove to be useless as evidence, akin to palm reading. But *Newsweek* had tapped two very well-placed sources for its revelations: the FBI's Van Harp and Roscoe C. Howard Jr., the United States attorney for Washington, D.C.[41]

Even amid the highly publicized scrutiny, Hatfill had managed to land a job teaching public safety personnel how to respond to acts of terrorism. The $150,000-a-year position, at Louisiana State University, was funded by a grant from the Justice Department. Yet soon after he began drawing his paycheck, a Justice administrator ordered the university to terminate his contract. Attorney General Ashcroft and five FBI officials would later say under oath that they knew of no other instance in which the government had forced an investigative target—as yet charged with no crime and presumed innocent—out of a nongovernmental job.[42] The Justice Department's action was in line with the public condemnation of Hatfill by Ashcroft. On the morning of August 6, the attorney general, appearing on CBS-TV's *Early Show*, labeled Hatfill—by name—as "a person of interest," a designation that Ashcroft applied to no other subject of the anthrax investigation.

By August 2002 the FBI was all over Steven Hatfill. FBI director Mueller had briefed President Bush with details about the investigation's "person of great interest."[43] Consistent with Mueller's directive to make the prevention of another terrorist attack the top priority, the bureau placed Hatfill under twenty-four-hour surveillance. If he traveled to seek a job, if he went to the store, a caravan of agents photographed and videotaped him. At one point an FBI employee drove over Hatfill's foot. After learning that the incident was related to surveillance with the anthrax investigation, Washington police ticketed Hatfill for "walking to create a hazard."

Hatfill moved from his now notorious unit at Detrick Plaza to the Washington apartment of his female companion, Peck Chegne. Some of his friends severed contact with him, fearing they, too, would be tarred by leaks from the investigation. He considered himself a patriot, a man who had trusted the government, including the FBI. He was confident of his innocence. Yet he also realized that, no matter the outcome, he was damaged goods. He could never reclaim a normal career.[44]

EIGHTEEN

LESS THAN A TEASPOON

On the first anniversary of the crimes, the anthrax attacks remained the FBI's highest-profile case. And its biggest challenge.

No eyewitness had emerged to identify a perpetrator. No fingerprints were found on any of the four recovered mailings, addressed to Senators Daschle and Leahy, NBC anchor Tom Brokaw, and "Editor" at the tabloid *New York Post*. By using prestamped envelopes and sealing them with tape, the mailer had denied forensic examiners any DNA-yielding saliva. The block-letter printing on the envelopes and in the letters appeared to have been disguised, perhaps by the mailer's use of his off writing hand.[1] And in Palm Beach County, Florida, where Robert Stevens had died of inhalational anthrax, no envelope or letter was found.

The attacks had killed five people and infected seventeen others. Of these twenty-two confirmed anthrax cases, eleven were the inhalational form and the remainder were cutaneous infections, contracted through the skin. Nasal swabs showed that at least thirty other people had been exposed to anthrax on Capitol Hill. The fear of infection was such that health officials recommended that some ten thousand Americans, including President Bush and First Lady Laura Bush, go on an antibiotic.[2]

Uncertainty surrounded the safety of Washington's most important public buildings. On and around Capitol Hill, anthrax was detected in seven of twenty-six buildings tested.[3] Operations of Congress and the Supreme Court were disrupted for days at a time.[4] Determining when a once contaminated structure was safe for occupancy boiled down to a vexing question: How clean is clean? The Environmental Protection Agency spent $27 million to pay for the scrubbings of the contaminated facilities on Capitol Hill alone. Officials had great difficulty assessing how widely the contaminated mail might have been disseminated. The U.S. Postal Service itself shut down for protracted cleanups of the two major centers that processed the anthrax-laced letters—Brentwood, in Northeast Washington, and the facility in Trenton where the letters had been postmarked.

Much more was at stake. Although no credible evidence linked any foreign entity to the mailings, the Bush administration was continuing to suggest Iraq's complicity, while marching the United States toward war. On September 18 and 19, 2002, Defense Secretary Donald Rumsfeld made the administration's case in appearances before the House and Senate Armed Services committees.

Rumsfeld said that Saddam Hussein "has amassed large, clandestine stockpiles" of anthrax and other biological weapons, posing an immediate threat to the United States. "Iraq has these weapons. They are much simpler to deliver than nuclear weapons, and even more readily transferred to terrorist networks, who could allow Iraq to deliver them without fingerprints." Rumsfeld added: "It is this nexus between a terrorist state like Iraq with WMD [weapons of mass destruction] and terrorist networks that has so significantly changed the U.S. security environment. . . . We still do not know who is responsible for last year's anthrax attacks. The nature of terrorist attacks is that it is often very difficult to identify who is ultimately responsible."[5]

On October 7, 2002, President Bush himself amplified the fear of biological weapons as he made his arguments for war in a nationally televised address. Speaking from the stage of the Cincinnati Museum Center, Bush said that Saddam Hussein's regime was seeking nuclear weapons—and that it already had anthrax and other pathogens "capable of killing millions." Those bioweapons could be easily deployed, the president said: "All that might be required are a small container and one terrorist or Iraqi intelligence operative to deliver it." [6]

Three nights later, the fears and unknowns would be distilled into votes on the floor of the United States Senate. Senators who privately held doubts about the basis for war faced an unpleasant choice: They could stay true to their skepticism and hope no proof ever emerged that Saddam Hussein retained weapons of mass destruction or that his regime had played a role in the September 11 attacks or the anthrax letters. Or, the senators could vote to give Bush the authority he wanted to launch war. Similar considerations had propelled Congress to pass, with relatively little reflection, the USA Patriot Act, the first leg of the president's antiterrorism agenda.[7]

On the night of October 10, 2002, the Iraq war resolution was coming to a final vote. The trauma inflicted by the events of one year earlier could be heard in the remarks of Senator Tom Harkin, a liberal Democrat from Iowa: "I understand the grave danger posed to America and the whole international community by weapons of mass destruction in the hands of a reckless dictator like Saddam Hussein. Since the terrorist hijackings and anthrax attacks in America last year, which wantonly took the lives of more than 3,000 people, all Americans are rightly concerned about the safety of our homeland."[8]

Harkin voted for authorizing war against Iraq, as did Senate majority leader Daschle and twenty-seven other Democrats.[9] When the voting ended, at 12:50 A.M. on October 11, the resolution passed, 77–23. A few hours earlier the House of Representatives had passed the same resolution, 296–133.[10]

The anthrax attacks continued to resonate in the clamor for war. On February 5, 2003, Secretary of State Colin Powell appeared before the United Nations to lay out President Bush's case for attacking Iraq. Powell, a centrist who carried with him the credibility earned as an architect of the U.S. coalition's victory in the first Gulf War, tried to put into perspective the threat he said America faced.[11]

Holding up a pinkie-size vial of white powder in his right hand, Powell said: "Less than a teaspoon full of dry anthrax in an envelope shut down the United States Senate in the fall of 2001. This forced several hundred people to undergo emergency medical treatment and killed two postal workers, just from an amount just about this quantity that was inside of an envelope."

Noting that Iraq in the 1990s had once acknowledged possession of 8,500 liters of liquid-form anthrax and that U.N. inspectors estimated Saddam may have produced nearly three times that amount, Powell said that if concentrated into dry form, "this would be enough to fill tens upon tens of thousands of teaspoons." He added, "Saddam Hussein has not verifiably accounted for even one teaspoonful of this deadly material." With CIA director George Tenet seated just behind him, Powell cited "the thick intelligence file we have on Iraq's biological weapons," and said Iraq was hiding mobile biological agent factories—capable of producing anthrax in dry powder form and botulinum toxin, enough in a single month "to kill thousands upon thousands of people."

No Iraqi stockpiles of anthrax were ever found and the mobile germ warfare labs turned out to be fictitious.[12] Powell's assertions not only relied on faulty intelligence, but also appeared disconnected from the findings of the scientific experts who had been consulted by the FBI. Though Powell did not directly accuse Iraq of perpetrating the letter attacks, his presentation invited the lay public to make such a connection. In fact, by mid-2002, the engineers at the Sandia National Laboratories had found that the anthrax used in the attacks was in no way chemically treated, as would be expected with material produced by a state-sponsored program.[13] And, as early as the fall of 2001, the geneticist Paul Keim had established that the anthrax in the letters was the Ames strain. Based on the known history of Ames anthrax, it most likely came from Fort Detrick or elsewhere in

the U.S. biodefense establishment or from a close ally's program.[14] Unless Iraq had somehow acquired the Ames strain—and
Powell offered no hint of any such evidence—Saddam could not
be plausibly associated with the anthrax attacks.[15]

On the eve of this new conflict, Bruce Ivins was transcending
even his glory days of the first Gulf War. At a Pentagon ceremony
on March 14, 2003, the Defense Department bestowed on Ivins
and three colleagues its highest honor for nonuniformed personnel, the Decoration for Exceptional Civilian Service. The award
was for their efforts to revive the long-troubled anthrax vaccine
made by BioPort Corp. This achievement, said supervising
Army Colonel Erik Henchal, "underscores the enormous value
of USAMRIID to the war fighter and to the nation's defense
against biological threats."[16]

Five days later, on March 19, 2003, President Bush announced
the launch of war against Iraq. America and its allies, Bush said,
"will not live at the mercy of an outlaw regime that threatens the
peace with weapons of mass murder."[17]

The vilifying of Saddam Hussein did nothing to remove Steven
Hatfill from the crosshairs of the criminal investigation. If indicted and convicted for the five anthrax murders, he might be
sentenced to death. By the summer of 2002 he had retained a
civil rights lawyer, Victor M. Glasberg, to counter what Glasberg
regarded as the "bullshit investigation" and spurious media accounts.[18] Glasberg began writing to Nicholas Kristof and to editors at the *New York Times*, challenging the columns pounding
his client. Glasberg had distinguished himself over the years as
a defender of free speech. But he did not specialize in criminal
defense—or in fighting major media organizations.

Hatfill was disconsolate and angry. He began looking for another lawyer, one with criminal defense experience who would
also be capable of confronting the torrent of damaging publicity.
He made an appointment in downtown Washington with
Thomas G. Connolly, a hard-nosed former federal prosecutor
who had recently entered private law practice. Connolly, raised

in an Irish Catholic family in south-central Nebraska, had a knack for distilling unwieldy facts into a traceable narrative.

By the end of their nearly three-hour meeting Hatfill made it clear that he wanted Connolly to represent him. Connolly, however, wasn't sure if he and his firm, Harris, Wiltshire & Grannis, should take the case. Connolly had not seen any evidence linking Hatfill to the anthrax mailings. On the other hand, Connolly knew relatively little about this man. Representing him might well become a major commitment of the firm's resources and his own time. He told Hatfill that he would get back to him.

Over the next couple of weeks, Connolly read all the news accounts he could find. He assessed the maelstrom engulfing Hatfill. And he recoiled at some of the tactics: The incessant leaks of investigative details. News helicopters hovering over the FBI's supposedly confidential searches of Hatfill's apartment. The use of the bloodhounds, with whispers of sensational, yet entirely unproven, suppositions. There was more. After having found anthrax spores in one New Jersey mailbox, at 10 Nassau Street, the main thoroughfare of Princeton, investigators showed local shopkeepers and residents a photo of only one man: Steven Hatfill.[19]

Connolly surmised that the federal investigation's leadership must be incompetent. What else, he reasoned, could explain the single-minded focus on a man who worked with viruses, not bacteria, a scientist with no known experience handling anthrax? In Connolly's view, it was as if FBI Headquarters had learned no lessons from the debacles of Richard Jewell, falsely accused as the bomber of the Atlanta Olympics, or Wen Ho Lee, the Los Alamos nuclear engineer fingered as a Chinese spy, yet never proven to be one.

Whatever his flaws, Hatfill was suffering a beating from two of America's most powerful forces, the federal government and the news media. Connolly wanted to accept Hatfill as a client; now he had to sell it to the firm. Hatfill had no money to pay up front. The firm would be lucky to recoup its costs. But this case, the forty-year-old Connolly told his colleagues, was why they had gone to law school. No one at Harris, Wiltshire & Grannis objected.[20] As of October 2002 Hatfill had a new advocate.

———

The director of the FBI was making a change of his own. Robert Mueller had inherited Van Harp, the wily bureau veteran, as the chief of the Washington Field Office, and the anthrax case had fallen to Harp upon the discovery of the letter addressed to Senator Daschle. Harp was well liked by veteran agents who saw him as old-school, an institutional loyalist who delegated responsibility but did not duck his own.

Yet the high-profile anthrax case had quickly gained Harp critics in high places. Leadership of this, one of the most important and complex cases ever undertaken by the FBI, demanded the delicate tending of prickly officials in Washington, plus familiarity with cutting-edge microbial forensics. Harp was privately ridiculed by some Senate staffers and their bosses, who did not think the FBI leadership took seriously enough the letter attacks which had jeopardized *them*. And his mastery of the complex details was doubted within the White House.[21]

Effective October 5, 2002, Mueller quietly replaced Harp with Inspector Richard L. Lambert, from the bureau's San Diego office. Among his other qualifications, Lambert had impressed Mueller with a detailed rebuttal of congressional concerns that the Saudi royal family may have bankrolled the terrorist attacks of September 11, 2001.[22] Harp would keep his title as an assistant FBI director and continue to have an advisory role in the anthrax case as head of the Washington Field Office. But from Lambert's first day on the job, he alone was Mueller's point man to lead it.

———

The searches of Steven Hatfill's apartment and his personal belongings had yielded nothing that linked him to the attacks. As investigators reviewed the hundreds of seized items, however, their curiosity was piqued by something recovered from Hatfill's black 2000 Chevrolet Camaro: It was a worn, hand-drawn map of a mountainous area of woods and several shallow, spring-fed ponds in the shadow of Catoctin Mountain, just a few miles northwest of Fort Detrick.

The map had been given to Hatfill three years earlier by a colleague at USAMRIID who was interested in teaching wilderness skills. The FBI theorized that Hatfill may have used the secluded area to dispose of anthrax-laden materials or equipment. Before a decision was made to search the ponds, the FBI in November 2002 brought the Southern California bloodhounds to the forest area, where, according to their handlers, the dogs indicated they'd found the scent of both the anthrax used in the letter attacks and Steven Hatfill. Bureau officials then planned an exhaustive search within the seven-thousand-acre Frederick Municipal Forest. The first job would be to explore the ponds for evidence, difficult work with the onset of winter snow.[23]

As the investigators made final arrangements for the major search operation, they consulted local government agencies and requested support at the site from the American Red Cross. When Red Cross officials looked through their files for volunteers to assist those searching the ponds, they noticed the name of a new volunteer. It was Bruce Ivins—who had signed up with the Frederick County chapter eleven days after September 11, while citing his position as an anthrax researcher.[24] Asked in an e-mail if he wanted to help the next day "with canteening the FBI," Ivins said yes.[25] Though the operation was supposed to be a closely guarded secret, four aerial photographs and the top story in that morning's *Frederick News-Post* had left little doubt about the activity in the forest: FBI agents were said by the newspaper to be "apparently seeking evidence in the government's anthrax investigation."[26]

On Saturday, December 14, 2002, Ivins reported to the forest where the Red Cross had set up a large green tent, reminiscent of the kind used by wartime surgical units. Not more than an hour after he arrived, he watched the commotion as flatbed ATVs ferried provisions to one of the ponds, where divers in wet suits waited their turn. It was rainy, with temperatures in the 30s. As Ivins surveyed the scene, another man on hand approached some

FBI agents. "Hey," he gestured, "do you know who this guy is?" The agents did not. "Well, he's Bruce Ivins, one of the top an-thrax experts at Fort Detrick." The agents asked Ivins for his identification and searched a backpack he had brought along. They ordered him to leave the area as soon as Red Cross person-nel could arrange for him to be driven off the mountain.[27]

"Oh my Lord, the FBI freaked out when they found out he was up there," recalled Miriam Fleming, a fellow volunteer who was alongside Ivins that day. Ivins, she said, professed to be con-fused by the FBI's reaction. "He was like, 'Well my name was on the list, they knew I was coming.'"[28]

Three days later, on December 17, 2002, Ivins applied to be a formal member of the Red Cross chapter's disaster response unit. "Perhaps I could help in case of a disaster related to biological agents," Ivins wrote. His reputation grew within the chapter, the brainy Fort Detrick anthrax guy who cheerfully did whatever was needed, the scientific Samaritan, humiliated by the FBI through no fault of his own.

Around the same time, Ivins wrote another lengthy e-mail to Mara Linscott, his former lab technician, hinting at dual person-alities within while borrowing from nursery rhymes:

I made up some poems about having two people in one (me + the person in my dreams): . . .

> *I'm a little dream-self, short and stout.*
> *I'm the other half of Bruce—when he lets me out.*
> *When I get all steamed up, I don't pout.*
> *I push Bruce aside, then I'm Free to run about!*
> *Hickory dickory Doc—Doc Bruce ran up the clock.*
> *But something happened in very strange rhythm.*
> *His other self went and exchanged places with him.*
> *So now, please guess who*
> *Is conversing with you.*
> *Hickory dickory Doc!*
> *Bruce and this other guy, sitting by some trees,*
> *Exchanging personalities.*

It's like having two in one.
Actually it's rather fun![29]

The investigative operations in the forest continued on and off
through the spring of 2003, when the once icy ponds brimmed
with torrential downpours. After using nine teams of divers and
spending an estimated $250,000, not including the time ex-
pended by dozens of federal agents, the FBI found no anthrax or
anything else of investigative value.[30]

Like the earlier searches of Hatfill's apartment, the FBI's work
was covered extensively by camera crews and reporters, who had
been tipped off to the ostensibly confidential operations. Once
again, much of the coverage made clear that the searches were
aimed at gathering evidence against Steven Hatfill. A front-page
article in the *Washington Post*, "New Find Reignites Anthrax
Probe; Evidence from Pond May Indicate Killer's Method," centered on the recovery of a clear plastic box with large-diameter
portals. "Some involved in the case," the *Post* reported, "believe
that the killer may have waded into shallow water to delicately
manipulate anthrax bacteria into envelopes, working within a
partly submerged airtight chamber." The article added, "The
water theory has increased investigators' interest in Hatfill, who
formerly lived in an apartment outside Fort Detrick's main gate
that is about eight miles from the ponds."[31]

The scenario as described entailed great difficulty: The perpetrator would have had to maintain a watertight seal with the plastic box while loading dry, powdered anthrax into envelopes. After
the FBI hauled the box from the mountain for further examination
at USAMRIID, John Ezzell, the veteran scientist and anthrax
handler, looked it over. He found the water theory unbelievable:
Keeping the powder dry under the water's surface would be next
to impossible.[32] Another USAMRIID scientist, Henry S. "Hank"
Heine, constructed a crude replica of the device and displayed it
in Building 1412, with a mocking sign: "FBI Turtle Trap."[33]

For Hatfill the damaging news coverage kept coming. Within
hours after the *Post* article appeared, CNN reported that the
searching of the ponds "turned up an item with traces of an-

thrax." The CNN exclusive, attributed to one anonymous government source and posted on the network's Web site, said, "the findings have once again focused investigators on Steven Hatfill." An article the next morning in the *Baltimore Sun* sought to summarize the significance of both media accounts about the FBI's scouring of the ponds: "Yesterday's reports from CNN and the Post were the first indication that those searches produced potentially valuable evidence." [34]

Yet no sooner had readers opened the *Sun* with their breakfast than an on-air CNN correspondent told viewers something else: "Actually in the preliminary testing of this item they thought it was anthrax, but subsequent testing . . . proved that to be negative." Nonetheless, said the correspondent, Hatfill remained the only figure named as a person of interest, adding, "Government interest in him remains high." [35]

On May 8, 2003, *CBS Evening News* anchor Dan Rather told viewers that "investigators believe they know who the culprit is." Correspondent Jim Stewart picked up from there against a backdrop of videotape depicting a search of the mountain ponds: "Divers went to the bottom, but came up empty-handed. Privately, however, agents say it would only have been icing on the cake because they believe they already have their man. . . . Bioweapons researcher Dr. Steven Hatfill, sources confirm, remains the FBI's number one suspect in the attacks." Stewart added, "And now one possible outcome, sources suggest, is if the government could bring charges against Hatfill unrelated to the anthrax attacks . . . if they become convinced that's the only way to stop future incidents. Not unlike, for example, the income-tax-evasion charges finally brought against Al Capone when evidence of racketeering proved elusive." [36]

One month later, on June 9, 2003, ABC's Brian Ross reported that the still ongoing draining of one of the ponds "may be the FBI's last best shot at proving that former government scientist Steven Hatfill is responsible for the anthrax letters." [37]

The months-long explorations in the Frederick forest had provided some cinematic moments for the broadcast media, but to what end? As the Amerithrax investigation neared its third year, a pattern was emerging: Whether they brought in bloodhounds, conducted fiber-by-fiber examinations of his belongings, or deployed divers to explore icy ponds, the FBI was not finding any evidence that implicated Hatfill.

The costs were mounting. The 24/7 surveillance continued to tie up vast amounts of investigators' time.[38] If nothing else, the spectacle surrounding Hatfill created the appearance that the FBI was vigilantly engaged. Senior bureau officials told the media that the surveillance reflected Director Mueller's vow to prevent another round of deadly terrorism.[39] In his many meetings with President Bush and members of Congress, Mueller reinforced that Amerithrax was the FBI's top priority. The top-down pressure translated to a gauntlet of pre-briefings, briefings, and after-briefings held throughout the FBI chain of command. The number of subpoenas sought, each agent's volume of interviews conducted, and the total hours worked—these were the coin of the realm at headquarters.

Some FBI hands questioned the extraordinary investigative measures and worried that other potential leads and suspects were getting too little attention. Said Brad Garrett, one of the agents who dealt directly with Hatfill, "Did it make any sense at the time? No, it didn't. Is it overkill? I think the answer is yes." Garrett made clear that the outsized focus on Hatfill came from the top, not from agents working the case. "Particular management people felt, 'He is the right guy. If only we put this amount of energy into him, we'll get to the end of the rainbow.' Did it take energy away? It had to have. Because you can't pull up another hundred agents and say, 'You go work these [leads] that these guys can't, because they're just focused on Hatfill.'"[40] But looked at another way, so long as agents were tailing him, videotaping him, and monitoring his conversations, the FBI was preventing the presumed perpetrator from striking again. And this had become the FBI's paradigm: a media-reinforced show of interdiction first, law enforcement second.

Away from public view, Hatfill's lawyer, Thomas Connolly, approached Agent Garrett with an alternative: In exchange for

ending the bumper-lock tactics, Hatfill would surrender his pass-
port, agree to wear a satellite-guided tracking device, and allow
an FBI agent to remain with him at all times. This would provide
the bureau unfettered monitoring of Hatfill. And it would allow
him to move about in public without the stigma of overt 24/7
surveillance. Garrett conveyed Connolly's offer to his supervisor,
Bob Roth, who presented it to the top officials overseeing the investigation.

"It was not accepted," said Roth, adding: "There were specific reasons that we did not accept that offer, but not because it
was judged as insincere."[41]

When Connolly first agreed to represent Hatfill, it was with
the expectation that his work would be confined to that of a criminal defense lawyer. His top priority would be to persuade the authorities not to seek Hatfill's indictment or, failing that, to defend
him in court against charges of murder.[42] But on August 26, 2003,
Connolly announced a more aggressive tack: He was suing the
Justice Department and the FBI for the many leaks of investigative information, the order to fire Hatfill from Louisiana State
University, and other actions that Connolly alleged violated Hatfill's right to privacy. If a federal judge allowed the lawsuit to go
forward, Connolly would get the opportunity to question under
oath virtually every official involved with the investigation, along
with an unknown number of journalists.

Several months later, on December 5, 2003, a reminder of
the attacks unfolded in Northeast Washington: The once heavily
contaminated Brentwood mail-handling facility at last reopened—
and it was renamed in honor of Thomas L. Morris Jr. and Joseph P.
Curseen Jr.—the two postal workers who died after inhaling spores
there.

NINETEEN

SOME NEW ANTHRAX VACCINE

We refuse to remain idle when modern technology might be turned against us. We will rally the great promise of American science and innovation to confront the greatest danger of our time.

—President George W. Bush at the signing
of the Project BioShield Act, July 21, 2004

The anthrax attacks had transformed American life. People were afraid to handle the mail at the office or at home. Members of Congress cited the attacks as they rushed to enact the USA Patriot Act, its potential to infringe on civil liberties notwithstanding. President Bush, Secretary of State Colin Powell, and Defense Secretary Donald Rumsfeld invoked the threat of anthrax, either the deadly letters or the claim that Saddam Hussein had large stocks of the bacterium, while pushing the country to war.

The mailings also helped spark a significant change in federal funding for biomedical research. Support was building within the administration and Congress for legislation that could draw some of the nation's best scientific talent into what had been a backwater: the development of vaccines and other products to defend against biological terrorism.

This new commitment would put a spotlight on experimental treatments that had been stalled on laboratory shelves, and among those who stood to benefit was Bruce Ivins. One of the first products to get a fresh look would be his own baby—rPA, the genetically engineered anthrax vaccine that he had co-invented. Ivins had long argued that his vaccine was superior to the existing, government-approved vaccine, which many military service members had blamed for causing serious side effects. As those who worked closely with him were well aware, Ivins was frustrated by the lack of government support for this next-generation vaccine. After the letter attacks, those who had heretofore been unable to propel rPA out of the hot suites at USAMRIID and toward actual use were once again hopeful.

Ivins and other promoters of the new vaccine stressed that it would cause fewer side effects and immunize people far more quickly than the old vaccine, which required six injections over eighteen months, plus yearly boosters. The old vaccine frequently caused swollen arms and muscle and joint pain and was so controversial that some members of the armed forces, the people ordered by the government to take it, had risked disciplinary action by refusing it. The product's shelf life was just three years, meaning that inventories would constantly have to be replenished.

In February 2002, the Institute of Medicine, part of the National Academy of Sciences, called for development of a vaccine "free of these drawbacks." The independent scientific advisors called the old vaccine "reasonably safe," but "far from optimal" and concluded: "A new vaccine, developed according to more modern principles of vaccinology, is urgently needed."

One of the first companies to respond to the promise of bioterror-related funding was VaxGen Inc., a publicly traded company based in South San Francisco, California. VaxGen had been spun off as a new entity in 1995 by Genentech Inc., the company recognized as the earliest and arguably the biggest success story in biotechnology. VaxGen's stature was enhanced in 2001 with the arrival of a new CEO, Lance K. Gordon, who had invented and developed a new, enhanced vaccine, the first of its kind for infant meningitis, and who had considerable biodefense experience. In collaboration with the Army, VaxGen set about trying to advance the development of rPA.

Uncertainty over the demand for a new anthrax vaccine had discouraged most major pharmaceutical companies from entering this arena. Company executives wondered: Why invest in a vaccine for which there might be only one customer? And for how long would the government be interested?

Bush offered an answer during his January 2003 State of the Union address. The president told a nation on the cusp of war that America's gravest danger came from "outlaw regimes that seek and possess" biological, nuclear, and chemical weapons. "It would take one vial, one canister, one crate slipped into this country to bring a day of horror like none we have ever known." Bush announced a new initiative—Project BioShield—aimed at helping industry develop products that would counter a biological attack. With BioShield, Bush proposed spending almost $6 billion to protect against anthrax, botulinum toxin, Ebola, plague, and other agents. This money was to be in addition to the $1.5 billion a year that administration officials would soon begin spending to build more than a dozen high-security laboratories to handle these agents and develop vaccines and antidotes.[1]

Although Congress did not act immediately on BioShield, the president's speech energized government and industry efforts to determine which biological threat required the most urgent attention. Two of the most important players in the administration were Philip Russell and D. A. Henderson, who, respectively, had led the Army's medical command and the World Health Organization's successful fight to eradicate smallpox. Russell and Henderson, both physicians, worked closely with aides to Vice President Cheney and Anthony Fauci, a director at the National Institutes of Health—and later in the year these officials decided to seek the purchase of 75 million doses of a next-generation anthrax vaccine. This would provide a three-dose treatment regimen for 25 million

Americans, enough to respond to simultaneous anthrax attacks on New York, Washington, and Los Angeles. The decision to commit to 75 million doses for the civilian Strategic National Stockpile was also based on a desire to keep the manufacturer operating continuously, so that production could ramp up quickly in the event of a crisis.[2]

The contract for the 75 million doses remained up for grabs. Meanwhile, Fauci had overseen the award of the earlier contracts to VaxGen and a British competitor, Avecia Biologics Ltd. Each company was developing a genetically engineered vaccine. Although it was not put in writing, the assumption was that the company with the most promising early results would be in line to win the upcoming contract for supplying the 75 million doses.

Based on the results of the early tests at USAMRIID, in which animals injected with rPA were "challenged" with live anthrax, Fauci and his staff at the National Institutes of Health decided to place an interim bet by investing the government's money in this next-generation vaccine. Beginning in September 2002 and again one year later, they awarded contracts totaling $101.2 million to VaxGen.[3] This was very good news for Bruce Ivins and his co-inventors at USAMRIID.

In an e-mail to Nancy Haigwood, Ivins mentioned the funding. "We learned that VaxGen just was awarded a contract to produce some new anthrax vaccine," Ivins wrote on October 22, 2003. "They're using a B. anthracis strain that we patented here that produces high levels of protective antigen, but is non-sporulating."[4]

His casual reference to "some new anthrax vaccine" gave no hint of Ivins's deep personal stake: Aside from the validation of seeing his invention rise to prominence, Ivins and four of his colleagues at USAMRIID who jointly shared patent rights could collect future royalties.

Under terms of the agreement with USAMRIID, which granted VaxGen the exclusive rights to bring new anthrax vaccine to market, the company began paying patent-related fees to the institute as of late November 2003—and, the next month, Ivins received his first check, for $3,500. A year later he would be paid another \$2,600. These modest initial payments, eventually totaling \$12,100, continued as VaxGen worked to complete development of the vaccine.[5]

When Project BioShield at last came before the Senate for final consideration on May 19, 2004, the anthrax attacks loomed over the debate. Republican senator Bill Frist of Tennessee, who had succeeded Tom Daschle as majority leader the year before, portrayed biological agents as the nation's most fearsome threat. "Bioterror agents are more powerful than traditional weapons of mass destruction, are more powerful than chemical weapons, are more powerful than nuclear weapons," Frist said, adding, "With the anthrax, three years ago, the reality was being demonstrated that bioterror is here, it is on our own soil. It hit this nation. It hit this Capitol. It hit the entire East coast. Indeed, it was deadly."[6]

Frist, trained as a heart and lung transplant surgeon, was outspoken on the risk posed by biologic agents, such as smallpox and anthrax. Yet no verification existed that smallpox was in the hands of a hostile regime or terrorist group. And even if smallpox were used as a weapon, the U.S. government, through the efforts of Drs. Russell, Henderson, and Fauci, had amassed more than enough vaccine by 2004 to contain an outbreak. Anthrax, of course, is not contagious, and the people exposed to it on Capitol Hill had been treated preventively, and successfully, with antibiotics. The administration had already placed in the Strategic National Stockpile enough life-saving antibiotics to treat more than forty million people for up to sixty days. It was with all of this in mind that administration officials who were directly involved saw no need to preemptively vaccinate civilians against anthrax.[7]

Frist's doomsday scenario also appeared to overlook the great difficulty of wielding anthrax outdoors, where wind can easily dissipate the bacterium, preventing it from reaching lethal concentrations. In the more measured opinion of Anthony Fauci, another domestic anthrax attack "would create massive panic in this country. It would create economic and other real, logistical problems. But at the end of the day, you're not going to kill as many people as you would if you blasted off a couple of car bombs in Times Square."[8] Not to mention the nuclear weapons cited so dismissively by Dr. Frist. Project BioShield cleared the Senate by a vote of 99–0. When Bush signed it into law two months later in the Rose Garden, he was flanked by Vice President Cheney, Health and Human Services secretary Tommy Thompson, Fauci, and a bipartisan cast of lawmakers. Cameras showed the president signing the legislation while seated at a desk outfitted with an embossed placard, "Protecting America."

With billions of dollars promised for the rise of a fledgling biodefense industry, companies and their lobbyists were now exploring the new opportunities. Bush had emphasized that BioShield was aimed at rapidly developing new vaccines and treatments "based on the latest scientific discoveries."[9] Skeptics noted that the biodefense buildup came as federal support declined for other basic microbiological research, including efforts aimed at far more common diseases and infections.[10]

First in line for funding under Project BioShield would be the next-generation anthrax vaccine. VaxGen was reporting positive test results. In the opinion of Fauci's staff of scientists, the South San Francisco company appeared to be a bit ahead of the British competitor, Avecia.

Fear and confusion stemming from the unsolved anthrax mailings continued, providing strong momentum for amassing millions of doses of a new vaccine. On November 4, 2004, Tommy Thompson announced that his department was awarding a contract worth $877.5 million to VaxGen. The money would be payable when the company started to deliver the 75 million doses of its next-generation anthrax vaccine. It was the first contract under Project BioShield. "Acquiring this new anthrax vaccine," Thompson said, "is a key step toward protecting the American public against another anthrax attack."[11]

The contract called for the company to make the first delivery of vaccine in just two years. In preparation for that moment, VaxGen scientists continued to confer with Bruce Ivins and others at USAMRIID, seeking to better understand the genetically engineered vaccine. They found Ivins and his colleagues to be knowledgeable and willing to help.

The contract terms specifying what Ivins could be paid were kept confidential by the Army and VaxGen. The payment of patent royalties was, indeed, a significant point of contention in negotiations involving VaxGen, the Department of Health and Human Services, and the Army: Aides to Thompson opposed paying any royalties to the Army and its inventors, saying that one arm of the government should not, in effect, be allowed to charge another for work already paid for by the taxpayers. The final agreement specified that VaxGen would pay royalties at a rate related to sales of the vaccine for the U.S. civilian stockpile. Executives from the company estimate that Ivins stood to earn perhaps tens of thousands of dollars a year. Under federal law, each co-inventor was allowed to receive royalties of up to $150,000 per year.[12]

Whatever the financial implications, the psychic rewards for Ivins appeared to be considerable. Senior defense officials were suddenly quite interested in the vaccine. Ivins was summoned to the Pentagon to provide up-to-date details on the tests of the new product's effectiveness.[13] VaxGen scientists shuttled back and forth to Maryland to meet with the USAMRIID staff. One of Ivins's co-inventors, Arthur Friedlander, narrated slides at an early meeting with the company. For the USAMRIID scientists, this was their star turn.[14]

Regular conference calls were held to discuss production of the vaccine and how to design tests with animals. The animal experiments were especially important to VaxGen: The company wanted to assemble data proving that rPA protected animals against infection with anthrax—and that the vaccine was helpful after exposure as a supplement to antibiotic treatment.

VaxGen had arranged for many of the animal experiments to be carried out by a subcontractor, the Battelle Memorial Institute, a privately held, Columbus, Ohio–based entity that specializes in collaborations with the Pentagon and U.S. intelligence agencies. Battelle was one of the very few facilities in the nation equipped to use lethal, aerosolized anthrax in such experiments. Battelle, a not-for-profit corporation with no public shareholders, is stocked with retirees from the uniformed services, the CIA, and the Defense Intelligence Agency, and Battelle's policy is to shield the identity of its clients and operations. Emblematic of its need-to-know culture, Battelle invented a code name for the new anthrax vaccine, Project Goldfish.[15]

Bruce Ivins was not content to leave the development of his co-invention to latecomers. In addition to participating in the regular conference calls and the meetings with VaxGen on the new vaccine, he sought to intervene directly with Battelle. As early as spring 2002, he questioned its ability to carry out the animal tests, beseeching a supervisor to send him to Battelle to "help them get it right with respect to making the vaccine." Ivins added, "Think about it, please. No matter how much money we give them, if they keep screwing up, it's not going to accomplish anything."[16]

Knowing that a brisk pace was crucial, Ivins arranged for additional animal testing at another lab, in case the process at Battelle lagged. Ivins had personally handled USAMRIID's earlier transfers of Ames anthrax to both Battelle and to the lab he lined up as an alternative, which was affiliated with the University of New Mexico. Entries he made in his lab book and investigators' interviews with Battelle scientists would show that Ivins sent Battelle anthrax spores from the highly purified admixture that he had labeled RMR-1029.[17]

TWENTY

WE'VE GOT OUR MAN

an Harp, the FBI man who survived years of internal scrutiny over the siege at Ruby Ridge, was convinced that Steven Hatfill was the anthrax killer. But by early 2003, the fifty-six-year-old Harp had been displaced as chief of the investigation, and was nearing the end of his long career. Director Mueller alone had the authority to keep Harp in charge of the Washington Field Office—and a part of Amerithrax—by extending his upcoming retirement deadline. Mueller declined, delivering the message through an intermediary.[1]

As his May 2003 retirement date neared, Harp nonetheless made sure he got his final say on the anthrax case. He privately assured senior executive branch officials—including at least one member of President Bush's cabinet—that the FBI had essentially solved it. "We've got our man," Harp said. "We know who did it."[2] The FBI was confident, Harp said, that Steven Hatfill was responsible. Mueller and Deputy Director Bruce Gebhardt had told Harp privately that the evidence was not yet sufficient for prosecution—but they at no point instructed either him or Richard Lambert, the FBI inspector who in October 2002 had superseded Harp as chief of the investigation, to reconsider their theory of the crime.[3]

Lambert, who favored monogrammed shirts and shiny cuff links, was trained as a lawyer and had most recently served in the San Diego office of the FBI, where he was responsible for foreign counterintelligence investigations. Early in his career he worked for the FBI general counsel, focusing on civil litigation and employment law. He became best known, however, not for investigating crimes and sending offenders to prison but for matters of internal discipline and efficiency: Lambert worked in the Office of Professional Responsibility—which investigates allegations of misconduct by FBI personnel. And he served as a traveling team leader within the bureau's Inspection Division, whose duties include examining in granular detail the performance of FBI offices throughout the country.

For ambitious younger agents, taking a leadership role on Inspection Division audits was long an unwritten requirement for advancement.[4] And as it turned out, Lambert's performance there helped persuade Mueller to bring him to Washington to lead the anthrax case.[5]

Lambert applied his background in audits to the anthrax investigation, imposing meticulous organizational charts and lists of tasks. He conferred every day with the three FBI squad supervisors whose agents were working the case: Robert Roth, who, alone, became responsible for Squad 1 and conventional aspects of the investigation; geneticist Scott Decker, who eventually began overseeing Squad 2 and the scientific aspects; and Ann Colbert, whom Lambert had installed as head of Squad 3, the FBI's satellite office in Frederick, home to USAMRIID. Lambert also met regularly with supervising Postal Service inspector Thomas Dellafera, who provided abundant institutional memory about the investigation, and Kenneth Kohl, the prosecutor who was presenting witnesses and evidence to a grand jury.[6] Perhaps most important to Lambert, he met at least once a week with Director Mueller, who had handpicked him to lead Amerithrax.[7]

Lambert steered clear of Van Harp's practice of providing confidential briefings to broadcast and print journalists. Lambert appeared proud to say that he had "never spoken on back-ground to any reporter about this case."[8] Lambert's style was more to Mueller's liking, and his attentiveness toward authority also wore well on Capitol Hill.

Yet if Lambert's approach differed from Harp's, his bottom line was the same: Steven Hatfill was the most probable perpe-trator. Lambert's central plan quickly became clear inside the Amerithrax task force: The weakness of the case against Hatfill would be overcome by shoring up what evidence there was. Deputy Director Gebhardt thought that Lambert would secure Hatfill's indictment within two years, by the fall of 2004.[9]

As Lambert saw it, some of the evidence that might seal the case against Hatfill had been gathered two months before he came to Washington. It was on August 1, 2002, that the FBI had, for the second time, searched Hatfill's apartment in Frederick. Only this time the investigators had been accompanied by the team of bloodhounds from Southern California, whose handlers believed they "alerted" on Hatfill, indicating he matched the scent of the anthrax used in the letter attacks.

No trace of anthrax was ever found in Hatfill's belongings, but Lambert viewed the bloodhound evidence as persuasive, and he shared his opinion with Mueller. The director himself stood behind the promise of the evidence, notably on the evening of January 9, 2003, when he, Lambert, and other bureau officials briefed both congressional targets of the anthrax letters, Sena-tors Daschle and Leahy. Relying on Lambert's briefing materials, Mueller's team told the senators that the bloodhounds had iden-tified Hatfill around the time of the August 2002 search of his apartment. The senators also were told that, in November 2002, the dogs indicated that samples of scent from both Hatfill and the anthrax letters were "associated" with the ponds in the for-est above Frederick.[10]

"They gave us a very graphic description of how this works and their confidence in the dogs," Daschle recalled. "They said these investigative dogs had really amazing capacity to follow the scents—even a matter of miles. They said that every single dog that they put on the case ended up on Steven Hatfill's doorstep, and even led to the lake where they felt Hatfill had deposited some of his makeshift equipment." [11]

On March 31, 2003, Mueller and Lambert provided a similar briefing to John Ashcroft. Lambert gave to the attorney general a detailed summary of the case against Hatfill, whom he called "our principal subject." Lambert stressed that the bloodhounds—which he said were specially trained and had "extensive track records"—had "associated" Hatfill with all of the anthrax-laden envelopes. [12]

Months later, while awaiting the start of a meeting in the White House Situation Room, Deputy Defense Secretary Paul Wolfowitz prodded the Justice Department's new number two official, Deputy Attorney General James B. Comey: Was Hatfill another Richard Jewell—an innocent man, wrongly implicated? Citing the evidence provided by the bloodhounds, Comey was "absolutely certain that it was Hatfill," Wolfowitz recalled. [13]

All of which meant that Mueller and Lambert were both invested in the dog evidence—a commitment that would misdirect the investigation for years. Given the well-publicized failures in the bloodhounds' past, all of it could have been avoided. A check of the public record would have shown that by 2000—two years before Mueller placed Lambert in charge of the investigation—judges and jurors in Southern California had rejected the reliability of such bloodhounds to match the scent of suspects to the scenes of major crimes.

In March 1997, an Orange County Superior Court judge threw out a jury's conviction of a man accused of strangling and bludgeoning a woman to death. Noting that the conviction was based on a handler's interpretation of how one of the bloodhounds reacted to the defendant, the judge said the dog evidence "does not have the reliability that is necessary as to base a criminal conviction on." The dog's handler, said Judge Anthony J. Rackauckas Jr., was "as biased as any witness that this court has ever seen. . . . He just simply will not be open about whether or not the dog could be mistaken." [14] One year later in the same murder case, another judge barred prosecutors from introducing any of the dog-related evidence, and they dropped the case. [15]

In January 1999, authorities in Los Angeles County released a man who had been jailed for nearly four months on suspicion of committing nine sexual assaults in the upscale Belmont Shore section of Long Beach. Police had made no arrest until the night of the last attack, when TinkerBelle—one of the dogs that would later "alert" on Steven Hatfill—meandered with her handler for nearly two miles from the rape scene to the man's apartment. The suspect ultimately was saved by a forensic tool more reliable than the bloodhounds: human DNA collected from the crime scenes, which proved that a different man was responsible for all the sexual assaults. In November 2000, a federal jury awarded the wrongly accused suspect $1.7 million. (The actual rapist was later sentenced to more than 1,030 years in prison.)[16]

Both the overturning of the murder conviction and the ordeal of the falsely accused rape suspect received prominent media coverage, notably in the pages of the *Los Angeles Times*. And in February 1999, the detailed misgivings about the dog evidence in both cases were explored by *60 Minutes II*, the CBS network newsmagazine.[17] The dogs' failures in California were hardly a secret.

Nonetheless, Richard Lambert persisted in making the dog evidence a pillar of the FBI's case against Hatfill. His approach raised concerns among some scientific specialists at the FBI. Said one of them, Agent Jenifer Smith, "Dogs work extremely well with explosives. They work really well with drugs. But a major investigation like this, you're going to suddenly start relying on dog technology? It was surprising to see those things used in an organization where we don't use psychics."[18]

The unavoidable problem with relying on the bloodhounds to pinpoint a killer or a rapist is that there is no way to know what scent or other factor a dog may be reacting to. It's one thing to envision a bedraggled convict, cornered by bloodhounds: He escaped, the dogs chased and found him. But how could a jury reliably interpret a bloodhound's response to Steven Hatfill? "They're fallible," said Dwight Adams, chief of the FBI laboratory from 2001 until his retirement in mid-2006. "And if you can't understand what it is that they're 'alerting' to, then it's very difficult to be able to interpret."[19]

There was an even more immediate cause for alarm: Hatfill was not the only person contacted during the anthrax investigation who elicited reactions from TinkerBelle and the other bloodhounds.

As of January 2003, Lambert and his investigators knew that the dogs had alerted on at least one other scientist, Patricia Fellows, who formerly worked at USAMRIID but was implicated by no credible evidence.[20] A document that Lambert prepared for Director Mueller's personal briefing of Senators Daschle and Leahy in January 2003 said that the bloodhounds had reacted to Hatfill and Fellows only, adding, "however, she assisted with the initial processing of the Daschle/Leahy evidence."[21]

By this Lambert was suggesting that although the dogs' identification of Hatfill remained significant, their reactions to Fellows could be discounted because she had helped the FBI handle the anthrax letters in the fall of 2001 and imparted her scent at that time to the materials that were later presented to the dogs. Others within the FBI saw the bloodhounds' identification of Fellows differently: It was another strong reason to abandon all of the dog "evidence."[22]

With his fifty-seventh birthday on May 29, 2003, Van Harp logged his last shift for the FBI. His departure was of little consequence to Richard Lambert, who had taken over the investigation the previous October and was working in lockstep with Mueller, who demanded an accounting of every move made. Hence the constant briefings at headquarters. The regular attendees knew the drill. Once and often several times a week, they would arrive by three or four in the afternoon, make their way to the seventh floor, and wait until a secretary waved them into the director's conference room.

Mueller sat at the head of a long rectangular table. Not given to humor or idle chatter, the director always wanted the latest, fast. When an official would begin to explain a complicated written analysis, Mueller would interrupt, cutting to the conclusion. The tenor of the briefings did not invite divergent opinions, let alone open challenge of the investigation's direction. In addition to Lambert, the meetings were regularly attended by the deputy director of the FBI, Bruce Gebhardt, as well as Van Harp's replacement at the Washington Field Office, Michael Mason, and the case agents, Robert Roth and Dave Dawson, and successive leaders of the bureau laboratory, Dwight Adams and Joseph A. DiZinno. "The director was always the leader of the anthrax investigation, period," Mason said.[23]

Mueller's approach imposed a relentless, quantity-over-quality imperative: Agents were pressed to leave no stone unturned— rather than taking the time to select more promising leads for deeper drilling. Even witnesses who seemed peripheral were subjected to exhaustive or multiple lie detector tests, sowing resentment in quarters of the scientific community. It was all of a piece: In the absence of an arrest or other tangible breakthrough, the total numbers of interviews and searches became the measure of investigative success.[24]

Savvy agents dread this phenomenon—the high-profile investigation led by headquarters. The telltale signs are recognizable across any number of celebrated cases: cumbersome prior approvals required for tasks that would ordinarily be routine, like tailing a subject for a day or traveling out of town to examine documents. Agents denied the autonomy to follow their own intuition. Finally, instead of proceeding to a conclusion through the considered exclusion of leads, there's a push to substantiate the original, high-profile hypothesis.

Director Mueller demanded some version of progress, or else. Jenifer Smith, among others, questioned the top-down pressure for action, any action. It led, said the twenty-year veteran agent, to "Brownian motion investigation" akin to the random darting of particles when viewed under a microscope. "The daily reporting puts a lot of pressure on people. What if they don't have anything to say? 'Well, we've got to have *something* to say.'" The result: a large number of FBI personnel who were consumed with robotic pre-briefing and briefing up and down the chain of command.[25]

Yes, Mueller wanted his agents to solve the case as quickly as possible. But the endless cycle of briefings had another purpose: to prepare Mueller for the important briefings *he* had to provide. The ritual would get underway between 8 and 9 A.M. just outside the Oval Office, where Mueller waited with Attorney General John Ashcroft and Tom Ridge, who joined the administration in early October 2001 as the president's homeland security advisor and later became a cabinet-level secretary.

Inside, CIA director George Tenet was presenting his daily summary on international terrorism to President Bush, Vice President Cheney, and National Security Advisor Condoleezza Rice.[26] When Tenet concluded, White House chief of staff Andy Card would open the door so that Mueller and the others could enter and brief the assembled officials on the latest in the anthrax investigation.

Mueller was questioned by Bush and Cheney in a way that would be familiar to those who met with the director during the afternoons at FBI Headquarters. What are you looking at? Anything uncovered? Any new leads? Where are we? They also pressed the FBI director on whether the anthrax mailings were linked to September 11.[27]

The Amerithrax investigators traveled widely seeking evidence of al Qaeda involvement in the mailings. In May 2004, they collected more than 440 samples from three sites in Kandahar, Afghanistan, where al Qaeda was believed to have tried to develop biological weapons. Although tests revealed no live anthrax, the FBI collected three samples with genetic markers possibly suggestive of an attempt to grow the bacterium. In the end, based on the investigators' additional work in Kandahar, interrogations overseen by the CIA, and other efforts that took the FBI to six continents, the bureau found no confirmation that al Qaeda succeeded in growing anthrax or had access to the crucial Ames strain. No evidence emerged that any foreign sponsor of terrorism had a hand in the anthrax attacks.[28]

Whether it was the White House, the Pentagon, or the Congress, officials clamored for both fresh information and assurances of public safety from the FBI. This magnified the role of headquar-

ters. It also ate up the time of Lambert and the downstream lay-
ers of bureau personnel called upon to assist Mueller's briefings.
Just as important, the investigation was burdened by Mueller's
pledge that preventing another terrorist attack would be the
FBI's top priority.

It was also becoming clear that Lambert's strengths did not
readily transfer to cracking a criminal case of such uncommon
complexity. Lambert was bright and well organized, and he aptly
accommodated the FBI director by crisply summarizing the day-
to-day activities of his agents. But his fluency as a briefer did not
translate to an ability to creatively analyze the possibilities. Some
of the investigators under Lambert questioned whether he sufficiently appreciated what he did not or could not know. They
viewed him as a linear thinker, more skilled at negotiating the cor-
ridors of power than at solving the ultimate puzzle: Who did it?

Lambert's zeal to bridge the gap of evidence against Hatfill
wound up pitting him against the scientists of the FBI laboratory
in Quantico. One confrontation centered on an almost infinites-
imal speck of dead skin found on the envelope addressed to
Senator Leahy. FBI lab director Dwight Adams and his staff concluded that given the circumstances, a more elaborate analysis of
the speck would not yield a result of any evidentiary value. Lambert rejected that advice and said he wanted the speck subjected
to a new testing procedure called Whole Genome Amplification,
or WGA—which he touted as "promising" in a March 2003
briefing to Ashcroft.[29]

The lab resisted, warning Lambert that applying WGA to the
speck was not apt to identify the perpetrator—but was far more
likely to point toward someone completely unconnected to the
crime, such as a mail handler or a person who helped manufac-
ture the envelope. The lab scientists believed that the real perpetrator had worn gloves and taken great care in preparing the
anthrax and loading the envelopes, all but eliminating the likelihood of leaving behind a trace of human DNA.

If the anthrax case ever went to trial, an irrelevant identification with WGA could boomerang: A defense attorney could use
the evidence to point jurors away from the accused and toward a

mythical villain, still at large. By opting for WGA, the bureau would be making a herculean effort—but to create evidence more likely to undermine than to help an eventual prosecution. The lab did what Lambert wanted.

In January 2004, preliminary results suggested that the DNA speck was left by a woman. The finding, Lambert said in an internal e-mail, "excludes Hatfill as the donor of the small amount of questioned DNA recovered from the Leahy envelope." But for Lambert the finding did not rule out Hatfill's girlfriend, Peck Chegne—and he demanded more of the whole genome testing.[30]

The WGA initiative would take about two years to complete. Ultimately, the testing found no additional DNA. As for the single speck of dead skin? It did not belong to Hatfill's girlfriend or anyone else of interest to the investigation. The skin was traced to a female technician who had accidentally contaminated the evidence soon after its arrival at the FBI lab and had resigned under pressure in June 2002 because of other irregularities, including falsification of data. She later pleaded guilty to submitting falsified DNA analysis reports in more than one hundred cases; the anthrax case was not among them.[31]

As the FBI scientists had anticipated, the Whole Genome Amplification initiative was at best a cul-de-sac, a waste of time. This and other turns of the investigation that seemed tilted toward nailing Hatfill left resentments among investigators and scientists alike. Focusing on Hatfill in the early stages of the investigation had made sense; plenty of provocative questions were raised about him. But as time wore on, it became apparent to more and more investigators that evidence of his involvement simply was not there.

Another protracted Hatfill-related inquiry centered on the hand-printed envelopes and letters used in the anthrax attacks. Soon after he came under investigation, Hatfill began complying with investigators' requests to submit samples of his writing. The FBI instructed him to print while sitting, standing, left-handed, and right-handed—even while wearing thick kitchen mitts. He agreed to still another session. "When they did it the third time, I realized that in this case, things had gone completely haywire," said defense lawyer Thomas Connolly.[32] There was a reason, not shared with Hatfill, why the task force sought more samples: When Postal Service handwriting expert Robert J. Muehlberger had compared Hatfill's first "exemplar" to the printing on the anthrax letters and envelopes, he did not see a match.[33]

TWENTY-ONE

EYE EXERCISE

Thanks to the foresight of Rita Colwell, the director of the National Science Foundation, an elite cast of outside experts—notably Paul Keim, the geneticist at Northern Arizona University, along with scientists at TIGR, the Institute for Genomic Research in Maryland—had been assisting the federal investigation since the fall of 2001.

The team's goal was to find within the mailed anthrax a DNA profile that would link the material to a laboratory, and Keim believed that if the killer had used a very rare batch of spores, DNA evidence might even clinch the case.[1] But this was not an hourly episode of *CSI: Crime Scene Investigation*. The complex science being applied to the anthrax case could not be rushed.

Keim and the other scientists had made some remarkable early contributions to the investigation—achievements that would have seemed impossible just a few years earlier. They had quickly determined that all the anthrax recovered from the mailed envelopes was the Ames strain, and, by analyzing blood or other body samples from the victims, they had confirmed that the Ames strain killed them.

There were also setbacks, limiting the extent to which science

could actually help solve the case. Attempts to discern the geographic origin of the water used to prepare the anthrax yielded
nothing of value.[2] Elaborate efforts to find a link between a contaminant found in some of the anthrax letters (*Bacillus subtilis*)
and a potential perpetrator's batch of anthrax proved unsuccessful. The Amerithrax scientists were hampered as well by false in-
dications of anthrax. This happened with material retrieved from
one of the ponds above Frederick, the remains of the Flight 93 hijackers, and three of the samples retrieved from Kandahar,
Afghanistan. In each instance, the FBI and its top experts, including Keim, concluded that the initial lab readings were invalid and
that no anthrax was present.[3]

Another disappointment involved the efforts to compare the
DNA from USAMRIID's original inventory of Ames strain anthrax, derived from the Texas cow felled in 1981, with that of the
bacterium that killed photo editor Robert Stevens. To make the
comparison, the FBI asked USAMRIID to send to Paul Keim's lab
in Arizona a vial of the anthrax cultured from the dead cow. With
difficulty, Keim was able to extract DNA from both the anthrax
that had killed the cow and the anthrax that, twenty years later,
killed Stevens. Keim then sent the separate DNA samples to the
TIGR group in Maryland, whose work with the investigation as
of mid-2002 was being led by a Ph.D. microbiologist, Jacques
Ravel. Utilizing his institute's advanced technology, Ravel se-
quenced the DNA—that is, he mapped the order of the chemical
building blocks in DNA from both anthrax cultures.[4]

The scientists were hoping to see some differences that would
distinguish the anthrax in the first letter attack from the original
Ames "ancestor" material. A unique genetic characteristic might
enable investigators to trace the attack material to a specific batch
and to a perpetrator. To his chagrin, Ravel, who speaks with an
accent that echoes his upbringing in eastern France, found what
he called the anthrax equivalent of identical twins.

"We had a strain that was grown in 2001 out of the spinal
fluid of Mr. Stevens, and a strain that was grown in 1981. That's
the mother of all Ames. There's no other isolate that could be
more the mother. It's really just one culture step removed from

the real cow. So when we compare that one to Florida there was absolutely no genetic difference between the two," Ravel said. "And that was the point where we were very disappointed. Because we all thought that genomics was not going to help." [5]

But Ravel's despair was short-lived. Adhering to standard FBI practice, the bureau had compartmentalized certain aspects of the scientific work. Even these most trusted outside specialists were not told what certain other scientists were doing on behalf of the investigation. The approach was intended to prevent scientific bias and, when possible, to keep the investigative details confidential. As a result, neither Ravel nor Keim knew in 2002 that another scientist, USAMRIID microbiologist Patricia Worsham—Bruce Ivins's close colleague—was sharing some very intriguing observations with the FBI.

Worsham, more so than anyone else assigned or hired to help the investigation, had considerable experience studying how spore-forming bacteria produce colonies in a Petri dish. Results of her earlier research into irregular anthrax colonies had been published in the scientific literature, and Worsham's expertise came to the attention of the FBI in the fall of 2001. [6] This was soon after another USAMRIID scientist, Terry Abshire, first noticed the irregular colonies that sprouted from the anthrax cultured from the material mailed to Senator Daschle.

Worsham picked up where Abshire had left off, growing anthrax in hundreds of Petri dishes. Her skills and experience made her uniquely suited for the tedious job of identifying and counting the single, irregular colonies—the morphs—that emerged occasionally amid the regular-shaped colonies of newly grown anthrax. The process took far longer than the typical high-volume growing and harvesting of anthrax spores for USAMRIID's animal experiments. She had to work very deliberately, scrutinizing each Petri dish of anthrax cells at regular intervals. First, she cultivated material from the Leahy letter, then the Daschle letter, and then the one to the *New York Post*. [7]

Worsham assigned grades to the emerging morphs to track the rate at which they developed. Only one out of every fifty or so colonies might develop into these morphs, identifiable by their yellowish tinge. The surfaces of the morphs also appeared rougher and less translucent, less like ground glass. "It took a lot of eye exercise," Worsham recalled.[8] The FBI labeled the samples so that Worsham did not know which scientist had submitted the individual quantities of anthrax she was testing. Her efforts, however, were generally known to colleagues, and Worsham once found that someone had affixed a sticker to her office door: "FBI Rat."[9] Importantly for the investigation, her work was establishing an unbroken pattern: The morphs grew consistently from cultures of the anthrax that had been used in the letter attacks. Worsham found the opposite when she repeatedly cultured the original anthrax that USAMRIID had received from Texas in 1981—the "mother" of all Ames strain anthrax: No morphs appeared in that material.

Beginning in early 2002, Worsham regularly reported her observations to FBI agent Scott Stanley, who was at USAMRIID on almost a daily basis. As Stanley discussed all of this with Agent Scott Decker, the two agreed that the consistency of Worsham's results might be pointing the way to a distinct characteristic in the DNA of the anthrax in the letters.[10]

Stanley and Decker realized that if a unique genetic characteristic were identified in the mailed anthrax, the FBI might be able to exclude from suspicion most of the labs using Ames strain anthrax. Stanley approached TIGR with an idea: Could the institute genetically sequence the particular morphs that Patricia Worsham was finding? If so, investigators could apply conventional law enforcement methods to trace which individuals may have had access to what became the attack material.[11]

Following a colleague's departure from TIGR in spring 2002, Jacques Ravel enthusiastically assumed the challenge. Worsham's work, he saw, indicated that the morphs were "the only thing that's different" between the anthrax used in the attacks and the material harvested from the Texas cow and used for over two decades in experiments at USAMRIID and other biodefense labs.

Over the ensuing months the ensemble of laboratories assisting the FBI carried out a rhythmic series of delicate tasks, super-

vised by Agent Stanley. Patricia Worsham at USAMRIID grew
and handed over to the FBI the live morphs, which the bureau
delivered in test tubes to Paul Keim, whose lab in Arizona ex-
tracted the DNA and routed it to Jacques Ravel in Maryland for
analysis at TIGR. Other outside labs were enlisted, and some of
the extractions of DNA were performed at the Naval Medical
Research Center, in Silver Spring, Maryland.

In contrast to the spectacles that surrounded the searches of
Steven Hatfill's apartment and the mountain ponds, the scientists' work proceeded methodically and quietly.[12]

TWENTY-TWO

PLAY IT STRAIGHT

gent Lawrence Alexander joined the anthrax investigation in
January 2004 with proven skill in the brick-by-brick building of criminal cases. He had spent the previous six years on
Operation Safe Streets, an FBI task force that targeted violent
drug crews wreaking havoc in Washington, D.C. The experience
helped Alexander appreciate the difficulty of cultivating informants against the backdrop of violence. He understood that in
some cases the cooperation of one witness—the right witness—
was worth more than an impressively large number of empty interviews. He was also skilled at extracting threads of meaningful
data from the FBI's voluminous databases, enabling him to see
connections that others might not.

Alexander had an affable personality, but he carried himself
like the former Marine Corps officer that he was. He grew up
near Washington, in Dumphries, Virginia, and graduated with a
biology degree from Virginia Military Institute, where he com-
peted as a middle-distance runner.

Alexander had enjoyed the action of Safe Streets, but he tired
of witnessing the family dysfunction and squalor: adults who
constantly lied; their kids doomed to grow up in the squalor of

dirty beds, chaos, and despair. He was seeking a new challenge with Amerithrax. Robert Roth, the FBI supervisor who recruited him for the assignment, told Alexander that the indictment of Steven Hatfill was imminent. Over the next several weeks Alexander reviewed the confidential case summary to get up to speed. And then he shared his first impressions with Roth. "I don't see it," Alexander said. "I don't see any facts pointing in his direction."[1]

Hatfill struck Alexander as a loudmouth, a braggart, an exaggerator—but a man lacking the essential skills to have pulled off the letter attacks. There was nothing in his known qualifications or experience that would have enabled Hatfill to grow, harvest, and dry anthrax. And there was no evidence that he had had the help of an accomplice.

Apart from his investigative skills, Alexander brought a special asset to the task force: the freedom of expression that comes with not seeking a promotion. By this point the anthrax investigation was hardly a plum assignment. "A lot of burnout issues," recalled Michael Mason, who had replaced Van Harp as head of the Washington Field Office. The FBI was under tremendous pressure to solve the case quickly. And yet the chances of doing so dimmed with each passing month. Some bureau veterans were privately comparing Amerithrax to the eighteen-year hunt for the Unabomber.[2] The worry was that, without a tip from a family member or other stroke of luck, the anthrax attacks were akin to those dead-end cases languishing in what Agent Roth called the "zero file."[3]

As he immersed himself in the case, Alexander learned that many of the other agents were puzzled by its direction. They, too, did not see compelling evidence against Hatfill. But voicing that view carried a risk because an agent would stand a far better chance of winning a better assignment elsewhere if he or she was in the good graces of top management. And though he insisted he was keeping an open mind about potential suspects, it was obvious to his subordinates that Richard Lambert, with the backing of Director Mueller, was driving the investigation in one direction, toward Hatfill's indictment.

Alexander was assigned to Squad 1, responsible for carrying out conventional investigative tasks from the Washington Field Office. In addition to interviewing witnesses, Alexander sifted through the information gathered about Hatfill. And he reviewed a mountain of e-mail traffic obtained from USAMRIID. The e-mails, sent or received by scores of Army scientists, spanned the periods before, during, and after the fall 2001 anthrax attacks.[4] By late 2004, Alexander had reached two conclusions: First, Hatfill had nothing to do with the attacks. Second, another scientist—Bruce Ivins—merited the most rigorous scrutiny possible.

Numerous e-mails sent by Ivins suggested to Alexander that at minimum the man was mentally unstable. Ivins was of course well known to the investigation as one of the Army's senior anthrax specialists. He had conversed regularly with the FBI agents stationed at USAMRIID as the letters addressed to the two U.S. senators and the New York media figures were first analyzed. But Ivins, in contrast to the former USAMRIID virologist Hatfill, was generally well liked by his colleagues, some of whom went out of their way to describe him as a guileless, harmless eccentric. It was said that if Ivins did anything—let alone something horrible—he would have been unable to keep quiet about it. Over time the refrain of "Bruce being Bruce" had taken hold within the Amerithrax task force, too.

Alexander came to distrust these benign assumptions. He was not prepared to dismiss Ivins as the quirky but trustworthy guy who could hurt no one. Alexander made his points in group meetings and personally with his supervisor. He found an ally in Thomas Dellafera, Amerithrax's senior postal inspector. Dellafera earlier in his career had investigated mail theft by postal employees, and it taught him a lasting lesson: The can-do clerk, the trusty employee always willing to sacrifice and stay a little later, was uniquely positioned to commit the most audacious of crimes.

Dellafera was mindful of this as he reviewed e-mails that Lawrence Alexander shared with him. The postal inspector was struck initially by Bruce Ivins's comments just before and after the letter attacks. First, Ivins seemed to predict what was about to happen. Then, he appeared to bask in the excitement. "Why is it we don't think this is interesting?" Dellafera asked.

Alexander kept speaking out in the group meetings and he continued to tell his boss, Robert Roth, why he believed Ivins needed exhaustive scrutiny. Roth still tilted toward Hatfill as the perpetrator, but he encouraged Alexander to keep digging and speaking out. The two also discussed how the prosecutor assigned to the investigation, Assistant U.S. Attorney Kenneth Kohl, was at loggerheads with Richard Lambert over Hatfill. Kohl insisted that the evidence did not justify seeking Hatfill's indictment.[5]

In late 2004, the Amerithrax investigators learned of an exciting development: The scientific side of the task force had found an apparent genetic match between the material used in the letter attacks and a particular batch of Ames strain anthrax. Further testing was needed to verify the match. But this was evidence that held great promise.

After examining more than one thousand samples collected from eighteen biodefense facilities worldwide, the scientists assisting Amerithrax had narrowed the investigation's focus to this one batch of anthrax that might be the murder weapon. It would be up to the task force investigators to examine records and conduct interviews to see how widely the seemingly unique batch had been distributed.

At this point, the scientific evidence had traced the attack material to the flask labeled RMR-1029, maintained at USAMRIID, controlled by the scientist who created it, Bruce Ivins. The FBI had seized Ivins's flask in mid-2004, after investigators realized that he and other scientists at USAMRIID may not have submitted samples from all the isolates of Ames strain anthrax in their custody, despite a federal subpoena ordering them to do so. Based on their analysis of the flask and their scrutiny of all fifteen labs in the United States and the three abroad that had possessed Ames strain anthrax, the investigators eventually concluded that Ivins had shared material from his flask of RMR-1029, which was his unique mixture of Ames anthrax, only with his colleagues at USAMRIID and with researchers at the Battelle Memorial Institute.[6] Once the task force collected small quantities from those specific shipments of RMR-1029, testing found a genetic resemblance to the material used in the letter attacks.

Lawrence Alexander saw the scientific breakthrough as a domino, falling in the direction of Ivins. And it looked as if Ivins had tried to cover his tracks: The sample from RMR-1029 that Ivins had submitted in April 2002 in response to the subpoena had *not* matched the attack material. Yet when the task force subsequently arranged for testing of anthrax that investigators themselves withdrew from Ivins's flask of RMR-1029, it *did* match the material used in the attacks.[7] This raised for Alexander and some of his colleagues the possibility that Ivins had deliberately submitted a false sample.

Ivins's colloquies with the investigators up to this point demonstrated the edge that he held when it came to understanding important subtleties. For instance, on August 13, 2003, when the investigators first questioned Ivins about the sample of RMR-1029 that he had submitted more than a year earlier, they had no way of knowing that it lacked the genetic similarities that should have been present. But almost as if he were preparing for the day when his questioners might be more knowledgeable, Ivins said during that conversation that the sample had probably been prepared by one of his senior lab technicians, not himself. This claim would be disproved by evidence gathered later, when investigators learned how Ivins had used his skills to submit what was, in fact, a bogus sample.[8] And while the potentially incriminating details of Ivins's sample were unknown to the investigators when they spoke to him on August 13, 2003, Ivins appeared to be worried. Six days earlier he had hired a criminal defense lawyer.[9]

The FBI's top human DNA expert, Bruce Budowle, was insisting privately that the novel genetic techniques being applied to crack the case must be shared with the broader scientific community.[10] Budowle had in mind Supreme Court rulings that generally revised the standards for using evidence in court from new scientific techniques. The court held that a new technique should first be subject to scrutiny in a peer-reviewed publication; that an error rate for the technique should be established; and that the technique should be generally accepted by outside scientists.

Going public with the techniques being used by Jacques Ravel posed a delicate challenge. The general aim was to win acceptance among geneticists and microbiologists outside the investigation— while not revealing details that could in any way compromise the case. Ravel prepared a series of slides to present in February 2005 at an annual meeting of the American Society for Microbiology.

He planned to explain how he had begun sequencing the four separate morphs grown from a sample of *Bacillus anthracis*. Before he made the presentation, Ravel drove to an office of the FBI in northern Virginia, near Washington, to confer with Agent Scott Decker. As he reviewed each of Ravel's slides, Decker decided what could and could not be presented to the assembled microbiologists.

"I could not use the word 'Amerithrax,'" Ravel recalled. "And it had to be presented as 'We made this spore preparation up and we wanted to test how we could find differences.' So there was no mention of the context, which was, in reality, the investigation. It was presented as just a hypothetical, a 'case study.' There was no mention of the letters."

The day that he presented the slides, at Baltimore's Waterfront Marriott, Ravel noticed a familiar face, one he'd often seen at such meetings. It was Bruce Ivins. Ravel thought nothing of Ivins's presence. "He looked, you know—he always looked weird. But you know, which scientist doesn't look weird?"[11]

By early 2005 the Amerithrax task force had moved out of downtown Washington to more spacious offices a few miles away, in Tysons Corner, Virginia. Inspector Richard Lambert maintained an open-door policy, and one day Lawrence Alexander dropped by for a conversation. The two men knew they disagreed about the evidence concerning Hatfill. In earlier group meetings,

Alexander had always stood up from the table to ask his questions and voice his skepticism, which he enunciated in careful but stark terms. Lambert had at times appeared discomfited by his direct style.

Now Alexander was appealing to the leader of the investigation with a less frontal approach: "Let's not bicker over whether Hatfill did the crime. We need to resolve all the issues with Ivins before we even think of taking Hatfill to trial."

Alexander's message was that, unless the task force could find a rationale that convincingly cleared Ivins, lawyers for Hatfill could defend their client by pointing a jury to the many suspicious circumstances surrounding Ivins, the Army anthrax specialist.

Alexander ticked off a few of the issues, including Ivins's unfettered access to RMR-1029 and his proficiency in handling anthrax. Ivins, he said, may have obstructed the investigation by submitting a bogus sample in April 2002. And, Alexander pointed out, a cursory reading of Ivins's e-mails showed that the scientist had psychiatric troubles that predated the letter attacks. Lambert listened, but Alexander walked away believing that he had gotten nowhere.

Soon afterward, Lambert informed the investigators that he would seek to personally question Ivins as quickly as it could be arranged. Lambert's decision set off a storm of protest among a number of members of the task force who believed that without more time and meticulous preparation, such an interview would do more harm than good.

Why rush to interview the possible culprit when the investigators still knew so little about his disputed submission of the sample in 2002? Why not first thoroughly analyze Ivins's many self-revealing e-mails? Why not take a bit more time to get better prepared?

It appeared to some of the investigators that Lambert saw Ivins not as a viable suspect but as a witness: As the keeper of RMR-1029, Ivins was positioned to say whether this now crucial mixture of anthrax had ever been kept where someone who had worked at USAMRIID but did not ordinarily handle bacterial cultures could have had access to it. That someone would be Steven Hatfill, who worked at USAMRIID from 1997 to 1999. And since Hatfill had no demonstrated skill in handling anthrax, questioning Ivins about who had access to RMR-1029 might also help identify a person who could have served as Hatfill's accomplice.

Ivins, based on his own attentive tracking of the investigation over the past year, appeared to believe that he might be in the clear. As of August 2004, his lawyer, Richard P. Bricken, went so far as to mark his year-old file on the case "closed." But in early March of 2005, Ivins returned to the lawyer with word of a new development indicating to him that the hunt for the perpetrator had returned foursquare to USAMRIID. The FBI, he said, had just scheduled interviews with ten to thirty colleagues, although not yet with him.[12] That changed once Lambert set a date for an interview with Ivins later that month.

In the days leading up to the interview, several senior members of the task force met with Lambert to voice their concerns. Each of them—Robert Roth, Tom Dellafera, and prosecutor Kenneth Kohl—told Lambert the interview was premature and would impair a rigorous investigation of Ivins.

"You need to protect the investigation of Ivins," Dellafera said. "Whether you think it's him or not, you need to play it straight."

If Lambert insisted on going forward, the investigators recommended a simultaneous search of Ivins's house, vehicles, and other possessions. Otherwise, they said, Ivins would be apt to throw away anything related to the anthrax attacks that he might still have. Perhaps he had kept the original letters that were photocopied and sent through the mail in the fall of 2001. Lambert said he would not be opposed to such a search—if it could be organized "right away" to coincide with the interview.

The investigators pointed out that this was not possible. The task force's protocol for searching a location with suspected anthrax required coordinating with a specially outfitted hazardous materials team, along with notifications to local safety authorities. All of this would take a week or more. No, Lambert said, he would not wait.[13]

On Thursday, March 31, 2005, Ivins met with Lambert and FBI agent Ann Colbert without an attorney. The agents prefaced their questions about RMR-1029 by revealing that the investigation had found genetic similarities between it and the anthrax used in the attacks. Ivins acknowledged that he was the custodian of RMR-1029. But it made no sense, he said, that the sample he submitted in April 2002 did not show whatever characteristics the investigation's scientists had found through separate testing of RMR-1029.

The agents asked Ivins where he had stored the flask over the years. Without naming him, Lambert and Colbert showed great interest in determining whether Steven Hatfill could have gotten access to RMR-1029. The agents knew that Hatfill had worked in USAMRIID's Building 1412, a facility separate from Building 1425, where Ivins was based. They showed Ivins one of his own inventory documents, which suggested that the RMR-1029 flask was once stored in Building 1412, where the institute's animal experiments were conducted. The document was wrong, Ivins said; at all times the flask had remained in Building 1425.

This meant that during Hatfill's two-year tenure at USAMRIID, he would have lacked access to the central stocks of anthrax secured in Building 1425, and to the crucial flask that Ivins had kept there. But the interview left a glimmer of an opening for Lambert to insist that Hatfill might have had access to RMR-1029: Ivins said that tiny anthrax samples, or aliquots, that he withdrew from RMR-1029 for animal experiments were stored for brief periods in Building 1412.

This information could keep alive the possibility that, before leaving USAMRIID in 1999, Hatfill had the opportunity to abscond with a vial of liquid-form anthrax derived from the RMR-1029 flask. This did not alter the fact that Hatfill, with no proficiency in handling anthrax, would have faced great difficulties: First, he would have needed to grow the larger amount of anthrax necessary for the letter attacks. He would have had to convert the liquid anthrax to dry powder. And, as of the time he left USAMRIID in 1999, he had no access to a specially outfitted biocontainment lab, without which the anthrax could have escaped and killed anyone who was not vaccinated.

As the interview unfolded, Lambert and Colbert asked Ivins about the string of late nights he had spent at USAMRIID in the weeks before the letter attacks. He'd kept those hours, Ivins replied, because of strains in his home life. Shifting to other questions, the agents revealed to Ivins that investigators had read his e-mails to Mara Linscott—including those about his "paranoid personality disorder" diagnosis. Ivins replied that he was now in better mental condition and had stopped taking Celexa, the antidepressant. Agent Colbert's summary of the interview added, "When asked whether his psychological condition had ever caused him to do anything which surprised him, IVINS responded in the negative. IVINS offered that he does not 'act out' and has never hit his wife."

Ivins agreed to allow the FBI to enter his home later the same day for the purpose of examining his personal computer. As technicians copied its contents, Agent Colbert reopened their earlier conversation about RMR-1029. After thinking about it, Ivins revised his stance.

He still had no specific memory of storing the RMR-1029 flask in Building 1412, but now Ivins thought it was possible that he did so. "It would make sense to him that he might have stored RMR 1029 in 1412," Agent Colbert wrote in her summary of the day's second interview. "He is devastated to learn that someone may have used his Ames material to commit a crime and that people are dead because of it." Ivins phoned Colbert the next day to offer a few more comments—and to say that he was going back on antidepressants.[14]

The March 31 interview appeared to reawaken Ivins's fear. He once again retained the services of defense attorney Richard Bricken, telling him he was worried that the FBI would "leak embarrassing information to the media," based on material of a personal nature stored in his computer. "I'm happy to provide information on anthrax," Ivins said, but he was "not willing to drag old skeletons out of the closet." If the FBI sent the blood-hounds to his house, Ivins said, they would not find anthrax. He added that his scent was mixed within the anthrax sent to Senator Daschle—because he had personally handled the envelope after it was brought to USAMRIID.[15]

If only Ivins had known what was really happening within the Amerithrax task force: After meeting with him, Richard Lambert made clear to his subordinates that he did not think Ivins was the perpetrator. For Lambert, the issues surrounding Ivins appeared to have been resolved.[16]

Lawrence Alexander and Thomas Dellafera were disgusted by Lambert's conclusions. The issues important to them were surely *not* resolved. For starters:

Ivins had yet to credibly explain his remarkable string of late nights in the hot suite just before the mailings—a pattern that set him apart from all other USAMRIID scientists. He did not have a verifiable alibi for the blocks of time when he could have driven to Princeton to mail the letters. He had offered contradictory claims regarding his submission of the suspicious sample of anthrax from RMR-1029. His secretive cleaning of his personal office with bleach remained a mystery. Ivins's inventory book did not account for approximately 220 milliliters of anthrax missing from RMR-1029, and he offered no explanation for this other than to claim that he was not good at math. Moreover, the investigators had yet to explore the depths of Ivins's psychiatric troubles in the run-up to the letter attacks.[17]

Alexander and Dellafera had opposed Lambert's decision to interview Ivins. Now they were convinced the interview had undermined the task force's opportunity to investigate him effectively. They were furious at Lambert for alerting Ivins to sensitive discoveries by the investigation, notably, the apparent genetic match of RMR-1029 with the material used in the attack letters. Just as bad in their view was letting Ivins know that investigators had read his e-mails to Mara Linscott.

The way Alexander and Dellafera saw it, the apparent genetic link between RMR-1029 and the attack material was a bomb-shell that should have been saved for maximum investigative leverage. Now that Ivins knew agents had examined his e-mails to Linscott, investigators would be hard-pressed to recruit her to draw more information out of him. Within days of the interview Ivins had lawyered up, informing the FBI that he wanted his attorney present for any further questioning. Because Lambert had been unwilling to delay the interview to accommodate a simultaneous search of the house, the possibility also loomed that Ivins would now destroy or discard any items remaining that could tie him to the attacks. Ivins would later acknowledge that, although he had kept them as of March 2005, he decided subsequently to throw away certain things that would, indeed, have been prized by the investigators. These included materials he had amassed regarding Kappa Kappa Gamma—notably the addresses of particular college chapters.[18]

In the interview's aftermath the investigators were kept busy with other tasks. There remained dozens of scientists who needed to be scrutinized because of their possible entrée to RMR-1029. Alexander and other investigators continued to seek a greater understanding of Ivins—but now they did much of this research on their own time. Such was the case when FBI agent Robyn Powell, assigned to Squad 3, based in Frederick, began reading through a colleague's notes describing how Nancy Haigwood had voiced suspicions about Ivins in a phone call to the bureau three years earlier, in 2002.

Agent Powell set about trying to verify what Haigwood had said about the counterfeit letter she said Ivins had sent to the *Frederick News-Post* under her name. (This was the letter, published on May 9, 1983, that strongly defended hazing rituals by Haigwood's former sorority, Kappa Kappa Gamma.) Powell, by feeding search terms into Google, found verification for Haigwood's account in a book, *Broken Pledges: The Deadly Rite of Hazing*, which quoted the counterfeit letter at length. The author of the book, unaware that the letter had been written under a false name, made no mention of Ivins.[19]

As of spring 2005, agents Powell and Alexander were intrigued by the extent of Ivins's obsession with Kappa Kappa Gamma. Yet there was nothing in the investigators' hands that linked the obsession in any way to the anthrax letter attacks. Until, that is, Agent Powell Googled other groupings of words, including "Princeton" and "Kappa Kappa Gamma."

Powell's search elicited an address for the sorority in Princeton, New Jersey, at 20 Nassau Street. This was adjacent to 10 Nassau Street—site of the only mailbox where spores of anthrax matching those used in the letter attacks were found. Powell shared her discovery with Lawrence Alexander. The significance was obvious to them: a nexus between Ivins's obsession and the mailing location. Powell entered the information into the FBI's database, where, regardless of the leanings of Richard Lambert, it would remain a part of the Amerithrax case file.

The discovery by Powell boosted the morale of some investigators, including Alexander, who pushed even harder with the Web searches on his own time. This led to another breakthrough, when Alexander, with the assistance of other agents, unearthed the charitable contributions Bruce and Diane Ivins had made to the American Family Association, a Christian advocacy group. Alexander verified that the couple had resumed donating just a month after the group publicized its filing of a federal lawsuit involving a fourth-grade student at Greendale Baptist Academy, near Milwaukee, Wisconsin. Over the objections of the school, two state government social workers had questioned the student regarding a tip about corporal punishment at Greendale.[20] Alexander immediately saw a connection that seemed chilling in the context of the investigation. The anthrax-laced envelope sent to Senator Daschle's office in October 2001 had borne this partial return address:

4TH GRADE
GREENDALE SCHOOL

Alexander believed he'd found something important. Without informing Lambert, he also set out to compress the reams of data from the electronic access cards into a concise form that would show how extraordinary were Ivins's late-night hours leading up to the mailings. He first used an Excel spreadsheet and, with the help of colleagues, produced bar charts that sharply magnified the essence of the data. Alexander hoped the day would soon come when it would be impossible for the FBI to disregard the weight of the gathering evidence against Bruce Ivins.[21]

———

John Ezzell had regarded Ivins as a strong scientist—and a colleague whose antics provided a welcome touch of humor at an institute that worked year-round with the world's most frightening pathogens. If Ivins's quirkiness caused an eyebrow to be raised now and then, Ezzell, like so many others, dismissed the strangeness as "Bruce being Bruce." Ezzell looked forward to Ivins's hyperkinetic banter in the hallways, and he had never regretted serving on the three-member panel that hired Ivins as an Army civilian microbiologist at Fort Detrick.

Ezzell had been upset to learn the Daschle envelope was removed in October 2001 from the holding area without his or the FBI's authorization so that Ivins could examine its contents. Yet he at no point blamed Ivins for it; he realized that it was the request of someone else at USAMRIID, probably Peter Jahrling, that had prompted a lab tech to loan out the envelope. Nor did Ezzell harbor any suspicion that Ivins had actually perpetrated the attacks. The truth was that John Ezzell was still a fan of Bruce Ivins.

Ezzell, then, would have been shocked to know that Ivins was implicating *him* as the anthrax killer. On July 30, 2005, Ivins laid out his allegation in a letter to Richard Bricken, his criminal defense lawyer. First, Ivins pointed out, accurately, that FBI scientists had worked with the Army's Dugway Proving Ground in Utah to try to replicate the anthrax powder recovered from the attack letters. The material that most closely resembled the anthrax used in the letters, Ivins now claimed, was not produced at Dugway; it was "material which had been covertly made by Dr. John Ezzell at USAMRIID."

Ivins cited one other basis for his grave charge—comments that he claimed Ezzell had made in November 2004 while attending a scientific conference in Illinois. This much was true: Ezzell—along with Ivins and a dozen or so other researchers from USAMRIID—had visited the Argonne National Laboratory near Chicago for a two-day conference about anthrax and biodefense. Ezzell was a featured dinner speaker and he gave a general description of the work that USAMRIID had done to assist the FBI investigation. Ivins, however, recounted a shocking scene that he said occurred offstage at the same event.

"You may remember from a previous conversation that I told you that last November Dr. Ezzell told several people at a conference in Illinois that he would confess on his deathbed to being the anthrax letter perpetrator," Ivins wrote to his lawyer in the July 30, 2005, letter. Ivins also alleged that Ezzell "clearly benefited from the letter attacks." As Ivins told it, Ezzell benefited because he "had a book—'The Anthrax Letters'—written about him."

Ezzell's supposed declaration about a deathbed confession was corroborated by no one. The book Ivins cited, *The Anthrax Letters*, published in fall 2003, mentioned Ezzell only once, and it in no way could have benefited Ezzell.[22] As for the similarity between the powder that he produced in the 1990s and the material used in the letter attacks, Ezzell had used Ames strain anthrax, but he irradiated the spores before drying them to render the material harmless to humans. Ivins also tried in his letter to implicate Ezzell's boss, Colonel Erik Henchal, suggesting that the anthrax mailings led to Henchal's promotion in spring 2002 to USAMRIID commander.[23]

A month before Ivins alleged to his lawyer that Ezzell and Henchal may have been perpetrators, he came close to saying the same to lab technician Patricia Fellows. In an e-mail to her titled "Hot news!," Ivins suggested there was something sinister about Ezzell's work in the 1990s with anthrax spore powder: "I've got his e-mail admitting it," Ivins wrote, adding he'd heard that the material Ezzell produced "was virtually identical to the spore powder in the letters."[24]

As the four-year anniversary of the anthrax mailings approached, in September 2005, Ivins traveled to Santa Fe, New Mexico, for a meeting of the International Conference on *Bacillus anthracis*.

Paul Keim was chairman of the group's steering committee, and he was once again counting on Ivins's participation on the panel. Since meeting at the conference in Britain in 1998, the two had helped each other in their separate efforts to locate new sources of anthrax that could be used to test the effectiveness of new or experimental vaccines.

Keim thought of Ivins as bright but not brilliant. More important for a chairman assembling an international conference, Ivins could be relied on to take his committee assignments seriously. The work entailed screening other scientists' technically dense research summaries and helping to select the featured speakers.

Ivins, however, was not his jocular self in Santa Fe. This was evident late one afternoon, when attendees gathered on the third floor of the La Fonda hotel for complimentary drinks and hors d'oeuvres. From here they could socialize while gazing east at the nearby St. Francis Cathedral Basilica. When one of the scientists mentioned that a man in their midst, the microbiologist Douglas Beecher, worked for the FBI, Ivins did not bother introducing himself. He loudly reproached Beecher, saying that the FBI had been harassing him in connection with the anthrax attacks. Beecher, although he had worked on the case scientifically from the outset, was not an agent and did not know Ivins's status. He said nothing and walked away, stunned.

Ivins was not under surveillance and he was not, by any rational measure, being hounded. On the other hand, the chance encounter with Beecher provided Ivins with an opportunity to play the role of victim—and to sow sympathy and support among his scientific colleagues.

During the waning hours of the Santa Fe conference, Ivins informed Keim that this would be his last as an organizer and that he would no longer participate on any of the committees. He was resigning. Ivins hinted at unspecified health issues but went no further. Keim, surprised by the development, thanked him and said goodbye.[25]

While the team of government and outside scientists made quiet headway in their hunt for a matchable DNA profile, Steven Hatfill was on the verge of getting some traction of his own. His law-yer, Thomas Connolly, had sued the Justice Department and the FBI in August 2003, claiming that the many investigative leaks violated Hatfill's privacy and severely damaged both his reputa-tion and ability to earn a living as a scientist.

Not mentioned in the court papers was Hatfill's despair at what had befallen him. Jobless and isolated from his friends, who were still leery of being swept up in the furor, Hatfill con-tinued to drink heavily. He made angry nighttime calls to jour-nalists, castigating them and their work.[26] Hatfill was no longer in contact with his old friend William Patrick, the retired biowar-fare scientist who had faced questions regarding whether he had in any way trained Hatfill how to handle anthrax; Patrick was wary of being further sullied by leaks from the investigation. The FBI had brought the bloodhounds to the hillside home that Patrick shared with his wife above Frederick, sniffing for any trace of anthrax, and more than a dozen agents eventually inter-viewed Patrick.[27]

Connolly, in order to prove the allegations lodged in the civil lawsuit, sought to force numerous officials—everyone from the case agents to the director of the FBI and the attorney general of the United States—to answer his questions under oath. The gov-ernment resisted by persuading a federal judge to grant more than a year of delays, contending that allowing Hatfill's suit to proceed could undermine the investigation into the anthrax mailings.

Finally, in March 2005, the judge overseeing the Hatfill lawsuit, Reggie B. Walton, permitted the first witness to be questioned. Three months later, an FBI spokeswoman, Debra Weierman, ac-knowledged in a sworn deposition that a litany of print and broad-cast reports implicating Hatfill appeared to be based on leaks of confidential investigative information. During questioning that spanned almost ten hours, Weierman also confirmed that, although senior agency officials would occasionally seek to clarify news re-ports that reflected badly on them or the investigation, no such ef-forts were made regarding accounts that appeared to falsely malign Hatfill.[28]

At the conclusion of the deposition, Connolly sensed he had the upper hand. He turned to his colleagues and said, "We're gonna get these guys." [29]

In November 2005, Connolly gained far greater insight into how and why information about the FBI's investigation of Hatfill might have gotten out: Almost everything learned and planned by the agents working the anthrax investigation was filed in a centralized database, called Automated Case Support, or ACS—and that database was open to thousands of FBI employees, plus certain officials from other agencies, including the Justice Department. Robert Roth, the FBI agent who supervised traditional aspects of the investigation, testified that "a vast majority" of the leaks affecting Steven Hatfill could have come straight from the database. "ACS is an open book. . . . So if someone wants to watch the case remotely they can get some really good information."

Did anyone at the FBI ever try to trace who might have leaked confidential details to the media from ACS? "We did at one time print out some period of time that wasn't very long to see who had been viewing our case and we got a blizzard of paper back," Roth testified. "It was massive. It was—to say it was unexpected is just an understatement. It was a huge group of people."

Did that huge group include people with no legitimate basis to be peering into the Amerithrax investigation? "It would take an Amerithrax investigation to figure it out because it was that voluminous." [30] It would emerge later that one of the higher-level providers of information from within the investigation was the U.S. attorney for the District of Columbia, Roscoe Howard, who served as a confidential source to both *Newsweek* and the *Washington Post*. [31]

The flow of leaks from the investigation was weighing on another official—one with power over Mueller's FBI: U.S. District Court Judge Reggie Walton, who was presiding over all pretrial decisions related to the fate of Hatfill's lawsuit. The judge was a former federal prosecutor and public defender who had also served as a crime policy advisor in the White House of President George H. W. Bush. Walton was nominated to the District Court in 2001 by President George W. Bush and was known for his reliably strict bearing.[32]

After Connolly stood before him and read from recent *Washington Post* accounts that cited unnamed law enforcement sources saying that Hatfill remained a "key focus of the probe" and a "person of interest," Walton, who had earlier granted the FBI's requests to stall the lawsuit, erupted. The anonymous leakers, the judge bellowed, were "undermining what this country is supposed to be about—that is, that we treat people fairly. If you don't have enough to indict this man, then it's wrong to drag his name through the mud." The judge directed his next remarks at the Justice Department: "That's not a government I want to be a part of. It's wrong—and you all need to do something about it."[33]

Connolly was gaining momentum with each deposition. And now he appeared to have a supportive judge. Still, the power to ask questions under oath could boomerang: Hatfill remained the top suspect in the murder by anthrax of five people—and Connolly knew that the civil lawsuit gave the government a far-reaching opportunity to question his client. The danger therein was that Hatfill's own answers could send him to life in prison or to his execution.

Yet Connolly assumed that if he did not push forward with the lawsuit, "they would continue to try him in the press forever."[34]

———

In June 2006 a visiting team of some two hundred FBI employees arrived at the bureau's Washington Field Office. They were sent there on a mission familiar to Richard Lambert, the FBI inspector who remained in charge of the anthrax investigation: This was the FBI's Inspection Division, within which Lambert had built his early career. The visitors were there to conduct a full-scale audit of the office's efficiency and effectiveness.

Lawrence Alexander and other agents were frustrated by Lambert's years-long emphasis on Hatfill, but they had felt powerless to appeal decisions they viewed as counterproductive. Until now. The Inspection Division's arrival gave these agents the opportunity to lay out their misgivings, and they did. Alexander met privately with the visiting questioners for about two hours, during which he detailed "all issues and concerns" regarding the management of the anthrax investigation.[35]

The Inspection Division's findings are off-limits to both the Congress and the American public—but not to the director of the FBI. Mueller at no point made any public statement about what he learned.[36] But on August 25, 2006, bureau headquarters announced through a press release that Lambert was leaving Washington to become the head of the FBI's office in Knoxville, Tennessee.[37] Lambert had steered the investigation as hard and as long as he could toward the indictment of Steven Hatfill.

TWENTY-THREE

SOME CHANGES

B ased on the science alone, the anthrax attacks posed perhaps the most complicated challenge ever tackled by federal law enforcement. Making sense of it required leadership that could sift through logical leads while enduring the staggering burden of turning over every stone. Leadership that was self-confident enough to tell Robert Mueller about investigative disappointments—especially when the facts clashed with the director's expectations. Such candor had its risks. In an e-mail to the chief of the FBI laboratory, even the long-favored Richard Lambert had noted Mueller's "propensity to kill the messenger" bearing unwelcome information.[1]

With Lambert's departure, the investigation was at a crossroads. Mueller turned to the equivalent of the FBI's chief operating officer, Joseph Ford, to screen the list of potential replacements. One of the candidates Ford looked at was Edward Montooth, a nineteen-year FBI veteran whose rural Midwest mien and closely cropped white hair gave him an uncanny resemblance to Peter Graves, formerly the secret agent star of TV's *Mission: Impossible*.

Montooth was known within the FBI for the breadth of his successes. He had helped gather the evidence that in the late

1980s helped convict high-ranking Navy and Air Force officials in a Pentagon contracting scandal, dubbed Operation Ill Wind. In the 1990s he worked to solve a wave of homicide cases in Washington, D.C., during which he became acquainted with Mueller, who was then serving as a prosecutor. Later Montooth led international teams that investigated war crimes cases in the Balkans, and he helped win convictions against a group of Indonesian rebels in connection with the killings of two American educators in the eastern province of Papua. Montooth's on-the-ground work in both the Balkans and Indonesia required the sensitive eliciting of information from reluctant sources—not to mention the constant risk of getting killed.

On September 7, 2006, Montooth met with Ford at FBI Headquarters to discuss the anthrax investigation vacancy. As he walked out of the office, Montooth came face-to-face with another agent, Vincent Lisi, who also was interested in the leadership position. Lisi had known since he attended a Pittsburgh-area high school that he wanted to be an FBI agent and was a man of unflinching self-assurance.

Five years younger than Montooth and trained as an accountant, Lisi had distinguished himself with investigations of homicides and other street thuggery in D.C. In one memorable case Lisi learned about a shooting at a supermarket while driving through the same area. He found the armed perpetrator, Percy Barron, hiding in a backyard and arrested him single-handedly without a shot being fired.[2] Barron was later sentenced to 409 years in federal prison for his role in two murders, including the shooting at the supermarket, and several other robberies and assaults.[3]

Lisi was skilled at developing informants and he pursued cases tenaciously. Yet he also stayed dispassionate enough to recognize evidence that established a suspect's—even a convict's—innocence. He had earned respect for assisting defense lawyers to win the release of a man, Steven Dewitt, who was imprisoned thirteen and a half years for a killing he did not commit.[4]

One of the first things Lisi told Ford was that, if Montooth wanted the job, "You should hire Ed." That's interesting, Ford told Lisi—because Montooth moments earlier said much the same about his younger colleague: " 'You won't go wrong having him lead the investigation.' " [5]

Mueller approved elevating both men. Montooth was given top responsibility for leading the investigation and Lisi was installed as number two. Their first challenge was to learn what had been done, what was in the works. There were so many details that each man likened his entering the investigation to drinking water from a fire hydrant.

They were made more deeply aware of complaints aired about Richard Lambert's leadership during the recently concluded audit by the Inspection Division. Lisi and Montooth put out the word to the long-dispirited corps of FBI agents and postal inspectors that composed Amerithrax: "*This is your investigation.*" It would be a fresh start from the ground up—without a management-down imperative to tilt in any one direction. [6]

The new leaders learned about the arc of the investigation from Agent Lawrence Alexander, who had been examining Bruce Ivins's past on his own time, using his home computer. Montooth and Lisi also debriefed two investigators who had been there from the outset: Thomas Dellafera, the senior official from the U.S. Postal Inspection Service, and FBI agent Scott Decker, the Ph.D. geneticist who oversaw the scientific work. Dellafera summarized various developments, including the discovery of tiny printing defects in each of the thirty-four-cent "federal eagle" envelopes used in the attacks, and the determination by postal inspectors that envelopes with these defects had been shipped for sale to five post offices in Maryland and two in Virginia on March 21, 2001. Decker informed them about the genetic sequencing and the possibility that the morphs, the irregular-shaped colonies of anthrax, might provide distinct DNA evidence. Within just a few weeks on the job, Montooth and Lisi would conclude that Steven Hatfill was no longer a top suspect.

Based on the genetic testing, it seemed likely that the anthrax used in the letter attacks had originated at USAMRIID, or at a lab that had received a batch of Ames anthrax from there. And although more testing was needed to be certain, it looked as though the anthrax used in the letters had been cultured from the RMR-1029 batch of Ames that was created and stored by Bruce Ivins at USAMRIID. The additional tests, and other scientific aspects of the investigation, would continue to be carried out largely in Paul Keim's lab in Arizona and at the TIGR lab in Maryland under Agent Decker's supervision.

Yet even if those efforts eventually confirmed that RMR-1029 was the attack material, this would not automatically identify the perpetrator or other conspirators. Yes, pinpointing RMR-1029 would narrow the list of presumed suspects to people who had worked at USAMRIID or the Battelle Memorial Institute in Ohio: These were the only two labs that had possessed not just Ames strain anthrax, but the RMR-1029 batch. To catch whoever was the killer, however, Lisi and Montooth knew that Amerithrax would have to thoroughly investigate many innocent scientists—dozens or more—who may have had access to RMR-1029.

Montooth expected that he, too, would eventually face criticism. Second-guessing went with the territory of high-profile work—and Montooth had enough real-world experience to resist being distracted by those forces beyond his control.

His rise could be traced to preparation and perseverance, befitting his upbringing in a small Illinois farming community, where his mother stayed at home to raise four children, his father was a high school teacher, and Ed was the lanky teenager neighboring farmers could rely on for a solid day's work. There was no shortage of it. He picked soybeans and corn, baled hay, slaughtered pigs, cows, and sheep, mended fences, and cleaned the manure from cramped chicken houses in summer.

Montooth played the major sports in high school and then paid his own way through Western Illinois State University. Like Lisi, he'd known that he wanted a career in law enforcement since he was a boy, and so he majored in criminal justice. When he learned he would likely need more diverse preparation if he were ever to be hired by the FBI, he took a paid internship with a local company, work that trained him how to untangle complicated financial crimes. He earned his degree at Western Illinois while working days at the company, a Fortune 500 retailer, and taking classes four nights a week. After graduating, Montooth managed the firm's credit card fraud investigations for seven years. The experience showed him the type of evidence needed to get search warrants, along with how to collaborate with local, state, and federal authorities to build successful white-collar cases. In May of 1980, he left to join the FBI.

Whether he was working on drug trade murders in Washington, ethnic cleansing in Bosnia, or the cold-blooded killings of the two Americans in Indonesia, Montooth felt an obligation to the victims and their survivors. It was no different with the anthrax attacks. He wanted to assure the families of Robert Stevens, Thomas Morris, Joseph Curseen, Kathy Nguyen, and Ottilie Lundgren—along with the victims who had survived exposure to the attacks—that their losses, their suffering, would not be forgotten. Everything possible, he wanted them to know, would be done to bring to justice whoever was responsible.

On Friday, October 27, 2006, Montooth, Lisi, and Lawrence Alexander met for the first time with a group of those victims and survivors. Postal inspector Dellafera was on hand, along with other senior investigators. As the meeting unfolded at bureau headquarters, it was obvious that after five years of waiting for a breakthrough, some were eager for any shred of promising news and others were angry or frustrated. Montooth said that his team would always remain open to them. He encouraged questions. The investigators circulated their cards. Still, the people who had come to Washington with hopes of seeing concrete signs of progress were disappointed. The secrecy required to avoid compromising the investigation prevented Montooth from providing any but the barest details.

One man asked whether the FBI was investigating a certain scientist at USAMRIID—a fellow named Bruce Ivins. Montooth deflected the question with a poker face, as he did when a couple of other names were raised. "We're continuing the investigation. We're reviewing everything. We're looking at everybody," Montooth said.

For Agent Alexander, it took an effort to remain quiet. He

was moved by the emotion in the room, but he could not tell this man or the others about the war he had waged inside the FBI to see to it that Ivins would be thoroughly scrutinized. Each time Alexander had read the "302" form summarizing the FBI's first interview with Robert Stevens's widow, Maureen, he had teared up. Alexander's solace was knowing that, with Montooth and Lisi in charge, the investigation was at last on track.[7]

Within the bureau, Montooth was known to speak his mind, even when it risked offending the boss. As a homicide investigator he had clashed with then prosecutor Robert Mueller over which witnesses should testify and other decisions. After Mueller was appointed FBI director, he became so riled by Montooth during one briefing that he ordered him from the room. Yet more than a decade after their first clash, Mueller had put Montooth in charge of the FBI's biggest investigation.

Now, with Lambert gone, Montooth needed to have a frank discussion with the director about the perennial chief suspect, Steven Hatfill. Before doing so, Montooth gathered his senior investigators for a point-by-point discussion of the available evidence. After going through all of it, Montooth and his team agreed: Hatfill did not have access to the crucial flask of RMR-1029, he did not have access to a laboratory suitable for handling anthrax during the two years leading up to the letter attacks, he did not have the expertise to prepare the spores. Hatfill was not the one. When Montooth delivered this news to Mueller, the FBI director did not contest the point.

Lambert had met often with Mueller, through some periods as often as daily.[8] Montooth was eager to scale back these briefings. In his view investigations progressed best when driven from the ground up, not from on high. "Headquarters effect" had hindered the Amerithrax task force, which for years was freighted with stay-in-motion tasks that supplanted evidence-inspired investigation. Montooth was not afraid to share with colleagues his bottom line: "Too much time in front of the director is a bad thing." He also did not see the value in tying up a dozen or more investigators, management personnel, and other staff with the incessant briefings.

When he first took the reins of Amerithrax, Montooth met every two weeks with Mueller, on Friday afternoons. These were actually not the first anthrax case briefings that Montooth had delivered to the director. In the bedlam of October 2001, Montooth had for a few days served as a substitute briefer on the fledgling investigation. These and Montooth's other encounters with Mueller had taught him to be wary of when to share investigative details with the director. The catch-22 with Mueller was that he wanted the most up-to-date information—but at a pace that often did not allow enough time to first vet the more murky details. This carried the risk of setting the director's expectations too high, at a level that was at odds with the evidence or what was feasible to accomplish.

Montooth preferred not to raise false hopes. So, he risked the director's wrath by slowing the tide of real-time details that had yet to be confirmed. Soon enough, his briefings of Mueller were adjusted to once every three weeks.

On the last Friday before Christmas, 2006, Montooth, with only Vince Lisi and his chief scientific investigator, Scott Decker, in tow, went to headquarters for one such briefing.

"How's it going?" Mueller asked. "What's going on? You've been there three months. Where do you stand?"

Montooth was hesitant. He had not yet told the director about a man who had become an object of great suspicion. Trying his best to keep expectations modest, Montooth let the director in on some news. "Just for transparency and some visibility for you: There's a guy that we can't wash out, no matter what we're doing. It makes us more suspicious." Montooth explained that this man was a civilian scientist at Fort Detrick, Bruce Ivins.

Mueller asked for and received more details, then braced Montooth with what, for close observers of the director, was a predictable question: "When were you going to tell me about this?"

"I was going to wait," Montooth replied. "But I figured I better tell you, because we're going to look at him pretty hard here."

Not long afterward, the mandatory three-week meetings were scrapped. Mueller instead kept time open on his schedule every Friday afternoon. Once a week, the director's secretary would call Montooth to ask if it was necessary for him to brief the director. Only rarely did the chief investigator deem that it was. Control of the case was now firmly in the hands of Montooth—not headquarters.[9]

The first signal to an outsider that the new FBI leadership was moving the investigation beyond Steven Hatfill came around the same time, in late 2006, when the beleaguered suspect was preparing to travel outside the mid-Atlantic region. His lawyer, Thomas Connolly, had routinely made courtesy calls to contacts within the FBI to alert them to Hatfill's itinerary. Connolly's unstated purpose was to avert any further scenes that would impede his client's travel or, worse, foil a new job offer. By making these courtesy calls, Connolly deadpanned, "I knew he'd be the most protected man in America." This time Connolly called Agent Lisi, an acquaintance from the days when Connolly was a prosecutor. "Tommy, you don't need to tell me his travel plans. . . . We've been working on a lot of things here. Your guy's not a priority."

Representing Steven Hatfill for the previous four years had kept Connolly awake many nights. It had become personal. As they fought together against the FBI, the Justice Department, and the credulous coverage of too many news organizations, Connolly and Hatfill had developed something deeper than a lawyer-client relationship. When Connolly's second child was born, Hatfill came by the house and assembled the crib. After Connolly mentioned that he wanted a used pickup—nothing special but sturdy enough to haul things on weekends—Hatfill found a $500 bargain, in Ona, West Virginia. The truck, Hatfill beamed, bore the Mountain State's unofficial color: primer gray. Now, for the first time since they met, Connolly could rest easier knowing that his client—his friend—was no longer in imminent danger.[10]

While the future was suddenly looking brighter for Steven Hatfill, a matter unrelated to the investigation was not turning out well for Bruce Ivins. The federal contract with VaxGen, worth a whopping $877.5 million for making the next-generation anthrax vaccine, the product for which Ivins had such high hopes, was in dire trouble. The contract had come with a catch: VaxGen was required to deliver the first of 75 million doses of the vaccine on a tight schedule. When the California company proved unable to overcome a scientific problem, the Bush administration refused to make any advance payments, even though the Project BioShield law had allowed for some. Without the stopgap revenue, VaxGen was in an even weaker position to carry out the new rounds of experiments demanded by federal regulators as a prelude to testing the vaccine in humans. The company also proved unable to compete effectively in the power corridors of Washington, where its chief rival, BioPort, the maker of the existing anthrax vaccine, deployed fifty-two lobbyists compared to VaxGen's six.

On December 19, 2006, the government terminated VaxGen's $877.5 million contract.[11] The best chance for bringing into use the new vaccine—Ivins's career-defining achievement—was dead. A year earlier, he had unexpectedly resigned from the committee of international anthrax researchers, dimming his prominence in the field. Now he was sixty years old, and his career prospects were very different from what they had seemed in the fall of 2001.

By the late fall of 2006 the Montooth and Lisi–led investigation was focused relentlessly on solidifying the list of those government and outside scientists believed to have had access to RMR-1029. In November, the FBI conducted what was intended as a discreet nighttime search at USAMRIID, with no advance notice to the staff. This marked a shift from the bureau's previous approach, whereby scientists had been allowed to submit samples of anthrax that had been prepared with no witness present, let alone an FBI agent. Top suspect Steven Hatfill had left USAMRIID in 1999, which, along with concerns about interfering with the Army's biodefense mission, appeared to account for the FBI's trusting treatment of the remaining scientists. Under Montooth and Lisi, the approach tightened.

When the FBI's nighttime operation became grist for discussion by USAMRIID scientists who gathered at a holiday party, Ivins reacted with the kind of us-against-them rhetoric that played well among his colleagues. The FBI, he opined, was overstepping its bounds to the potential detriment of those at USAMRIID. Ivins had displayed similar indignation since the earliest days of the investigation. This time his reaction provoked reassuring but firm advice from the commander of USAMRIID, Army colonel George Korch: "[Y]ou are not to discuss what was said or mention the FBI visit to anyone. . . . Please come speak to me on Monday and we can discuss the situation. Please do not worry about this FBI situation, it is under control." [12]

In response, Ivins complained that the FBI may have "taken or altered" samples for which he or other scientists were responsible. "If we can't be assured that none of our select agent material was disturbed," Ivins wrote Korch in an e-mail on December 18, 2006, "then we can't make any assurances when inventory time comes that we have exactly what we're supposed to have." [13]

Ivins was seriously focused on the investigation—and, increasingly, on what it meant for him. Soon after he had complained about the FBI's nighttime search at USAMRIID, he wrote to Mara Linscott, naming the staff scientists who were being questioned by investigators:

Now the Postal Service people are all over RIID. They talked to [four USAMRIID researchers], and others, and they're going to talk to [another researcher] at the end of the month. What's more is that all of the people above have come back and said the same thing—"They were asking lots of questions about you." ("You" meaning me.) They asked [a researcher] about my showing him how to use the lyophilizer. They talked to [two other researchers] about the fermentor that was on my hand receipt, and then disappeared off it.

Ivins relayed more to Linscott a few days later. "The FBI are back too. Fun City. They talked to [a USAMRIID researcher] for a long time last week, and they talked to [one of the other researchers] for over three hours."[14]

Suspecting that the investigators were watching him, Ivins in late fall 2006 bought a device that would detect bugs on his phones and reveal whether anyone in his presence was using a tape recorder. He also purchased a tracking service to see not only when a recipient opened one of his e-mails but also to whom they forwarded it. The service, ReadNotify, also enabled Ivins to learn approximately when and where his e-mails were opened. This particularly alarmed the investigators, who advised Nancy Haigwood and certain other cooperating witnesses to take precautions in order to prevent him from finding out who might be forwarding his e-mails to the FBI.[15]

Ivins was troubled not only by the investigators but by what other scientists might be saying about him. Although he had no evidence for his suspicion, he told family members that one colleague in particular, microbiologist Hank Heine ("HINE-ee"), was implicating him to the FBI. And at roughly the same time, Ivins was suggesting to the FBI and others that Heine might be the anthrax killer.[16] Ivins had welcomed Heine when the latter arrived at USAMRIID in December 1998 as a civilian scientist in the Bacteriology Division, and Heine had later invited Ivins and his son, Andy, to his mountain cabin in West Virginia for several all-guys weekends of target shooting.

In earlier times the two men seemed to have appreciated each other's sense of humor. But now Ivins complained bitterly to Andy and Amanda about e-mails that he received from Heine. The messages displayed pictures of doughnuts covered with white powder, a reminder of the material used in the letter attacks. The capper had come in April 2006, when Heine, while attending a scientific conference in Princeton, addressed an envelope to Ivins at USAMRIID: "Hello Bruce," began Heine's enclosed note, handwritten on Hyatt hotel stationery. "A gift from Princeton. Enjoy the postmark." The postmark was Trenton, New Jersey—exactly as had appeared on the anthrax-laced letters in the fall of 2001.

Heine regarded the stunt as gallows humor, intended to boost morale. And when Ivins opened the envelope at his office, he called Heine's cell phone, sounding to Heine like a fellow prankster, in on the joke: "Hank—this is great." Yet Ivins professed outrage over Heine's mailing to both his family and the FBI.[17]

As he tracked the investigators, and obsessed about who might be betraying him to them, Ivins also continued to court the goodwill of the person who had once confronted him about his deceptions, who knew firsthand that the cheery, helpful Bruce Ivins was a man capable of twisted duplicity: Nancy Haigwood.

During this period Ivins was sending Haigwood scores of e-mails, with subject lines like "For Animal Lovers," "To brighten your day," "Happy Monday Morning!!," "Beware of infant terrorists!!!!," "Happy Wednesday," "Smiles for the weekend!," "Cute Kittens and puppies." One of his e-mails, "do you remember fender skirts????," included twenty-seven attached photographs. Another, "Happy Friday!!," attached sixteen photos of various animals, most of them kittens.[18]

Haigwood viewed the barrage of cuddly messages as one more stratagem. "I think Bruce believed that as long as he sent me pictures of kitties and happy little notes every now and then, pictures of what a wonderful day and hope you're happy, that he could somehow stay on my good side, that I would never tell the FBI what I knew about him. . . . I think he loved manipulating people. 'Look, I'm smarter than Nancy Haigwood.'"[19]

Her role in the investigation had changed abruptly in late 2006 with a phone call from Washington. It was Agent Lawrence Alexander, who made it clear there had been "some changes" in the people who were running the case, and that the investigation was on a new path. He told Haigwood the FBI was taking "a greater interest" in the lead that she had provided back in early 2002, after she had read the letter from the FBI soliciting help from members of the American Society for Microbiology. Since calling the FBI's toll-free number (within minutes of reading the letter) she had heard occasionally from an agent assigned to the case, but their conversations yielded no results.[20]

Alexander spoke with Haigwood by phone and met with her in person, in both Seattle and in Washington, D.C. Agents also met with Carl Scandella, Haigwood's fiancé in 1983, whom she had later married and from whom she was recently divorced. Each recalled, vividly, the harassment and Haigwood's suspicions about Ivins. The FBI eventually told Scandella that Ivins had for years appropriated his name, renting a post office box and receiving mail as Carl Scandella.

Haigwood, who for so many years had been reluctant to make any active move to cut off contact with Ivins, was gaining confidence. She saw that she could help in bringing Ivins to justice—not for tormenting her, but for the five anthrax deaths. "I knew how smart and cunning Bruce was. My goal was to get the truth out."[21]

TWENTY-FOUR

GO TO THAT SAMPLE

The law office of Richard Bricken is a gray nineteenth-century row house on the western edge of historic downtown Frederick. The three-story building abuts what was once called the National Road, linking Baltimore and St. Louis. Its high-ceilinged rooms are crammed with the files of a solo practitioner who shuttles to and from the nearby county courthouse, representing misdemeanor and felony defendants. The lore is that these used to be slave quarters. Bricken's conference room is in the back, up one long step. The furnishings consist of little more than the overflowing file cabinets that are Bricken's concession to decor.

It was here that Bricken's scientist client was first questioned by Agent Lawrence Alexander, who had spent more time than anyone else at the FBI trying to dissect the bundle of contradictions that was Bruce Ivins. Alexander was accompanied by Agent Darin Steele, who had been with the anthrax investigation from the outset and was deeply grounded in the scientific details. Steele had taken the very first picture of the Daschle letter, held by John Ezzell in the glass-partitioned lab at USAMRIID. Steele and Ivins had long since been on a first-name basis. As the agents

sat down with Ivins on February 27, 2007, they planned to proceed gingerly. They had arranged the interview with the excuse
that they wanted to hear Ivins's thoughts about who could have
perpetrated the letter attacks. They saw an opportunity to start a
longer-term dialogue—and to test how aggressive Bricken might
be in curbing his client's answers.

The agents guessed, correctly, that Ivins would be eager to
voice his suspicions and intense dislike for his former colleague
Joseph Farchaus, who, Ivins claimed, had bullied him.[1] The task
force had already concluded that Farchaus was not responsible
for the mailings. But raising his name with Ivins was a way to
spark the conversation. Ivins had first fingered Farchaus as the
possible perpetrator in November 2001. And now, more than
five years later, he said that Farchaus remained "at the top" of
his list.

In addition to recounting details related to patenting the next-
generation anthrax vaccine that he and Farchaus had both
worked on as co-inventors, Ivins described the loose security that
used to prevail at USAMRIID. Anthrax or just about any other
germ, he suggested, could have been spirited out of the buildings.
He recalled a colleague who took home samples in paint cans.[2]
Ivins's unstated point was this: The lax controls meant that any
number of people could have had access to the anthrax used in
the letter attacks.

Bruce Ivins had a new secret. Unlike so many of his other in-
trigues, he had decided to share a part of this with at least one
confidante—his daughter, Amanda, now twenty-three years old.
They had built a close bond. Though some of his quirks had em-
barrassed her, Amanda had always been more open with her father than with her disciplinarian mother. She could tell him
things. During her high school days, Amanda was a bright and
athletic teenager, with light-colored hair and almond brown
eyes. But during her senior year, she felt isolated by "mean girls"
in her class. By January 2002, the situation had driven her into a
very dark place.

She was still conscious when her mother had found her at

home, overdosed on Tylenol and painkillers. Amanda acknowledged that she had attempted suicide.[3] After emergency treatment at the closest hospital, she was transferred to a facility for adolescents about thirty miles away, in Rockville, Maryland. Bruce visited her every night, and they talked about depression and the need to ride it out in the expectation of better days to come. During her college years he had helped with her coursework and paid many of her expenses. As adults, they still enjoyed going to movies or lunch together. Now Bruce wanted to discuss something especially sensitive. She could tell no one—especially not her mother. Amanda agreed, and he explained.

Several days earlier, on Sunday, March 4, 2007, he had signed legal papers changing the terms of his will. He volunteered no specifics, and Amanda assumed that her father was making plans for a very distant day. He would turn sixty-one in a month and he appeared to be in good health. Yes, he had his dark days, when he would sit silently in the living room, head down, rubbing his palms and fingers together, deep within himself. Just as often, though, he seemed as spirited as always.

With his new will, however, Bruce Ivins had devised a way to inflict a final cruelty on his wife. He assumed that Diane, a devout Catholic, would insist on a traditional burial and funeral, should she survive him. He knew that the scattering of ashes was frowned upon by the Catholic Church, which only recently had loosened its prohibition against cremation. Yet his new will stated: "Under no circumstances should my body be buried. . . . I do not want a funeral, but a memorial service may be held in my family's discretion."

The will set forth other, more pointed provisions:

1. If my remains are not cremated and my ashes are not scattered or spread on the ground, I give to Planned Parenthood of Maryland, its successors or assigns, the sum of Fifty Thousand Dollars ($50,000.00).
2. My Personal Representative [Ivins's estate lawyer] shall either provide to the Orphans' Court of Frederick County, Maryland, or to the court having jurisdiction over my probate es-

tate, if elsewhere, or to Planned Parenthood of Maryland detailed proof of my cremation and satisfactory evidence that
my remains have been scattered or spread on the ground, or
my Personal Representative shall make this gift to Planned
Parenthood of Maryland.

For Diane, the leader of Frederick County Right to Life, the
idea of a bequest to Planned Parenthood, an organization that
provides abortions on demand, would be deeply hurtful. And
it might trouble their children, for not only had both parents
always emphasized that adoption was the "right choice" and
abortion "selfish," but Amanda and her twin brother were themselves adopted. Bruce offered no explanation for the changes, either in the will itself or in his private conversation with his
daughter.

Amanda kept her word and said nothing about it.[4]

Ivins had redrawn his will just five days after meeting with the
FBI agents. In an interview that appeared to be entirely low-key,
the agents had not pressed him with any questions aimed at establishing his guilt or innocence. Yet Ivins did not appear to be
mollified and he stayed closely attuned to what the FBI was
doing. On April 6, 2007, he e-mailed his attorney, Richard
Bricken, to say that 130 lab notebooks had been subpoenaed at
USAMRIID, including some in his possession. Ivins also told
Bricken that he would not be opposed to the FBI's questioning
his psychiatrist, Dr. Allan Levy of Frederick.

Despite his anxiety about the FBI's interest in him, Ivins was unable to resist yet another opportunity to indulge his obsession
with Kappa Kappa Gamma. What animated him this time was a
gunman's rampage in April 2007 at Virginia Tech, resulting in
the deaths of thirty-two students, including a member of KKG.

As in the past, Ivins seemed to derive pleasure from assuming
public poses at odds with his true feelings. Having for decades
used subterfuge to ridicule campus sororities—also known as
Greek Letter Organizations, or GLOs—Ivins now affected a

smarmy respect for them. At 10:01 on the night of the campus killings in tiny Blacksburg, Virginia, Ivins posted a message to the Web site GreekChat.com, voicing sympathy and adding: "I would also like to suggest that if the shooter had been in a GLO—I've heard nothing to suggest he was—he would more than likely have received support and help through whatever difficult times he was going through, and—I'm just being truthful here—we may well have not seen the awful tragedy that unfolded today."

He went on to say: "[I]t does give us pause to know that the deep relationships that are made through families and social or ganizations can help us through our darkest moments." Ivins signed his posting as Goldenphoenix, one of his many Web pseudonyms.

Ivins made several other posts to GreekChat.com about the Virginia Tech killings, one of which suggested that he identified in some way with the perpetrator: "My heart goes out to the family of the shooter, but he knew what he was doing, he didn't go to get professional help (medication and counseling), and he coldly and methodically plotted his evil deeds."

Ivins soon turned his focus to nineteen-year-old Caitlin Hammaren, the victim who had been a member of Kappa Kappa Gamma. In addition to making pseudonymous posts about her on GreekChat.com, Ivins signed his own name to a tribute on another Internet guestbook.[5] And he sent condolences to Nancy Haigwood, a strange gesture since she had had no involvement with Kappa Kappa Gamma for thirty years, had never visited Virginia Tech, and was not acquainted with the deceased sophomore or her family.

"Dear Nancy," Ivins wrote to Haigwood on April 20, 2007, four days after the killings, "I just want to express my sympathy to you and other members of Kappa for the loss off [sic] your sister Caitlin at Virginia Tech. Everything I've read about her says that she was a beautiful human being, warm and bright, and always ready with a smile and an ear to listen."[6]

Writing under yet another pseudonym, jimmyflathead, Ivins had been trying to post changes—about one hundred of them—

to Kappa Kappa Gamma's Wikipedia page, some notably focusing on connections he wanted to draw between KKG and terrorism and murder.

In his first such posting, on December 27, 2005, he expanded the list of "Notable Kappas" by adding the name of Angela Atwood, a former high school cheerleader and student at Indiana University who became a founding member of the Symbionese Liberation Army, the band of armed radicals that in the 1970s kidnapped heiress Patty Hearst and killed two people. Atwood and five other SLA founders died in a shootout with Los Angeles police.

When another writer lamented that the Wikipedia pages for sororities other than Kappa Kappa Gamma did not contain such negativity, Ivins, again writing as jimmyflathead, defended his handiwork as "honesty."

"It is correct to assume that other fraternal organizations have 'Other Facts' that they would rather people not know," Ivins posted on July 25, 2006. "For example, Symbionese Liberation Army member and confessed murderer Emily Harris was a Chi Omega. Charles 'Tex' Watson, mass murderer and member of the Charles Manson 'Family,' was a Pi Kappa Alpha."

Still writing as jimmyflathead, Ivins flaunted his knowledge of Kappa Kappa Gamma's secret customs—saying that he "at one time" possessed the sorority's Book of Ritual. Unless a person had "the KKG Cipher" or other means of decoding, he wrote, "simply having the Book of Ritual won't do you any good."[7]

Ivins also added Nancy Haigwood to the list of "Notable Kappas," a mention later removed from the sorority's Wikipedia page at her request.

On April 9, Ivins received a subpoena to testify before a federal grand jury in Washington. In the cover letter, Assistant United States Attorney Kenneth Kohl wrote, "You are not a target of this investigation." A dozen or so of Ivins's colleagues received subpoenas with the same assurance.[8]

Kohl's letter to Ivins also invited the microbiologist to meet voluntarily with him on April 30, a week before his scheduled testimony. The session with Kohl would be held at FBI offices in Frederick, where agents had invited Steven Hatfill five years earlier.

After meeting with the prosecutor for several hours, Ivins told his lawyer that he expected to face questioning at the grand jury about his psychiatric condition; his co-invention of the next-generation anthrax vaccine and how its development could benefit him financially; and his anger over the Senate's delay in passing the USA Patriot Act immediately after September 11, 2001.[9]

The E. Barrett Prettyman Federal Courthouse is on Constitution Avenue, a short walk west of the Capitol. Built during the administration of Harry Truman, the courthouse has hosted some of the nation's highest-profile criminal proceedings. Shortly before 1 P.M. on Tuesday, May 8, 2007, Ivins strode inside and made his way to the grand jury alone. It is common for witnesses to bring defense lawyers, who wait outside the closed doors of the grand jury room. A witness may leave and reenter for as many consultations as desired. But Ivins had decided not to avail himself of this protection.

Hours later he headed home with deeper concern for his future than when he arrived. The questioning was more adversarial than he had expected and lasted until late in the day. Since the session ended before prosecutor Kohl asked all his questions, Ivins would have to return in a couple of days. Kohl had pressed him at length about the anthrax samples that Ivins submitted in early 2002. Ivins now knew that his biggest immediate problem was his submission of what was supposed to have been material from RMR-1029. Curiously, the sample had turned out not to have contained any of the morphs, the irregular-shaped anthrax colonies that characterized other RMR-1029 samples.[10] He might yet be able to devise a satisfactory explanation. But Ivins's answers to the grand jury were given under oath and were now part of a body of evidence that could be used against him.

It was apparent to Richard Bricken that Ivins needed a new lawyer, someone experienced in the federal courts and who could handle matters in Washington without the hundred-mile round-trip. At Bricken's recommendation, Ivins hired Paul Kemp, a former state prosecutor whose office in Rockville was near a Metrorail station with frequent service to downtown Washington. The fifty-seven-year-old Kemp had also served as a state and federal public defender, roles in which he represented defendants accused of violent crimes. In more recent years his practice tilted toward white-collar defense, defending companies under investigation by the Securities and Exchange Commission.

Kemp first met with his new client on May 12, 2007, when Ivins drove to Rockville to describe his view of the case. Kemp would need more time to master the scientific issues, but he was struck by what Ivins said about the lax security for deadly pathogens at USAMRIID through the fall of 2001. To hear Ivins tell it, the United States Army Medical Research Institute of Infectious Diseases—a supposed pillar of the nation's biowarfare defense—was almost an open-access building. Ivins said there had been no rigorous accounting of anthrax drawn from storage for experiments.

Kemp would have advised Ivins against appearing at the grand jury unless his lawyer was in the courthouse, available outside the closed door. Yet from what he could see initially, Kemp was not convinced that the FBI was seriously focused on Ivins. His new client struck Kemp as a harmless, absentminded-professor type, though markedly uneasy about the course of the investigation. Kemp surmised that representing him might be mostly "witness hand-holding."

Ivins continued to grouse to his colleagues about the damage being inflicted by the investigation. He said that he was asked "gotcha" questions in front of the grand jury and that the investigators "know everything" about the scientists' personal and professional lives. "Eventually a trial will come, and we'll be dragged up to the witness chair to testify, and that's when the other side wil[l] start dragging us through the dirt," Ivins said in an e-mail to Mara Linscott on May 23, 2007. "It's a lawyer's job to sully the personal and professional reputations of witnesses on the other side. For me it means people finding out that I'm a slob, keep poor records, am lousy at math, and see a psychiatrist." [11]

There was other serious investigative activity underway that Ivins and his lawyer were not in a position to see. The team of scientists Rita Colwell had assembled after the letter attacks was still hard at work. And at the Sandia National Laboratories in New Mexico, Joseph Michael and his colleagues had long since established that the spores used in the letters showed no signs of having been treated with an additive to make the material lighter and more deadly. This buttressed an important conclusion: Whoever perpetrated the mailings did not need additives associated with state-sponsored offensive biological warfare programs, like silica or bentonite. The purified Ames strain spores were deadly enough on their own.

Although the 2002 Sandia findings, along with what investigators were learning about RMR-1029, strengthened the likelihood that the killings could be traced to USAMRIID, the new leaders of Amerithrax, the FBI's Ed Montooth and Vince Lisi, emphasized internally that no conclusions should be drawn yet. Both said they were wary of tunnel vision that could close an investigator's eyes to unexpected clues.

By the summer of 2007 the last of the investigation's most eagerly anticipated scientific tests were unfolding in strict secrecy at the Institute for Genomic Research, located in Rockville, just four miles from Paul Kemp's law office. At TIGR, the microbiologist Jacques Ravel was helping to identify the unique set of four morphs that appeared repeatedly in cultures of the anthrax recovered from the letters. It had first been the idea of the FBI's Scott Stanley and Scott Decker to sequence the morphs in search of distinct DNA evidence that matched the attack material—and TIGR had been working on this since early 2002, making steady progress, morph by morph.

There was just one more test for TIGR to complete, assessing the last of the four morphs, "Morph E." The results would show whether the morphs could yield DNA evidence matching RMR-1029 to the anthrax letters.

The samples that Ravel worked with had been coded by the

FBI in such a way as to prevent both him and his lab technician, Sara Koenig, from identifying the source of the material they were handling. This type of "blinding" is a precaution against overt or subconscious bias that might tilt the results of an experiment. What Ravel did know, however, was that TIGR's work with the other three morphs was complete. This was to be the final test of the final morph.

The results were ready. At 10 A.M. on Wednesday, September 5, 2007, two FBI scientists, Jason Bannan and Matthew Feinberg, arrived at TIGR. Feinberg in the previous years had logged many weeks as a visitor at Paul Keim's genetics lab in Flagstaff to ensure that the work there met the FBI's standards, and Bannan had actually applied to the FBI at the encouragement of Keim.

The two FBI men knew full well the significance of the pending results because they had *not* been blinded to the earlier data, and they were aware that Ravel's sequencing of the first three morphs had matched samples of RMR-1029. They also knew that those samples had been obtained from only two places, USAMRIID and the Battelle Memorial Institute.

Ravel had assembled the new data in TIGR's main conference room. As he began to methodically explain the results, Bannan cut him off. Pointing to a number on one of the documents, he asked, "Can you go to that sample?" Ravel pulled it. Bannan and Feinberg checked the relevant data. No words were necessary—and no amount of blinding could mask the excitement that Ravel saw in their faces.[12]

Morph E had checked out the same as the first three. After years of slogging, the Amerithrax task force had a DNA profile that linked RMR-1029 to the anthrax mailings.

The heaviest scientific lifting was over. The Amerithrax investigators had traveled the world and examined 1,070 samples of anthrax from eighteen labs in four countries. In the end they found a total of only eight samples—each apparently descended from Bruce Ivins's parent flask of RMR-1029—that matched the anthrax found in the letters. Seven of the samples came from USAMRIID; the other came from the anthrax inventory at the

Battelle Memorial Institute—and it, too, had its origins in spores Bruce Ivins had sent to a Battelle scientist in May and June of 2001.[13] (The transfer was aboveboard and well documented.)[14]

The genetic evidence alone, however, could not finger the perpetrator. Now the Amerithrax investigators had to complete their efforts to scrutinize anyone known to have had access to RMR-1029. Ed Montooth and Vince Lisi were leading an investigation that was no longer foundering in pursuit of the wrong man. They could focus on determining which people with access to RMR-1029 had plausible alibis, and which didn't.[15]

The investigators' earlier interviews (more than one hundred Battelle scientists were questioned in 2002) and checking of Battelle's records had found that a total of forty-two people entered the Ohio lab where RMR-1029 was stored between May 9, 2001, when the material was received from Bruce Ivins, and early October 2001, when the last anthrax-laced letters were mailed. Investigators pored over laboratory notebooks to see in which experiments Battelle had used anthrax from RMR-1029. Then, after questioning and conducting background investigations of all forty-two employees who had potential access to RMR-1029, the investigators concluded that fewer than twenty of them had the technical ability to work with anthrax. The others were animal handlers, maintenance workers, administrators, and clerical staffers.

Battelle functioned as a commercial lab, with more stringent access procedures than at USAMRIID. At Battelle, every minute spent in a hot suite was supposed to be accounted for and billed to a client. No researcher there was allowed to be alone in a suite. There was only one span of days during the critical period— from June 13 to 16, 2001—when any Battelle employees were known to have been in a suite after normal business hours. During those nights there were always two employees in the suite where RMR-1029 was stored—and each of the four nights it was a different pair.[16] Could a determined person have subverted Battelle's controls to prepare the anthrax used in the letter attacks? Perhaps—but it would be far more difficult than under the looser conditions at USAMRIID that had allowed Bruce Ivins to work in a hot suite night after night, alone and unmonitored for hours on end.

There was also an issue of practicality: The mailbox on the street in Princeton where the letters were dropped was, depending on the route chosen, a round-trip of seven to eight hours from USAMRIID. Driving from Battelle, in Columbus, to Princeton and back would take about eighteen hours.[17] On September 17 and 18, 2001, the day the first anthrax letters were postmarked, thirty-seven of the forty-two Battelle employees with access to RMR-1029 worked full eight-hour shifts. Of the remaining five employees, one was on administrative leave and the others were animal specialists who the investigators found did not have the expertise to handle anthrax.

After further scrutinizing these final five employees and taking into account the larger body of evidence, the investigators concluded that the anthrax mailings most probably did not originate at Battelle.[18]

By fall 2007, the investigative hunt had been narrowed to the scientists who had worked at USAMRIID. Investigators were by then familiar with all the microbiologists, technicians, and animal handlers who had access to RMR-1029. Many had been interviewed repeatedly, subjected to lie detector tests, and brought before the grand jury in Washington. Yet nearly all of them had credible alibis or did not appear to have been proficient enough to complete all the steps taken by the anthrax killer.

The investigators were looking for an anomaly, in this instance a person who, for whatever reason, stood out. They found just one.[19] During the pivotal weeks before the first anthrax-laced letters were dropped into the mailbox in Princeton, it appeared that Bruce Ivins had been on a mission. Beginning on August 31—and for twelve consecutive nights—he was alone in the hot suite. During three nights leading up to September 18, when the first anthrax letters were postmarked, Ivins worked alone in the hot suite for a total of 7 hours, 7 minutes. He was there on the night of Friday, September 14, from 8:54 P.M. to

12:22 A.M. On Saturday the 15th he was there from 8:05 P.M. to 11:59 P.M. And on Sunday the 16th he was again there, alone, from 6:38 P.M. to 9:52 P.M.

Amid his flurry of solitary activity, Ivins had taken the time to alert Mara Linscott on September 12 to "BIG security" just imposed at Fort Detrick—while foreshadowing a new genre of terrorism: "I don't know if there will be any further events, but we've been told to prepare for possible biological events." (If by "we" he was referring to USAMRIID's Bacteriology Division, within which he worked, Ivins was exaggerating. As he well knew, the plans for handling materials related to any biological events were the responsibility of two other divisions at the institute.)[20]

———

The many nights he spent in the hot suite would have given a microbiologist with Ivins's skill enough time to prepare the anthrax used in the first letters—those sent to American Media in Palm Beach County, Florida, to the *New York Post*, and to Tom Brokaw at NBC News in New York.[21] If, as investigators suspected, Ivins had an unaccounted-for stash of anthrax in his lab's refrigerator, all he needed to do was purify and dry it, averting the chore of growing more spores. Did Ivins also have enough time to drive the letters to the mailbox in Princeton?

Based on postal collection schedules, the letters postmarked on September 18 had to have been dropped into the mailbox on Nassau Street between 5 P.M. on September 17 and noon on September 18. On September 17 Ivins worked until about noon and then took off the remainder of his shift as annual leave, but he attended a group therapy session nearby, which would have made an afternoon drive to Princeton improbable because the round-trip from Fort Detrick would take at least seven hours. If Ivins, as investigators suspected, had taken a slightly more circuitous route to avoid the fixed cameras at toll plazas, the trip would have taken closer to eight hours.

Ivins returned to USAMRIID at 7 P.M. that day, and the electronic card records showed that he stayed for thirteen minutes before leaving. His best opportunity was during the next twelve hours, when he could easily have driven to Princeton, dropped the letters under cover of darkness, and been back at Fort Detrick for work the next morning at 7:02 on Tuesday, September 18. As he ultimately acknowledged to investigators, it was not unusual for him to take long nighttime drives with no questions asked by Diane.[22] She was a prodigious snorer and they had long slept apart, Diane's bedroom in a separate, ground-level extension of the house. Typically she was asleep before he went to bed, unaware of his whereabouts or comings and goings.[23]

The second batch of letters, those addressed to Senators Daschle and Leahy, contained anthrax powder that was of higher quality. It was fluffy, with a consistent, creamy tan color. This was in contrast to the anthrax sent to Brokaw and the *New York Post,* which was granular, with flecks colored off-black, tan, and white, similar in appearance to the contents of a diner's pepper shaker. The finer texture and consistent color of the powder in the Daschle and Leahy letters suggested more elaborate preparation.

This is in line with the irregular hours that Ivins kept in the critical days preceding October 9, 2001, when the envelopes to the senators were postmarked: From Friday, September 28, through Friday, October 5, Ivins worked eight consecutive nights alone in the hot suite—totaling 15 hours, 17 minutes. On seven of the eight nights he did not leave the building until after at least 10 P.M. A federal holiday, Columbus Day, fell on Monday, October 8. Based on Ivins's time spent at USAMRIID and the postal collection schedule, he had multiple-hour blocks throughout the three-day weekend when he could have traveled between Frederick and Princeton and dropped the letters in the mailbox in time for them to be postmarked on October 9.

The electronic card records at USAMRIID showed that from mid-August through mid-October of 2001, Ivins spent more nighttime hours in the hot suite than he did during any other such period since 1998 when the security system, first installed in the late 1980s, was expanded to the interior labs. And taking into account that each of the anthrax-laced letters was a photocopy— the originals were never found—there was another wrinkle to cast suspicion on him.

During the same periods when he was logging such unusual amounts of time in the hot suite, Ivins also made three brief visits during off-hours to the USAMRIID library, which was equipped with a photocopier. On Sunday, September 16, 2001, two days before the first anthrax letters were postmarked, he was in the library from 2:11 P.M. to 2:25 P.M. On Saturday, September 22, he was there from 8:22 P.M. to 8:36 P.M. And on Friday, September 28, he returned for a final visit, from 10:42 P.M. to 10:55 P.M. Ivins was the only researcher in the library during his last two visits; on September 16, two others had been present. No librarians worked at night or on weekends. And when investigators checked the available electronic records, they found no other period when Ivins made such a series of visits to the library.[24]

Could there be a benign explanation for Ivins's unusual hours at USAMRIID in the days preceding each of the two rounds of anthrax mailings? His lab notebooks, which documented his official work, offered none for the period preceding the first round of letters. As for the second round, when he worked alone in the hot suite for eight consecutive nights, Ivins's notes said that on the first five of those dates, he had checked on the health of rabbits being used in a colleague's experiment. Observing and documenting dead rabbits would have taken far less time than Ivins spent in the hot suite on the first three of those five nights: 1 hour, 42 minutes; 1 hour, 20 minutes; 1 hour, 18 minutes. On the fourth and fifth nights, Ivins was in the hot suite for 20 minutes and 23 minutes, respectively. His hours in the hot suite lengthened markedly during the sixth, seventh, and eighth consecutive nights, when he was alone there for 2 hours, 59 minutes on October 3, 2001; 3 hours, 33 minutes on October 4; 3 hours, 42 minutes on October 5. Ivins's only other explanation for all these hours was that he went to the hot suite to escape family tensions.[25]

In addition to the unusual hours he spent in the hot suite, there was the e-mail Ivins had sent to his former lab tech—using language that paralleled the photocopied letters, not yet publicized, mailed eight days earlier to Brokaw and the *New York Post*. "Osama Bin Laden has just decreed death to all Jews and all Americans," Ivins wrote to Mara Linscott, on September 26, 2001. The anonymous, anthrax-laced letters mailed on September 18 had said, in part:

DEATH TO AMERICA
DEATH TO ISRAEL.
ALLAH IS GREAT.

The same sequence of threats was included in photocopied letters addressed to Senators Daschle and Leahy and postmarked October 9, 2001, thirteen days after Ivins's e-mail to Linscott. Stealthily scapegoating others—in this case, by implication, Islamic terrorists, notably Osama bin Laden—to serve his own purposes was a hallmark of Bruce Ivins. And using Islam in his inflammatory manipulations was also within his repertoire. Ivins once disparaged a local Islamic leader's modest call for interfaith dialogue, writing in a 2006 letter to the *Frederick News-Post*, "By blood and faith, Jews are God's chosen, and have no need for 'dialogue' with any gentile. End of 'dialogue.' " [26]

As the six-year anniversary of the first anthrax-mailing death passed, Ivins bantered with an acquaintance about his own impending death, saying that he was going to have a heart attack, "the big one." He also talked about his increased drinking of tequila while taking Ambien, one of his prescription sleep medications.[27] At about this same time, Ivins joined his middle brother, C.W., on a Caribbean cruise.

While Bruce Ivins ordered Bahama Mama cocktails aboard the *Sovereign of the Seas*, Ed Montooth and Vince Lisi remained in Washington, planning a new turn in the anthrax investigation. They conferred with the key investigators, including Agents Lawrence Alexander, Darin Steele, Scott Decker, and the case's senior postal inspector, Thomas Dellafera. Under the earlier leadership of Van Harp and then Richard Lambert, the Amerithrax task force had conducted some 9,100 interviews and carried out a total of sixty-seven searches. But the task force had not searched Bruce Ivins's house. Yet.

TWENTY-FIVE

THE REST OF US

Those now in charge of the case could see that Amerithrax's long and intense focus on Steven Hatfill had been a costly mistake.

Investigators had twice searched Hatfill's apartment, thoroughly scoured his and his girlfriend's belongings, and brought in the bloodhounds from California to sniff him and other acquaintances. For years he was followed, his every public move videotaped. What might have been found if investigators had rolled past Hatfill's apartment and the main gate at Fort Detrick and gone around the corner another two hundred yards to the home of Bruce Ivins? What was inside Ivins's cluttered house and vehicles? The address of Kappa Kappa Gamma's chapter in Princeton? The original letters from which the photocopies were made for the anthrax mailings?

The case had been bungled, but Ed Montooth and his team had reasons to be optimistic. They had DNA evidence linking the RMR-1029 batch of anthrax to the letter attacks. They had the electronic keycard records showing Ivins's extraordinary night-time hours in the hot suite in the periods just before both sets of mailings. They had Ivins's September 26 e-mail to Mara Linscott, using language similar to that in the soon-to-be-infamous anthrax letters.[1] The investigators were learning more about Ivins's serious mental problems, including his acknowledged paranoid delusions and his fear, which he voiced before the letter attacks, that he might do "terrible things."[2]

Montooth and Lisi agreed: There was no use waiting any longer. But they were determined not to make the search of Ivins's house a spectacle. Montooth won an important bureaucratic battle, enabling the task force to proceed without bringing in the moon-suited hazardous materials specialists. This in turn eliminated any requirement to reveal the search in advance to the mayor or any others not directly involved in the investigation. Montooth wanted no TV cameras, no circling helicopters. No "Hatfill." When he shared the strategy with Mueller, the FBI director doubted that the search could be kept a secret but did not stand in its way.

This time the task force would do what Inspector Richard Lambert did not do on March 31, 2005: move broadly and in unison to question Ivins, his wife, and each of their adult children while at the same time launching searches of the family home on Military Road and their vehicles.

The first overt move came at 4 P.M. on Thursday, November 1, 2007, when the FBI's Lawrence Alexander and Darin Steele arrived at the office of the USAMRIID commander, Colonel George Korch. The agents informed Korch that they wanted to question Ivins—but in a way that would minimize attention. Ivins was in his office, Room 19. If the FBI men went there, it would surely set off a commotion. They persuaded Korch to quietly inform him that he had two visitors waiting—in the commander's conference room. The agents had complementary strengths: Alexander, through interviews and his review of Ivins's massive output of e-mail, had become an expert on Bruce Ivins. And Steele, "Dr. Darin" within the FBI, was so steeped in the science that Ivins could not lead him astray.

As Ivins entered the conference room and made eye contact with them he asked, "Do I need my attorney?"

The agents said they were there to share some important information. They laid out why they suspected he had misled the investigation regarding RMR-1029—what Ivins called the Dugway spores—the batch he had created in 1997 and had under his control through the fall of 2001 and beyond.[3]

Steele pointed out that cultures from the second sample of RMR-1029 that Ivins had submitted, in April 2002, did *not* include the morphs. And here is where the saga of the samples could get confusing. But not to Agent Steele, who had carefully reconstructed what really happened.

Earlier, when Ivins had not followed FBI instructions in submitting the first sample of RMR-1029, in February 2002, he, along with many other scientists in the field, believed that it was impossible to tell one batch of Ames anthrax from another. However, in the time between his submission of his first and second samples, Ivins had gleaned inside information from the investigation that challenged this view: On March 29, 2002, he and a handful of other USAMRIID scientists gathered for a discussion that explained why the samples they submitted had to be drawn from a broad swath of anthrax colonies.

The session was led by FBI agent Scott Stanley, also a Ph.D. scientist. Stanley took notes during the meeting and drew a diagram showing where Ivins and every other participant was sitting.[4] After Stanley described the procedure for drawing the samples, Ivins's newly anointed supervisor, Patricia Worsham, explained why this was so important. This precise method was mandatory, Worsham explained, because submitting the broadest variety of colonies was the most reliable way to capture genetic diversity—in the form of any morphs that might exist. Worsham made clear that the investigators were hunting for these morphs as a means of tracing the genetic origin of the anthrax in the attack letters.

It would be unacceptable, Worsham said, to prepare a sample by picking a single colony from a Petri dish. The morphs emerged at a rate of only 1 out of every 50 to 100 colonies, so picking just one colony almost certainly would not yield the morphs. "We knew that if you took a single-colony pick, we'd get screwed,"

Stanley recalled.[5] If a scientist submitted a sample by the prohibited single-colony pick method, this would violate the subpoena.[6]
(It would also invite suspicion that the scientist had reason to fear
the discovery of a genetic match with the attack material.) The
instructions and explanation from Worsham and Stanley likely
led Ivins to believe that the rejection of his earlier sample was an
extraordinary stroke of luck. As far as he knew, it was null and
void.[7]

On April 10, 2002, twelve days after hearing Agent Stanley's
and Worsham's explicit instructions, Ivins submitted his second
sample. When the Amerithrax scientists examined it, they found
none of the telltale morphs that could link Ivins's sample to the
attack material. Ivins's defense lawyer, Paul Kemp, would later
say that his client had in fact prepared the April 10 sample by
using the single-colony pick method. Ivins did this because he believed it would produce a legitimate "pure-culture" sample,
Kemp said.[8] The Amerithrax investigators suspected that Ivins
either used the verboten single-colony method—or he submitted
anthrax that was not from RMR-1029. Either way, they believed
that Ivins knowingly violated the subpoena.

Now, on November 1, 2007, agents Alexander and Steele were
sharing their curiosity with Bruce Ivins: His sample contained
none of the morphs. But when the FBI's scientific team cultured
material directly from his parent flask of RMR-1029, the
morphs *did* emerge. What could explain the discrepancy? Alexander and Steele did not let on that part of Ivins's original sample, the reject, had been inadvertently shipped by USAMRIID to
Paul Keim's lab. The material sat in a locked metal cabinet, un-
touched, until late 2006 when Keim noticed it and alerted the investigators. The FBI then arranged for another laboratory to test
Ivins's sample, and it was found to contain three of the four
morphs.[9]

The interview, meanwhile, was becoming a spirited chess
match. On the crucial issue of why his April 10, 2002, submission from RMR-1029 did not contain the four telltale morphs,
Ivins would not even acknowledge that he had personally pro-

vided the sample. He reiterated a claim he had made earlier to the FBI—that it was a lab technician who submitted the second sample of RMR-1029, on April 10, 2002. Now the agents informed Ivins that this was impossible: His hand-printed labeling was on the test tubes. And the keycard records and other evidence showed that he had hand-delivered the material.

When the agents thought they had locked him into one explanation or another, he would suggest a different scenario, or claim a faulty memory. Alexander tried to break Ivins's rhythm. Leaning across the table with his palms open, the agent interrupted: "*Look—stop talking.*" Alexander wanted him to listen to these questions and to think about his answers. Alexander had prepared a spreadsheet with scores of statements Ivins had made over the previous six years. Item by item, Alexander was able to flag the inconsistencies.

Ivins, wearing a plaid shirt with his customary plastic pocket protector, was undeterred, rattling off new explanations. He suggested that the morphs were absent because the material submitted was *not* from RMR-1029. Alexander pointed out an e-mail from Ivins to the FBI on April 9, 2002, in which he said he would draw material from RMR-1029 and submit it. Indeed, Ivins submitted the sample the very next day. Ivins pivoted: The FBI scientists who analyzed the sample must have made a gross mistake. Steele noted that Ivins had submitted separate test tubes of the material. If there was such a gross error, the agent said, it would likely not have occurred twice.

While the agents and Ivins sparred, the task force had begun questioning Diane Ivins, whom they approached as she ended her shift at a local eatery. Alexander occasionally left the conference room at USAMRIID to call Montooth. The interview was tense, he reported, but Bruce Ivins was still talking. Try to keep it going, Montooth said. As planned, the investigators could use the extra time for their questioning of the other three family members. As soon as the interview with Bruce Ivins ended, the cell phone calls would commence and everyone might clam up.

The search of the house would begin after nightfall to avoid attracting attention from the media or anyone else.

At 6:45 P.M., with just a tinge of fading light left in the western sky, the investigators entered the house on Military Road, having presented the search warrant to Diane Ivins. Once inside, they placed blackout material on all the windows to mask their activities.

Across the street at Fort Detrick, the interview was approaching three hours. Agent Alexander now shifted the discussion away from the science. He asked about a detail that revealed just a hint of the FBI's knowledge of the compartmentalized life led by Bruce Ivins. Alexander asked about a person whose name Ivins used on one of his post office boxes. At this Ivins abruptly pushed back from the table, crossed his arms and legs, and said that he was asserting his Fifth Amendment right against self-incrimination. When prompted again, Ivins stayed firm. He would not discuss this person whose name so obviously unsettled him. It was Carl Scandella, who was engaged to Nancy Haigwood when Ivins started secretly appropriating his name. Ivins now had to wonder what else the agents knew.

About 8 P.M., Colonel Korch reentered the conference room to retrieve a set of keys. At that point Ivins announced he would not answer any further questions and that he wished to leave. The agents told him they had something else of importance to share: His home and vehicles were being searched. Every effort was being made to ensure discretion. But Ivins could help avert any media coverage by remaining calm and staying away from the house. Bruce, Diane, and their son, twenty-four-year-old Andy, who was still living at home, could spend the night at a local hotel, where rooms would be provided at the government's expense. The agents told Ivins that Diane and Andy were being questioned separately.

Agent Alexander, anticipating that Ivins would be driven by investigators to the hotel, and knowing that he owned handguns small enough to conceal, told him he would need to pat him down. Ivins followed instructions and faced away, placing his outstretched palms on a wall of the conference room. When Alexander finished, Ivins turned around and presented his hands—as if expecting to be placed in handcuffs. He was not.[10]

It was 8:25 P.M. Ivins accepted the offer of a ride to the nearby Hilton Garden Inn with two other investigators, both of whom were familiar to him. He got into the front passenger seat of the FBI's idling Ford Explorer. Postal inspector Tom Dellafera, all the while chatting with Ivins, took the middle of the back seat. Behind the wheel was FBI agent Scott Stanley, who had once been a near-constant presence at USAMRIID. Without a trace of humor or compassion, Ivins peppered Stanley with details of a serious car crash the agent had been in a few months earlier, citing particulars that Stanley assumed would not have been known to any outsiders. When he asked how Ivins had come by this knowledge, he got no reply. Gamesmanship, the agent thought.

Stanley asked Ivins if he was worried about the searches. Yes, Ivins said, he was. After a few moments of silence, Ivins explained himself. He had a habit, he said, of doing things a "middle-age man should not do." Things that would "not be acceptable to most people." He elaborated. In the basement—the same area where he stored his juggling gear—he kept a bag of materials that he used to "cross-dress." Stanley assured him that neither he nor Dellafera were there to judge his lifestyle. What he did privately was his business, so long as he didn't hurt anyone.

After having shared this highly personal detail, Ivins remained visibly anxious. Stanley asked if something else was bothering him. There was. Ivins did not want to be labeled a "mass killer or a terrorist." He could not believe that the investigators viewed him as the "anthrax mailer." Stanley offered Ivins an out. Never, Stanley said, had he believed that the mailer intended to harm anyone: The envelopes were taped shut. The letters pointed out the presence of anthrax and the photocopied message sent to Tom Brokaw and the *New York Post* even warned recipients to take penicillin, an effective treatment. The agent's implication was that any resulting harm, including the five deaths, had been an accident. Then Stanley asked a question that invited Ivins to be not a suspect, but an analyst. "What kind of person do you think would have done this?" Ivins jerked violently out of his seat and flush against the door, and stared at the floorboard. He said nothing in response. In less than fifteen minutes they had reached the hotel.[11]

Dozens of investigators, resembling a crew of technicians and movers, were quietly at work inside the house. Others were sealing and preparing for transport to another location the three family vehicles: a rust-red 1996 Dodge van, a blue 1993 Honda Civic, and a blue 2002 Saturn SL1 sedan. Once the vehicles had been moved and unsealed, technicians could swab the interiors and the compartments for traces of anthrax. Other investigators were at USAMRIID, searching Ivins's office and wall lockers and duplicating all the information on his computer's hard drive.[12]

The investigators inside the house gathered copies of sixty-eight letters that Ivins had sent in his own name over the years to members of Congress and to a range of media outlets, such as *Newsweek*, the *Washington Post*, and the *Frederick News-Post*. Ivins had written about various political issues, including abortion and biodefense research. The letters were of interest because each of the recovered anthrax-laced envelopes had been mailed to a member of Congress or to a media organization. Ivins had also saved news articles, notably a printout of an April 11, 2003, account in the *Baltimore Sun*, "Tests point to domestic source behind anthrax letter attacks."[13]

At the hotel, Ivins left a phone message for his defense lawyer, Paul Kemp, who lived on land with horses west of Frederick in rural Washington County, Maryland. About 9 P.M., Kemp returned the call.

"They tell me I'm not in custody but they took me to this hotel and I'm not sure what I am," Ivins said rapidly.

"Just be cooperative," Kemp advised him. "And try not to say anything."

Kemp arrived at the Hilton within an hour. Diane was calm. Bruce was not. "What's happening to me? What's happening to my family?" He was agitated, and kept gesturing and repeating the questions. With Kemp now in the room, Inspector Dellafera again explained to Bruce and Diane the purpose of the search, how long it was expected to last, and that they were free to leave the hotel if they wished. Kemp tried to soothe his panicked client: We don't know yet what the search means. We'll have plenty of time to sort it all out. A few minutes later investigators handed over to Ivins medication that he had requested from his house—Ambien, a sleeping aid; Celexa, an antidepressant; and Valium, an antianxiety drug. It was shortly after 10 P.M.

Andy, who would turn twenty-four in a few days, was meeting in a separate room down the hallway with two other investigators who were seeking his cooperation—and any incriminating information he might have about his father. They informed him that the Amerithrax task force was offering a reward of up to $2.5 million for information leading to the conviction of the anthrax killer.[14] Andy began shouting. He loved his father and was fiercely loyal to him. After the interview he told his parents and Kemp that the investigators referred to his father as a murderer.[15]

Earlier in the evening Andy had thought of his sister, Amanda, who lived in an apartment in Hagerstown, Maryland, about thirty miles northwest of Frederick. They had not communicated in any way since the investigators descended and he had no way of knowing what was going on with her. Andy sent his twin a text: "Call me when they leave." He had guessed right: Two female investigators, one from the FBI and the other from the Postal Inspection Service, were questioning Amanda.

As Amanda recounted, the investigators first described their interest in solving a potential mail fraud case in the Hagerstown area. After what seemed like a half hour or more, the subject shifted: Did she know about the anthrax attacks of 2001? "I need my lawyer," she said, recalling that months earlier her father had given her the business card of Richard Bricken, who was then representing him, with instructions to call Bricken if any investigator ever contacted her.

The investigators told her about the Amerithrax reward money. Amanda could best avoid trouble, one of them said, if she told the truth. They asked if she knew about her father's decades-long obsession with Kappa Kappa Gamma. She did not. When did she first realize that her father was depressed? What medications did he take? Did her father or the family ever travel to the Northeast United States?

The postal inspector displayed five photographs. These, she said, were the people murdered by the anthrax killer. They were real victims. And they and their loved ones deserved justice.[16]

The cars and the house in Frederick all came up negative for anthrax. Yet the search provided insight into Bruce Ivins's tendencies—and his impulse to implicate even his closest colleagues in the anthrax deaths. Among the items recovered was a printout of an accusatory e-mail that Ivins had written and sent to himself on November 19, 2005, using two different screen names. In this e-mail Ivins listed twelve points in support of a theory that his former colleagues Mara Linscott and Patricia Fellows, both of whom had obsessed him for years, might have perpetrated the letter attacks to exact revenge on him and to boost their own careers.

Ivins's accusations showed his chameleon-like quality, the darker side of "Bruce being Bruce." On the same day that he printed out his twelve-point, self-addressed rant, he sent three friendly e-mails to Fellows, who had continued to work in the Frederick area after leaving her position with the Army.[17]

In an e-mail to Fellows a few weeks after the November 1, 2007, search, Ivins once again fingered John Ezzell, the senior microbiologist who had served as USAMRIID's chief liaison with the FBI. Ivins alleged that Ezzell knew "how to make anthrax into a bioweapon, he's made millions off the letters. . . . The rest of us are trying to scrape by." (In the 1990s Ezzell did produce the powdered anthrax used for approved experiments, and the material was irradiated to render it nonlethal to humans. Ezzell said that he derived no outside compensation from any of his official duties, including his work for the FBI.)

The search of Ivins's home raised other concerns about what he could yet be up to. Investigators found Internet monitoring software and other equipment that would allow him to identify eavesdropping devices. The search also found both handwritten and MapQuest directions to the new residence of Mara Linscott, his former lab tech. Having in the past driven more than ten hours round-trip to drop off gifts for Linscott in Ithaca, New

York, he now appeared ready to visit her near Providence, Rhode Island, where she was working as a physician.

It also turned out that Ivins, who had once disparaged his middle brother as a "gun nut," was himself well armed.[18] Beginning in fall 2004 and continuing over the next two years, he had bought a Beretta 21 Bobcat, a concealable 22-caliber pistol; a Glock 27, an easy-to-conceal 40-caliber weapon used by police as a backup; and a Glock 34, a 9-caliber long-barrel handgun. Ivins also had bought an extra barrel for the Glock 27. (Investigators wondered why he would need the extra barrel. Was it to be a replacement that could foil efforts to trace bullets fired with the first barrel?)[19] It was obvious that the basement had been used as a firing range, with telephone books arranged to absorb the bullets. Ivins also owned three types of stun guns and a supply of pepper spray. Among the stun guns he preferred the Taser model, because it could propel a dart into a target from the longest distance.[20]

The family members were allowed to reenter their home the next afternoon. Ivins made no secret of the search, lamenting to colleagues about the abuse he said had been heaped upon his two adult children. Word of the search and of the investigators' questioning of Amanda and Andy Ivins circulated among the USAMRIID staff scientists, many of whom sympathized with their beleaguered colleague and his family.

Army officials now barred Ivins from all the hot suites where anthrax or other deadly agents were stored. Yet none of these developments leaked to the news media. Soon after the search, Ivins called Paul Kemp and told him that he was buying a T-Mobile cell phone, solely for the purpose of communicating with him. He said he believed that any other phone at his disposal was bugged.

A few days later, by which time all the family cars had been returned, Bruce, Diane, Amanda, and Andy Ivins drove to Rockville to meet with Kemp. Although Kemp saw no potential wrongdoing on the part of the twins, he recommended that separate attorneys be retained to represent them. On the way back the family stopped for a late lunch, sharing a booth at a Red

Robin diner in Germantown. The conversation was strained. Bruce ordered a sandwich and ate little of it, staring in silence.[21]

What Paul Kemp had first envisioned as a "witness hand-holding case" now looked far more serious. He scheduled a meeting with Kenneth Kohl, the prosecutor who had told Bruce Ivins in writing on April 9, 2007, "You are not a target of this investigation." On November 19, 2007, Kemp, accompanied by colleague Thomas DeGonia II, visited Kohl in Washington and said he was surprised by the search warrant and the entire Amerithrax operation on November 1.[22]

As both Kohl and Kemp were aware, the prosecution was under no obligation to explain a change of heart toward Ivins or to declare that he was now a target. Kohl gave Kemp his personal opinion, that Ivins was not at that point in time seen as the anthrax killer. But there was concern, Kohl said, about Ivins's truthfulness. Kohl was alluding to investigators' belief that on April 10, 2002, Ivins had deliberately obstructed the task force by disobeying the instructions for preparing his sample of anthrax from the RMR-1029 batch.[23] Now Ivins would have to account for his actions.

TWENTY-SIX

NOT A SCINTILLA OF EVIDENCE

On the night of Wednesday, November 7, 2007, a handful of investigators quietly took up positions around the home of Bruce Ivins. In a few hours, sometime before dawn, a trash truck would arrive for the first neighborhood pickup since the major search carried out six nights earlier. The investigators were there, as they had been on other trash nights, to retrieve whatever Ivins might decide to throw away. Ed Montooth was pleased that he had no shortage of volunteers for duty that would be cold and tedious.

It was now just after 1 A.M. on Thursday. For the first time that the investigators had observed on a trash night, the front door opened and Bruce Ivins came outside and stood for a while in long underwear. He faced the two-lane street and, just a few yards beyond it, the darkened expanse of Fort Detrick. Ivins looked around, verified that his own and his neighbors' curbside trash cans remained unemptied, and returned inside. A few minutes later, the truck from Allied Waste Services arrived, took the trash, and headed north on Military Road. An agent hailed the crew with his badge—and lifted out the just collected household materials.

Seven minutes after the truck had cleared his house, Ivins reemerged under the porch light, still wearing his long underwear and still on the lookout. He walked to the street, verified that the trash can was empty, and pulled it back up into his driveway. He then turned and walked back toward the street. He checked his neighbor's can. It, too, was empty. Then he went out onto the empty street, peering straight into the hedgelike canopy of evergreens that line the perimeter of Fort Detrick. Just a few feet from Ivins was the FBI's closest spotter, Agent James Griffin Jr., who stood frozen against one of the fir trees, hands glued to his sides. About a minute later, Ivins returned inside.

The agent's ability to remain unseen saved what could be an important investigative edge: Ivins had no inkling the FBI had grabbed the trash that he was so focused upon. His interest in the fate of this particular load was clearly unusual. The FBI would conduct a total of eighteen "trash covers" at the house, along with numerous other twenty-four-hour surveillances; this was the only time that Ivins ever came outside to check any of the cans.[1]

As investigators sifted carefully through the recovered trash, they found two items that might account for Ivins's odd behavior: *Gödel, Escher, Bach: An Eternal Golden Braid*, a sprawling book that discusses DNA coding and coded messages within messages;[2] and "The Linguistics of DNA," a lengthy scientific article written by David B. Searls and published in 1992, comparing the grammatical structures of the genetic code and common English.[3] Neither the book—extensively dog-eared and with underlined passages and Ivins's notations in the margins—nor the article had drawn the attention of the investigators who searched inside the house the week before.

The task force had long suspected that the nine boldfaced Ts and As in the photocopied letter sent to both the *New York Post* and anchorman Tom Brokaw conveyed some sort of coded message:

09-11-01
THIS IS NEXT
TAKE PENACILIN NOW

DEATH TO AMERICA
DEATH TO ISRAEL
ALLAH IS GREAT

And now the investigators had just watched Bruce Ivins covertly dispose of literature focusing on coded messages.

"Holy shit," Montooth said. The evidence against Ivins appeared to be building.[4]

The discovery of *Gödel, Escher, Bach* gave Agent Lawrence Alexander an idea. Given Ivins's fixation with Nancy Haigwood, perhaps Ivins would open up about *GEB* during a face-to-face meeting with her. It helped that Ivins and Haigwood had discussed the book many years earlier, soon after its publication. After being Ivins's victim for so long, Alexander told her, this would be an opportunity to turn the tables.

Haigwood agreed and asked Ivins if he would like to catch up over coffee or lunch the next time she was in the Washington area on business. Ivins said yes. Alexander's plan was for Haigwood to engage Ivins in conversation about *Gödel, Escher, Bach*. Once they were trading observations about its brilliance, Haigwood, wearing a hidden microphone, would make a boast of sorts. She would say she had applied *GEB*'s message-within-a-message paradigm to analyze the photocopied letter sent to Tom Brokaw and the *New York Post*. And she had found what appeared to be coded messages. Amid the repartee, perhaps Ivins would drop his guard.

Haigwood wanted to do it—but she was worried that the encounter could spin out of control. Alexander assured her that agents would be in the restaurant, and they would be armed. She was rattled by the prospect, however remote, of guns being drawn. Before she could make a final commitment, she told Alexander, she needed to talk it over with her two teenage sons. They advised her not to do it. Haigwood, citing a complication, told Ivins that she would not be able to make the trip east after all.[5]

Bruce Ivins grew up in a household dominated by his violent mother, whose beatings of Bruce's father, Randall Ivins, were an open secret to acquaintances in Lebanon, Ohio. Mary Ivins once summoned a physician neighbor: "Ralph, come down here. I've killed Randall." *(Reprinted with permission from the archives of the Warren County Historical Society, Lebanon, Ohio.)*

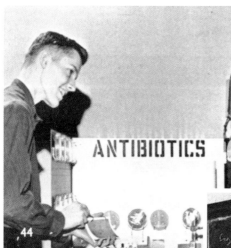

As far back as his school years in Lebanon, Bruce Ivins distinguished himself in science. He earned consistent As in biology and chemistry participated with other top-performing teenagers in a summer science program at Ohio State University. Ivins is shown with his exhibit at Lebanon High's science fair in 1963, during his junior year. *(Trilobite, Lebanon High School)*

Though he was a high-achieving student at Lebanon High School, Bruce Ivins struggled to fit in. Said one teacher, "Some of the questions he would ask would cause some of the other students to turn their heads. He was different." *(Trilobite, Lebanon High School)*

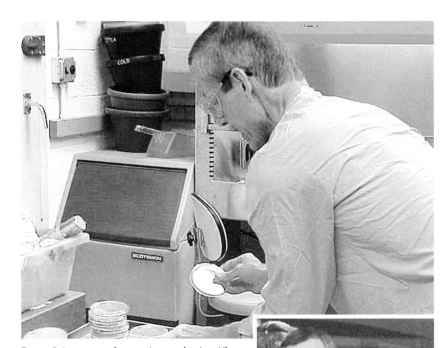

Bruce Ivins coveted attention and scientific distinction, and the anthrax attacks provided him with both. On November 14, 2001, Ivins widely e-mailed this photo of himself handling what he said were cultures of "the now infamous 'Ames' strain of Bacillus anthracis." *(USAMRIID)*

On March 14, 2003, the Defense Department awarded Ivins and three colleagues its top honor for civilian personnel, marking a turnabout: Until the September 11 hijackings and the anthrax attacks, the entire anthrax vaccine program—and with it Ivins's hopes for a new vaccine he co-invented—was at risk. *(USAMRIID/U.S. Army)*

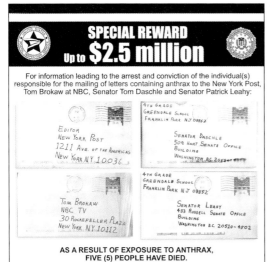

SPECIAL REWARD
Up to **$2.5 million**

For information leading to the arrest and conviction of the individual(s) responsible for the mailing of letters containing anthrax to the New York Post, Tom Brokaw at NBC, Senator Tom Daschle and Senator Patrick Leahy:

EDITOR
NEW YORK POST
1211 AVE. OF THE AMERICAS
NEW YORK NY 10036

4TH GRADE
GREENDALE SCHOOL
FRANKLIN PARK NJ 08852

SENATOR DASCHLE
509 HART SENATE OFFICE
BUILDING
WASHINGTON DC 20510

TOM BROKAW
NBC TV
30 ROCKEFELLER PLAZA
NEW YORK NY 10112

4TH GRADE
GREENDALE SCHOOL
FRANKLIN PARK NJ 08852

SENATOR LEAHY
433 RUSSELL SENATE OFFICE
BUILDING
WASHINGTON DC 20510-4502

AS A RESULT OF EXPOSURE TO ANTHRAX, FIVE (5) PEOPLE HAVE DIED.

The person responsible for these deaths...
 • Likely has a scientific background/work history which may include a specific familiarity with anthrax
 • Has a level of comfort in and around the Trenton, NJ area due to present or prior association

Anyone having information, contact **America's Most Wanted** at **1-800-CRIME TV** or the **FBI** via e-mail at **amerithrax@fbi.gov**

All information will be held in strict confidence. Reward payment will be made in accordance with the conditions of Postal Service Reward Notice 296, dated February 2000. Source of reward funds: U.S. Postal Service and FBI $2,000,000; ADVO, Inc. $500,000.

The U.S. Postal Service and the FBI faced steep challenges in cracking the case of the deadly anthrax letter attacks. The government offered a huge cash reward for information leading to the arrest and conviction of whoever was responsible. *(U.S. Postal Service)*

A decontamination crew in hazardous materials suits at the Senate Hart Office Building, November 7, 2001. The nine-story structure, work site for half the members of the Senate and hundreds of staffers, was closed for three months because of anthrax that spilled from the letter addressed to Majority Leader Tom Daschle. *(Stephen Jaffe/AFP/Getty Images)*

LEFT: A schism developed within the Amerithrax task force over the investigation's years-long focus on Steven Hatfill. Senior postal inspector Thomas Dellafera (left) and FBI agent Lawrence Alexander struggled along with other investigators to turn the probe toward another scientist: Bruce Ivins. *(Jim Carpenter)*

RIGHT: Beginning in December 2002, the FBI searched and drained ponds in forested land above Frederick, Maryland, seeking materials used to prepare the anthrax letters. On January 9, 2003, FBI director Robert Mueller led bureau officials who told Senators Tom Daschle and Patrick Leahy, targets of the attacks, that bloodhounds had traced the scent of both Steven Hatfill and anthrax from the letters to one of the ponds. *(Associated Press)*

Steven Hatfill declared his innocence to a gathering of reporters in August 2002. Hatfill was vilified in numerous media accounts, including columns written by Nicholas D. Kristof of the *New York Times*. Hatfill ultimately sued both the FBI and the Justice Department, alleging that leaks of investigative information had violated his right to privacy, and he won a $5.82 million settlement from the government in June 2008. *(Associated Press)*

It was in a mailbox at 10 Nassau Street, Princeton, New Jersey, that investigators found anthrax spores matching those sent in the letter attacks. An office of Kappa Kappa Gamma, the sorority that obsessed Bruce Ivins, is located on the fourth floor of the building almost directly behind and overlooking the mailboxes. *(© 2011 Beverly Schaefer)*

On February 5, 2003, Secretary of State Colin Powell argued at the United Nations for confronting Iraq. "Less than a teaspoon" of anthrax, Powell said, had closed the U.S. Senate, forced hundreds to undergo medical treatment, and killed two postal workers. Though Powell did not directly accuse Iraq of perpetrating the letter attacks, his presentation invited the public to make the connection. *(Reuters/Ray Stubblebine)*

The United States Army Medical Research Institute of Infectious Diseases, where Bruce Ivins was hired as a civilian scientist in December 1980. As a senior Army official conceded in writing to the author in September 2008, the service at no point sought to evaluate Ivins's mental fitness to handle anthrax. *(USAMRIID/Getty Images)*

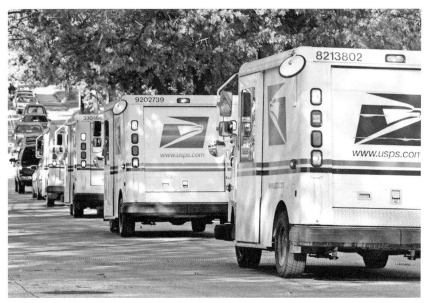

Colleagues pay final respects to Joseph P. Curseen Jr., one of two mail handlers in Washington, D.C., who died from anthrax in October 2001. Though congressional staffers were given Cipro the day the anthrax-laced letter to Senator Tom Daschle was opened, postal workers were overlooked. *(Associated Press)*

Nancy Haigwood first met Bruce Ivins in the mid-1970s at the University of North Carolina while she was a doctoral student and advisor to the sorority Kappa Kappa Gamma and he was a bacterial researcher. Ivins stole Haigwood's lab notebook, continued to torment her anonymously, and told a psychiatrist he had planned how to murder her. In early 2002, Haigwood alerted the FBI that Ivins might be the anthrax killer. *(Kimberli Ransom Photography)*

Joseph P. Curseen Jr., forty-seven, worked at the U.S. Postal Service's Brentwood plant in Washington, D.C. It was at Brentwood, through which all mail addressed to members of Congress is routed, that Curseen was exposed to anthrax that leaked from a letter, perhaps the one intended for Senator Tom Daschle. Curseen died on October 22, 2001. *(Reuters/William Philpott)*

Popular with colleagues, Thomas L. Morris Jr. was a twenty-eight-year postal employee who contracted inhalational anthrax at the Brentwood plant in Washington, D.C. Morris, fifty-five, was one of five Washington-area mail handlers stricken by inhalational anthrax. Three of the others survived. Morris died on October 21, 2001. *(Associated Press)*

Ottilie Lundgren, a ninety-four-year-old resident of rural Oxford, Connecticut, became the fifth and final victim of the anthrax attacks on November 21, 2001. No spores were found in her home or belongings. However, sorting machines at a regional postal facility in Connecticut were found to be contaminated, raising the likelihood that Lundgren was infected by a cross-contaminated piece of mail. *(Associated Press)*

Kathy Nguyen, a sixty-one-year-old hospital stockroom worker in New York City, died of inhalational anthrax on October 31, 2001. No anthrax was found in Nguyen's apartment or where she worked—evoking expressions of fear from health authorities that even the most minuscule amount of the bacterium could be spread by the mail system and kill. *(FBI)*

On October 5, 2001, Robert Stevens, a photo editor in South Florida for the parent company of the *National Enquirer*, became the first person in the United States to die from inhalational anthrax in more than two decades. Tests quickly found that Stevens was killed by the Ames strain—a type of anthrax used for laboratory research but found only once in the wild—indicating to two scientists who led the testing that a bioterrorism event had occurred. *(Getty Images)*

As the holidays passed and 2008 dawned, Ivins continued to complain to colleagues and friends about the investigative scrutiny. He still bristled at the questioning the previous fall of Amanda and Andy, saying that investigators had tried to turn the twins against him. He vilified Agent Alexander, who had frisked him for concealed weapons before the drive to the hotel in Frederick, calling him "the gay Black guy." (Alexander is African American and the father of three children; he is heterosexual.)

In Ivins's telling, he and his colleagues at USAMRIID were loyal government servants—brutalized by clueless investigators hell-bent to close the case. Ivins's complaints about the investigation elicited sympathy from many of his acquaintances. They struggled to understand how it was possible that the man they knew as nothing but gentle could be a target of the anthrax investigation.[6]

Thanks largely to the painstaking work of Alexander, the new leadership of the task force appreciated that this one-dimensional portrait of Ivins was in fact a mirage. His vindictive obsession with Kappa Kappa Gamma, his homicidal impulses toward both Nancy Haigwood and Mara Linscott, his manipulation of the emotions of strangers—including a mother whose son had died in a college hazing incident—these were not the actions of a gentle, harmless man.

Montooth, along with prosecutors Kenneth Kohl and Rachel Carlson Lieber, who had recently been brought on the case, believed that it would be important for jurors at trial to see for themselves the well-camouflaged side of Bruce Ivins. In his own words. They arranged for a new interview with Ivins and his lawyers—the first such session since the house search. The interview would be led by Ed Montooth and Vince Lisi, whom Ivins had not met.

The pair prepared for the interview with the hope that this would be the first of several conversations with Ivins. Yet for all they knew, Ivins's lawyers could decide there was too much risk for their client and move to cut off this or any future interviews. Their minimum goal, the investigators agreed, was to coax Ivins to admit at least some of the conduct that could undermine the

sunny image that he had so successfully manufactured. Lisi
would take the lead, with Montooth assuming a more detached,
senior-figure role. Their hope was to develop a connection between Ivins and Lisi. Prosecutors Kohl and Lieber would sit in as
observers.

On Wednesday, January 16, 2008, Ivins and his lawyers, Paul
Kemp and Tom DeGonia, arrived for the interview at the U.S. attorney's office in Washington. Following introductions, which
highlighted the extensive crime-fighting experience of the two
new agents, Montooth framed the context: "We're new to this.
We're obviously bringing a new perspective to this—but there's
things we just can't get our arms around."

Lisi began gently, asking Ivins about his "interest" in Kappa
Kappa Gamma. "You don't understand," Ivins said. "It's not an
interest. It's an *obsession*."

Ivins explained—at length. It began in the 1960s, when he
asked a coed for a date at the University of Cincinnati and she
declined. She was a member of the sorority. He then started scanning the school newspaper for mentions of Kappas and regularly
spent time observing the campus sorority house. In the late
1970s he began compiling a list of "dozens and dozens and
dozens" of Kappa chapters throughout the Eastern United
States. Part of his research involved copying contact information
from telephone directories at the Library of Congress. He visited
Kappa sorority houses at the University of North Carolina in
Chapel Hill, at the University of Virginia in Charlottesville, at
the University of Maryland in College Park, at West Virginia
University in Morgantown, at the University of Tennessee in
Knoxville. He was interested in Kappa's presence at the University of Pennsylvania, but when he tried to call there he found out
the chapter was closed.

Lisi was listening attentively, emotionlessly, saying only
enough to keep the dialogue flowing. A few minutes later he
asked Ivins if he had visited the Kappa chapter at Princeton University. "Oh no," Ivins said. "No Ivy League schools." But what
about Ivins's interest in the University of Pennsylvania chapter?
"Penn's an Ivy League?" (Well into the conversation Montooth's

cell phone vibrated. It was his sister on the line and he excused himself from the room to take the call. Their father, the former high school teacher, had just died. Grieving would have to wait; Montooth returned directly to the interview.)

Ivins was animated, recalling more and more precise details. In the late 1970s and early 1980s, he had escalated his vendetta against the sorority: He used something to "jimmy" open a window at the Kappa house in Chapel Hill. After wandering among the cabinets and drawers he found the KKG cipher—the manual that could decode the sorority's Book of Ritual. He stole both the cipher and some ritual-related materials. A few years later, he said, he had planned and executed another burglary. This time it was the Kappa house in Morgantown. Again, he broke in by prying open a ground-floor window. Inside, he found and stole the sorority's prized Book of Ritual, the storehouse of Kappa Kappa Gamma's passwords and secrets.[7]

Lisi, knowing the correct answers to many of the questions he was posing, tried another: What became of this purloined Book of Ritual? Ivins obliged. He copied the entire book, he said, and he returned it by U.S. mail to the Kappa chapter in West Virginia. He included a phony personal note with the book, saying that although another fraternity brother stole the book, he wanted to return it to its rightful owners. In the aftermath of the September 11 attacks, Ivins said, he decided to throw away all of his long-treasured KKG artifacts, including the Book of Ritual, the cipher, and the list of the sorority's locations.

Only once, Ivins said, had a Kappa representative contacted him. It was through a letter thanking him for his $150 donation to the sorority, which he made in memory of Caitlin Hammaren, the KKG member killed in April 2007 by the gunman at Virginia Tech.

Within the previous year, Ivins had described in some detail his adversarial relationship with the sorority on a Web site called AboveTopSecret.com. "Kappas are noted for being lovely, highly intelligent campus leaders," Ivins wrote under one of his pseudonyms, Goldenphoenix. "Unfortunately, they labeled me as an enemy decades ago, and I can only abide by their 'Fatwah' on me. I like individual Kappas enormously, and love being around them. I never choose an enemy, but they've been after me since the 1960s, and REALLY after me since the late 1970s. At one time in my life, I knew more about KKG than any non-Kappa that had ever lived." [8]

The interview by this point had exceeded the investigators' original goals. Now Lisi steered the conversation toward Nancy Haigwood, whom Ivins had met in the mid-1970s at the University of North Carolina. Ivins wound up confirming everything she had suspected.

Yes, he stole Haigwood's lab notebook—holding all of the materials upon which her pursuit of a doctoral degree depended. Yes, he deposited the notebook in a U.S. mailbox on or near the campus in Chapel Hill. Yes, he informed Haigwood where the notebook could be found, possibly by way of an anonymous note. Yes, he anonymously vandalized the sidewalk, fence, and vehicle outside Haigwood's home in Gaithersburg, Maryland. Yes, he wrote the letter to the Frederick newspaper in Haigwood's name, defending hazing by college sororities. Yes, he opened one of his post office boxes in the name of Haigwood's husband, Carl Scandella. Yes, he bought advertisements in *Mother Jones* and *Rolling Stone* offering, in the name of Carla Sander, Kappa Kappa Gamma's closest-held secrets. Yes, he stole Patricia Fellows's computer password by watching her log in at USAMRIID, enabling him to hack into her e-mails. Yes, he used an array of pseudonyms, including an e-mail address called Bigsky, under which he sent leering e-mails to Mara Linscott. He said he stopped this when he learned that Linscott, fearing she was being stalked, was about to bring in the police. And yes, he subscribed to *American Family Association Journal* (the evangelical publication that publicized the filing of a lawsuit in connection with events at the Greendale Baptist Academy). The investigators did not point out that the letters to Senators Daschle and Leahy carried a return address that seemed to allude to the school and the fourth grader who was at the center of the controversy that sparked the lawsuit.

Ivins commented on a few other subjects of high interest to

the investigators: His wife, he said, knew nothing about his decades-long fixation on Kappa Kappa Gamma. He had pursued the obsession while maintaining what amounted to a dual existence for the entirety of their marriage.

The interview was halted after about two hours because one of Ivins's lawyers had another appointment. Ed Montooth was delighted with the outcome: Ivins had described in great detail conduct that completely belied the chipper, one-dimensional image familiar to colleagues and others who dealt with him.

The investigative team prepared even more extensively for a follow-up interview that Ivins and Kemp agreed to, which was to take place a month later, in February 2008. A dozen or more of the investigators gathered, for hours at a time, to sort through what questions needed to be asked, how to ask them, and in what general sequence. (One FBI agent and a postal inspector were deployed to Lebanon, Ohio, where they visited the basement of what used to be the family drugstore, searching for anything related to the letter attacks that Ivins may have returned to stash.)[9] Montooth invited a psychiatrist, Dr. Gregory Saathoff, to the meetings for advice on how Ivins might react to certain questioning.

The careful planning paid off. As the next interview unfolded on February 13, the investigators elicited more revealing details from Ivins, including his obsession with bondage, which he traced back to when he was five or six years old, and he would place blindfolds on his teddy bear or other stuffed animals. Over time, he said, the obsession had taken on a sexual focus. Yes, he had posted anonymous Internet messages regarding USAMRIID's work on the anthrax vaccine to "stir the pot," he said. Lisi steered the conversation to the Daschle letter. Ivins recounted his original analysis of the spores, whose quality, he said, indicated they had been grown in a laboratory, not a garage. Without prompting, Ivins volunteered that one of his former colleagues, Patricia Fellows, "was the spore queen."

Stealing the Book of Ritual and being able to decode Kappa Kappa Gamma's secrets, Ivins said, gave him a sense of "power." Ivins also told the investigators that, to the extent she ever knew about them, his wife viewed his long nighttime drives as a form of therapy. On some of those occasions, he told her that he was at the lab. She never, Ivins said, questioned where he had gone or what he might have been doing. Her unawareness of his activities appeared to eliminate Diane Ivins as a potential alibi witness for solo drives that her husband may have made to Princeton.

The results of their first and second interviews with him indicated that Montooth and Lisi had succeeded in forging a rapport of sorts with Ivins. At some points during the sessions, Ivins would resemble a disturbed child, gesticulating and rocking determinedly in his chair. While Montooth questioned Ivins politely but persistently, Lisi reacted with open-minded understanding to whatever Ivins might say. In turn, Ivins became more forthcoming with the two senior FBI agents than he had been with other investigators.

Montooth was struck by Ivins's disciplined sense of purpose, not least in his methodical, unhurried ransacking of the two Kappa Kappa Gamma houses. In Montooth's experience most burglars break in, grab what they want, and flee as quickly as possible. They fear getting caught. Ivins, however, had admitted that he'd spent about an hour roaming the Kappa house in North Carolina and a half hour inside the West Virginia house.

When Montooth took stock of the back-to-back interviews and the other evidence already in hand he saw a highly educated professional who for decades operated in a cold, calculating fashion—a dangerous man whose dark side was hidden from those who thought they knew him well.[10]

———

Ivins's ongoing complaints about the investigation continued to elicit the sympathy of many of his acquaintances, among them Bill Hirt, who in 1975 had been best man at Bruce and Diane's wedding. In January 2008, Hirt and his wife, Ann, stopped for a brief visit while driving through Frederick. They returned to their home in Ohio shaken by the condition of their old friend. To them, Bruce now seemed about eighty years old.[11]

In a follow-up e-mail, Ivins thanked the Hirts for their loyal support. Writing from one of his nongovernment addresses on Saturday, February 2, 2008, he recounted at length some of his troubles: He described his mental illness and his deep dependence on a former lab technician whom he did not name (Mara Linscott), and referred, indirectly, to factors that might have put him in jeopardy with the federal investigation:

> It's been very difficult, and gotten more so recently, ever since I developed Major Depressive Disorder in the mid to late 90s. I had my first really bad episode when a technician left to go to medical school. She was quite honestly my confidante on everything, my therapist and friend. When she went to buffalo to medical school it was crushing. There are a whole series of signs and symptoms for the disorder, and I displayed everyone or [sic] them.
>
> You honestly don't feel like life is worth living and some times may even prepare to end it because of the mental, emotional and spiritual torture you go through. Fortunately in 2000, I started getting psychiatric help and antidepressant medicines which brought me back to a functional human within several weeks.

Ivins referred to the fact that his two longtime friends had been questioned recently by the federal investigators. Later in his e-mail, Ivins appeared to refer, indirectly, to omissions or inaccuracies in his official lab notes that were causing suspicion among the investigators.

"I am neither a mass murderer nor a terrorist—it's just not in me—but I admit to making errors (like notebook entry errors, math errors, forgetting entries) at my desk and I have screwed up in the lab." Ivins added, "my memory is going the way of my father's—which is south very fast. I'd never deliberately mislead investigators or try to impede their investigation." [12]

Unfortunately for him, Ivins had lost the asymmetric edge in knowledge that had enabled him to prevail in past schemes. The scientific advances made by the investigation had toppled any original assumptions he may have had about the traceability of RMR-1029, and now he had reason to suspect that this was going to put him in great legal peril.

————

The Amerithrax task force was further boosted by the arrival of the second prosecutor on the case—intense, fast-talking assistant U.S. attorney Rachel Lieber. A graduate of Villanova University and Georgetown law school, with experience in working homicide cases, Lieber was a quick study and she worked to build relationships with investigators and defense attorneys alike.

Kenneth Kohl's day-to-day availability, meanwhile, had been diluted by his assignment to another major case—a happy coincidence, actually, because it was obvious by late 2007 that he and Vince Lisi were at odds. Although Kohl had earlier sided with Agent Lawrence Alexander and the other investigators who wanted to more thoroughly scrutinize Bruce Ivins, Kohl's instinct now was to slow down. After having fought internally against prosecuting Steven Hatfill, Kohl was wary of moving too soon against Ivins. Lisi was chafing at Kohl's less-than-full-time engagement with the anthrax case, and he believed the evidence justified moving forward to resolve the questions about Ivins.

Lieber wanted to keep the investigators' momentum going. In early January 2008, she convened a day-long meeting of all the Amerithrax investigators to review where the case stood. What would the FBI's experts be able to say under oath about certain evidence? What holes needed to be filled? Lieber guided the conversation toward setting deadlines for finishing all the remaining work—propelling the case on a path toward criminal charges.

Lieber and the lead investigators had concluded that Bruce Ivins was the top suspect and that Steven Hatfill did not appear to be the perpetrator. Yet while the investigation may have been done with Hatfill, the former Army researcher and his lawyer were not prepared to meekly fade away.

Within the same federal courthouse on Constitution Avenue where the grand jury was reviewing evidence from the refocused criminal investigation, Hatfill's lawsuit against the government was gaining force. The lawsuit continued to be presided over by

U.S. District Court judge Reggie Walton, who earlier had decried the many damaging leaks of investigative details to the news media. It was Walton who had allowed Hatfill's lawyers to pursue the origins of the leaks by questioning journalists and dozens of federal officials under oath, including former attorney general John Ashcroft and FBI director Robert Mueller.

At a hearing on January 11, 2008, the Hatfill case was about to get much more painful for the government. What appeared on Judge Walton's docket was titled innocuously a "status conference" regarding the Hatfill lawsuit. It proved far from perfunctory. One of Hatfill's lawyers, Mark A. Grannis, informed Walton that recent sworn depositions had identified three federal officials who anonymously leaked investigative details harmful to his client.

"Some of the most damaging information leaked in this case [came] straight out of the U.S. attorney's office," Grannis said, before naming the leakers: Roscoe Howard, who from 2001 to 2004 served as United States attorney for the District of Columbia; Daniel S. Seikaly, who served as Howard's Criminal Division chief; and a former media spokesman for the FBI, Edwin Cogswell. Journalists had revealed Howard, Seikaly, and Cogswell as sources after the three men released them from their earlier pledges of confidentiality.[13]

Hatfill's lawyers were eager to push the case to trial. The Justice Department wanted none of it. A department lawyer, Elizabeth J. Shapiro, asked Judge Walton to direct both sides to try to resolve the case out of court. A private settlement would avert an embarrassing public spectacle for the government. Walton told the attorneys to pursue mediation over the next two months—but he went on to say that he expected that a trial on the lawsuit could begin in his courtroom within the year.[14]

The judge delivered a more devastating message to the Justice Department at a hearing the next month. On February 19, 2008, Walton—who had unique access to all the sworn testimony in the lawsuit, along with confidential FBI summaries about the ongoing criminal investigation—declared, "There is not a scintilla of evidence that would indicate that Dr. Hatfill had anything to do with this." [15] With one simple statement from the judge, the man who for years had been branded as the likely anthrax killer was all but officially pronounced innocent.

———

No matter what happened, Amanda Ivins knew that she would always love her father. But she was frightened. There was so much to take in, and it was all so hard to understand. Her father's secret amending of his will. The traumatic night of November 1, when investigators had placed before her eyes pictures of the five people killed by the anthrax letter attacks. The removal by the federal task force of her twin brother and her parents from their home in Frederick for a top-to-bottom search. The suspicions of culpability her father had shared with her about several present and former colleagues. In their conversations in recent months Bruce Ivins had returned repeatedly to his misgivings about Patricia Fellows and Mara Linscott, scientists whose integrity and decency Amanda had never before doubted. As a young girl she had been to Fellows's house and met her children. Mara Linscott's older sister was Diane Ivins's best friend and had been Amanda's swim coach and occasional math tutor. And yet her father, the man whose judgment she had always relied upon, was connecting Fellows and Linscott with awful crimes.

Now Amanda was learning for the first time some of the details of her sixty-one-year-old father's obsession with, of all things, a college sorority. It shocked her. Amanda was questioning not her devotion to her father, but what else she might not know about him.

She waited until they were alone in the car one day. As they drove to lunch, she asked the question: "Did you do this?"

"I've never cheated on my wife. I've never cheated on my taxes. And I didn't do this, Amanda."

Later at a restaurant Amanda asked, "Why do they think you did this?"

"I don't know." [16]

TWENTY-SEVEN

CRAZY BRUCE

The thrust of the investigation was now unmistakable. The FBI was watching Ivins, often twenty-four hours a day, and ever since the November 2007 search of his house, the Army had continued to ban him from working in the hot suites, relegating him to handling nonlethal pathogens. Ivins was still taking a battery of powerful prescriptions—pills for depression and anxiety, pills to help him sleep. He was also drinking heavily at home—vodka, mixed with juice. And he remained fixated on Patricia Fellows and Mara Linscott.

The two former lab technicians (along with all the other scientists who had worked alongside Ivins) had been interviewed extensively by the Amerithrax investigators, who shared with them some of the relevant details. When Fellows confronted Ivins about one such matter—his backstabbing speculations about her and Linscott as perpetrators of the anthrax attacks—he blamed another side of himself. This, he wrote to her in an e-mail on March 11, 2008, was " 'Crazy Bruce,' who surfaces periodically as paranoid, severely depressed and ridden with incredible anxiety."[1]

Ivins elaborated the next day in another e-mail: "I hope that someday people can understand mental illness . . . that people can understand that we don't want to hurt people. . . . I'm sorry if working with me was so ugly and regrettable and disgusting that you had to write to others about how bad a person I was. . . . I never would have deliberately hurt you. However it seems as though I have been selected as the blood sacrifice for this whole thing."[2] Ivins struck the same morbid tone in a flurry of e-mails the night of March 12, 2008, to Ann and Bill Hirt, his old friends from Cincinnati, appealing to what he knew were their liberal sentiments:

> I have this terrible, dreaded feeling that I have been selected for the blood sacrifice, like we saw with Mrs. Weaver at Ruby Ridge, and with women and children at Waco, and with Richard Jewel[l] in Atlanta. I would jump off a bridge before hurting innocent people like those in your families. I wanted my life to be dedicated to helping humanity, but now it seems that the people in power have determined that I must suffer and die in order to appease the Bush/Cheney/Rumsfeld types. It used to be that talking about freedom and rights and liberties was considered patriotic. Not anymore. I think that Patrick Henry would be considered right along side Al Quaida.

Ivins added, in the same e-mail:

> I don't have a killer bone in my body, but that doesn't make any difference. It doesn't matter who they sacrifice, just so long as they sacrifice somebody—and I think that I'm that somebody. Please know that whatever happens, there is love in my heart for people and for our planet. I hope that evil will never triumph, and that goodness, mercy, love, virtue, and willing sacrifice will save our nation from those who would change it into another "Third Reich."

In one of several subsequent e-mails to the Hirts that night, Ivins wrote: "The investigators have selected a blood sacrifice, and I truly think that it's me. . . . I'm not happy about it, but I guess I have to accept it." He concluded at 10:03 P.M.: "I may have to be sacrificed to appease the political God of Revenge. I'm ready. When you and Bill come together [to visit], I'll talk to you, if I still exist."[3] Ivins's choice of words echoed his remarks eight years earlier, when he had described himself to a counselor as an "avenging angel of death."

In an e-mail on March 17, 2008, to Cheryl Linscott—best friend of his wife and the older sister of Mara—Ivins had switched back to castigating the thirty-two-year-old Mara, saying she "isn't satisfied with winning. She isn't satisfied until she makes somebody lose. I've seen her. I know. I've seen her play scrabble, boggle, soccer, and wiffle ball. She has to make somebody lose. . . . That's why she's proud of hurting me. I used to think of her as my confidante. Now I know what she and [Fellows] wrote back and forth. I have seen. I know."[4]

On that same day, Ivins had a mishap while preparing liquefied spores of the Sterne strain, a nonlethal type of anthrax, spilling onto his pants several milliliters of the material. Although this did not pose a threat to him or anyone else, safety procedures required him to report the incident immediately to his supervisor. Instead Ivins walked the short distance to his home, where he washed and dried his pants before returning to USAMRIID and disclosing the spill.

Army officials had done nothing to discipline Ivins in April 2002 when they learned that he had kept secret for several months his bleaching of what he suspected was lethal Ames anthrax in the office that he shared with Fellows and another scientist. Now, with the newly focused investigative scrutiny bearing down on USAMRIID, Army officials could no longer afford to let Bruce be Bruce.

Having already banished him from the hot suites, the Army now stripped Ivins of access to all lab facilities for the technical violation of not immediately reporting his spill of the nonlethal Sterne spores. Until further notice he would be assigned to "administrative" duties.[5] He would still draw a paycheck—but his career as a prominent government scientist appeared to be over.

The next day, on March 18, Ivins wrote directly to Mara Linscott, his bitterness and self-pity fully unsheathed:

I'm sorry that you have abandoned me. You were the one person I knew I could bare my soul to and tell everything to, and now you have abandoned me. You have put me on your dark list . . . I lose my connections. I lose my years. I lose my health. I lose my ability to think. I lose my friends. What do I have left but eternity?

————

Just before 2 P.M. on Wednesday, March 19, Diane Ivins arrived at home to find her husband unconscious upstairs. She told the 911 dispatcher that she suspected he might have taken too many sleeping pills or Valium. Alcohol, she said, might also be a factor. The paramedics rushed him to Frederick Memorial Hospital, just over a mile away. He was evaluated but released to come home that evening. At about midnight, Ivins sent an e-mail to Mara Linscott and her sister, Cheryl Linscott, in which he appeared to take stock of his career—and to apologize for past transgressions, not all of which he specified:

I miss the days that all would say that I was sane without a snicker. I miss the days when I felt that we were doing what was worthwhile for our soldiers. I miss the days when I believed that our undertakings were worthy and honest and sacrificial. I miss the days since I could talk to you!

O, Healer! [referring to Mara Linscott's status as a medical doctor]

O devoter of your life to the lives of others! I can hurt, kill, and terrorize, but others place me with the vilest of the vile . . . Go down low, low, low as you can go, then dig forever, and you'll find me, my psyche. I can kill none but myself. I can terrify none but myself, but I can love and hug and turn toward the good, all who are willing. Give[n] my longdistant and productive past. Our pasts shape our futures, and mine was built on lies and craziness and depression, and thievery, and things that make an honest man and woman

cry. Alone. The farther I go, it's alone. The state smells its car-
nivorous death-blood sacrifice. I look into the mirror and cry
out who it is.[6]

Diane Ivins, who was trained as a registered nurse, told
Amanda that she believed Bruce had tried to kill himself. Diane
also contacted his psychiatrist, Dr. Allan Levy, and asked him not
to prescribe any more Ambien or Lunesta—sleeping pills that
seemed to impair Bruce's thinking. It was not easy to sort out
which if any of the pills was affecting his behavior because he
took so many different medications. In addition to Ambien and
Lunesta, he had in recent years used a litany of mood-altering
prescription drugs, including Celexa, Cymbalta, Zyprexa, Valium, and Trazodone.[7]

Both Andy and Amanda remained solidly supportive, but the
possible suicide attempt rocked them. Andy wrote his father a
note, imploring him to stop the self-destructive behavior. The
family needed him, he said. Amanda learned from Andy that
their father had been drinking—heavily. This disturbed her because she had never known him to drink.[8] Not long afterward,
on the night of April 21, 2008, investigators watched as Ivins
walked in a cold rain to his house, where he placed what he was
carrying into a trash can set by the curb. When they sorted
through the trash, the investigators would find that Ivins had
dumped something unusual—a collection of women's panties.
He had them in various colors and styles, including red and pur-
ple thongs and Girl Wonder apparel decorated with blue and
pink cats.[9]

Later in April, Ivins entered an alcohol abuse treatment program at Suburban Hospital in Bethesda, close to the Defense Department university where he had first worked upon arriving in
Maryland some thirty years earlier. From the hospital he could
look straight across the street and see the sprawling campus of
the National Institutes of Health, where Dr. Anthony Fauci's
staff had awarded over $100 million in grants to VaxGen to fast-
track Ivins's co-invention, the next-generation anthrax vaccine,
which was now consigned to oblivion. Amanda visited and pre-

sented her father with a poem to celebrate his birthday. On April
22, Bruce Ivins had turned sixty-two years old.

After a week-long stay at Suburban Hospital, he left and entered a second program for the treatment of alcoholism, at a
state psychiatric hospital in the western Maryland town of Cumberland. Ivins appeared to do well during his month-long stay
there, in the Joseph S. Massie Unit of the Thomas B. Finan Center. He played piano for the staff, and he admitted to Amanda
that his drinking had gotten out of control. "I was drinking to
mask what I was feeling," he said.[10]

On May 19, 2008, Bruce Ivins returned home to Frederick.
He still had a job at USAMRIID, though without any lab privileges. He conferred with Paul Kemp about retiring from the
Army as of September, when he would be in line for a government pension. He talked of visiting Andy, who had left Frederick
and expected to be certified as a firefighter in North Carolina.
And he told various family and friends that he might seek part-
time work, as a greeter at Walmart or a lecturer at Hood College
in Frederick.

Ivins remained under the care of psychiatrist Allan Levy, who
also treated Amanda. On one occasion Levy met jointly with father and daughter. It was an opportunity for Amanda to raise the
subject she'd shied away from when Bruce was institutionalized.

Amanda tearfully gave voice to her greatest fear: "Promise me
you won't hurt yourself."

Bruce Ivins had the look of a father pained that his daughter
feels the need to voice such a plea. He promised Amanda: He
would not kill himself.[11]

TWENTY-EIGHT

NOT A KILLER AT HEART

By May of 2008 it had been eight months since the DNA tests showed a match between RMR-1029 and the anthrax used in the letter attacks. After scrutinizing those who had access to RMR-1029, the Amerithrax task force investigators were now assembling the evidence that could support the indictment of Bruce Ivins for the five anthrax murders.

It was becoming apparent to some of Ivins's present and former colleagues that he was a serious suspect. The FBI had questioned many of them about him, and Ivins was openly despairing about the ongoing scrutiny. Yet in contrast to the circus that followed Steven Hatfill, not a single news account mentioned that Ivins was now a target of the investigation. Ivins's predictions of damaging FBI leaks about himself were not coming to pass.

On Wednesday, May 14, the geneticist Paul Keim flew into the Washington area at the request of the FBI. As he walked into a small conference room in a hotel near Dulles International Airport, where the FBI had invited him for a private meeting, he didn't know why he had been summoned.

At 4 P.M., leaders of the task force filed in: Ed Montooth and Vince Lisi and scientists Scott Stanley and Jason Bannan, all from

the FBI; prosecutor Kenneth Kohl and his colleague from the
U.S. attorney's office, Rachel Lieber. The meeting proceeded innocuously at first, with questions jogging Keim's memory about
some of his earliest efforts with anthrax.

The officials asked about his groundbreaking work in distinguishing the differing strains of anthrax, such as Sterne, Vollum,
and Ames. This was the innovation for which Keim was saluted
at the 1998 international conference in Plymouth, England—and
where he had also met with Bruce Ivins for the first time. The
questioning proceeded to Keim's seminal contributions to the investigation of the 2001 letter attacks: How many in this specialized scientific community knew about his and his colleagues'
efforts to genetically distinguish between batches of Ames strain
anthrax? Could Keim explain the technology used? As of late
2001 and early 2002, what particular scientists were paying attention to this work?

After about an hour, Keim noticed that Lieber, Montooth,
and Lisi were looking at each other knowingly yet quizzically. It
was as if they had arrived at a moment of decision. They told
Keim they would break and return shortly. "We need a sidebar,"
one of them said. The room cleared, except for Keim and a couple of FBI officials.

When the questioning resumed, the officials asked Keim to
read and to discuss a series of e-mails that Ivins wrote in late
2001 and 2002. Some were e-mails that Ivins had sent to other
leading anthrax researchers in which he asked questions and
commented about the recent letter attacks. Ivins appeared to be
focused on the Ames strain, which he and others at USAMRIID
had been working with for longer than any other researchers in
the world.

Keim had not had any contact with Ivins since the conference
at Santa Fe in late 2005, when Ivins told him that he was resigning from further involvement with the international group. As
Keim now read what was handed to him and provided his off-
the-cuff speculations about Ivins's thoughts, it became obvious
to him for the first time: The investigators were trying to figure

out if Ivins had taken steps to cover his tracks. The quirky scientist that Keim had known and considered a valuable colleague for a decade was a suspected murderer. Keim's ashen expression revealed his shock.[1]

Beginning with Agent Lawrence Alexander's arrival in 2004, the Amerithrax task force had gained familiarity with Ivins's provocative e-mails and Internet postings. It was Alexander who had first pored through the e-mails, which provided invaluable insight into Ivins's conduct and state of mind. And ever since the search of his house in November 2007, the investigators had been reading in close to real time many of Ivins's outgoing messages, including some of those sent under his Internet pseudonyms. There was no shortage of material to comb through.[2]

That same month, Judith McLean, Ivins's former clinical counselor, was shocked to hear his voice on the phone. It had been nearly eight years since they had last spoken, soon after Ivins had detailed his plan to poison Mara Linscott. "Do you remember me?" Ivins began. Yes, she certainly did. Ivins was businesslike. He wanted to know if McLean had retained any records from their long-ago sessions. "My lawyer needs them." He didn't say why a lawyer was involved. McLean pointed Ivins to Comprehensive Counseling Associates, her former employer in Frederick. "They may have put them in storage—or they may have shredded them," she told him.[3]

In his e-mails to others both before and after the letter attacks, Ivins had expressed concern that he was capable of violence due to his mental illness.[4] Now, in the spring of 2008, the investigators wanted to explore whether Ivins would reveal more about himself—or possibly confess to the anthrax murders.

The FBI had tried but failed to arrange an information-eliciting meeting between Nancy Haigwood and Ivins. Investigators then approached another woman whom Ivins had victimized, his former lab technician, Patricia Fellows. Although they had been friends and colleagues at USAMRIID, Ivins had stolen Fellows's password and then used it to spy on her e-mails. He had also accused Fellows and their mutual friend, Mara Linscott, of possibly being responsible for the anthrax attacks. Unlike the many acquaintances who viewed his actions as merely "Bruce being Bruce," Fellows had become aware of his mendacious ways. She agreed to confer with Ivins over coffee as the FBI listened with the aid of a hidden microphone.

The conversation unfolded at a restaurant in Frederick on June 5, 2008, with Fellows reminding Ivins that he had earlier described his alternate personality in an e-mail to her. As the FBI recorded the conversation, Fellows began to lead Ivins toward saying whether his alternate self might have perpetrated the anthrax letter attacks.

> FELLOWS: I'm trying to be supportive and understanding. But I guess a part of what you said before to me in response to that was that, you know, there kind of seems to be another person at times. And if you don't remember doing that, I mean [pause], don't get mad [laugh], are you absolutely . . . ?
>
> IVINS: You were going to say how do I know that I didn't have anything to do with . . .
>
> FELLOWS: Yeah.
>
> IVINS: . . . I will [tell] you that it's, I can't pull that up. And a lot of times with e-mails, I don't know that I sent an e-mail until I see it in the sent box. And it worries me when I wake up in the morning and I've got all my clothes and my shoes on, and my car keys are right beside there. . . . I can tell you I don't have it in my heart to kill anybody.
>
> . . . And I, and I do not have any recollection of ever have doing [sic] anything like that. As a matter of fact, I don't have no clue how to, how to make a bio-weapon and I don't want to know.

Later in the conversation Ivins continued:

> The only reason I remember some of this stuff, it's because there's like a clue the next day. Like there's an

e-mail, or, you know, when you're, when you're in bed and you're like, you're like this, you know, that's, that's not real fun. It's like, "Oh shit, did I drive somewhere last night?"

FELLOWS: Right, yeah, yeah, that must be awfully scary.

IVINS: It really certainly is. Uh, because I can tell you, I am not a killer at heart.

When Fellows suggested that hypnosis might help him to recall whatever he did, Ivins indicated that this would terrify him.

IVINS: What happens if I find something that, that is like buried deep, deep, deep, and you know, like from, from my past or I mean . . . like when I was a kid or stuff like that you know?

. . . Oh, but I mean, you know, that would just, that would just like, like, like make me want to jump off a bridge. You know, that would be . . .

FELLOWS: What's that? If you found out that . . .

IVINS: If I found out I was involved in some way, and, and . . .

FELLOWS: And you don't consciously know?

IVINS: Have any clue. [*pause, ending with a groan*] Cuz like, I'm, I'm not uh, a uh, I don't think of myself as a vicious, a, a nasty evil person.

FELLOWS: Oh, no, no, me either, but I mean, unless there is a whole other side.

IVINS: Yeah.

FELLOWS: . . . That is buried down in there . . .

IVINS: Yeah.

FELLOWS: . . . For whatever reason.

IVINS: Because I, I don't like to hurt people, accidentally, in, in any way. And [several scientists at USAMRIID] wouldn't do that. And I, in my right mind, wouldn't do it [laughs] . . . . But it's still, but I still feel responsibility because it [RMR-1029] wasn't locked up at the time. . . .

Ivins also told Fellows, "My lawyers have told me that an indictment is coming and I should be prepared to face the death penalty."[5]

Agent Lawrence Alexander was at the FBI's office in Frederick, listening in as the conversation unfolded. As he followed the back-and-forth, Alexander looked forward to the day when a jury would hear Ivins stammering and equivocating about whether he committed the anthrax letter attacks. That night, Rachel Lieber listened to a tape of the conversation and resolved that she would play excerpts from it during opening arguments at the future murder trial of Bruce Ivins.[6]

From the time that he inherited the case, defense lawyer Paul Kemp had advised Ivins to be more circumspect. Cooperate with the authorities, Kemp had told him on the night of the search, but "try not to say anything." Ivins, however, remained far from a quiet client. He vented to colleagues about his predicament with the investigation. He continued to fire off revealing e-mails and Web postings, using no fewer than eleven pseudonyms.[7]

Kemp faced another challenge. He now questioned the sincerity of prosecutor Kenneth Kohl's April 2007 letter in which he had told Ivins, "You are not a target of this investigation." Kemp's goal was to guide Ivins to retirement with an intact pension—and to avert his indictment for the five anthrax murders. Yet Kemp continued to believe that Ivins could do himself more good than harm by answering the Amerithrax task force's questions, which is why he had twice accompanied Ivins to Washington, in January and February of 2008, for the interviews with the FBI.[8]

Kemp at this point was touching base regularly with Lieber, who was taking a more prominent role in all aspects of the case. They negotiated an arrangement that might provide benefits to both sides.

Ivins would sit for one more round of questioning—this time in exchange for a promise that he would not be prosecuted for any answer he gave, so long as he answered truthfully.[9] The formalized, "off-the-record" ground rules would allow Ivins perhaps a last opportunity to persuade the government not to seek his indictment for the murders. On the other hand, Lieber and the FBI would get an in-depth preview of how Ivins and Kemp might try to parry the accusations at a trial.

The interview was scheduled to take place at Kemp's law offices in Rockville. As with the two sessions earlier in the year, the FBI's Ed Montooth and Vince Lisi would take the lead. For this session the agreed-upon participants—Montooth and Lisi, the prosecutors Rachel Lieber and Kenneth Kohl, the defense lawyers Paul Kemp and Tom DeGonia and their client, Bruce Ivins—settled into the black leather chairs of Kemp's third-floor conference room. Lisi sat directly across the rectangular table from Ivins. It was just after 10 A.M. on Monday, June 9, 2008—four days after Ivins told Patricia Fellows, "I am not a killer at heart" and "I, in my right mind, wouldn't do it."

After Kohl rereviewed for everyone the special off-the-record ground rules, the opening conversation became wide-ranging.

Ivins gave a self-contradictory account of when he first learned that anthrax colonies grown from spores removed from the Daschle letter visually resembled colonies grown from his flask, labeled RMR-1029. This was important because investigators believed that Ivins submitted a false sample of RMR-1029 in April 2002 to confound the FBI's hunt for matching DNA evidence.

Ivins acknowledged that he had accused various present or former colleagues of having possibly committed the anthrax attacks, including Patricia Fellows and Mara Linscott. Ivins's e-mails showed that he alternately loathed and desired the attentions of both. Now he was describing at length his fixation on them. The women, Ivins said, were attractive, hardworking, and very bright. They had quickly grasped the techniques for handling anthrax that he had taught them.

He conceded that he filched Fellows's computer access code, enabling him to read her e-mails. These included messages in which Fellows and Linscott referred to Ivins unflatteringly, and this left him feeling angry and betrayed. Accusing them of perpetrating the anthrax mailings, he said, was akin to his taking revenge against Kappa Kappa Gamma because of the undergrad who declined a date with him at the University of Cincinnati. Ivins also admitted that once, when Linscott was away from her desk working in a hot suite, he had made a duplicate of the key to her apartment. He was "quite taken" with Linscott, he said.

Agent Vince Lisi was questioning Ivins with his usual non-judgmental affect. He didn't let on, but the investigators were convinced that Ivins had written coded messages into the first anthrax letter—and that those messages alluded in some way to both Linscott and Fellows. Gently but inexorably, Lisi was trying to get inside Ivins's mind. Now Lisi eased toward his next set of questions by tapping into what he knew about Ivins's hostility toward New York. First, Lisi touched upon a feeling shared by many non–New York sports fans: dislike of the New York Yankees. Yes, Ivins said, he did not like the Yankees; they won too often. And yes, he had a strong dislike for New York City and for those who lived there.

At which point Ivins began to trace with animated gestures the origins of that particular obsessive enmity: It was the late 1960s and he was attending a microbiology conference in New York City. He had a waitress—a very rude New Yorker—who flung his order of spinach salad on the table. And then she just walked away. Reliving this affront now, some forty years later, Ivins stood as he loudly mimicked an authentic accent: "So what? That's the way New York is. If you don't like it, you can leave."

Ivins was revved up. Lisi was ready to move closer. He handed Ivins a copy of the anthrax-laced letter mailed to Tom Brokaw and the *New York Post*:

09-11-01

THIS IS NEXT

TAKE PENACILIN NOW

DEATH TO AMERICA

DEATH TO ISRAEL

ALLAH IS GREAT

Comments? Yes, Ivins did notice a few things. He questioned the need for the date, "09-11-01." In his opinion the block printing looked like that of a second grader. The writer, he said, "can't make Rs." The Rs did in fact resemble lowercase Os sitting atop two diagonal sticks. He noticed the misspelling of penicillin. One other thing: Ivins said that the writer had a "problem with Ts."

Now Ivins had helped deliver Lisi to the verge of his destination: the book and the scientific article that Ivins had jettisoned— or so he thought—with the household trash. Even a casual reader could see that the writer of the anthrax message sent to the New York recipients had boldfaced certain Ts and As. But Ivins, the microbiologist, would have known that these letters could signify two of the four nucleic acids in the DNA sequence of an organism: A for adenine, and T for thymine.[10] This was noteworthy when considered alongside the fact that he had gone to considerable effort to ensure that he had disposed of the book *Gödel, Escher, Bach: An Eternal Golden Braid* and the article "The Linguistics of DNA." Both the book and the article focused on coded language-like messages within DNA. And based on details provided by a witness who was contacted by the FBI, Nancy Haigwood was not the only person with whom Ivins had discussed his fascination with *Gödel, Escher, Bach*. Ivins had given the witness, Patricia Fellows, a copy of the book in fall 2006— and became angry when she told him later that she had not yet read it.[11]

Ivins was a man long fascinated by codes and cryptography, having burglarized Kappa Kappa Gamma's campus offices, where he stole the sorority's cipher and its Book of Ritual. He once described the gratification he derived from applying scientific skills to the unlocking of secrets. "For me, it's a real thrill to make a discovery, and know that I've just revealed something that no one else in the world ever knew before," Ivins wrote to Mara Linscott on July 26, 2000. "I feel like a detective, and that which is unknown dares me to try to find out about it, to decipher its code, to understand it, to fit it into the puzzle or 'Big Picture.'"[12]

To the seasoned investigators watching Ivins on that November 2007 night, he'd acted like a man intent on hiding something. Now Lisi would test this investigative hypothesis. What about, Lisi asked, these As and Ts in the anthrax letter? Did the conspicuously boldfaced letters suggest anything? Ivins acknowledged that he knew a bit about DNA sequencing—and that As and Ts match up, as do Cs and Gs. But Ivins said that he had never read anything about conveying messages by using these or other components of DNA.

Prosecutor Kenneth Kohl asked, "Have you read anything about the *linguistics* of DNA?" Never, Ivins said. Nor, Ivins said, had he ever sent any messages using As, Ts, Cs, or Gs. And, he had never read anything or had any discussions about how the genetic code of DNA could have some deeper or philosophical meaning. Ivins's responses amounted to a flat denial that he had read—let alone so carefully and furtively thrown away—the now highly relevant scientific article, "The Linguistics of DNA." It was time for Vince Lisi to play the card he had been holding back until this moment. He reached into an accordion file at his feet and slid the hefty tome that is *Gödel, Escher, Bach* across the table. "Hey Bruce, what about this?" To which Ivins replied, "*Gödel, Escher, Bach.* That's cool." He had bought a copy of this same book a few years ago for a friend, and another for himself, he said. "I've got a book just like that one at home." Ivins said he had read about three fourths of the book and found it fascinating, "really cool." It is about, he said, "Truths that cannot be proven within the system you're trying to prove them in." He noted from memory that *Gödel, Escher, Bach* also analyzes Johann Sebastian Bach's *Magnificat,* which he said proclaims "generation, upon generation, upon generation, shall call me blessed."

Without saying a word about what the investigators had found in Ivins's household trash, Lisi then brought his attention to page 404. And there it was: six lines of text—but with a scattering of single boldfaced characters intended to convey coded messages within the original message. Ivins said he knew nothing about this: He actually hadn't read as far as page 404—just a tad over halfway into the 777-page book. Lisi did not bother to remind Ivins he had just said that he had read about three fourths of the book. Nor did Lisi point out the similarity between the boldfaced characters in the book and those in the anthrax-laced letters sent to Brokaw and the *New York Post*. But what about *Gödel, Escher, Bach*'s discussion of DNA and the nucleic acids A, T, C, and G? He hadn't read that far, either, Ivins said.[13]

Privately, the investigators had already applied a basic understanding of DNA structure to theorize that the boldfaced As and Ts in the letter to Brokaw and the New York newspaper contained at least two coded messages: "PAT," the nickname for Patricia Fellows. And "FNY," perhaps reflecting Ivins's hostility toward the state where Mara Linscott had relocated when she left USAMRIID.[14]

The theorized messages were teased out initially by one of the FBI scientists, Darin Steele, who saw that the first three boldfaced characters in the Brokaw–*New York Post* letter were TTT. Assuming that TTT represented three consecutive nucleic acids, this sequence would code for a specific amino acid, a building block of DNA called Phenylalanine. The next three boldfaced characters in the New York letter were AAT, which coded for another amino acid, Asparagine. The final three boldfaced characters were TAT, which coded for a third amino acid, Tyrosine. Hence **PAT**, derived from the first letter of each coded amino acid. Finally, each of the three amino acids has a single-letter designator: F for phenylalanine, N for asparagine, and Y for tyrosine.

In the interview, Ivins told the FBI that although his lab routinely had used amino acids for growing anthrax spores, he knew nothing about the single-letter designators. For example, he said that he did not know which amino acid is represented by TTT. He was not, Ivins said, much of a "gene jockey." However, the FBI had found an e-mail indicating that Ivins was at least familiar with how a person could convey ideas by pairing the As, Ts, Cs, and Gs that represent the nucleic acids of DNA.

Said the e-mail, which Ivins forwarded to Mara Linscott on July 27, 2000: "Biopersonals: I have single-stranded too long! Lonely ATGCATG would like to pair up with congenial TACGTAG."

Ivins added his own note to the e-mail, "this is some cute humor for anyone who has ever had anything to do with biochemistry or molecular biology."

The possibility that Ivins had planted hidden messages within the first anthrax letter added a twist that fit with his obsession with codes and secrets. Yet given the information available, it would be difficult to say with certainty whether PAT and FNY were intentional or the result of chance. The most persuasive evidence investigators had that the anthrax mailer tried to communicate through the language of DNA was Bruce Ivins's own consciousness of guilt: Why, otherwise, would Ivins suddenly want to throw away both the 1992 article about DNA linguistics and such a cerebral, "really cool" book, *Gödel, Escher, Bach,* and do so with such determined secrecy? Why, otherwise, would Ivins falsely deny to the FBI that he had ever read or discussed anything about DNA-coded messages?[15]

When the hours-long interview had ended on June 9, Paul Kemp knew that Ivins was in serious legal jeopardy. His client's most obvious exposure, he believed, centered on the sample of anthrax he submitted to the FBI repository in April 2002. (Ivins told colleagues the day after the interview that he was "extremely interested" in seeking an Army buyout of up to $25,000, to be paid if he retired by the end of September.)[16]

In the interview, Ivins had said he received no instruction for how to submit the disputed sample until more than a month later, in May 2002. The investigators did not challenge Ivins on this—but they were confident that his claim could be refuted at trial.[17] Ivins again suggested that the sample may have been prepared and submitted by either of his lab technicians. Yet neither technician confirmed Ivins's suggestion when questioned by the FBI. Other evidence had further contradicted Ivins's statement: The test tubes bore labels filled out by Ivins. And the electronic keycard records at USAMRIID and a handwritten log both showed that Ivins personally submitted the sample on April 10.[18]

Although Kemp still held out hope that the task force would stop short of seeking Ivins's indictment for murder, he prepared his client for the worst: charges with a possible death sentence upon conviction. In Washington, meanwhile, Rachel Lieber, now with the support of her colleague Kenneth Kohl, was writing a formal prosecution memo—a step toward eventually seeking the grand jury's indictment of Ivins for the five anthrax murders.

Mounting an adequate defense could cost in the range of $2 million. Even if he drained every cent of equity from his home, this was money that Ivins did not have. Kemp notified authorities at the Federal Public Defender office that he would seek a subsidy to pay for the defense of his client. Kemp instructed Ivins to fill out a sworn affidavit in which he listed the family's income, assets, and debts. The public defender's office recommended to a federal judge that, given Kemp's breadth of experience, he should continue as Ivins's lawyer at taxpayer expense. The recommendation was made to the presiding U.S. District Court judge in Washington, Royce C. Lamberth.[19]

Ivins, whose ability to cope had seemed to be improving a month earlier at the rehab facility in Cumberland, was regressing. He still had a job and his desk in Room 19 of USAMRIID's Building 1425. But he was back to drinking alone at night. Both colleagues and family sensed that he was deeply troubled.

C. W. Ivins grew concerned when he called to see if his brother was interested in another vacation getaway—possibly a train trip through the Canadian Rockies. The two had not spoken since C.W. suffered a heart attack on March 5, followed by bypass surgery. Bruce told him that leaving the country would "cause too many problems." C.W. asked Bruce about the FBI.

"How're things coming along with your three-letter friends?"

"You have no idea. You don't want to know. I can't even tell you over this phone."[20]

When twenty-four-year-old Amanda received a subpoena in late June, requiring her to appear the next month before the grand jury in Washington, Bruce Ivins had a new injustice to declaim about.[21]

It was late on the afternoon of Friday, June 27, 2008, a pleasant day in Washington, D.C.—an extraordinary day for a particular middle-aged man who was waiting by himself for a transit bus on the north side of downtown Washington.

Steven Hatfill was of a powerful enough build to discourage an opportunistic mugger. But when a stranger in coat and tie approached to introduce himself, Hatfill flinched, as if wary of assault. Hatfill, whose face had been well publicized during his years as the prime suspect in the anthrax killings, felt the need to be on guard whenever he ventured out in public.[22] Even at this sweet moment: Court papers that had just been filed represented glorious vindication. The Justice Department and the FBI had agreed to pay Hatfill $5.82 million to settle the lawsuit his lawyers had brought against the government five years earlier. He would receive $2.82 million immediately, and a tax-sheltered annuity of $150,000 a year for the next twenty years.[23] But from Hatfill's standpoint, it was hardly an occasion to celebrate.

"I can't believe this could happen in this country." He was not talking about the monetary settlement.[24]

On the morning of Sunday, July 6, Bruce Ivins was in his usual place, playing the electronic keyboard for the nontraditional mass at St. John the Evangelist Roman Catholic Church in Frederick. His old friend and boss, Dr. Russell Byrne, could see that Ivins was in a roiled frame of mind. When the service was over and Ivins had unplugged his instrument, he flung a table across the stage. Byrne had been aware of the investigative scrutiny over the previous months, and he could not fathom that the man he thought he knew so well was in fact the anthrax killer. "Sooner or later this is going to pass," Byrne had told himself. "They'll figure out he's not the one."[25]

On that Sunday night a team of investigators following Ivins watched him meander through the streets of downtown Frederick, talking to himself. His odd behavior continued the next day: After the FBI received a call from a concerned colleague at USAMRIID, prosecutor Rachel Lieber telephoned Paul Kemp on July 7 to alert the defense attorney that his client was acting in a bizarre fashion. He was said to be flailing his hands around and making no sense when he spoke. One co-worker feared for her safety. Lieber voiced concern about Ivins's state of mind. Kemp called Ivins and tried to calm him.[26]

Ivins was back on the Internet that same night, disguised by pseudonyms as he gave new voice to his obsessions with sororities and homicide. Ivins in earlier years had often shown unusual interest in female celebrities. Now he was preoccupied with Kathryn Price, a Stanford Law School graduate and aspiring writer who in early 2001 had appeared in episodes of *The Mole,* an ABC-TV reality game show. (The show revolved around ten contestants who tackled various physical and mental challenges while trying to discern who among them was "the mole," a saboteur planted by the show's producers.)

At 11:05 P.M., Ivins, posting as Goldenphoenix on the Web site GreekChat.com, wrote: "Kathryn Price, who starred in 'The Mole,' was in a sorority at Kansas University. Could someone please tell me what she was in? Thanks!!!!!" When a respondent the next evening, on July 8, provided an answer, Kappa Alpha Theta, Ivins weighed in with other details about Price:

> Thanks!!! I have a friend who's been a big fan of hers ever since "The Mole." She'd love to meet her, maybe at a book signing or at the opening of one of the movies she's written or produced. I appreciate the help. You can really, REALLY be proud of her. Did you know that she also finished second in her class at Stanford Law School? Hopefully somebody at chapter headquarters might have some more info on her. What Cindy (my friend) really wants is a picture standing beside her.
>
> Congrats to Theta!!!!!!!![27]

Ivins had more to say about Kathryn Price in July 2008. Writing as bruceivi, he posted comments to YouTube, this time voicing a bloodlust that he may have been harboring for the more than seven years since the show had aired:

> Steve had a great chance to kill Kathryn that would go down as the primo moment in reality TV. After the fake fainting

he'd say, "Kathryn, do you know what a mole is? It's a blind useless animal that humans hate. And do you know what we do to moles? We kill them."

With that he should have taken the hatchet and brought it down hard and sharply across her neck, severing her carotid artery and jugular vein. Then when she hits the ground, he completes the task on the other side of the neck, severing her trachea as well. The "Blind" mole is dead and Steve is a hero among heroes! I personally would have paid big money to have done it myself.

Maybe something really dreadful will happen to Kathryn Price. If so, she will richly deserve it! The least someone could do would be to take a sharp ballpoint pin [sic] or letter opener and put her eyes out, to complete the task of making her a true mole![28]

Having referred, as Goldenphoenix, to the curiosity of his friend, "Cindy," and having voiced his desire as bruceivi to kill Kathryn Price, Ivins posted under yet another name—Cindy Wood—to seek information regarding Price's upcoming whereabouts:

I've been a HUGE fan of Kathryn Price ever since she was the Mole on Season 1. She was great. I understand that she's now writing and producing. Can somebody, even one of her sorority sisters at Kansas University, tell me how to reach her? I'd LOVE to get an autograph from her and have my picture taken with her, perhaps at a book signing or at a movie release. Does she have an email, or does she have an agency where she can be reached by email? I hope, hope, hope she reads this! I really do want to meet her! Any help out there from anybody will be greatly appreciated!!!![29]

Why Kathryn Price? What could explain this obsession? Unlike two earlier celebrity fixations of Ivins's, the astronauts Sally Ride and Christa McAuliffe, Price was not an iconic figure. Perhaps Ivins was motivated by Price's combination of brains and fresh-faced beauty. Perhaps it was the format: *The Mole* was a test of the intelligence of both cast and audience as they sought to identify the producers' plant. The Amerithrax investigators found another possible explanation: In one episode of *The Mole* Kathryn Price was blindfolded—a fetish of Ivins's. One of the computers the FBI had taken from him in November 2007 showed that he had viewed scores of pictures of women who were blindfolded, bound, and nude.[30]

TWENTY-NINE

I'M NOT GOING DOWN

Since early 2008, Bruce Ivins had been meeting for one-on-one therapy with Jean C. Duley, an addictions counselor in Frederick who worked under Ivins's psychiatrist. At their first meeting, Ivins focused on a framed display showing Duley's membership in an honor society, and he quizzed her at length about both that and her IQ. Counselor and client developed a rapport and, at Ivins's request, Duley had a session with Amanda Ivins.[1]

After his hospitalization in May, Ivins also began attending weekly group therapy sessions led by Duley. She noticed that he would light up when discussing scientific details of the anthrax used in the letter attacks, or when explaining why he believed a certain ex-colleague was the perpetrator. She also saw that Ivins was a meticulous planner.[2] At one session he pulled a scrap of paper from his wallet to show her. It was a kind of recipe: Based on his body weight of roughly 160 pounds, Ivins had calculated the amount of alcohol and pills he would need to kill himself.[3] Though he was known for his cheery affect, Ivins's behavior at another group session revealed a far different side. The session was overseen by both Duley and his psychiatrist, Dr. Allan Levy, who encouraged those present to engage in a role-playing "psy-chodrama," the goal being to reenact memories, some painful. It began with one of the clients engaging in a simulated conversa-tion with his father, for whom he held unresolved feelings. When that part of the exercise ended, the same client volunteered to take the role of father, while Ivins played himself as a child and young adult. This was not the reticent "Bruce the Goose" of Lebanon, Ohio. Jabbing his finger into the other man's chest, Ivins unleashed anger that seemed long in the making. "You were never there for me," he shouted. "You were a coward." Duley, unsure where the exchange might lead, lightly touched Ivins on the arm to reel him in. He was slow to respond, but took a seat and stared silently at the floor.[4]

On the evening of Wednesday, July 9, 2008, Ivins arrived for another round of group therapy. As usual for his mental health appointments, he was early. On this night it was as if he were a different real-life Bruce. He snarled when he made his co-payment, prompting a receptionist to alert Duley, "There's some-thing wrong with Bruce."[5]

Ivins was noticeably jumpy and angry as other members of the group began discussing their problems. A colleague of Duley's, counselor Wendy Levy (Allan Levy's wife), also sat in. Asked if there was something he wanted to say, Ivins let loose: He had been walking late at night recently in the "ghetto" of Frederick, hoping to lure someone to attack him so he could stab the person with his sharp writing pen. He was ready, he said, to call out, "Come on, nigger boy!"[6] This was an echo of what he had said shortly after 9/11, when he e-mailed Mara Linscott telling her that he had walked, armed with a gun, in a "bad part of town," hoping to encounter trouble.[7] Now he insisted that Jean Duley feel for herself the sharp tip of the pen—the same type object he had mused about wielding against the reality TV performer Kathryn Price in his macabre posting on YouTube.[8]

Ivins told the group more than he had said previously about his status as a suspect in the anthrax letter attacks of 2001. He was about to be indicted, he said, and he was angry at the gov-ernment investigators who were after him, angry at the system that had dealt him this hand. He planned to exact revenge on those who had wronged him—colleagues at USAMRIID and others. He had a list of those he intended to kill. He had a bulletproof vest and was going to obtain a Glock handgun with the help of his son.[9] One group member, a veteran with post-traumatic stress disorder, rose abruptly and left. Why, others in the group asked Ivins, would he do these things if he were innocent? Ivins avoided a direct response, saying that he planned to go out blazing. "I'm not going down for five capital murders. . . . I'm going to get them all." Throughout this recitation of his plans, Ivins maintained a snarling, fixed grin. Duley had not seen this before, and it frightened her.[10]

Later that night, Duley contacted Ivins's attorneys, Paul Kemp and Tom DeGonia, and relayed her concerns. Kemp suggested that she arrange a consultation between Ivins and his psychiatrist, Allan Levy.[11] After conferring the next morning, July 10, 2008, by phone with Dr. Levy, who was away from the area, Duley contacted Frederick police. As a professional courtesy, a detective promptly informed the FBI about what Duley had reported.[12]

Ivins, meanwhile, was reporting for work at USAMRIID. Inside the main building, a longtime colleague, Dr. Arthur O. Anderson, approached him in the hallway and started a conversation. Over the previous several months Ivins had vented to Anderson about the federal investigation. Now Ivins again appeared incensed, saying that the investigators had told Amanda that her father was a "murderer." Citing Amanda's brush with suicide as a teenager, Ivins told Anderson he was concerned about how vulnerable she was emotionally to what he described as aggressive investigative tactics.[13]

Ivins attended a midday ceremony honoring researchers who had made progress with a vaccine against plague, the flea-borne pathogen long feared as a potential biological weapon. Ivins's former supervisor, Jeffrey Adamovicz, noticed him in the auditorium and approached to say hello. The last time they had spoken was in March, when Adamovicz had tried to comfort the visibly agitated Ivins on a roadway inside Fort Detrick. Now Ivins was irreverent, cracking jokes. They talked about the experimental plague vaccine, a project that Adamovicz had focused on for years before retiring from the Army to work at a private research institute nearby. Ivins told him that he, too, was getting ready to retire. Based on their brief conversation, Adamovicz saw no cause for alarm.[14]

Others did after learning of Ivins's threats at the group therapy session. At 2 P.M., a team of officers from the Frederick Police Department arrived at Fort Detrick and made their way to USAMRIID.[15] At the officers' request, Ivins was summoned to a conference room. The police informed him that, based on the threatening remarks he had made the previous evening in group therapy, he would be driven by ambulance to Frederick Memorial Hospital for psychiatric evaluation. Ivins reacted angrily but did not resist. As a few of Ivins's colleagues watched, Detective Bruce DeGrange escorted him from the building where he had arrived twenty-eight years earlier as an eager, thirty-four-year-old microbiologist.[16]

The Army had already taken away his lab privileges. Now that Duley had reported his threats of violence, it was all but certain that Ivins would never work another day at USAMRIID.[17] Once he caught sight of the waiting ambulance, Ivins became more agitated, fulminating against "the government" and the FBI, whose agents observed from a distance. "Identify yourselves! I know you're here!" Ivins shouted.[18]

Unlike his brief stay at Frederick Memorial in March, on this occasion Bruce Ivins was kept overnight. He was irate about being confined—and he blamed Jean Duley, the counselor who had reported his remarks to the police.[19] At 4:25 A.M., he called her office from Frederick Memorial and left a message in an emotionless voice: "Hello, Jean. This is Bruce. And I want to thank you for getting me arrested at Fort Detrick and roughed up, threatened with being handcuffed, guarded by two police officers with guns in the room and incarcerated. And also I want to thank you for destroying the client-patient relationship. So now the FBI can come and get all the information from you and Dr. Levy." At

4:28 A.M., Ivins called back to say, "I'm going to be leaving both you and Dr. Levy as a therapist, a psychiatrist." [20]

Later that day, Friday, July 11, 2008, Ivins was transferred to Sheppard Pratt, a 117-year-old psychiatric hospital in Towson, a northern suburb of Baltimore. At 11:17 A.M. the next day, Ivins again called Duley, voicing further resentment over the likelihood that damaging secrets from his past, revealed in psychotherapy, would be revealed to the FBI.

Though Duley was mindful of a patient's right to confidentiality, she had a countervailing duty to warn authorities of a patient's threat to harm himself or others. Still, she had not acted impulsively. She checked with her boss, Dr. Levy, before contacting the police. Based on the police's subsequent heads-up to the FBI, two Amerithrax investigators arrived without notice on July 11 to question Duley about Ivins's threats at the group therapy session. The investigators questioned Duley at Comprehensive Counseling together with Wendy Levy, the other counselor who had attended the session. She corroborated Duley's account.

Yet until Duley arrived for work on Monday, July 14, 2008, she had no inkling of any previous homicidal threat by Ivins. On that morning, however, a secretary approached her with a paper file. "I think you should see this." For the first time, Duley read about Ivins's admitted plan in 2000 to poison Mara Linscott and about the earlier evaluation by another psychiatrist, Dr. David Irwin, who termed him the "scariest" patient he had ever treated. Duley called one of the Amerithrax investigators, FBI agent Daniel G. Borsuk, and alerted him that new information had emerged. [21]

When Borsuk and postal inspector Armando R. Garcia reinterviewed her in Frederick, Duley described details from the file. Among the revelations was that Ivins had participated in the individual therapy sessions in 2000 with Judith McLean—the mental health counselor to whom he confided his plan to poison Linscott. Based on this information, the Amerithrax task force eventually obtained a judge's order to review the file and other mental health records, including those reflecting Ivins's conversations not only with Duley but with other mental health professionals dating back to 1978.[22]

Aside from his phone call to her the previous November, McLean had not spoken to Ivins since the summer of 2000, when he rebuked her for reporting his plot against Linscott to the police. Along with McLean's written observations, the file on Ivins at Comprehensive Counseling contained his statements about buying bomb-making ingredients. McLean had left Frederick within a year or so to practice in central Pennsylvania—but she never forgot Bruce Ivins. This became clear to Agent Borsuk when he reached her by phone and explained that the FBI was interested in a man she had once counseled. Before Borsuk mentioned a name, McLean interrupted: "There's only one client in my twenty-five years of counseling who the FBI would ever contact me about. There's only been one client that I ever felt was that dangerous, that scary and that I had a sense of evil about." That client was Bruce Ivins.[23]

McLean's vivid account of her experience with Ivins gave investigators new insight into his capacity for vengeance. The information also answered a question that had gnawed at Agent Lawrence Alexander, who had spent hours combing through Ivins's voluminous correspondence: Alexander had never been able to make sense of a statement by Ivins in his e-mail of March 4, 2001, when he wrote that a previous mental health counselor had "wanted to put me in jail." Now Alexander realized this must have referred to McLean.[24]

Over the weekend the task force searched Ivins's house again, as well as his vehicles, his office at USAMRIID, and the wallet he had with him at Sheppard Pratt in Towson. At the house investigators found a late-model bulletproof vest, which Ivins had referred to when making his threats in the group therapy session, along with homemade body armor and 236 rounds of ammunition. In addition, the investigators found seventeen rounds of .40 caliber, hollow-point bullets, plus a large canister of smokeless handgun powder.[25] The discovery of these items, in combination with the threats Ivins had made, led investigators to suspect that he had been planning a siege at USAMRIID. More likely, thought some on the task force, was that Ivins would barricade himself and brandish a weapon to provoke their fire: suicide by cop.[26]

On Monday, July 14, Amanda Ivins went to Washington to appear before the grand jury. She and her lawyer met privately for an hour with two FBI agents and Rachel Lieber before the prosecutor led her into the grand jury room, where Amanda was asked about her father's depression, his dealings with Mara Linscott and Patricia Fellows, his visits to Hank Heine's cabin in West Virginia. Lieber also asked whether the Ivins family had ever traveled in the area of Princeton, New Jersey; Amanda said they had once driven to New York when she was a child. Did Bruce Ivins ever talk to her about Kappa Kappa Gamma or any sororities or fraternities? No, Amanda said.[27]

Twice over the next week and a half Paul Kemp drove to Sheppard Pratt, where he advised Ivins not to submit to the FBI's request for a sample of cells from inside his mouth. Ivins, however, said he did not want to fight it. On July 23, an agent with a DNA-swabbing kit and a judge's order in hand, accompanied by a Sheppard Pratt security guard, collected three inner-cheek swabs. Ivins seemed calm, as if he were now resigned.

Sheppard Pratt planned to release him the next morning.[28] Lieber, who had contacted Kemp on July 7 to alert him to Ivins's erratic behavior, now feared worse: suicide. While Ivins was still within the facility, she called a lawyer for Sheppard Pratt and urged that he be held for further evaluation. "Look, you really don't want to release him," Lieber said. "Because we do think he's a danger to himself." Her plea made no impact. Ivins would be released as planned.[29]

As a precaution, the FBI's Daniel Borsuk informed counselor Jean Duley about the development. She, too, called Sheppard Pratt and unsuccessfully urged a staff psychiatrist to hold Ivins there. As Duley was well aware, once Ivins was out, he would be just an hour's drive from Frederick. Shortly before ten the next morning, Thursday, July 24, Duley, sitting on a courthouse bench, hurriedly filled out a petition asking a local judge to bar Ivins from making any contact with her. Duley's petition described his threats of murder at the earlier group therapy session and cited matters that were documented in the mental health files to which the federal investigators had just gained access.[30] Duley, accompanied by her attorney, Mary McGuirk Drawbaugh, presented the petition to Maryland District judge W. Milnor Roberts.

> DRAWBAUGH: At this time, Ms. Duley, are you fearful for your personal safety?
> DULEY: I am and so is the FBI.
> DRAWBAUGH: Why . . . are you fearful?
> DULEY: . . . He is a revenge killer. When he feels that he's been slighted—or has had—especially toward women, he plots and actually tries to carry out revenge killing. He has been forensically diagnosed by several top psychiatrists as a sociopathic, homicidal killer. . . . And through my working with him I also believe that to be true.

Duley added in a clear, loud voice, "I'm scared to death."

Judge Roberts had heard enough. He signed an order prohibiting any contact between Ivins and Duley. The order called for both Ivins and Duley to appear for a final hearing one week later, on July 31 at 9:45 A.M.[31]

Soon after Duley's court appearance in Frederick, Diane Ivins picked up her husband at Sheppard Pratt. It had been two weeks since he was led out of USAMRIID and confined for emergency psychiatric evaluation. Back at home on Military Road, he could gaze over the barbed wire fence that separated him from Fort Detrick, but he could not do any work there. He was barred from even the office areas, let alone the labs. His personal computers had been seized in the most recent federal search, leaving him without access to the Internet.

Shortly after noon Ivins set out for the Giant Eagle supermarket on Seventh Street, a two-minute drive. He had a short shopping list: whole wheat bread, 2 percent milk, orange juice, Welch's grape juice—and something for his headache.[32]

Once inside he went to the pharmacy section, its row after row of bright and densely stocked shelves a far cry from the small-town feel of Ivins Drugs in Lebanon, Ohio. He reached for a package containing seventy pills of Tylenol PM, the potent over-the-counter painkiller and sleeping aid. After gathering the other items on his list, Ivins checked out at 12:31 P.M. with a Giant Eagle discount card. Slightly over an hour later, he paid for the filling of three prescriptions: Celexa, the antidepression drug; Seroquel, an antipsychotic approved for treatment of schizo-phrenia and manic episodes of bipolar disorder; and Depakote, for mania and migraine headaches.

That evening he visited the county library branch on East Patrick Street, just two miles away in downtown Frederick. Ivins made his way to the second floor, where scores of computers were available to the public. Library policy limited to one hour a person's use of any single computer.[33] From 7 P.M. to 8:30 P.M., FBI agents who were tailing him watched as Ivins logged on and off one, and then another, computer to check various e-mail accounts—and to review a Web site dedicated entirely to devel-opments in the anthrax investigation.[34]

That same Thursday evening Ivins called his daughter. They had talked only once when he was at the psychiatric hospital, after her appearance at the grand jury. He always seemed ill at ease on the phone and was no less so now. They had planned to have lunch the next day, but Bruce said he needed to cancel be-cause of a bad headache. He and Amanda agreed to postpone until Monday or Tuesday.

"I love you, Dad," Amanda said as they were hanging up.

"I loved you first."

Strange, Amanda thought. He'd never said that before.[35]

That night Diane Ivins placed a letter on the end table in her husband's upstairs bedroom:

Bruce,
    I'm hurt, concerned, confused, and angry about your ac-tions over the past few weeks. You tell me you love me but you have been rude and sarcastic and nasty many times when

you talk to me. You tell me you aren't going to get any more guns then you fill out an on line application for a gun license. You pay Paul Kemp an enormous amount of money then ignore his advice by contacting Pat [Fellows] and Mara [Linscott], going into work at odd hours, and walking in the neighborhood late at night. You are jumpy and agitated from the extreme amount of caffeine you drink each day. Peter [a financial advisor] asked us not to cash any more EE bonds because we pay so much tax on them and you cashed one in June. The FBI is convinced you're having an affair with Mara every time you email her they are more suspicious.[36] Can you honestly say you are following the plan you developed at Massie [*sic*] Clinic for stress reduction and coping with this?

Bruce Ivins scribbled a response on the back of Diane's note: "I have a terrible headache. I'm going to take some Tylenol and sleep in tomorrow. . . . Please let me sleep. Please."

On Friday, July 25, Ivins called Paul Kemp and they scheduled an appointment for the following Monday, July 28, at the law offices in Rockville. By getting a judge's permission to tap federal funds to pay for legal fees in the event of capital murder charges, Kemp and Ivins were preparing for the worst. Kemp nonetheless held out hope that any charges, if they came, would be limited to Ivins's allegedly false statements about the disputed sample of RMR-1029. Kemp informed Ivins that he and the other defense lawyer, Tom DeGonia, were scheduled to meet with the Amerithrax team on Tuesday, at which time the prosecutors were expected to provide a detailed account of the evidence.[37]

On Saturday, July 26, Ivins stayed in bed most of the day. He remained upstairs in his room as evening approached, with plenty of sunlight still washing over the west-facing house. On a small end table next to his bed he had placed a quart-size plastic water bottle containing a reddish orange liquid, perhaps a mixture of the grape and orange juice he bought at Giant Eagle. Next to the bottle was a green glass, which Ivins had filled with what appeared to be the same mixture. At 7 P.M. and again at

9 P.M. Diane went up to check on him. She returned downstairs to read a book on a couch, where she fell asleep.

At some point thereafter Bruce Ivins rose and went into the upstairs bathroom. Just he and Diane were in the house. At about 1 A.M., Diane awakened and went upstairs for another look. She found him sprawled straight out from the toilet seat on the bathroom floor, his head at the doorway, his eyes closed. He was on his right side, wearing underpants and an undershirt. He was breathing but unresponsive to Diane's voice. The former registered nurse checked his pulse and pinched his arm in an attempt to rouse him. No reaction. Lying in a pool of his own urine, he was very cold to the touch. She called 911.[38]

At 1:47 A.M. on Sunday, July 27, the ambulance delivered Ivins to the emergency room at Frederick Memorial Hospital. Diane drove separately and arrived a few minutes later. His breathing was rapid, his blood pressure extremely low. A doctor suspected a drug overdose or a stroke. Yet by 8 A.M. Ivins improved somewhat, according to an intensive care unit nurse who was monitoring him. Ivins, she wrote at the time, was "arousable—and able to nod head to yes\no questions."

The nurse, Megan Shinabery, took the opportunity to pose a crucial question. "Did you intentionally try to commit suicide?" Nurse Shinabery's handwritten notes underscored Ivins's response: "pt nodded yes."

Ivins then began pulling out the tubes that were delivering his medication, notably an antidote for Tylenol overdose. The nurse and other hospital personnel placed soft leather restraints on his wrists and ankles. Faint writing in blue ink was visible on the inside of Ivins's left leg, an illegible scrawl that would interest, to no avail, investigators seeking some kind of parting message.[39]

Diane asked Shinabery to see to it that Ivins's involvement with the anthrax investigation, which was already known to at least one of the doctors, be kept quiet within the hospital.

Amanda arrived later that morning. "Dad, open your eyes." He did.[40]

At 9 P.M. on Sunday, a nurse noted, "Patient opened eyes slightly to loud name call, twitched left foot when asked to wiggle toes. No response when asked to grip RN's fingers."[41] Tests of Ivins's blood showed drastically elevated levels of acetamino-phen, the active ingredient in Tylenol. The results also showed the presence of a benzodiazepine—perhaps a consequence of his frequent use of Valium.[42] Diane told the police that she found no suicide note. But she agreed with the doctors and nurses who concluded that he had, indeed, attempted suicide. By Monday, July 28, he was failing—suffering from severe liver damage and acute kidney failure, likely from the overdose of Tylenol. With those vital organs damaged, toxins were building up in his body.

Paul Kemp, who learned of Ivins's apparent suicide attempt early that morning from Rachel Lieber, arrived at the hospital for a visit. His client was unconscious with no signs of movement.[43] Diane told one of the doctors that she did not want her husband placed on a list for a possible liver transplant (a decision consistent with her declining of another offer, to treat his Tylenol over-dose with the additional therapy of kidney dialysis). "Bruce did not wish to live in this manner," she said. Based on Diane's "fairly adamant" statement, the hospital as of 3:08 P.M. also put in place orders not to attempt to revive him if he suffered cardiac arrest.

On the morning of Tuesday, July 29, Diane gathered Amanda and Andy with her at the bedside. On Sunday, her father's re-sponsiveness had given Amanda hope. Now he was comatose and yellow with jaundice, a result of liver failure. Amanda held his hand and said softly, "You can go, Dad."[44]

At 10:47 A.M. Bruce Ivins was dead.[45]

———

Two of the books Ivins kept in his bedroom described men whose lives had faint echoes of his own lost promise. *Arrow-smith*, the 1925 novel by Sinclair Lewis, depicts the rise from a small town in the Midwest of a scientifically gifted man who achieves acclaim as a bubonic plague researcher but is buffeted by the temptations of recognition and power.[46] Ivins, who as-pired to Mensa, might also have related to the protagonists of *A Madman Dreams of Turing Machines*. Janna Levin's 2006 novel chronicles the anguished lives of Kurt Gödel, the storied mathematical logician (whose work is examined in *Gödel, Escher, Bach,* the book that would provide a key to the mystery of the anthrax letters), and Alan Turing, who helped break the German military code during World War II and whose "universal Turing machine" was the archetype for the modern computer. The deaths of both were self-inflicted—Gödel, by intentional starvation due to his paranoia over being poisoned; Turing, by eating a cyanide-laced apple.

After Amanda had attempted suicide in high school, Ivins had assured his daughter that no matter how dark things may seem, light is always at the end of the tunnel. He had looked out for her, and she could not recall his ever breaking a commitment to her.[47] Bruce Ivins, however, had always been painfully aware of his total self, not least his odd looks and the scary thoughts that crowded his gifted mind. Unlike a simple sociopath, he knew and at times resented his dark side—the impulses that led him to plot acts of revenge, up to and including homicide. He had sought help through counseling and medication. But there would be no light at tunnel's end. He had failed to quell the evil within himself and now faced the likelihood of life in prison or even a death sentence. His recourse was a final act of revenge—against himself.

Nothing could shake her love, but as the family member closest to him, Amanda Ivins was stunned to learn some of the details of her father's secret life. His obsession with the sorority, his use of false names to send letters, packages, and e-mails, the details of his fixation with Mara Linscott and his plan to poison her—until the wrenching weeks before and after his suicide, Amanda had known about none of it. She continued to have faith in his innocence, but the revelations left her dumbfounded. "I'm close to him," she said. *"Why don't I know about these things?"*[48]

In the predawn hours of Thursday, July 31, the Amerithrax investigators again sifted through the Ivins household's trash. In it they found forty-five wedding photos of Bruce and Diane Ivins, along with an empty container of Tylenol PM.[49]

———

Diane Ivins never publicly discussed the allegations against her husband or his death.[50] She did assist Monsignor Richard Murphy in selecting the hymns and readings of scripture for her husband's memorial on August 9 at St. John the Evangelist. One theme of the service, which drew among others C. W. Ivins, Bill and Ann Hirt, and Mara Linscott, was that God is the only one who can judge man.[51] Consistent with his wishes, Bruce Ivins was cremated, and his ashes were scattered on land in western Maryland.[52]

Following her husband's suicide, Diane Ivins paid Paul Kemp and his law firm to defend Ivins as an innocent man. Kemp did just that in numerous media interviews, saying the evidence did not prove that he was the anthrax killer. Kemp also rebuked conspiracy theorists who spun the suicide as something more sinister.[53]

Paul Kemp never wavered publicly in his defense of Ivins. In private, he did on at least one occasion. At 1 P.M. on July 29, 2008, just over two hours after Ivins died, Kemp and his colleague, Tom DeGonia, entered the eleventh-floor conference room of the U.S. Attorney's Office in Washington for the meeting where, as Bruce Ivins had been informed the week before, the government's evidence was to be spelled out for his lawyers. Prosecutor Rachel Lieber had completed her draft of the confidential memo summarizing the case against him four days earlier. Now she and her colleagues Ed Montooth, Vince Lisi, Tom Dellafera, Ken Kohl, and Lawrence Alexander greeted the defense lawyers. For the better part of two hours, Lieber laid out the case, providing details that had not previously been shared outside the investigation.

Kemp was saddened by his client's death, and his eyes moistened when he recalled his last conversations with Ivins. As the participants rose to leave, he looked toward Lieber and said: "It would've been a fun case. Would've been a fun case to try. You would've cooked our goose."[54]

EPILOGUE

I n an ordinary criminal investigation, the suicide of the sole remaining suspect would lead to the quiet closing of the file.
Officials might talk about continuing their pursuit of the
truth and following the facts wherever they led, but it would
likely be just that—talk. The case of the anthrax letters, however,
was not like any other investigation.

Ivins's family and friends and colleagues were owed a thorough accounting of the evidence. So were the families of the
victims—and the entire country. How, otherwise, could anyone
be confident that the Amerithrax task force had at last gotten it
right, that there was not a killer lurking in our midst?

There were other questions to be answered that bore on the
conduct of high officials and prominent scientists, and on policy
decisions made in response to the attacks. In the run-up to war
senior Bush administration officials, including members of the
president's cabinet, had cleared time to meet with a Fort Detrick
virologist who told them the anthrax used in the attacks appeared to be chemically treated—and perhaps linked to Iraq.
Why, then, did none of these officials seek out the scientists at the
Sandia National Laboratories who, by mid-2002, had demon-

strated otherwise? If Ivins and not a foreign enemy was responsible for the attacks, should Congress and succeeding administrations reassess both the safety risks and the costs of the multibillion-dollar efforts to develop products to counter the deadly pathogens of biological warfare? Should the breakneck pace of building more labs for this work be slowed or halted? And, apart from whether or not to maintain the still mandatory vaccinations for the military, is there a sufficiently plausible threat of a large-scale anthrax attack to justify continually replenishing the nation's civilian stockpile with up to 75 million doses of the vaccine?[1]

There surely are significant lessons to be drawn. But they are unlikely to be learned if the most basic question—who did it?—remains unanswered.

For leaders of the FBI, a satisfactory answer hinges on laying to rest doubts about the bureau's competence. After the well-chronicled debacles of Richard Jewell and Wen Ho Lee and, more recently, the $5.82 million payout to Steven Hatfill, the bureau's credibility has been severely compromised. Many Americans would be unwilling to accept that it had solved this high-profile case. Whereas a trial would have subjected each piece of evidence against Ivins to a jury's scrutiny, his suicide left officials of the FBI and the Justice Department only the court of public opinion in which to present their case.

The FBI has a positive story to tell: Ed Montooth and Vince Lisi took a long-foundering investigation, refocused it on suspects who had access to the strain of anthrax used in the letter attacks, and cracked the case. The task force of FBI agents and postal inspectors used traditional investigative methods to complement the scientific efforts that had yielded the distinct DNA evidence.

But to persuade the public that Ivins was the right man, the FBI would have had to acknowledge the mistakes its leaders made in single-mindedly pursuing Steven Hatfill. By embracing the dubious bloodhound evidence against him, the FBI leadership stayed fixed on a researcher who had never worked with anthrax or other bacteria—while looking past another scientist, squarely within their sights, who had the skills, the easy access to anthrax, and the necessary equipment to perpetrate the letter attacks. If the FBI had been so wrong for so long about Hatfill, why should the public believe it was right about Ivins? The circumstances demanded an admission of error.

In the *Los Angeles Times* of August 1, 2008, I broke the news that Ivins, a man who was an unknown to the general public, had apparently committed suicide as authorities prepared to charge him as the anthrax killer.[2] Five days later, the FBI and the Justice Department held a news conference to discuss for the first time the abrupt resolution of the case. It quickly became apparent that there would be no owning up to error regarding any of the investigation's wrong turns.

When asked about Hatfill, Jeffrey A. Taylor, the U.S. attorney for Washington, D.C., and Joseph Persichini Jr., an assistant FBI director and head of the bureau's Washington Field Office, repeated variations on the same theme: The investigators followed the evidence where it led. The implication was that until the scientists were able to link RMR-1029 to the letter attacks, there was no reason to focus on Bruce Ivins.

When I pressed the two officials to reconcile the intensive focus on Hatfill with the fact that he had never worked with anthrax during his stint at USAMRIID, Taylor replied, "With respect to the other individual you mentioned, we were able to determine that at no time could that individual be put in the presence of that flask from which these spores came."

Although Taylor's oblique statement absolved Hatfill, the U.S. attorney's failure to utter the name of the longtime chief suspect was no accident. He and the other federal officials at the news conference had been advised by a senior Bush administration appointee not to speak Hatfill's name.[3] This smacked of damage control, not a full and open accounting.

Hatfill's lawyer, Thomas Connolly, complained vigorously to the Justice Department about the obvious refusal to recognize his client by name and to acknowledge that Hatfill was no longer under any suspicion. In response, U.S. Attorney Jeffrey Taylor sent Connolly a letter, explicitly exonerating Hatfill. While the letter was accessible on the Justice Department's Web site, the exoneration was not conveyed in a press release or other public statement and certainly could not undo the years of frenzied leaks, tying Hatfill to murders he did not commit.[4]

Something else was peculiar about the news conference: The men who led it, Taylor and Persichini, were virtual unknowns on the national stage, and their roles in the investigation were limited. The one top-level official who had been integrally involved from start to finish—FBI director Robert S. Mueller III—chose not to attend. At this, his moment to publicly preside over the resolution of one of the most important cases in the annals of American law enforcement, the FBI director stayed away.

His absence seemed of a piece with his other miscalculations. After installing Inspector Richard Lambert and supporting his misguided leadership, Mueller in the end offered no congratulations for a job well done to Ed Montooth, Vince Lisi, Tom Dellafera, Lawrence Alexander, or the others who steered the investigation away from Hatfill to Bruce Ivins.

Looking back on the investigation, Mueller must have had regrets. He had participated in the detailed confidential briefings of Senators Daschle and Leahy and Attorney General Ashcroft, at which the FBI touted the prowess of the bloodhounds, each of which was said to have led investigators to Hatfill's doorstep, even to the ponds above Frederick. Mueller's backing of Inspector Lambert stifled dissent among investigators and helped to keep the task force sidetracked.

On August 7, 2008, the day after the news conference, the FBI director traveled to Vermont to announce a locally focused counterterrorism initiative and to meet privately with Leahy. When reporters asked about missteps in the anthrax investigation, including the $5.82 million settlement of Hatfill's lawsuit, Mueller took a hard line. "I am unapologetic. I do not apologize for any aspect of the investigation that was undertaken over the years. And I think it is erroneous to say there were mistakes."[5]

By refusing to yield any ground, Mueller missed an opportunity to assure the public that a just conclusion had been reached.

The FBI abetted the misinformation surrounding the anthrax mailings by not promoting more rapid disclosure of the scientific details. At the time of Ivins's death, more than six years had passed since the Sandia National Laboratories had determined that the anthrax in the letters was not enhanced with any additive. Yet the FBI still had not authorized the publication of that finding in a scientific journal. Had Sandia's results been made public in mid-2002, the claims of weaponized spores, linked to Iraq or al Qaeda, might have been relegated to a circle of conspiracy theorists.

The vacuum was filled, predictably, by rumor and conjecture that fed the twenty-four-hour news cycle. No speculation was too extreme for some blogs. After Ivins's suicide, even respected news outlets seemed to resist the idea that this unknown figure, not Hatfill, had carried out the attacks. Among the most vocal doubters to emerge were Army colleagues of Bruce Ivins, including the same supervisors who had never questioned his mental fitness to handle anthrax.

The myth of weaponized spores could be traced to October 2001, when both Bruce Ivins and the virologist Peter Jahrling opined repeatedly about the supposedly spectacular, weapons-grade characteristics of the powder sent to Majority Leader Daschle. Ivins did much of his talking among colleagues at Fort Detrick. Jahrling carried photographs of the spores to the Pentagon and to the White House to buttress his contention that the material appeared to have been treated with an additive, perhaps linking the bioterrorism to Saddam Hussein.

Jahrling's analysis was scientifically discredited as of spring 2002 by the results at the Sandia national labs. But the staying power of his assessment was on vivid display six years later, after Ivins's suicide. On August 18, 2008, the FBI called a second news conference in Washington, featuring a handful of top scientific experts who had helped the investigation. Among them was Joseph Michael, the leader of the Sandia team, who described in detail the basis for concluding that the spores had not been enhanced with an additive. But at least one of the assembled journalists, Gary Matsumoto, was not ready to let go of the early hypothesis. Referring to Jahrling and his technical assistant, Thomas Geisbert, Matsumoto said: "Dr. Jahrling and Dr. Geisbert said they actually saw the silica on the surface of the spores." [6]

Michael tried to explain: The microscope used by Jahrling and Geisbert could see the "signal" of silicon or silica, but was not capable of detecting whether the material was inside the spores, or coating the exteriors. This was a crucial distinction, because only through coating could the spores have been enhanced, or *weaponized.* [7] Sandia's more powerful electron microscope had shown, definitively, that there was no exterior coating on the spores. A month after the August 2008 news conference, Jahrling acknowledged that he had gotten it wrong.

"I believe I made an honest mistake," Jahrling told me by e-mail on September 16, 2008, adding that he had been "overly impressed" by what he thought he saw under the microscope. "I should never have ventured into this area. . . . [I]n retrospect, I believe I was mistaken, and defer to the experts." [8]

Jahrling's admission of error, which I reported in the next day's *Los Angeles Times*, did not catch up with the loose talk about weaponized anthrax. That same morning, in a spacious, wood-paneled hearing room of the Hart Building—the very building that seven years earlier had been shut down because of the anthrax-laced letter to Senator Daschle—FBI director Robert Mueller appeared before the Senate Judiciary Committee. Among the spectators were a few defenders of Bruce Ivins, including one of his former bosses, Dr. Russell Byrne. And in the front row sat Steven Hatfill, flanked by his attorney, Thomas Connolly. The committee chairman, Democrat Patrick Leahy of Vermont, the other senator to whom an anthrax-laced letter had been addressed, erupted with the fervor of an aggrieved victim.

"I have watched your testimony," Leahy said, interrupting Mueller's recitation of prepared remarks. "You briefed me in Vermont [on August 7]. I have read the material. These weapons that were used against the American people—and *they are weapons. They're weapons.* The weapons that were used against the American people and Congress."[9]

Leahy's vehemence implied a dispute that didn't exist: No thinking person would question the lethality of the anthrax in the letters. The material killed five people. But Joseph Michael's research at Sandia revealed a nuance that Leahy did not understand or would not acknowledge: There was no evidence that this already deadly anthrax had been treated with a lethality-boosting additive, the presence of which could have suggested sponsorship by Iraq or a state-sponsored terror group. Mueller could have publicly reminded Leahy that the FBI had in fact informed the senator and his top aides on several occasions about the results from Sandia, and that those results showed that the mailed anthrax was not weaponized with an additive—but he did not.[10]

Leahy proceeded to his rhetorical climax, alleging a conspiracy of unknown proportions: "If he [Bruce Ivins] is the one who sent the letter, I do not believe in any way, shape, or manner that he is the only person involved in this attack on Congress and the American people. I do not believe that at all. *I believe there are others involved, either as accessories before or accessories after the fact. I believe there are others out there. I believe there are others who can be charged with murder.*"[11] Leahy did not cite any basis for these assertions, either at the hearing or when given the opportunity afterward.[12]

Theatrics aside, there was a legitimate question regarding the attack material. Yes, the scientists at Sandia had documented that the silicon in the anthrax was inside the spores, where it did not enhance lethality. And it could be inferred that the silicon was not there due to any sinister origin. But what could explain the absence of a similar level of silicon in the parent flask of RMR-1029 maintained by Bruce Ivins? The reasoning of experienced microbiologists who assisted the investigation is as follows:

The anthrax spores in the letters appeared to have resulted from the culturing, growing, and harvesting of material from the parent flask. The process entails using a brothlike material, or culture medium, to grow the spores. The medium can contain trace amounts of silicon, which can be absorbed by the anthrax and deposited in the layer beneath the spore's outermost covering, where it would in no way enhance the lethality of the powdered anthrax. Additional experiments might help to explain why the silicon in the letters reached particular concentrations, approximately 1.2 percent to 2.3 percent of the weight of the anthrax spores.[13]

Although scientifically sound, this explanation is subtle enough to be drowned out when government officials and conspiracy theorists join to promote dramatic scenarios. It's also true that although there is no evidence the silicon in the spores made them more lethal, determining exactly how the silicon got there might be impossible, even with additional research. FBI Director Mueller sought to address such uncertainties by arranging for the National Academy of Sciences to appoint a committee, in mid-2009, to examine the investigation's scientific methods and conclusions.[14] Out of public view, the Justice Department later that year won a federal judge's permission for another outside review, this one focusing on Ivins's mental health history and seeking lessons to be learned "that may be useful in preventing future bioterrorism attacks." [15]

Some critics of the investigation never backed away from their original assertions about the origins of the anthrax letters. Richard Spertzel, the retired USAMRIID deputy commander and United Nations bioweapons inspector, clung to his belief that Iraq was likely the source.[16] Randall J. Larsen, who served as executive director of the Congressional Commission on the Prevention of Weapons of Mass Destruction Proliferation and Terrorism and is a retired Air Force colonel, believes the mailings were the work of al Qaeda. "I can't prove it beyond reasonable doubt—but neither can they," Larsen told me, referring to the FBI.[17] His reasoning is worth parsing: Although there is no credible evidence that al Qaeda or Iraq ever obtained the Ames strain—let alone RMR-1029—it's also impossible to prove that any terrorist organization or rogue nation did *not* do so.

Thomas Inglesby, one of the two lead authors of the May

2002 *JAMA* article that described the mailed anthrax as having been "treated to reduce clumping," never provided a basis for his article's claim, or a published correction. The claim was cited without qualification by other scientific journals.[18] Yet the article caused no apparent professional repercussions for Inglesby. To the contrary, in June 2009, the National Academy named him to the committee that would judge the scientific aspects of the Amerithrax investigation. The other lead co-author of the 2002 *JAMA* article, Dr. Tara O'Toole, won an appointment from President Barack Obama in 2009 to serve as undersecretary of science and technology in the Department of Homeland Security.[19]

———

The FBI's Ed Montooth sensed it the instant he got the call informing him that a comatose Bruce Ivins had been rushed to Frederick Memorial Hospital: If Ivins died, the conspiracy theories and skepticism would eclipse a fair-minded evaluation of the evidence. *"They better save his ass,"* Montooth snapped as he hung up his phone.

The agent's worry was well founded. Perhaps the most exotic conjecture held that the letter attacks may have resulted from a covert operation set in motion by the U.S. government. This notion had been floated in 2002 by the anti-biowarfare activist Barbara Hatch Rosenberg—and it was revived after Ivins's suicide by others. One of those often quoted in this regard was Meryl Nass, a physician and well-known critic of the military's anthrax vaccine program. In postings on her Web site and in media interviews, Nass ridiculed the evidence against Ivins. And in February 2010, when the Justice Department issued its final investigative summary of the case, Nass posted a list of criticisms along with her own dark conclusion:

'[T]here are reasons a conspiracy makes better sense. If the FBI really had the goods, they would not be overreaching to pin the case on a lone nut. JFK, RFK, George Wallace, Martin Luther King, all felled by lone nuts. Even Ronald Reagan's would-be assassin was a lone nut. Now Bruce Ivins. The American public is supposed to believe that all these crimes required no assistance and no funds. Does the FBI stand for the Federal Bureau of Invention?[20]

Similar thoughts were voiced by Frederick attorney Barry Kissin, a onetime candidate for Congress whose views on the anthrax case have appeared in the *Frederick News-Post* and the *Washington Post* and on other Internet sites. In February 2010, Kissin wrote that the Justice Department and the FBI "and the powers above them that directed the farce called Amerithrax should be very satisfied if all that people suspect is that this was a botched investigation." Sounding like Barbara Hatch Rosenberg eight years earlier, Kissin added, "Amerithrax is a deliberately 'botched investigation,' otherwise known as a cover-up. The powers that be know exactly where the anthrax attacks came from, and so should we."[21]

Another persistent critic, blogger-novelist Lew Weinstein, said "the most likely scenario" is that FBI officials "do know who did it but they won't tell us." Weinstein in late 2010 posted this comment on his Web site, Case Closed, which offers a steady menu of conspiracy-rich statements about the investigation.[22]

Rosenberg herself reprised her theory of government complicity: On July 22, 2010, she and two other critics of the investigation sent a letter to the National Academy of Sciences review committee, suggesting that the attacks may have been carried out by an "authorized" person who obtained spores prepared not at USAMRIID, but at the Battelle Memorial Institute. Rosenberg, together with anthrax researcher Martin Hugh-Jones and Stuart Jacobsen, a chemist in the semiconductor industry, also wrote that the spores in the letters "may have come from the leftover remains of production runs that had authorized purposes." They did not say who the perpetrator might be. Rosenberg and her associates instead asserted that the FBI had not investigated thoroughly enough to disprove their ideas.[23]

Of all the weapons of mass destruction allegedly possessed or coveted by Iraq, anthrax was the one most immediately familiar to Americans. It was the dread of massive anthrax casualties that

Secretary of State Colin Powell—conjuring the memory of the letter attacks—invoked at the United Nations during his argument for ousting Saddam Hussein in February 2003. Yet the anthrax investigation's own experts had already reported to the FBI that the powder in the letters was *not* treated with an additive—that is, it was *not* weaponized—a finding that undercut the notion of linkage to Iraq. Moreover, the anthrax used in the mailings was of the Ames strain, material that at no point was found to be in the hands of anyone in Iraq.

Had the Bush administration accepted the scientists' findings, Powell might have steered clear of invoking the anthrax mailings, and a pretext for war would have been denied the credibility supplied by America's distinguished secretary of state.

Powell later conceded the failure to find any biological, chemical, or nuclear weapons in Iraq, and he voiced uncertainty about the basis upon which he helped prod the nation into war—a war that cost some $750 billion and took the lives of more than 5,000 Americans and in excess of 100,000 Iraqis.[24] Tom Ridge, who served as Bush's advisor and cabinet-level secretary for homeland security, acknowledged that there had been a rush to judgment. He said that in the run-up to the war many administration officials had been adamant that Iraq had a role in the anthrax attacks. "There were certain people at the White House who were absolutely positive," Ridge recalled, saying that, in retrospect, their opinions amounted to "conclusions without facts."[25]

No second thoughts were to be found among the Bush administration's ardent hawks, including Deputy Defense Secretary Paul Wolfowitz, who continued after the war's outset to emphasize the anthrax letter attacks while framing the threat of Iraqi weapons of mass destruction. "There was no oversell," Wolfowitz said in May 2003. "I mean, let's go back and remember what changed the whole world, which is 3,000 Americans were killed on September 11th by commercial airliners. And a couple of weeks later we got a warning of what somebody could do with envelopes filled with anthrax."[26]

When asked in late 2010 why he had believed there was a

connection between Iraq or al Qaeda and the anthrax mailings, Wolfowitz said, "It struck me as a rather remarkable coincidence that this happened so soon after 9/11. It strongly suggested a connection."[27] His opinion with the benefit of more than seven years of hindsight? Wolfowitz said he did not know what to believe.[28]

This was a replay of what Defense Secretary Donald Rumsfeld had told Congress about the anthrax mailings in advance of the Iraq War: "The nature of terrorist attacks is that it is often very difficult to identify who is ultimately responsible."[29] For his part, George W. Bush commented only cryptically about the mailings in his 2010 memoir: "The biggest question during the anthrax attack was where it was coming from. One of the best intelligence services in Europe told us it suspected Iraq." The former president did not identify which intelligence service or its basis for implicating Iraq.[30]

The willful discounting of the investigation's scientific findings had practical implications that went beyond the launching of the Iraq War. The one-two punch of September 11 and the anthrax letters triggered a major commitment of federal resources to biological defense. One of the first beneficiaries was, of course, the long-languishing next-generation anthrax vaccine co-invented by Bruce Ivins, a product boosted by the first contract awarded under Project BioShield.

The Bush administration and Congress also began funding a several-fold increase of laboratories—and lab personnel—to work with the most dangerous biological pathogens, including the Ebola and Marburg viruses, tularemia, plague, and anthrax.[31]

These new Level 3 and Level 4 labs—called Regional Centers of Excellence for Biodefense and Emerging Infectious Diseases—continue to be scattered around the country. The labs have been funded at upwards of $1.5 billion a year on the implicit promise that they will make us safer by developing new antidotes or other products to counter the instruments of biological terrorism. Perhaps such benefits will come to fruition.

The more immediate consequence of these labs, staffed by

more than fifteen thousand researchers and technicians, is an enormous security risk inherent in the greatly increased number of people and institutions with access to the deadliest pathogens.[32] This is the Strangelovian legacy of the anthrax attacks, crimes that, according to the best available evidence, were committed by a trusted researcher at the most presumptively secure of American biodefense facilities. Yet many prominent biodefense scientists appear unfazed by this recent history. They oppose as overly intrusive and costly the enactment of tighter federal controls over the labs.

Their mind-set was starkly displayed on April 3, 2009, about eight months after Ivins's suicide, in a crowded hotel conference room in Bethesda, Maryland, where a federal advisory panel was meeting to consider procedures for "enhancing personnel reliability among individuals with access to select agents and toxins." None of the printed materials prepared for the panel referred to him by name, but as several speakers noted, the "elephant in the room," the man whose fate had made this gathering necessary, was Bruce Ivins.[33] But what to make of this elephant? Those speakers who mentioned him by name were, with rare exception, careful to opine that Ivins's guilt remained unproven. One audience member, a scientist from the FDA, drew applause when she said that her deceased acquaintance deserved a "presumption of innocence."

Denial of Ivins's culpability permeated the resistance to any new federal controls on those who work in the labs. One panel member, retired Army Colonel David R. Franz, a biologist and former USAMRIID commander from the 1990s who remains prominent in the biodefense field, likened new regulation to America's habit of "always fighting the last war." In this case, the "war" would be the anthrax letter attacks, the lessons from which, Franz suggested, were unworthy of being applied to future lab operations. Franz, without ever having examined the powder, had been among the first to publicly assert that the anthrax attacks must have been sponsored by "some proliferant nation" in league with terrorists.[34] And now, if the actual culprits remained unidentified—meaning that the attacks might yet be tied to a *foreign* sponsor—why impose more stringent controls on U.S. researchers?[35]

Other opponents of tougher U.S. government policies, mainly university officials with burgeoning biodefense budgets, made clear that they want the new federal money for their institutions to be free and clear of additional security requirements. No one bothered to point out the tighter federal restrictions on workers who handle nuclear or chemical weapons.

The changes that were up for discussion seemed modest: One would require that at least two researchers always be present for work with anthrax or other lethal pathogens—a "two-person rule" that would have complicated or prevented Bruce Ivins's string of late nights, toiling alone in the hot suite. Also discussed and roundly criticized was the idea of standardized psychological evaluations. This, too, might have kept Ivins away from anthrax.

Having observed the room's overwhelming hostility to new restrictions, one of the invited lab chiefs began a personal reminiscence of Ivins. Dr. P. Frederick Sparling, the director of a regional biodefense research complex at the University of North Carolina, had approved Professor Priscilla Wyrick's hiring of Ivins as a postdoctoral researcher in 1975.

"I knew Bruce," said Sparling, illuminated at the podium. "He was *certifiably* strange, at the very best. No doubt about it. And yet people who worked with him very closely, going way back to his youth—and also his colleagues at Detrick—couldn't recognize what was up. So I find that very disconcerting. . . . It's very difficult to know what is normal."[36]

During the next break another former USAMRIID commander, the now-retired Colonel George Korch, who in December 2006 had assured Ivins that "this FBI situation . . . is under control," promptly sought out Sparling and upbraided him. Korch ridiculed the idea that Ivins had been dangerously unstable.

Sparling's cautionary remarks soon would be disregarded. The next month the National Science Advisory Board for Biosecurity issued a handful of tepid recommendations, with no call for either standardized psychological evaluations or for the two-person rule in the hot suites, or for any other new federal requirements. After all, said the board's upbeat report, "local institutions already do an extremely effective job at screening individuals." [37]

This was not to say that all the board members believed Ivins was innocent. On a steamy late summer night in 2010, I met with one of them at a hotel bar in Rockville, Maryland. Paul Keim had always deflected the paramount question surrounding the anthrax investigation, saying that the answer was outside his discipline as a scientist. But as we began conversing over burgers and cold beers, I asked him directly: How would he vote if he were a juror weighing Ivins's guilt or innocence? The circumspect geneticist replied without hesitation: "I think he did it." [38]

THE CASE AGAINST BRUCE IVINS

Some valid questions persist about the case against Ivins—questions that prosecutors would have had to confront at a trial. Among them:

Did Ivins have both the expertise and the opportunity to prepare the anthrax?

Some of Ivins's defenders argued that he could not have perpetrated the letter attacks. "The bottom line is, Bruce didn't have anything to do with it. And USAMRIID didn't have anything to do with it," former Bacteriology Division chief Gerard "Gerry" Andrews, who worked with plague, not anthrax, told me.[1] Richard Spertzel, the former deputy USAMRIID commander who asserts that the spores were treated with a chemical additive, told the *Washington Post* within a week of Ivins's suicide, "I don't think there's anyone there [at USAMRIID] who would have the foggiest idea how to do it." Ivins, he said, lacked "the opportunity, the capability."[2]

Yet Ivins himself, by casting suspicion on present or former colleagues, repeatedly suggested that it was, indeed, possible for a USAMRIID scientist to have pulled off the attacks. Moreover, on September 20, 2001—two days after the first anthrax-laced letters were postmarked—Ivins had boasted of his expertise in preparing spores. He told an outside scientist that his mastery of "nuances in methodology" enabled him to rapidly produce "stable, pure, unclumped" spores.[3]

It's not necessary to rely on Ivins's own assessment of his proficiency. Several microbiologists with experience growing bacterial spores told me they were convinced that a skilled hand such as Ivins could have prepared all the anthrax used in the letter attacks.

"It's almost an insult to say he didn't have the capability," said the ex-USAMRIID anthrax specialist John Ezzell, in one of our many conversations.[4] Ezzell, himself an accomplished microbiologist, had a unique vantage point: He helped hire Ivins and worked alongside him, he personally had grown and dried anthrax spores (though they were irradiated for safety), and he led the evaluations of all the attack letters brought to USAMRIID. Not wanting to run afoul of a then binding nondisclosure agreement he had signed with the FBI, and wary of offending the defenders of Bruce Ivins, Ezzell at first spoke with me only with great reluctance. Over the next two years, however, we discussed the science and the related circumstances surrounding the letter attacks on more than eighty occasions. As he spoke, Ezzell often drew diagrams to show how anthrax could be grown, purified, and dried at USAMRIID.

Ezzell estimated that Ivins would have needed "less than a week" to prepare the material sent to the *New York Post*, Tom Brokaw of NBC News, and American Media Inc. in Palm Beach County, Florida. Ezzell also said he suspected that Ivins had sufficient anthrax stored in his lab's refrigerator. If this was the case, Ivins would not have had to go through the time-consuming process of growing the material. All he would have had to do was purify and dry the spores. (Though Ezzell believes the evidence points toward Ivins's guilt, he said he had stopped short of so judging him.)[5]

Assuming that Ivins saw the September 11 attacks as the perfect cover for the anthrax mailings, he had to rush to get that batch out by September 18, the date the first letters were post-marked, and it showed: The dried anthrax was of a relatively crude texture. The particles were not microscopically small and included many flecks of blackish brown, dead anthrax cells, demonstrating that time had not been taken to both centrifuge and wash the batch over and over to high purification.

As for the remaining two letters recovered by investigators—the envelopes addressed to Senators Daschle and Leahy—both the off-tan color and the finer texture of the powder suggested preparation that was more meticulous. Ezzell opened the Leahy envelope under the observation of the FBI and weighed the anthrax at 0.85 gram.[6] But because each of the other envelopes had been unsealed before the FBI got hold of them, there is no way to know how much anthrax they contained. (The limitations of carbon dating prevent that technology from pinpointing whether all or a portion of the anthrax put into the letters was grown before, or after, September 11.)[7]

The FBI's Douglas Beecher, whose work on the case began in early October 2001, sought to learn firsthand whether a microbiologist with common skills and know-how could grow anthrax with the high concentration of spores found in the letter attacks. Using standard lab equipment and working over a period of days with Bacillus cereus, a spore-forming bacterium closely related to anthrax, he was able to do just that: Beecher's batch contained 2.3 trillion spores per gram of finished material—similar to that found in the letters to Daschle and Leahy and far purer than the material addressed to Brokaw and the New York Post.[8]

Professor Peter Setlow of the University of Connecticut, a biochemist and microbiologist with decades of experience in the field, said that preparing the necessary amount of purified spores would not have been difficult for a microbiologist with access to anthrax, an up-to-date vaccination, standard lab equipment—and the safety provided by a biocontainment suite.

"It doesn't take phenomenal sophistication to make spores or to purify them, despite what people have sometimes said," Setlow said. As for drying the spores, "Anybody who ever worked with spores would know how to do it." In addition to expertise, Ivins had easy access to a hot suite with negative-air controls to remove loose spores that would otherwise contaminate the lab.[9]

Ivins clearly had not only the ability but the opportunity to prepare ample quantities of anthrax. He had unlimited access to RMR-1029, the special batch of spores that he had created in 1997 and that geneticists matched through DNA analyses to the attack letters. And his all-hours access to the well-equipped facilities in the USAMRIID hot suites would have enabled him to work in secrecy.[10]

Ivins was able to go in and out of the hot suites at any time of the day or night, when no other scientists were present. Using one of the standard-issue centrifuges, he could have isolated and then washed away dead cells and other debris to make the anthrax spores purer and more deadly. He could have dried the material, using either a lyophilizer or a centrifuge equipped with a moisture-eliminating vacuum, equipment also available in his lab. Finally, with a razor blade and a mortar and pestle—just like the ones his pharmacist father used—Ivins could have chopped and ground any dried clumps of spores into a powder.

The laboratory where Ivins worked was cluttered and the Army gave him wide latitude in how he maintained his supplies of anthrax. He kept his original batch of RMR-1029 in his lab's walk-in refrigerator, where he was able to store this and numerous other flasks without any concern about the possibility of random inspections.[11] Ivins could have grown and stored spores under arbitrary labels known only to him, and no video cameras were in place to monitor what he or others were doing.

As Ivins ultimately acknowledged in his interviews with the FBI, there was an apparent shortage in the amount of accounted-for anthrax in the parent flask of RMR-1029, of which he was the sole custodian. This discrepancy between the anthrax actually in the flask and the quantity Ivins recorded in his logbook was approximately 220 milliliters.[12] This was less than the quantity needed for the letter attacks, but the discrepancy was a sign of lax controls at USAMRIID that could be exploited by a determined insider.[13]

Did the presence of silicon in the attack spores show that the material was weaponized, that is, treated with a chemical additive?

The scientists at the Sandia National Laboratories provided the data that seemingly answered the question in 2002: After applying state-of-the-art analytical techniques, they found that the material was not treated with any additive.

Yet this finding went widely unnoticed, even among scientists and officials paying relatively close attention. There are various explanations for why the Sandia results did not gain traction. Although the FBI did brief executive branch officials and a few members of Congress and their senior aides about the results in 2002 and 2003, the bureau refused until early 2010 to approve publication of Sandia's data. Second, certain supposed experts outside the investigation—the widely quoted Richard Spertzel and Thomas Inglesby come to mind—never retreated from their original assertions that the anthrax *was* treated with an additive.

It was in December 2001 that Spertzel originally suggested that Iraq could have used a compound of silicon—"pharmaceutical grade silica"—to weaponize the anthrax.[14] On August 5, 2008, four days after the news of Ivins's suicide, Spertzel reprised his old claims in service of a new conclusion: Ivins could not have weaponized the material—and therefore he was not the perpetrator. "Apparently," Spertzel wrote in an essay published by the *Wall Street Journal*, "the spores were coated with a polyglass which bound hydrophilic silica to each particle."[15]

Polyglass? A review of available scientific literature shows that polyglass is a product used for making partial dentures—but not pharmaceutical powders. When I asked him to explain, Spertzel conceded that he was unsure about this alleged additive. "Polyglass is used as a coating, I believe, in the pharmaceutical industry. I'm not 100 percent sure."

Yet Spertzel said that he stood by his published statements that pharmaceutical silica and polyglass had been used to weaponize the anthrax because, as he wrote in the essay, a former subordinate had told him that the FBI "briefed it to the German Foreign Ministry" in fall 2001. Asked if he knew who or what level of official in the FBI had briefed the Germans, Spertzel said: "No, because I was just collecting information. I can't even use the word 'collect.' The information was falling on me." For Spertzel, hearsay about what someone in the FBI supposedly said to unspecified German officials trumped the data and analysis by the experts at Sandia.[16]

Spertzel was not alone in making the case that the spores bore a telltale coating. Journalist Gary Matsumoto published two articles suggesting that the spores were artificially treated. The first article, with Matsumoto as a co-author, was published October 28, 2002, on the front page of the *Washington Post*.[17] In November 2003, Matsumoto was the sole author of a longer account, published by *Science*, a peer-reviewed weekly journal, in which he wrote that a "laboratory analyzing the Senate anthrax spores for the FBI reported the discovery of what appeared to be a chemical additive." Matsumoto did not identify the laboratory but added, "U.S. intelligence officers informed foreign biodefense officials that this additive was 'polymerized glass.'"[18]

The presence of "polymerized glass" would have been news to Sandia lab engineer Joseph Michael, whom the FBI assigned to analyze the Senate anthrax in early 2002.[19] Nonetheless, a scientific journal article published years later, in March 2007—citing Matsumoto's magazine account—reasserted the claim that the Senate anthrax was treated with polymerized glass.[20]

Matsumoto had been among the first journalists to claim that the mailed anthrax was artificially treated: As a producer at ABC News, he was cited as a contributor to investigative correspondent Brian Ross's explosive but ultimately discredited account, on October 26, 2001, that tests at Fort Detrick and elsewhere had found bentonite, a signature of Iraq's biowarfare program, in the anthrax sent to Tom Daschle.[21]

In February 2011, the committee appointed by the National Academy of Sciences to review scientific aspects of the case agreed with the results reached nearly nine years earlier at Sandia: The committee said it saw no evidence of bentonite or that the anthrax in the letters had been in any way chemically treated, or weaponized, so as to prevent the spores from clumping together. "Silicon was present in the letter powders but there was no evidence of intentional addition of silicon-based dispersants," the committee concluded, adding that "no silicon was detected on the outside surface of spores where a dispersant would reside." [22]

If the silicon-containing material was not added—how did it get inside the spores?

A likely source would be the brothlike culture medium in which anthrax cells are sometimes grown. [23] This could help explain why the parent flask of RMR-1029 maintained by Ivins contained no measurable amounts of silicon, while the anthrax that investigators believe was cultured from material that had been removed from RMR-1029 did. The scientific literature affirms that silicon exists in anthrax and other *Bacillus* spores—and the propensity of the spores to absorb silicon during growth has been described by researchers, including a team at the Lawrence Livermore National Laboratory in Livermore, California. [24]

In its review of the investigation, the National Academy of Sciences committee pointed out the difficulty of reconstructing precisely how silicon came to be in the attack material. The committee also noted the complexity of measuring the amounts of silicon in the anthrax recovered from the letters: The refined uniformity of the Leahy powder may have lent itself to more consistent measurements of silicon, unlike the coarse, granular material mailed to the *New York Post*. [25]

Laboratories of differing expertise did produce divergent results for the *Post* material. Though the Sandia National Laboratories found that the amount of silicon in the *Post* and Leahy letters was about the same, an initial test at the FBI lab in Quantico, Virginia, had suggested a far higher level for the *Post* material. It was after that test in the fall of 2001 that the FBI contracted with Sandia to provide more sophisticated analyses of the recovered anthrax. The laboratories had different equipment and methods: Sandia examined the percentage of silicon for each spore; the FBI lab measured silicon not by spore, but on the entire sample. The FBI's "bulk" method was less precise, and more vulnerable to a misleading result, especially because of the crude composition of the *Post* anthrax.[26]

In the opinion of the National Academy committee, the "detection sensitivity" for silicon at Sandia was superior to that of any other lab that examined the anthrax from the Leahy and *Post* letters. Noting the instruments and methodology employed at Sandia, the committee said, "These enhanced capabilities greatly aided the measurements and the conclusions that could be drawn from them."

Nonetheless, the committee faulted the FBI for not providing a "compelling explanation" for the disparity in the results for the *Post* letter. "Lacking this information," the committee said, "one cannot rule out the intentional addition of a silicon-based substance to the *New York Post* letter, in a failed attempt to enhance dispersion."[27] The committee's speculation on this point neglects other potential explanations, and it conflicts with its own finding that there was "no evidence of intentional addition of silicon-based dispersants."

Dwight Adams, who was director of the FBI lab during the first several years of the investigation, had enlisted Sandia to provide more precise data. "You can't give equal weight to both analyses," Adams told me, referring to the initial finding by his lab and the work done by Sandia. "That's exactly why we went to a national laboratory like Sandia. Those are the results that I think are the most valid."[28]

How reliable were the four genetic mutations, or morphs, as evidence that the anthrax used in the letters was derived from RMR-1029?

The Amerithrax scientists found that of the 1,070 samples of Ames strain anthrax collected worldwide, only 8 had all four of the morphs detected in the powder from the letters.[29] All eight of those samples were traced to the parent flask of RMR-1029, maintained by Ivins. The numbers are impressive, but could the morphs have emerged in any of those eight samples irrespective of a lineage with RMR-1029?

In its review of the scientific aspects of the investigation, the National Academy of Sciences committee said that the genetic evidence was "consistent with and supports an association between the RMR-1029 flask" and the anthrax in the letters, but "did not definitively demonstrate such a relationship." The committee also faulted the FBI for not employing the newest technologies for analyzing anthrax, including morphs.[30] On this point, the committee looked past the real-world conditions under which the Amerithrax case played out. In consultation with outside experts, the FBI's scientific leaders used only those approaches that would conform to legal precedents requiring that new techniques must have been validated—that is, proven reliable through controlled studies that consistently reproduced the same results—in order for the related evidence to be admissible at a trial. As the investigation unfolded, some of the latest experimental methods were either not available or not validated, making them irrelevant to the work at hand. New methods that came on line may have sped some of the genetic testing, but there is no indication that the results would have differed.[31]

The National Academy committee did acknowledge that the data from the four morphs support the conclusion that the anthrax letters were derived from RMR-1029. As the committee pointed out, that support is not absolute, and this underscores the distinction between scientific certainty and the burden of proof for winning a criminal conviction: Prosecutors would have drawn upon both scientific and traditional evidence in trying to prove Ivins guilty beyond a reasonable doubt. This is not to be confused with "beyond a shadow of a doubt." Indeed, judges instruct jurors that the government is *not* required to prove guilt beyond all doubt—or to a mathematical or scientific certainty.[32]

How did *Bacillus subtilis*, a contaminant that was not present in the parent flask of RMR-1029, get into the attack anthrax?

This contaminant is a common, if unwanted, guest in laboratory settings. Because the attack material appeared to have been at least one step removed—cultured and grown—from the original batch of RMR-1029, the emergence of the contaminant is not a surprise to microbiologists. A speck of dust or a simple sneeze could have introduced it.[33]

Why the particular high-profile list of intended victims?

Ivins did not appear to have a firsthand connection with any of the addressees of the letters—Brokaw, Senators Daschle and Leahy, "Editor" of the *New York Post*, or anyone at the parent offices of the *National Enquirer*. Yet Ivins was a longtime student of the news media and national politics. He had written scores of letters to office holders and news organizations and, on some occasions, voiced contempt for tabloids, in particular, the *National Enquirer*.[34] He could have surmised that sending anthrax to the senators and the media targets all but guaranteed maximum attention, fear—and, very likely, policy reactions that would revive development of his co-invented anthrax vaccine.

> **Circumstantial evidence.** 1. Evidence based on inference and not on personal knowledge or observation.
> —*Black's Law Dictionary*, 8th edition

Did Bruce Ivins do it? Did he lace the letters with anthrax and mail them? Did he consign five people to their deaths, six other victims to the serious after-effects of inhalational anthrax, and eleven other survivors, including a seven-month-old boy, to the ghastly experience of anthrax skin infections?

The reasons to believe that Ivins prepared and mailed the anthrax letters are not provided by an outright confession or an eyewitness account. There is no toll road receipt from New Jersey, no videotape of a crime in progress, no single, dispositive piece of evidence that, by itself, establishes his guilt. But there is a chain of evidence—pieces that, considered as a whole, reveal Ivins to be the perpetrator.

Judges routinely instruct juries that circumstantial evidence of a defendant's guilt may be viewed as equal in weight to direct evidence, such as testimony from an eyewitness. What, then, is the circumstantial evidence pointing toward Bruce Ivins's guilt?

The extraordinary late hours alone in the hot suite. In the weeks before the first postmarked mailings, on Tuesday, September 18, 2001, Ivins had appeared to be on a mission known only to him. In just the month of August, he logged more nighttime hours alone in the B3 hot suite than during the previous seven months. Through September 11, he had spent parts of twelve consecutive nights there—and three straight nights immediately preceding September 18. Before the day of the next postmarked mailings, Tuesday, October 9, 2001, he spent eight more consecutive nights alone in the same hot suite, totaling more than fifteen hours on this round.

When the FBI asked him about these very unusual hours, Ivins could not offer a plausible explanation. His contemporaneous lab notes also offered no justification, other than the chore of checking for dead rabbits. Ivins said that, to escape unpleasantness at home, he went to the hot suite during some off-hours just to sit and think. To be sure, Ivins over the years did stop by the lab on weekends or during other off-hours. Yet investigators found that on those occasions his colleagues or his own lab notes generally gave a believable explanation for why he was there. The hours Ivins worked in proximity to the fall 2001 mailings were unlike any other period for him captured by the electronic card system since its installation in August 1998.[35]

Ivins's unaccounted-for hours stand in striking contrast to the work schedules of the other scientists known to have had access to RMR-1029, the parent batch of anthrax: Not one of them worked alone or for such intervals in a hot suite during the periods before the letter attacks.[36]

The mailbox in Princeton. Ivins had plenty of time to make the separate seven- to eight-hour round-trips to the mailbox in downtown Princeton, where the anthrax-laced letters were deposited. And he could have made those without attracting the notice of his wife, since they slept in different parts of the house and she did not question his absences.

Why Princeton? Only by knowing about his bizarre, decades-long obsession with Kappa Kappa Gamma can an outsider begin to fathom why Ivins would have chosen the mailbox at 10 Nassau Street: Nearly straight above the mailbox, on the fourth floor of an office building at 20 Nassau, is the Princeton chapter of Kappa Kappa Gamma. Ivins had painstakingly researched the locations of scores of KKG chapters throughout the East. He also knew that his ex-colleague from USAMRIID, Joseph Farchaus, lived nearby in New Jersey. Ivins—who had quickly pointed this out to investigators and repeatedly alleged that Farchaus could be the perpetrator—may have delighted in choosing a location that cast suspicion on the man he considered his tormentor.

The DNA profile linking RMR-1029 to the attacks. From the time that he inventoried it under the label RMR-1029 in the late 1990s, Ivins was the custodian of this mixture of Ames strain anthrax. He stored the material in B3, the same hot suite where he spent the many late nights preceding the letter attacks. The FBI traveled the world to collect 1,070 samples of the Ames strain. The bureau's team of scientific experts tested each—and found that only eight of the samples contained the same four genetically distinct morphs as the anthrax in the letters.

Those eight samples all came from either of two places: USAMRIID, where Ivins worked, and the Battelle Memorial Institute in Ohio, to whose scientists Ivins had sent RMR-1029. The exhaustive police work, including scrutinizing more than one hundred Battelle scientists in 2002, led the FBI to rule out every person who had access to those eight samples, except for Bruce Ivins.

The submission of the false sample of RMR-1029. In early 2002, as the FBI was collecting samples of anthrax for DNA testing, Ivins was among the first at USAMRIID to submit a sample. But despite the subpoena's clear instructions, he put the material in the wrong type of test tubes. Consequently, that sample was rejected.

A few weeks later, Ivins attended a meeting on March 29, 2002, led by his colleague Patricia Worsham and FBI agent Scott Stanley, at which Ivins and other USAMRIID scientists were given precise instructions about how to prepare their samples of anthrax. After withdrawing a small amount of anthrax from his flask of RMR-1029 and culturing it in a Petri dish, he was supposed to harvest and submit within test tubes a broad swath of emerging anthrax cells. The broad swath was crucial, those attending the meeting were told, because the investigators were hunting for possible genetic mutations that would likely not be found in individual, regular-shaped colonies of anthrax cells.

By his own acknowledgment to his attorney, Ivins deliberately picked only single colonies for his pivotal second sample, submitted on April 10, 2002. Not surprisingly, it contained none of the four signature mutations. Considering the instructions that he was given, his recognized expertise in growing and harvesting anthrax, and his newfound awareness that genetic identifications of specific morphs of anthrax might be feasible, his actions look like a cover-up—an attempt to conceal the true composition of the contents of his RMR-1029 flask.

Unknown to him, half of the first sample he submitted, on February 27, 2002, was preserved. Ivins was told at the time that the sample had been rejected because he used the wrong type of test tubes. But without the knowledge of Ivins or even the investigators, a mix-up at USAMRIID resulted in half of his sample being sent to Paul Keim's lab in Arizona, where it remained locked in storage for four years. When Keim came across the material in late 2006, he notified the FBI. The anthrax in this sample—submitted by Ivins *before* the March 29, 2002, meeting at which he and his colleagues were told about the investigation's possible identification of specific morphs—tested positive for three of the four mutations.

Why would Ivins have submitted a true sample on February 27 but a stalking horse on April 10? The likeliest explanation is that by the time he submitted the second sample, Ivins had been alerted, at the March 29 meeting, to the details of the FBI's hunt for distinct DNA evidence in the irregularly shaped anthrax colonies. The instructions provided at that meeting served to inform Ivins of the necessity of minimizing any chance that the incriminating morphs would be found in his sample.[37]

The furtive efforts to bleach away anthrax spores. In late 2001, Ivins said he hunted for loose spores of anthrax in the personal office he shared with two colleagues at USAMRIID. The office was well removed from the specially enclosed hot suites and there should have been no occasion for it to be contaminated with anthrax. Ivins apparently suspected otherwise. He swabbed a desk and other surfaces in the office and put what he collected in Petri dishes for culturing. When he checked the dishes the next day, he saw colonies of growth, which indicated his office was contaminated with anthrax.

Ivins then used bleach in an attempt to kill any loose anthrax spores and, contrary to safety procedures, he chose not to document or report any of what he did to the Army chain of command. This much Ivins admitted—but not until months later—after a lab mishap involving two junior colleagues gave him the opportunity to obscure the motive behind his earlier actions.

Ivins said that he had secretly hunted for anthrax in Room 19 because he suspected that a colleague was tracking spores into their shared office from the division of USAMRIID that was analyzing the attack letters on behalf of the FBI. But his explanation fell short: No contamination was ever found in that other division; and, after Ivins had tested and found what appeared to be anthrax in Room 19, he did not alert Kristie Friend, one of the lab technicians who shared the office and whom he privately accused of having caused the contamination. What is more, by his account, Ivins had swabbed for spores in the men's clean-change room, just outside the hot suites, but not the women's clean-change room—which Friend would have used. His story simply didn't add up.

Also in April 2002, Ivins claimed that he could not remember if he had verified in late 2001 whether he succeeded in eliminating all the loose anthrax spores from his office. "I honestly do not recall if follow-up swabs were taken of the area," he told the Army investigation. Ivins's professed forgetfulness on this critical issue was not credible: Room 19 was open to his own family members, to janitorial staff, and to other visitors—none of whom was vaccinated against anthrax.

Why was Ivins really seeking those loose spores in his office? One explanation is that Ivins had carried the anthrax-laced letters from the hot suite into his office before he mailed them—and he feared that some of those spores might have spilled.

Why would Ivins claim he couldn't remember making an essential verification of safety after his cleanup? If Ivins's original cleanup had been an innocent safety procedure, then he would surely have written down his findings. But if Ivins had swabbed in order to verify that his secretive bleaching eliminated evidence that could link him to the letter attacks, he would not have wanted to document any of what he did. His own explanation was that he did not keep records of his cleanup out of concern that the documentation would later be made public under the Freedom of Information Act. He also said that notifying his superiors about the presumed contamination in his office would have disrupted USAMRIID's work. His furtiveness and his conveniently faulty memory more likely reflected his consciousness of guilt.

The foreboding about inflicting harm. Well before the fall of 2001, Ivins was battling impulses to do harm. In June of 2000 he told a counselor, Judith McLean, that in the 1970s he began having urges to strike out at those who offended him. He had bought the components to make a bomb, and his urges, he confided to McLean, were growing. He wasn't sure he could contain them. He told Mara Linscott he worried that he had inherited violent tendencies from his mother, whom he regarded as schizophrenic. On July 4, 2000, he said that he might have "Paranoid

Personality Disorder," which, he said, was "seen frequently in blood relatives of schizophrenics, and it can be [a] preliminary sign of the onset of schizophrenia." Two days later, Ivins told Linscott, "When I see the terrible things that some paranoid schizophrenics have done, it honestly makes me want to cry," adding: "I may be heading toward becoming that kind of person." On August 12, 2000, Ivins elaborated: "I wish I could control the thoughts in my mind. It's hard enough sometimes controlling my behavior . . . I get incredible paranoid, delusional thoughts at times, and there's nothing I can do until they go away." When he felt that Linscott had crossed him that summer, Ivins mixed poison into a jug of wine and plotted to offer it to her. He saw himself as the "avenging angel of death."

The reveling in the attention surrounding the attacks. After the letters had been mailed, Ivins sent mysteriously predictive e-mails to Nancy Haigwood and Mara Linscott, whose attentions he sought so assiduously. On September 21, 2001—three days after the first batch of letters was postmarked in New Jersey, but weeks before the attacks became known to the public— Ivins told Haigwood that he and colleagues at USAMRIID were ready to reprise their selflessness of the first Gulf War. On October 3, 2001, the day before the first anthrax infection would be announced, Ivins told Linscott that, since she was vaccinated against anthrax, she would be able to play a prominent role in treating patients during a biological attack—although he was "hoping such an attack doesn't happen, of course."

Ivins was similarly prescient in his e-mail to Linscott on September 26, using language that echoed the anthrax letters, which were still unknown to the public. "I just heard tonight that the Bin Laden terrorists for sure have anthrax," Ivins wrote, adding, "Osama Bin Laden has just decreed death to all Jews and all Americans." [38]

Both sets of anthrax letters, postmarked September 18 and October 9 but not made public until almost three weeks after Ivins had sent his e-mail, declared, "DEATH TO AMERICA," and "DEATH TO ISRAEL." The October 9 letters also said, "WE HAVE THIS ANTHRAX." All of the letters began with a date, "09-11-01," and further invited an assumption of Islamic authorship by concluding, "ALLAH IS GREAT."

The blaming of colleagues. In conversations and e-mails with colleagues, Ivins went out of his way to trumpet the supposed inability of anyone at USAMRIID to prepare the material that was loaded into the letters. Yet as early as November 2001, he was quietly suggesting to others, including the FBI, that the crimes had been perpetrated by present or former USAMRIID researchers. Ivins's impugning of at least seven of his colleagues can be construed as an attempt to create confusion and divert the investigation away from his own deeds.[39]

The history of using deception and the U.S. mail to torment others. To his defenders, Ivins was the churchgoing family man, the gentle eccentric who wanted to help. And he could be those things. Yet Ivins was also a chameleon, skilled at obscuring the malevolent side of his personality. For more than two decades before the anthrax letter attacks, he had repeatedly used pseudonyms and ruses to torment others.

Ivins knew the trauma he was inflicting on Nancy Haigwood when he stole her lab notebook at the University of North Carolina and left an anonymous note, pointing her to a local mailbox, all the while jeopardizing her pursuit of a doctoral degree. Ivins was no less coldhearted in planting in the local newspaper a letter in Haigwood's name, defending hazing by college fraternities. Worse, he mailed a copy of this fabricated letter, as it had been published in the newspaper, to Eileen Stevens, the mother whose son had died in a campus hazing incident.

His many sadistic manipulations showed that Ivins enjoyed toying with people while concealing his actions and identity. Together with his recurring homicidal thoughts, his actions were consistent with a man capable of plotting an episode of greater evil.

The phony return address. The first mailings, to Tom Brokaw and the *New York Post,* bore no return address. But the second batch of letters, to Senators Daschle and Leahy, did have a seemingly innocuous return:

> 4TH GRADE
> GREENDALE SCHOOL
> FRANKLIN PARK NJ 08852

There was no Greendale School in New Jersey. But Ivins had reason to be familiar with a school of that name: Greendale Baptist Academy, in Wisconsin. It was in November 1999 that Ivins and his wife donated to a Christian group that had just publicized its lawsuit in connection with the disciplining of a young student at Greendale. The student was in the fourth grade.

Motive. Something, especially willful desire, that leads one to act.

—*Black's Law Dictionary,* 8th edition

In September of 2001 Bruce Ivins was at that stage of career where there were far fewer years ahead than behind. The twins were now seniors in high school and, in just a few years, he could retire from the Army and start anew, if he wished. He was fifty-six years old.

Why, then, would Ivins risk everything by launching the anthrax letter attacks?

Developing the next-generation anthrax vaccine was, for Ivins, a deeply personal matter, bound up with his excessive need for attention and longing for scientific distinction. By the year 2000, he was seething over the project's endangered status. And by mid-2001, the controversy surrounding the military's entire anthrax vaccine program had pushed the next-generation product "beyond the back burner," in the words of Major General Stephen Reeves. As the Army official directly responsible for these biodefense matters, Reeves believed that, absent a crisis, "the White House would have killed this program."

Ivins knew well the marvelously persuasive power of fear: In 1980, fear of what the Soviets were up to in the aftermath of the anthrax deaths at Sverdlovsk got him hired at USAMRIID. In 1990 and 1991, fear that Saddam Hussein might use anthrax in the first Gulf War brought Ivins to center stage as a scientist and gave a boost to his early work on the next-generation anthrax vaccine. For Ivins, a co-inventor and patent holder, bringing this product all the way into use held the promise of untold professional glory (and years of steady patent royalties).

As Lawrence Alexander had discovered by sifting through the prodigious e-mails and Web postings, Ivins was not the benign, eccentric scientist he portrayed himself to be. His Army superiors, including those who would defend him in death, had known nothing of his dark obsessions, least of all his fascination with poisons and his urge to kill those he believed had slighted him.

It was only after Ivins voiced his torrent of specific threats at the group therapy session in July 2008 that the FBI found a lever to begin questioning the mental health professionals who had treated him. His detailed medical records, including the contemporaneous notes of his psychiatrists and counselors, revealed Ivins in full: a man who created a mirage that misled most everyone he met.

The outside review of Ivins's behavioral history had been requested by the Justice Department and authorized by the chief U.S. District Court judge for Washington, D.C., Royce C. Lamberth. The nine-member panel, led by Dr. Gregory Saathoff, a psychiatrist at the University of Virginia medical school, had access to Ivins's medical records dating to 1978, to his boundless e-mails, and to the balance of the Amerithrax investigative file, including summaries of interviews with his family, friends, colleagues, and the mental health professionals who treated him. The Justice Department asked the panel to assess Ivins's state of mind before and after the anthrax mailings, "his possible motives—and the connections, if any, between his mental state and the commission of the crimes."

In August 2010, the panel completed its nearly three-hundred-page report, an unabridged version of which was distributed to government officials with national security responsibilities. The panel said that its review of Ivins's previously sealed psychiatric records alone found "considerable additional circumstantial evidence in support" of the FBI's conclusion that he was responsible for the anthrax attacks. As for lessons to be drawn, the panel noted that when Ivins was hired by the Army in 1980, he "had a significant and lengthy history of psychological disturbance and diagnosable mental illness." [40]

How much of that history might have been shared with jurors if Ivins had stood trial cannot be known. At the least, prosecutors would have sought to introduce his targeting of Nancy Haigwood as proof of his fixation with Kappa Kappa Gamma, an obsession that ultimately inspired him to drop the deadly letters in the mailbox next to the sorority's office in Princeton. If his lawyers had argued that Ivins's mental condition rendered him incapable of knowing right from wrong, most if not all of his background would likely have been aired at a competency hearing or at a trial.

Given all the circumstances pointing to him, it is reasonable to conclude that Ivins did it for reasons unique to both his psychosis and his professional self-interest. His well-honed cunning and advanced scientific skills enabled him to script America's worst bioterrorism event and a panic that, as he anticipated, instantly focused attention on USAMRIID, where he was able to insinuate himself into the FBI investigation. Other federal officials responded by doing what for years had been unthinkable: They committed hundreds of millions of dollars to speed the development of the next-generation anthrax vaccine, the baby of Bruce Edwards Ivins.

ACKNOWLEDGMENTS

This book would be something much less without the patience of the people who took time to talk with me. Many met me in laboratory buildings and government offices, some in diners, bars, or their homes. To each of the more than three hundred people who gave of your time to discuss the events described herein: thank you.

I could not have been more fortunate than to meet dozens of present and former residents of Lebanon and greater southwest Ohio, who recalled how their paths intersected with those of Bruce Ivins and his family. My particular gratitude goes to Pamela Wehby, Don Hawke, Ann Seeger, Ellen Heffner, Rick Sams, Dean Deerhake, Bill Jameson, Lana Davis, Joe Haven, and Bill and Ann Hirt.

Special thanks to Arne Trelvik, a high school classmate of Bruce Ivins, who not only shared his memories but guided me through the files at the Warren County Genealogical Society. I benefited as well from the expertise of John J. Zimkus, historian of the Warren County Historical Society.

I am deeply indebted to several former members of Kappa Kappa Gamma. The fortitude of these women in agreeing to be identified by name lends authority to important details of Bruce Ivins's obsession with the sorority. The recollections of those who became acquainted with Ivins at the University of North Carolina at Chapel Hill, including Elizabeth Brownridge Colacino and Lori Mail, helped provide authentic corroboration of Ivins's fixation. Further verification came from Gail Wertz, at the time a UNC faculty member. Nancy Haigwood, who first encountered Ivins as a doctoral student at Chapel Hill, gave me hours upon hours of her time, relating in detail her brushes with Ivins and how she became a witness in the FBI investigation. I owe heartfelt thanks to Eileen Stevens, whom Ivins plied with letters under false pretenses while posing as an opponent of fraternity/sorority exclusivity and cruelty after her son died in a campus hazing incident. Eileen opened her Long Island home to me and entrusted me with copies of letters that Ivins had sent her.

The scientist who was instrumental in hiring Ivins at Chapel Hill, Priscilla Wyrick, provided keen observations of what he was like in those years. She was also able to shed light on the first years of his marriage to the former Diane Betsch. I was similarly helped by colleagues of Ivins at the Uniformed Services University of the Health Sciences in Bethesda, Maryland, notably Lesley Russell and Alison O'Brien.

Philip Russell, Stephen Reeves, Anthony Fauci, Donald A. Henderson, Stewart Simonson, and Anna Johnson-Winegar provided essential information about how the administration of President George W. Bush dealt with matters related to both the established and the genetically engineered anthrax vaccine, co-invented by Bruce Ivins.

Thanks also to Robert Kadlec, Ari Fleischer, Tommy Thompson, and Tom Ridge, who provided inside perspective on how the anthrax attacks resonated at both the Pentagon and the White House. The firsthand observations of certain congressional officials helped flesh out the visceral impact of the envelope addressed to Senate Majority Leader Tom Daschle. My thanks to Eric Washburn and Kelly Fado, aides to Daschle who were there the day the envelope was opened. I also thank Laura

Petrou, former senator Daschle, Representative Henry Waxman, and Clara Kircher, an aide to Senator Patrick Leahy.

I gained a front-row seat at Bruce Ivins's rise to prominence as an anthrax researcher through the remembrances of C. J. Peters, Arthur Friedlander, and Charles Bailey, a former commander of USAMRIID. Army colonels all, these scientists worked with Ivins in the run-up to the 1991 Persian Gulf War. I thank those, including John Ezzell and John Parker, who described the frenzy at USAMRIID following the FBI's decision in October 2001 to house at the institute all the anthrax-laced letters that were recovered as evidence. My thanks as well to Caree Vander Linden, USAMRIID's spokeswoman.

The lawyers who represented Steven Hatfill, especially Thomas Connolly and Amy Richardson, accommodated my many questions and requests for documentation, encompassing nearly all of the sworn testimony from Hatfill's anthrax-related lawsuits. I also thank Richard Bricken and Paul Kemp, who illuminated their roles as defense lawyers for Ivins.

I'm indebted to members of the Ivins family, especially Amanda Ivins, the daughter of Bruce Ivins, as well as his middle brother, C.W. Ivins. Both C.W. and his wife, Juanita, opened their home and memories and shared family pictures dating to the late 1940s. They and the oldest of the three brothers, Thomas Ivins, deepened my understanding of Bruce and their parents, Randall and Mary Ivins.

The complexities of microbial forensics led me to test my welcome with a handful of scientists who assisted the federal investigation. John Ezzell, Paul Keim, and Joseph Michael exhaustively enhanced my familiarity with the microbiology, genetics, and elemental analyses integral to reconstructing the origins of the letter attacks. Peter Setlow spoke authoritatively yet accessibly about the culturing of *Bacillus* spores, and about the ubiquity of certain laboratory contaminants. Related thanks to James Burans, Rita Colwell, and Jacques Ravel. William C. Patrick III, one of the microbiologists from the nation's now-defunct offensive biowarfare program, provided not only historical sweep but also details of his experiences as an expert consultant to and, for a time, a potential target of the FBI investigation. Unlike other scientists I interviewed, Patrick was well acquainted with both Steven Hatfill and Bruce Ivins. Bill encouraged me to complete this book; I regret not being able to do so before his death on October 1, 2010.

A primary goal of mine was to gain the deepest understanding of one of the most consequential criminal cases in United States history. Whatever success I achieved in this regard is due in no small part to my conversations with numerous present and former investigators and federal scientists. From the FBI and the Postal Inspection Service, I especially thank those many members of the Amerithrax task force who spoke with me on multiple occasions and whose names appear in the narrative or footnotes. Thanks also to Michael Kortan and Kenneth Hoffman at FBI Headquarters for their responsiveness to my questions and informational requests. Among retired FBI personnel, Bruce Gebhardt, Charles Whistler, Brad Garrett, Jenifer Smith, Randall Murch, and Dwight Adams gave generously of their recollections and insights. I owe much to Gerald Richards, a retired bureau document examiner. I was helped as well by conversations with police officials in Frederick, including Gene Alston, Clark Pennington, and Matthew Burns. At the Centers for Disease Control in Atlanta, Von Roebuck provided information that was both reliable and timely. The same is true for Bill Kearney at the National Academy of Sciences.

The roots of this book are in my reporting for the *Los Angeles Times*, work that first led me to survey the booming arena of biological warfare preparedness. I left the *Times* to research and write the book; fortunately, my friendship with many top professionals who have worked there remains. Roger Smith, Jim Gerstenzang, John Carroll, Henry Weinstein, Jim Newton, and Dana Parsons each read and commented upon at least an excerpt from the draft manuscript. Karlene Goller, the paper's stellar newsroom lawyer, offered spot-on advice. My thanks also to John Arthur, whose competitive fire spurred me to join the paper and who provided support for the next eighteen years, and to Doyle

McManus and Tim Phelps. I also benefited from the readings and deft advice provided by former colleagues from our shared years at the Washington bureau of Knight-Ridder Newspapers: Mark Thompson, Thomas J. Moore, and Carl Cannon.

I can only struggle to properly thank two other journalists whose guidance helped lift this book. Bill Rempel became the editor at the *L.A. Times* most integral to my earliest discoveries about Bruce Ivins, and he remained a confidant through my completion of this manuscript. Marc Duvoisin, who is still on the masthead of the *L.A. Times,* is simply one of the finest editors working today. Marc, more so than any editor, recognized the importance of my early reporting into biodefense matters. After making me look better than I would have on those original articles, he encouraged me to take the leap of writing this book, for which he provided astute conceptual and line-by-line advice. Marc wound up editing nearly every paragraph, working after hours and on weekends to do so.

I owe a special category of thanks to Janet Lundblad, an indefatigable researcher, who for years enriched my work and that of others at *The Times.* It was my good fortune that Janet agreed to provide support for this book. Though I conducted every interview myself, when I was unable to monitor two peripheral events in Washington, I received comprehensive files from Cynthia Dizikes and Sunny Kaplan, former *Times* colleagues who attended in my stead. I was aided as well by *Times* reporter Nicole Gaouette, who shared notes bearing her meticulous observations from Frederick in the days following Ivins's death.

Phillip Ruiz, an information technology specialist and another *Times* alum, kept me up and running despite extreme weather and ever-brittle utilities. Blake Sell, a colleague from our beginning days at the *Pasadena Star-News,* was indispensable in helping to secure photographs. My thanks also to Tyrone Turner, Doug Stevens, and Howard Rosenberg, gifted journalists all. Friend and former *Times* colleague Alan Miller was generous in allowing me to hang my virtual hat on the Web site of his News Literacy Project.

John Flicker was the editor at Bantam Books who secured the

ACKNOWLEDGMENTS

rights to what would become *The Mirage Man*. I also owe much to Beth Rashbaum, a masterly and generous editor at Bantam, whose many suggestions were unfailingly wise. Luke Dempsey lent another set of smart eyes, and I benefited from Fred Chase's vigilant copyedit. Both Beth and Luke championed the manuscript inside Bantam, for which I am eternally grateful. Thanks as well to Bantam's Steve Messina and to Jessie Waters, whose sharp focus provided an important late-stage boost. Also in New York, original thanks go to my agent, David Halpern, whose advice was indispensable in helping me visualize and produce each stage of this book. David and his colleagues at the Robbins Office, including Kathy Robbins and Ian King, aided me at every turn.

Closer to home, I owe monumental thanks to Ned Feder, scientist and analyst, and to his wife, Eva, who never discouraged my endless late-night calls and visits to discuss the complexities of *Bacillus anthracis* and related challenges. Ned helped me to reliably interpret information that I had gathered, and to pose questions that would yield more clarity. He also read and commented on nearly all of the manuscript in its early stages. Hank Savage, Caroline L. Cunningham, John Gibbons, and Charles Curatalo provided important assistance and the generosity of friendship.

I am the grandson and son of postal workers, prompting a question that fueled my resolve: What if one of them had been moving the mail at Brentwood alongside Thomas Morris and Joseph Curseen? I owe much to my family, and I appreciate the support I've always enjoyed from my parents, Barbara and Kenneth Willman, who read and critiqued an excerpt. Most of all, I thank my wife, Joan Black, whose love, sage counsel, and humor have remained unstinting. Having encouraged me to write this book, Joan was an essential first reader and infinitely more. She and our children, Alison and Joseph, eased my journey with their kindnesses and unique inspiration. They have taken my life to heights I did not know.

—David Willman

NOTES

CHAPTER 1: SHE WOULD *KILL* YOU

1. Warren County (Ohio) Historical Society interview with T. Randall Ivins, conducted by Miriam Lukens, oral history project chairman, on August 22 and September 19, 1979; documents reflecting Ivins family history as maintained by the Warren County (Ohio) Genealogical Society and the New Jersey Historical Society; author's interviews with C. W. Ivins and William Jameson, June 2009.
2. Author's interview with C. W. Ivins and Juanita Ivins, June 17, 2009, and January 21, 2011; application for the marriage on December 26, 1933, of Thomas Randall Ivins and Mary Johnson Knight.
3. Author's interviews with C. W. Ivins and Juanita Ivins, June 2009 and January 2011, and Amanda Ivins, 2008 and 2009.
4. Author's interviews with C. W. Ivins, June 2009, and Martha Bladen (née Martha Leuzinger), June 30, 2009.
5. Author's interview with C. W. Ivins and Juanita Ivins, June 19, 2009, during which family pictures were circulated.
6. Summary of FBI interview with Bruce Ivins, February 13, 2008.
7. Author's interview with C. W. Ivins, June 19, 2009.
8. Ibid.
9. Ibid.; author's other interviews with C. W. Ivins, 2009 and 2010.
10. The family trip through Princeton was described by Bruce Ivins in an interview with the FBI on March 31, 2005.
11. Author's interviews with Martha Bladen (née Martha Leuzinger), June and July 2009.

12. Author's interviews with Jacqueline Stone (née Jacqueline Sams), June 14, 2009, and Martha Bladen (née Martha Leuzinger), June and July 2009.

13. Author's interviews with former employees of Ivins Drugs, including Jacqueline Stone, Ellen Heffner (née Ellen Leuzinger), and Martha Bladen (née Martha Leuzinger), June 2009.

14. Author's interview with Thomas Ivins, February 3, 2011.

15. Author's interviews with Elaine Steib (née Elaine Kraus), July 4, 2009, and Larry Buchanan, June and July 2009.

16. Author's interviews with Rick Sams, Larry Buchanan, Don Hawke, and Ellen Heffner (née Ellen Leuzinger), 2009 and 2010.

17. Author's interviews with Bob Edens, June 28, 2009, and December 7, 2010.

18. Author's interviews with Lana Davis (née Lana Neeley), June 2009.

19. Bruce Ivins's placing of thirteenth in the cross-country event in the fall of 1963 was documented on an index card filled out at the time by his coach, Dean Deerhake, who shared the card with the author on June 23, 2009.

20. Author's interviews with Dean Deerhake, January, June, and July 2009.

21. Author's interviews with Bob Edens, Nick Nelson, William Jameson, and Patricia McDaniel Brooks, June 2009.

22. Author's interview with Ellen Heffner (née Ellen Leuzinger), June 25, 2009.

23. Author's interviews with Elaine Steib (née Elaine Kraus), July 2009.

24. Author's interviews with Ellen Heffner (née Ellen Leuzinger), June 2009, and Pat West (née Patty Bercaw), July 19, 2009.

25. Author's interviews with Dean Deerhake, Rick Sams, and Elaine Steib (née Elaine Kraus), 2009 and 2010; "3 Local Students to Attend Summer Institutes in Biology," *Western Star* (Lebanon, Ohio), June 16, 1963.

26. Author's interviews with C. W. Ivins, William Jameson, and Martha Bladen (née Martha Leuzinger), June 2009.

27. Author's interviews with Rick Sams and Jackie Schrader-Hayes (née Jackie Schrader), June 2009.

28. Author's interviews with Joe Haven, January and June 2009.

29. Author's interviews with Pamela Wehby (née Pamela Thornbury) and *Maxine Lowe* cast members Elaine Steib (Kraus), William Jameson, and Nick Nelson, June and July 2009.

30. Author's interviews with Jacqueline Stone (née Jacqueline Sams), June 14, 2009, and Martha Bladen (née Martha Leuzinger), June and July 2009.

31. Author's interviews with Don Hawke and Rick Sams, June and July 2009.

32. Author's interviews with Jacqueline Stone (née Jacqueline Sams) and Ellen Heffner (née Ellen Leuzinger), June 14 and June 25, 2009.

33. Author's interviews with Don Hawke, Rick Sams, Victoria Tappy, Lana Davis (née Lana Neeley), and Marilyn McMurray, June and July 2009.

34. In an e-mail on March 24, 2003, to Mara Linscott, a former scientific colleague, Bruce Ivins wrote that he never heard Mary Ivins "say a SINGLE kind thing" about his father, adding: "I also saw her physically assault him (and draw blood) on occasions."

35. Author's interview with Ellen Heffner (née Ellen Leuzinger), June 25, 2009.

36. Author's interview with Don Hawke, July 14, 2009.

37. Author's interview with FBI agent Daniel G. Borsuk and postal inspector Armando R. Garcia, June 3, 2010. Borsuk and Garcia interviewed Bruce Ivins's college roommates.

38. Author's interviews with Ellen Heffner (née Ellen Leuzinger), June 25, 2009, and Martha Bladen (née Martha Leuzinger), June 30, 2009. Bruce Ivins and Martha Leuzinger saw the Monkees in concert on July 28, 1967.

39. Bruce Ivins described the genesis of his obsession with the Kappa Kappa Gamma sorority during an interview with federal investigators on January 16, 2008. His comments were represented in a summary of the interview prepared by the FBI. Author's interviews with Amerithrax investigators, 2010.

CHAPTER 2: YOU WILL ACCEPT ME

1. Certificate of death for Mary K. Ivins, Hamilton County, Ohio, Department of Public Health.

2. Author's interview with C. W. Ivins, November 19, 2009.

3. "Top Scholars' Initiation Set," *University of Cincinnati News Record,* May 10, 1968.

4. Federal Civil Service form by which Bruce Ivins applied for summer employment, May 23, 1968.

5. Author's interview with Peter Bonventre, April 13, 2009.

6. Author's interviews with Robert Baughn, April 13 and July 8, 2009, and March 3, 2010.

7. Letter from Bruce Ivins to Pamela Wehby (née Pamela Thornbury), February 22, 1990.

8. Author's interviews with Bill and Ann Hirt, January 30, 2010.

9. Ibid.; e-mail from Bruce Ivins to Ann Hirt, March 14, 2008.

10. Author's interviews with C. W. Ivins and Juanita Ivins, November 10, 2010. In a separate interview in early 2010, C. W. Ivins said that, before being apprised by the author of the claim that Bruce Ivins made in the March 14, 2008, e-mail, he had never before heard that his brother was conceived in response to a positive Pap smear test.

11. Author's interviews with Bill and Ann Hirt, January 30, 2010.

12. Author's interview with Mary Scherl (née Mary Westendorf), January 31, 2010.

13. Author's interviews with Priscilla Wyrick, April, June, and July 2009.

14. Priscilla Wyrick told the author on June 16, 2009, that Bruce Ivins "was serious about Mensa. He knew all the rules and regulations."

15. Author's interview with Elizabeth Brownridge Colacino (née Elizabeth Brownridge), June 20, 2009.

16. Ibid.; author's interview with Priscilla Wyrick, April 6, 2009.

17. Summary of statements made by Bruce Ivins during an interview with the FBI, February 13, 2008.

18. Author's interview with Lori Mail (née Lori Babcock), July 19, 2009, and January 7 and January 11, 2011.

19. Author's interview with Priscilla Wyrick, April 6, 2009.

20. Author's interviews with Nancy Haigwood, April 2009.

21. FBI summary of interview with Bruce Ivins on January 16, 2008.

22. The statements made by Bruce Ivins to a psychiatrist are referred to in the findings of a panel of outside analysts who, in 2009 and 2010, reviewed Ivins's previously sealed medical records. The documents reviewed by the panel included contemporaneous notes from several psychiatrists and behavioral

counselors who treated Ivins from the late 1970s until shortly before his suicide in July 2008. At the request of the Justice Department, U.S. District Court
judge Royce C. Lamberth authorized the panel to review Ivins's records. The
panel produced a report in August 2010, "The Amerithrax Case: Report of
the Expert Behavioral Analysis Panel," which was provided in unredacted
form to national security officials with the goal of improving the screening of
scientists entrusted with deadly microorganisms such as anthrax.

23. Author's interviews with Nancy Haigwood, April, May, June, and July 2009,
    and Gail W. Wertz, January 27, 2010, and January 21, 2011.

24. Summary of statements made by Bruce Ivins during an interview with the FBI,
    January 16, 2008.

25. Nancy Haigwood, Elizabeth Brownridge, and Lori Babcock each were former
    members of Kappa Kappa Gamma and each had unwelcome personal interac-
    tions at the University of North Carolina with Bruce Ivins, who ultimately ad-
    mitted to the FBI that he had tormented Haigwood. Ivins may not have limited
    his inappropriate focus in Chapel Hill to those three former Kappas. In inter-
    views with the author on January 21, 2010, and January 21, 2011, Gail W.
    Wertz, who served as an assistant professor of microbiology throughout
    Ivins's years at UNC, recalled that her home was broken into in the late 1970s
    by an intruder who stole only a jewelry box—and it contained her KKG mem-
    bership key and several pewter goblets. Less than a year after the break-in,
    which Wertz reported to Chapel Hill police, she received a phone call from a
    man who claimed to have been working on a bridge over the nearby Haw
    River, where he said he had found the KKG key, inscribed with her name. "He
    asked if I wanted my things back," said Wertz, adding that she rebuffed him.
    "It was just a creepy phone call. Too creepy for words." Wertz's affiliation
    with Kappa Kappa Gamma was known on campus; she provided career coun-
    seling to members of the sorority. Wertz recalled Ivins as a microbiology post-
    doc she would occasionally see walking the halls. Though she has no memory
    of ever conversing with him, Ivins was aware of her. In addition to her affilia-
    tion with KKG, Wertz, approximately Ivins's age, was strikingly attractive, a
    former Miss William & Mary. Ivins, in an October 9, 2007, e-mail to a mem-
    ber of Kappa Kappa Gamma in which he was discussing his attempts to add
    Haigwood to "Notable Kappas" listed on the sorority's Wikipedia page,
    lauded Wertz as a "noted virologist."

CHAPTER 3: SECRETS AVAILABLE

1. J. L. Middlebrook and D. R. Franz, "Botulinum Toxins," in F. R. Sidell, E. T.
   Takafuji, and D. R. Franz, eds., *Medical Aspects of Chemical and Biological
   Warfare* (Washington, D.C.: Office of the Surgeon General, 1997), p. 644; N. M.
   Covert, *Cutting Edge: A History of Fort Detrick, Maryland, 1943–1993*, U.S.
   Army, rev. ed., 1994.

2. A. Driks, "The Dynamic Spore," *Proceedings of the National Academy of Sciences,* March 18, 2003. The article reported that *Bacillus* spores "can survive
   most environmental challenges found on earth and even a few in outer space
   and can remain dormant in excess of millions of years."

3. G. Sternbach, "The History of Anthrax," *Journal of Emergency Medicine* 24
   (May 2003): 464.

4. J. W. Ezzell, P. Mikesell, B. E. Ivins, and S. H. Leppla, "The Genetic Basis of Pasteur's Attenuation of *Bacillus anthracis* Cultures," in *World's Debt to Pasteur* (Alan R. Liss, 1985).

5. Ibid.

6. Author's interviews with William C. Patrick III, November 2008, January 2009, April 2009, and May 20 and 21, 2010. The two simulants sprayed off the coast of San Francisco were *Serratia marcescens* and *Bacillus globigii*. Patrick, a microbiologist, was hired at Fort Detrick in 1951 to assist with biowarfare experiments and planning. As part of his work Patrick reviewed the data from the open-air testing initiated near San Francisco. Patrick retired from the Army in 1987 as a civilian scientist and later served as a consultant to the Defense Intelligence Agency and the CIA. Although the release of the simulants was a matter of secrecy at the time, some experts later criticized these and other such tests, saying that the simulants could be harmful to persons with weakened immune systems.

7. Author's interviews with Ken Alibek, former deputy director of Biopreparat, the Soviet Union's biological warfare agency, April 2007; V. Israelson, "Fighting Anthrax: A Cold Warrior's Confession," *The Washington Quarterly,* Spring 2002.

8. V. Israelson, "Fighting Anthrax: A Cold Warrior's Confession."

9. Defense Intelligence Agency report, "Biological Warfare Capabilities—Warsaw Pact," March 1990.

10. Central Intelligence Agency memorandum, "Soviet Biological Warfare Agent: Probable Cause of the Anthrax Epidemic in Sverdlovsk," declassified as of November 1987, and posted online by the nongovernmental National Security Archive; V. Israelson, "Fighting Anthrax: A Cold Warrior's Confession."

11. Author's interviews with Charles Bailey, John Ezzell, and C. J. Peters, 2008 and 2009.

12. Author's interviews with John W. Ezzell Jr., November 2008 and February 2009.

13. Ibid.

14. Army personnel file for Bruce Ivins, obtained under Freedom of Information Act, and author's interviews with current and former Army officials, 2009 and 2010.

15. Author's interviews in 2010 and 2011 with people familiar with the psychiatric care provided to Bruce Ivins; "The Amerithrax Case: Report of the Expert Behavioral Analysis Panel," August 2010.

16. Author's interview with John Ezzell, November 2, 2008.

17. E-mail from Bruce Ivins to Nancy Haigwood, September 22, 2006.

18. Bruce Ivins utilized a directory of colleges at the Uniformed Services University of the Health Sciences in Bethesda, Maryland, to compile his list of campuses in the East with Kappa Kappa Gamma chapters. On one of his visits to the Library of Congress, Ivins also checked out a book, *Sorority Girl,* written by Anne Emery and published in 1960 by Scholastic.

19. FBI summary of interview with Bruce Ivins, February 13, 2008, and author's interviews with Amerithrax investigators, 2009 and 2010. In an earlier interview with the FBI, on January 16, 2008, Ivins said that he broke into the sorority house in West Virginia between 1978 and 1980. Ivins revised his account in the subsequent FBI interview, saying that it took place in the early 1980s.

20. Letter to editor signed by "Bruce E. Ivins, Ph.D.," published by *Frederick News-Post*, February 19, 1982. Ivins's letter was preceded by news accounts in the *News-Post* that described the accidental burning of a West Virginia University student during a fraternity initiation. See "Student Burned in Fraternity Initiation," *News-Post*, January 14, 1982; and "Student Describes Initiation," *News-Post*, February 11, 1982.

21. Author's interviews with Nancy Haigwood, April, May, June, and July 2009, and Carl Scandella, March, April, and July 2009. Bruce Ivins admitted his actions as recounted by Haigwood and Scandella in an interview with the FBI on January 16, 2008.

22. In an interview with the FBI on January 16, 2008, Bruce Ivins admitted that he had fabricated the letter to the *Frederick News-Post*, published May 9, 1983, in the name of Nancy Haigwood.

23. Author's interview with Nancy Haigwood, April 11, 2009.

24. Letters from Bruce Ivins to Eileen Stevens, May 18, 1982, and May 29, 1983. (Ivins also sent Stevens letters or notes dated May 1, 1982; June 1, 1982; and May 26, 1986.) According to the author's interviews with Eileen Stevens in March, April, and July 2010, Ivins at no point explained what he had termed, in the letter of May 29, 1983, "some very exciting scientific developments . . . at Fort Detrick." He also did not explain what he meant by referring in the same passage to "the anthrax project." In his letter to Stevens dated May 18, 1982, Ivins said that he had once intended to write a book with the title "Convergence in the Codes, Rites, and Value Systems in American Collegiate Greek-Letter Societies," but had later "narrowed the scope of my research to sororities."

25. Letter from Bruce Ivins to Eileen Stevens, May 26, 1986. Stevens said in interviews with the author that, although she had not suspected Ivins was lying to her, she did not send him any testimonial that violated any victim's confidentiality.

26. Author's interviews with Eileen Stevens, July 31 and August 14, 2010.

27. "Not the One," letter to the editor of the *Frederick News-Post*, May 18, 1983. Nancy Haigwood's note to the newspaper was succinct: "I am not the Nancy L. Haigwood who was author of the May 9, 1983, letter to the editor (in the News-Post)."

28. Author's interview with Nancy Haigwood, April 11, 2009.

29. Classified advertisement composed by Bruce Ivins and published by *Mother Jones,* May 1984, p. 55.

30. FBI summary of interview with Bruce Ivins, February 13, 2008. Ivins also said during this interview that he made certain that he did not charge money for the sorority secrets to avoid violating copyright laws.

31. Letter to editor submitted by Bruce Ivins under the false name of Carla Sander, published by the *Frederick News-Post*, February 20, 1985. Bruce Ivins sent a subsequent letter in the name of Carla Sander to the *Frederick News-Post*, which published it on November 22, 1985. The letter praised the absence of sororities at Hood College, located in Frederick: "It is no mere coincidence with her deserved high rating that Hood has wisely chosen to eschew sororities. The administration and students realize that academics are more important than parties and long-lasting, inclusive friendships are better than an exclusive, ritualized 'sisterhood.' They truly know that although there are col-

lege *women* (such as the students at Hood), there are, in fact, only sorority *girls*."

32. FBI summary of interview with Bruce Ivins, June 9, 2008.

33. Jeffrey Zaslow, "Getting Even: Is an Act of Revenge Worth It?," *Chicago Sun-Times,* October 16, 1988.

34. Author's interview with Lauren Paitson, former executive director of Kappa Kappa Gamma, March 2, 2010. According to an FBI interview summary, Paitson relayed to the bureau details of Bruce Ivins's musical performance at the Kappa Kappa Gamma chapter in Knoxville, Tennessee, on August 10, 2007.

35. N. Luse, "Toss Up," *Frederick News-Post,* March 1, 1982.

36. Author's interview with Lawrence Alexander, July 15, 2010. Bruce Ivins's letter in 1987 to NBC also was mentioned in the Justice Department report on the anthrax investigation, "Amerithrax Investigative Summary," issued February 19, 2010. Ivins sent similar letters, all pitching his idea for a miniseries about the life of deceased teacher-astronaut Christa McAuliffe to the ABC and CBS television networks.

37. Author's interview with Eugene Haines, September 26, 2009. A program for the event at the elementary school in Germantown, Maryland, on April 26, 1988, listed Bruce Ivins and his performance at the outset of the ceremony, which included remarks from Christa McAuliffe's mother.

38. From August 13, 2006, through September 3, 2006, Bruce Ivins, writing as "Prunetacos," posted twelve messages about Sally Ride on GreekChat.com. Among his other statements, Ivins described in detail his attendance at the appearance by Ride at Goucher College on September 25, 2006. Ivins also wrote that he was soliciting information about Ride's possible affiliation with a college sorority because, "I just never got up the nerve to write Dr. Ride or Stanford or Swarthmore and ask the question." See also: L. Davis, "Sally Ride to Lecture," *Goucher Weekly,* September 19, 2006; and L. Davis, "Astronaut in Kraushaar," *Goucher Weekly,* October 3, 2006.

39. Author's interviews with Amanda Ivins, December 4, 2008; January 8, 2009; and June 30, 2010.

40. Author's interviews with Amanda Ivins, December 4, 2008; January 8 and 29, 2009; and June 30, 2010.

41. Author's interviews with C. W. Ivins, Thomas Ivins, Don Hawke, and Jean Duley, 2009, 2010, and 2011.

CHAPTER 4: BRUCE BEING BRUCE

1. B. E. Ivins, J. W. Ezzell Jr., J. Jemski, K. W. Hedlund, J. D. Ristroph, and S. H. Leppla, "Immunization Studies with Attenuated Strains of *Bacillus anthracis,*" *Infection and Immunity,* May 1986.

2. B. E. Ivins and S. L. Welkos, "Cloning and Expression of the *Bacillus anthracis* Protective Antigen Gene in *Bacillus subtilis,*" *Infection and Immunity,* November 1986.

3. B. E. Ivins, S. L. Welkos, G. B. Knudson, and S. F. Little, "Immunization Against Anthrax with Aromatic Compound-Dependent Mutants of *Bacillus anthracis* and with Recombinant Strains of *Bacillus subtilis* That Produce Anthrax Protective Antigen," *Infection and Immunity,* February 1990. See also B. E. Ivins, S. L. Welkos, G. B. Knudson, and D. J. LeBlanc, "Transposon

Tn916 Mutagenesis in *Bacillus anthracis,"Infection and Immunity,* January 1988.

4. Author's interviews with Charles Bailey, C. J. Peters, and Arthur Friedlander, 2008, 2009, and 2010.

5. Author's interviews with C. J. Peters, September 7, 2008, and November 24, 2009. Bruce Ivins and two of his colleagues in USAMRIID's Bacteriology Division also trained another government scientist who was on his way to heading a new laboratory in the Persian Gulf that could test whether any biological weaponry was being used against U.S. or other coalition forces. The scientist, James P. Burans, himself a microbiologist, told the author on October 2, 2009, that he learned from Ivins, Patricia Fellows, and Patricia Worsham how to handle and culture anthrax as well as other biological agents. Burans established the Navy Forward Laboratory within Saudi Arabia.

6. Author's interviews with Charles Bailey, beginning in March 2008 through August 2010. See also V. Dawson, "Diseased Cats Taken from USDA Lab in Md.," *Washington Post,* August 25, 1987; B. A. Franklin, "Going to Extremes for 'Animal Rights,'" *New York Times,* August 30, 1987.

7. Author's interviews with Charles Bailey, 2008 through 2010.

8. A. M. Friedlander, S. L. Welkos, M. L. M. Pitt, J. W. Ezzell, P. L. Worsham, K. J. Rose, B. E. Ivins, J. R. Lowe, G. B. Howe, P. Mikesell, and W. B. Lawrence, "Postexposure Prophylaxis Against Experimental Inhalational Anthrax," *Journal of Infectious Diseases,* May 1993.

9. Author's interviews with C. J. Peters, September 7, 2008; Charles Bailey, 2008 and 2009; and Arthur Friedlander, July 16, 2010.

10. Author's interview with Charles L. Bailey, September 9, 2008.

11. Letter from Bruce Ivins to Pamela Wehby (née Pamela Thornbury), February 22, 1990.

12. Christmas card from Bruce Ivins and family to Pamela Wehby (née Pamela Thornbury) and family, December 1990.

13. Author's interviews with Dr. Robert P. Kadlec, September 8, 2009, and February 2, 2010.

14. Ivins appears as a co-inventor on two patents for the recombinant Protective Antigen anthrax vaccine (rPA). Documents seeking the first patent were filed with the U.S. Patent and Trademark Office on November 23, 1994, and the patent was issued on November 13, 2001; the second patent was applied for on March 7, 2000, and issued on May 14, 2002.

15. Author's interviews with Charles L. Bailey, 2008 and 2009, and C. J. Peters, May and September 2008.

16. Holiday card from Bruce Ivins to Pamela Wehby (née Thornbury) and family, postmarked December 21, 1991.

17. Ibid.

18. Author's interview with Gerard Andrews, June 19, 2009.

19. Author's interview with Dr. W. Russell Byrne, November 16, 2008.

CHAPTER 5: DARK FAMILY MATERIAL

1. As an adult, Bruce Ivins lamented his upbringing with regularity. One late-in-life example came in an e-mail that he sent on March 14, 2008, to Ann Hirt,

who along with her husband was a friend from the years when Ivins was a graduate student at the University of Cincinnati. In his e-mail, Ivins wrote, "Your whole family was so welcoming, so open-armed, so friendly. I grew up in a family where none of that existed. . . . I felt as if I were really wanted for the first time in my life!"

2. Author's interviews with C. W. Ivins, June 8, 2009, and February 10, 2010.

3. "The Amerithrax Case: Report of the Expert Behavioral Analysis Panel," August 2010.

4. E-mail from Bruce Ivins to Mara Linscott, October 27, 1999.

5. Author's interview with Amanda Ivins, April 16, 2009.

6. Author's interviews with Priscilla Wyrick, C. W. Ivins, and Amanda Ivins, 2009 and 2010.

7. Author's interviews in 2010 and 2011 with people familiar with the psychiatric care provided to Bruce Ivins; "The Amerithrax Case: Report of the Expert Behavioral Analysis Panel," August 2010.

8. Letter to the editor of the *Frederick News-Post* from Carol Swick, published October 4, 1993.

9. Letter to the editor of the *Frederick News-Post* from William Long, published September 29, 1993.

10. Letter to the editor of the *Frederick News-Post* from Tom Caulfield, published September 30, 1993.

11. Letter to the editor of the *Frederick News-Post* from Bruce Ivins, published September 29, 1993.

12. A copy of Bruce Ivins's letter to *Newsweek*, dated January 2, 1992, was found by investigators during a search of his house on November 1, 2007. The magazine did not publish the letter.

13. Letter from Bruce Ivins published by the *Baltimore Sun,* "Marcia Clark's Children," March 25, 1995. Ivins's letter was in response to an earlier, sympathetic essay about Clark. In his letter Ivins wrote, "Marcia Clark is, of course, the brilliant prosecuting attorney in the O. J. Simpson case whose present to her husband on Christmas in 1993 was to tell him, 'You aren't intellectually stimulating enough for me. Get out!' . . . It was the decision of Marcia Clark, not her husband, to destroy their family and end the marriage."

14. FBI summary of interview with Bruce Ivins as he was driven from USAMRIID to a hotel in Frederick, Maryland, November 1, 2007; summary of FBI interview with Ivins on January 16, 2008.

15. Item within a year-end report of the American Family Association, http://www.afa.net/.

16. Sworn affidavit from U.S. postal inspector Thomas F. Dellafera in support of obtaining a warrant to search the residence and vehicles of Bruce Ivins, October 31, 2007; "AFA Takes Wisconsin to Court," *American Family Association Journal,* October 1999, http://www.afajournal.org/archives/23100000 166.asp.

CHAPTER 6: THIS WAS HIS BABY

1. The Russian research was led by Nikolai Staritzin and Andrei Pomerantsev, who were based at a biowarfare facility in Obolensk, about fifty miles south

of Moscow. See W. Orent, "After Anthrax," *The American Prospect,* November 30, 2002.

2. Holiday letter from Bruce Ivins to Pamela Wehby (née Pamela Thornbury) and family, December 1997.

3. T. Talton, "Corps to Track Marines Discharged for Refusing to Take Anthrax Shot," *Marine Corps Times,* April 28, 2008.

4. Holiday letter from Bruce Ivins to Pamela Wehby (née Pamela Thornbury) and family, December 1997.

5. E-mail to colleague from Bruce Ivins, "Trip to BioPort," April 24, 2000.

6. Author's interview with David L. Danley, September 15, 2008.

7. Ibid.

8. Ivins also began work in the late 1990s on another product with commercial potential. Called CpG, it was an adjuvant, to be added to a vaccine to boost its effectiveness. Beginning in 2000, Ivins was testing on animals whether CpG would improve immunization against anthrax. An application for a patent listed Ivins as a co-inventor of using CpG to "prevent infection from bioterrorism agents." The application was filed with the U.S. Patent and Trademark Office on October 31, 2003.

9. E-mails from Bruce Ivins on October 7, 1999, and November 19, 1999, to recipients whose identities were redacted by the U.S. Army in response to Freedom of Information Act requests.

10. E-mails sent and received by Bruce Ivins in communication with a USAMRIID colleague, April 7, 8, and 10, 2000.

11. E-mail from Bruce Ivins to Mara Linscott, June 28, 2000.

12. Author's review of statements made by Bruce Ivins in May 2007 to the anthrax investigation.

13. E-mail from Bruce Ivins to Mara Linscott, July 4, 2000.

14. E-mail from Bruce Ivins to Mara Linscott, September 21, 2000.

15. Author's interview with Rick Sams, May 6, 2010. In September 2000, Sams exchanged e-mails with Bruce Ivins in which Ivins complained about the lack of federal support for developing the next-generation anthrax vaccine, of which he was a co-inventor. In a reply to Ivins on September 26, 2000, Sams wrote, "I am sorry to hear about the funding decisions on your project." Sams told the author: "His [Ivins's] disappointment was toward the individuals who had made the decisions."

16. Holiday card from Bruce Ivins to Pamela Wehby (née Pamela Thornbury) and family, early 2001.

17. G. Matsumoto, "The Pentagon's Toxic Secret," *Vanity Fair,* May 1999.

18. Ibid.

19. E-mail from Bruce Ivins to W. Russell Byrne, May 21, 1999.

20. The first patent, "Method of making a vaccine for anthrax," was applied for on March 7, 2000, and issued on May 14, 2002. Bruce Ivins was listed as a co-inventor, along with Patricia Worsham, Arthur Friedlander, Joseph Farchaus, and Susan Welkos. The second patent, "Asporogenic B anthracis expression system," was applied for on November 23, 1994. The listed co-inventors were Worsham, Friedlander, and Ivins. Lance K. Gordon, the chief executive of VaxGen, which won federal contracts to complete development of the next-generation anthrax vaccine co-invented by Ivins, told the author on May 19, 2010, that the contracts prohibited adding the adjuvant

squalene to the product. Even without those contractual prohibitions, Gordon said, it was "very unlikely" that VaxGen would have chosen squalene.

21. E-mail from Bruce Ivins to Arthur Friedlander, August 28, 2001.

CHAPTER 7: AVENGING ANGEL

1. E-mail from Bruce Ivins to Mara Linscott, April 3, 2000.
2. Author's interviews in 2010 with behavioral specialists who conferred with Bruce Ivins, plus numerous e-mails that Ivins sent from 1999 to 2008 describing his symptoms.
3. Author's interviews with Judith M. McLean, April 30 and May 3, 2010, and January 9, 2011, and with others familiar with Bruce Ivins's psychiatric care, 2010 and 2011; "The Amerithrax Case: Report of the Expert Behavioral Analysis Panel," August 2010.
4. E-mail from Bruce Ivins to Mara Linscott, June 27, 2000.
5. Author's interviews with Judith M. McLean, April 30 and May 3, 2010, and January 9, 2011; "The Amerithrax Case: Report of the Expert Behavioral Analysis Panel," August 2010.
6. E-mail from Bruce Ivins to Mara Linscott, July 4, 2000.
7. E-mail from Bruce Ivins to Mara Linscott, July 7, 2000.
8. E-mail from Bruce Ivins to Mara Linscott, June 29, 2000.
9. Author's interviews with Judith M. McLean, April 30 and May 3, 2010.
10. Justice Department report on the anthrax investigation, "Amerithrax Investigative Summary," issued on February 19, 2010; author's interviews with government officials familiar with the anthrax investigation, 2009 and 2010.
11. Author's interviews with Judith McLean, April 30 and May 3, 2010, and January 9 and 25, 2011; "The Amerithrax Case: Report of the Expert Behavioral Panel," August 2010.
12. E-mail from Bruce Ivins to Mara Linscott, July 23, 2000.
13. E-mail from Bruce Ivins to Mara Linscott, July 30, 2000.
14. E-mail from Patricia Fellows to Mara Linscott, July 31, 2000. Fellows referred in the e-mail to Kristie Friend, a laboratory technician at USAMRIID who worked in the Bacteriology Division.
15. E-mail from Bruce Ivins to Mara Linscott, August 12, 2000.
16. E-mail from Bruce Ivins to Mara Linscott, August 14, 2000.
17. E-mail from Bruce Ivins to Mara Linscott, August 23, 2000.
18. E-mail from Bruce Ivins to Mara Linscott, March 4, 2001. Ivins was imprecise in how he characterized counselor Judith McLean's efforts. In July 2000, after Ivins told her how he had planned to poison Mara Linscott, McLean did, indeed, contact the local police and she did arrange for Ivins to be promptly evaluated by two psychiatrists. But McLean did not explicitly seek to have Ivins jailed.
19. Justice Department report on the anthrax investigation, "Amerithrax Investigative Summary," issued February 19, 2010; author's interviews with people familiar with Bruce Ivins's psychiatric treatment, 2010.
20. Response to Freedom of Information Act request filed by the author, signed by Army Major William A. Petrous, September 23, 2008.
21. "Personnel Security Program," published by U.S. Army, September 9, 1988; author's interviews with retired Army Major General Stephen Reeves and retired Army Brigadier General Stanley Lillie, August 4, 2009.

22. Author's interviews with present and former government officials familiar with the Army's immunization program at USAMRIID, March, April, and December 2010. Erik Henchal, USAMRIID commander from 2002 to 2005, told the author on April 27, 2010, that Army physicians kept any use of psychiatric drugs by employees confidential. Also see "The Amerithrax Case: Report of the Expert Behavioral Analysis Panel," August 2010.

CHAPTER 8: I AM AN ANTHRAX RESEARCHER!

1. Memo from Karl Rove to Paul Wolfowitz, April 25, 2001, titled, "GULF WAR SYNDROME AND ANTHRAX."
2. Author's interviews with Stephen Reeves, November 21, 2008, and Paul Wolfowitz, November 30, 2010.
3. Author's interviews with Stephen Reeves, November 21, 2008, and August 2 and September 30, 2010.
4. The specific nighttime hours that Bruce Ivins spent in his hot suite at USAMRIID were described in investigative documents compiled by the FBI.
5. E-mail from Bruce Ivins to Mara Linscott, August 20, 2001.
6. Bruce Ivins's e-mail of September 6, 2001, to Rick Sams did not cite the specific news reports, but he appeared to refer to accounts over the previous two days, beginning with a front-page article in the *New York Times* by reporters Judith Miller, Stephen Engelberg, and William J. Broad, "U.S. Germ Warfare Research Pushes Treaty Limits," September 4, 2001. See also V. Loeb, "U.S. Seeks Duplicate of Russian Anthrax," *Washington Post,* September 5, 2001.
7. E-mail from Bruce Ivins to Rick Sams, September 6, 2001.
8. E-mail from Bruce Ivins to Mara Linscott, September 7, 2001.
9. Author's interview on December 7, 2009, with Anna Johnson-Winegar, who in 2001 was U.S. deputy assistant to the secretary of defense for chemical and biological defense. Johnson-Winegar was pressing Army scientists at USAMRIID to focus less on anthrax vaccine research and more on products that could counter some of the other agents that might be used in a biological attack. "We don't want to be totally unprepared for some additional pathogen," Johnson-Winegar told the author. "I was concerned there was, essentially, no research effort on a number of different ones. And clearly glanders would have been one of those. I was just concerned about the priorities and the distribution of funds across many different work units."
10. Author's interviews with Jeffrey Adamovicz on November 27, 2009, Gerard Andrews on December 1, 2009, and with other present and former government officials, 2009; Justice Department report on the anthrax investigation, "Amerithrax Investigative Summary," issued February 19, 2010.
11. Author's interview with Anna Johnson-Winegar, June 14, 2009.
12. Ivins's e-mail on September 7, 2001, reflected a lack of certainty surrounding the issue of indemnification. Two senior officials said later that, so long as the contractor, Science Applications International Corp., performed to the satisfaction of the Army, the company would have been reimbursed for any reasonable costs due to litigation, according to author's interviews with both Anna Johnson-Winegar, who then was deputy assistant secretary of defense for chemical and biological readiness, and Army Major General Stephen Reeves, June 14, 2009, and August 5, 2009. Another official specializing in

vaccines who worked closely with Ivins, Army Colonel David Danley, said that indemnification posed "a real hornet's nest for the government. . . . It was an issue." Although Danley discussed the issue with Ivins, he said he did not know Ivins's basis for estimating indemnification costs of $200,000 per year for fifty years. Author's interviews with David Danley, September 15, 2008, and August 5 and 6, 2009; draft of memo from David Danley to Anna Johnson-Winegar, May 25, 2001.

13. Author's interview with Stephen Reeves, November 21, 2008.

14. Author's interviews with David Danley, August 5 and September 15, 2009. In an interview with the FBI on December 3, 2004, Ivins reiterated his scathing view of the scientists at BioPort. According to the FBI summary of the interview, Ivins described the company scientists thus: "Individuals with no science background, and essentially assembly line technicians hired to put out a product."

15. Author's interviews with Amanda Ivins, December 4, 2008, and January 29, 2009.

16. The letter Bruce Ivins wrote, citing an April 15, 1996, *Newsweek* article about the arrest of Ted Kaczynski, was not published by the magazine.

17. Author's interview with Jeffrey Adamovicz, December 7, 2008.

18. Author's interview with Amanda Ivins, December 4, 2008.

19. E-mail from Bruce Ivins to unidentified acquaintance, September 15, 2001. The e-mail was cited in a sworn affidavit by U.S. postal inspector Thomas Dellafera.

20. E-mail from Bruce Ivins to Mara Linscott, September 21, 2001.

CHAPTER 9: THIS IS NEXT

1. Author's interviews with acquaintances of Bruce Ivins and government officials familiar with the anthrax investigation, 2009 and 2010; Justice Department report on the anthrax investigation, "Amerithrax Investigative Summary," issued on February 19, 2010.

2. Investigators could not measure the exact amount of anthrax placed in any of the mailings because, with one exception, each envelope was unsealed before the FBI took custody of it. The exception was the letter addressed to Senator Patrick Leahy, discovered within a drum of quarantined mail on November 16, 2001. However, even with that letter, investigators noted that some spores may have been squeezed out during handling by the Postal Service's high-speed sorting machinery.

3. Author's interviews with Nancy Haigwood, 2009 and 2010.

4. Ivins's statement "It's believed that Fort Detrick may have been one of the possible targets" for United Airlines Flight 93, which crashed in Somerset County, Pennsylvania, on September 11, 2001, amounted to no more than unverified speculation, unsupported by any credible evidence. The author found that senior Army officials, including the commander of USAMRIID, at no point suspected that Fort Detrick was a target of the Flight 93 hijackers.

5. E-mail from Bruce Ivins to Nancy Haigwood, September 21, 2001.

6. "The Amerithrax Case, Report of the Expert Behavioral Analysis Panel," August 2010.

7. FBI summary of investigators' interview with Bruce Ivins on January 16,

2008; author's interviews with officials familiar with Ivins's statements in that session.

8. E-mail from Bruce Ivins to Nancy Haigwood, September 21, 2001.

9. E-mail from Bruce Ivins to a scientist at the privately owned Battelle Memorial Institute, September 20, 2001.

10. E-mail from Bruce Ivins to Mara Linscott, September 26, 2001. Ivins's statement "I just heard tonight that the Bin Laden terrorists for sure have anthrax and sarin gas" was buttressed by one media account. On that same date, the *CBS Evening News* reported that U.S. intelligence analysts "credited bin Laden with a rudimentary capability to produce both sarin gas and anthrax." See "New Hints of Emerging US Military Plan for the War on Terrorism in Afghanistan," *CBS Evening News,* September 26, 2001.

11. Bruce Ivins was off the mark, historically, when he said in his September 26, 2001, e-mail to Mara Linscott that Osama bin Laden "has just decreed death to all Jews and all Americans." It was actually five years earlier when bin Laden had issued a fatwa calling for the killing of Americans and Israelis. The fatwa, "Declaration of War Against the Americans Occupying the Land of the Two Holy Places," was published in August 1996 by *Al Quds Al Arabi,* a London-based newspaper.

12. FBI analysis of electronic access records at USAMRIID, showing Bruce Ivins's times of arrival and departure, dated February 11, 2008; Justice Department's report on the anthrax investigation, "Amerithrax Investigative Summary," issued February 19, 2010.

13. E-mail from Bruce Ivins to Mara Linscott, October 3, 2001.

CHAPTER 10: ON THE WRONG TRAIL

1. Author's interviews with Dr. Larry M. Bush, April 2009, and Dr. Jean M. Malecki, February 2007 and April 2009.

2. Ibid.

3. P. S. Brachman, "Inhalational Anthrax," *Annals of the New York Academy of Science* 353 (1980): 83–93.

4. Author's interviews with Ari Fleischer, September 4, 2009, and June 14, 2010. Fleischer consulted his contemporaneous notes to recount the remarks that President Bush made privately on October 4, 2001.

5. S. C. Suffin, W. H. Carnes, and A. F. Kaufmann, "Inhalational Anthrax in a Home Craftsman," *Human Pathology,* September 1978. The craftsman was infected from imported animal-origin yarn. J. C. Holty, D. M. Bravata, H. Liu, R. A. Olshen, K. M. McDonald, and D. K. Owens, "Systematic Review: A Century of Inhalational Anthrax Cases from 1900 to 2005," *Annals of Internal Medicine,* February 21, 2006.

6. Transcript of news conference at the White House, October 4, 2001.

7. Author's interviews with Arnold F. Kaufmann, retired epidemiologist for the Centers for Disease Control, November 10, 2009, and February 26, 2010.

8. Author's interviews with Dr. Larry Bush, April 14, 2009, and Dr. Robert P. Kadlec, September 8, 2009.

9. J. Long, "Sheila Stood at Center of Strange Plots at Rancho Rajneesh," *The Oregonian,* September 15, 1990; T. J. Török, R. V. Tauxe, R. P. Wise, J. R. Livengood, R. Sokolow, S. Mauvais, K. A. Birkness, M. R. Skeels, J. M. Horan, and

L. R. Foster, "A Large Community Outbreak of Salmonellosis Caused by Intentional Contamination of Restaurant Salad Bars,"*JAMA,* August 6, 1997.

10. E-mail from Bruce Ivins to Arnold F. Kaufmann, October 4, 2001. Ivins's time spent alone in the hot suite at USAMRIID was described in the Justice Department report on the anthrax investigation, "Amerithrax Investigative Summary," issued February 19, 2010. Before Ivins e-mailed Kaufmann that night, he had spent more than three and a half hours alone in a hot suite at USAMRIID. Ivins left the building at 10:12 P.M.

11. Author's interviews with Arnold Kaufmann, November 10, 2009, and February 26, 2010.

12. Author's interview with Paul Keim, March 18, 2009.

13. Author's interviews with Paul Keim and James Schupp, March 2009; Paul Jackson, October 21, 2010; and James Burans, October 22, 2010.

14. A. P. Pomerantsev, N. A. Staritsin, Yu. V. Mockov, and L. I. Marinin, "Expression of Cereolysine AB Genes in *Bacillus anthracis* Vaccine Ensures Protection Against Experimental Hemolytic Anthrax Infection," *Vaccine,* December 1997.

15. Holiday letter from Bruce Ivins to Pamela Wehby (née Pamela Thornbury) and family, December 1997.

16. Army inventory documents obtained by the author. In an interview with the FBI on March 31, 2005, Ivins described his first handling of the mixture of spores that he inventoried as RMR-1029.

17. Author's interviews with Mike Vickers, April 10 and May 15, 2009. See also W. J. Broad, "Geographic Gaffe Misguides Anthrax Inquiry," *New York Times,* January 30, 2002.

18. Ibid.; J. Warrick, "One Anthrax Answer: Ames Strain Not from Iowa," *Washington Post,* January 29, 2002.

19. Author's interview with Paul Keim, January 6, 2009.

20. Following weeks of antibiotic treatment, Ernesto Blanco survived and was able to leave the hospital.

21. D. B. Jernigan, P. L. Raghunathan, et al., "Investigation of Bioterrorism-Related Anthrax, United States, 2001: Epidemiologic Findings," *Emerging Infectious Diseases,* October 2002; author's interviews with present and former government officials familiar with the anthrax investigation, 2008, 2009, and 2010.

22. Remarks by Tom Brokaw on September 10, 2008, to a hearing of the Congressional Commission on the Prevention of Weapons of Mass Destruction and Proliferation and Terrorism; author's interviews with present and former government officials familiar with the anthrax investigation, 2008, 2009, and 2010.

23. Ibid.; author's interviews with Arthur O. Anderson, one of the two USAMRIID physicians who spoke by phone with Tom Brokaw and his aide, Erin O'Connor, on October 9, 2001. The author also reviewed Anderson's contemporaneous notes of his role, which included analyzing the sample of tissue from O'Connor's shoulder. Anderson concluded on October 11 that O'Connor's wound was negative for anthrax and was more likely from an insect or spider bite. Anderson turned out to be wrong. A second tissue sample was sent from New York to the CDC in Atlanta. On October 12, a CDC specialist concluded that O'Connor did have a cutaneous anthrax infection.

24. Author's interviews with present and former government officials familiar with the anthrax investigation, 2008, 2009, and 2010. See also D. B. Jernigan, P. L. Raghunathan et al., "Investigation of Bioterrorism-Related Anthrax, United States, 2001: Epidemiologic Findings," *Emerging Infectious Diseases,* October 2002; E. Lipton, "Taking Baby to the Office, Then Living a Nightmare," *New York Times,* October 17, 2001.

25. Prepared testimony of J. T. Caruso, an FBI deputy assistant director, presented to the House Subcommittee on Terrorism and Homeland Defense, October 11, 2001. Although the available scientific findings contradicted Caruso's statement that "there is no evidence" the anthrax found inside the American Media building resulted from a "terrorist act," he was on solid ground in disavowing any known connection between that event and the airliner hijackings of September 11.

CHAPTER 11: IN CIPRO WE TRUST

1. Author's interviews with Stewart Simonson, August 2009; Donald A. Henderson, August 27, 2009; Philip K. Russell, September 3, 2009; Tommy Thompson, October 6, 2009; and Paul Wolfowitz, November 30, 2010. See also D. J. Feith, *War and Decision* (HarperCollins, 2008). See also findings of Dark Winter exercise, posted on Web site of University of Pittsburgh Medical Center, Center for Biosecurity, http://www.upmc-biosecurity.org/website/events/2001_darkwinter/findings.html.

2. M. Enserink, "Bioterrorism: How Devastating Would a Smallpox Attack Really Be?," *Science,* May 31, 2002; author's interview with Richard H. Ebright, professor of chemistry and chemical biology at Rutgers University, August 24, 2009.

3. Health and Human Services secretary Tommy Thompson announced his intention to assemble 300 million doses of smallpox vaccine on October 17, 2001.

4. Author's interview with Dr. Philip K. Russell, September 3, 2009.

5. Author's interviews with Laura Petrou, November 20, 2008, and Kelly Fado, January 22, 2010.

6. Author's interviews with Kelly Fado, January 22, 2010, and Clara Kircher, January 25, 2010.

7. Author's interviews with Laura Petrou, November 20, 2008; Eric Washburn, January 13, 2010; Kelly Fado, January 22, 2010; and Scott Stanley, August 10, 2010.

8. Thirty-one of 150 nasal swabs taken from persons at the Hart Senate Office Building ultimately came back positive, which indicated exposure but did not prove that infection was present. Officials familiar with the matter further told the author that all persons who tested positive were prescribed Cipro or given the choice of whether to take the antibiotic.

9. Federal News Service transcript of press availability with President George W. Bush, who was joined at the White House by Italian prime minister Silvio Berlusconi, October 15, 2001. Bush learned about the powder-bearing letter during a telephone conversation with Tom Daschle that had first focused on other matters.

10. E-mail from Patricia Fellows to Mara Linscott, October 16, 2001.

CHAPTER 12: BENTONITE?

1. Author's interviews with John Ezzell, 2008, 2009, and 2010, and with Scott Decker, July 27, 2010; and internal chronology of investigative events maintained by the FBI.

2. Author's interviews with John Ezzell and other former or present officials familiar with the anthrax investigation, 2008, 2009, and 2010.

3. The anthrax-laced letter addressed to "Editor" of the *New York Post* was found there by the FBI on October 19, 2001, the day after health authorities informed the *Post*'s Johanna Huden that analysis of her blood showed that the lesion on her right middle finger was caused by anthrax. A total of three *Post* staffers ultimately were diagnosed and treated successfully for cutaneous anthrax infections: William Monagas, a mail room worker; Mark Cunningham, an editor for the opinion pages; and Huden, an assistant for those pages whose duties included opening the mail. See J. Huden, "Giving the Finger to Bioterrorists: Post Editorial Staffer Tells of Spore Horror," *New York Post*, October 20, 2001; M. Weiss, A. Miller, and A. Geller, "Post Gets 2nd Letter: Handwriting Matches Other Anthrax Hate Mail," *New York Post*, October 21, 2001; transcript of remarks made at a news conference on October 19, 2001, by New York City mayor Rudy Giuliani and Neal L. Cohen, the city's commissioner of health; D. B. Jernigan, P. L. Raghunathan et al., "Investigation of Bioterrorism-Related Anthrax, United States, 2001: Epidemiologic Findings," *Emerging Infectious Diseases,* October 2002.

4. *NewsHour with Jim Lehrer*, PBS, October 17, 2001.

5. Transcript of hearing held by House Committee on International Relations, December 5, 2001; Spertzel's remarks to the committee were featured that night on *Fox News Special Report with Brit Hume*.

6. *Hardball with Chris Matthews*, MSNBC, October 17, 2001.

7. Transcript of news conference of President George W. Bush, appearing in Shanghai, China, October 19, 2001.

8. Author's interviews with John Ezzell, 2008, 2009, and 2010, and Henry S. Heine, April 23, 2010. Heine conducted the tests that found the anthrax mailed to Senator Daschle was susceptible to no fewer than ten antibiotics.

9. A committee appointed by the National Academy of Sciences described the mishandling of the anthrax-laced letter addressed to Tom Brokaw by the New York City Department of Health. See *Review of the Scientific Approaches Used During the FBI's Investigation of the 2001 Anthrax Letters* (Washington, D.C.: National Academies Press, 2011).

10. Author's interviews with Erik Henchal, April 27, 2010, and John Ezzell, 2008, 2009, and 2010.

11. E-mails exchanged between Bruce Ivins and Peter Jahrling on February 12, 2003. In his response to Ivins, Jahrling wrote at 10:01 A.M.: "Yes, I asked you to do this. And yes, you did provide me with the data. I can probably resurrect that data, given a little time, if you need it. Is there a problem that I should be sensitive to?"

12. Author's interviews with John Ezzell, 2009 and 2010; summary of FBI interview with an unidentified colleague of Bruce Ivins, March 1, 2007.

13. Author's interviews in 2010 and 2011 with people familiar with the psychiatric care provided to Bruce Ivins; "The Amerithrax Case: Report of the Expert Behavioral Analysis Panel," August 2010.

14. The dirty, cluttered condition of the B3 hot suite and its surrounding laboratories was documented in an Army investigation report authored by Colonel David Hoover in May 2002, "Anthrax Contamination at USAMRIID."

15. Author's interviews with John Ezzell, 2009 and 2010; FBI agent Darin Steele, March 9, 2010; Erik Henchal, July 9, 2010; and Scott Stanley, August 10, 2010. Bruce Ivins, in an interview with the FBI on March 31, 2005, acknowledged the disarray of the B3 hot suite.

16. Author's interview with Jeffrey Adamovicz, December 8, 2008.

17. Author's interview with Gerard Andrews, retired USAMRIID Bacteriology Division chief, June 19, 2009.

18. Author's interview and exchange of e-mails with Priscilla Wyrick, June 16, 2009, and January 6, 2010.

19. Author's interviews with John Parker, September 21 and 23, 2009.

20. Author's interviews with Robert Kadlec, C. J. Peters, Anthony S. Fauci, and Stewart Simonson, 2008 and 2009.

21. Author's interviews with John Parker, Stewart Simonson, and Tommy Thompson, 2009 and 2010.

22. Author's interviews with Robert Kadlec, September 8 and 17, 2009; John Parker, September 23, 2009; and Paul Wolfowitz, November 30, 2010. On January 26, 1998, Wolfowitz and the man who would three years later become the U.S. secretary of defense and his boss, Donald Rumsfeld, had been among eighteen analysts who challenged President Bill Clinton to force Saddam Hussein from power. Doing so, they told Clinton in an open letter, was America's "only acceptable strategy." The letter's eighteen signatories: Elliot Abrams, Richard L. Armitage, William J. Bennett, Jeffrey Bergner, John Bolton, Paula Dobriansky, Francis Fukuyama, Robert Kagan, Zalmay Khalilzad, William Kristol, Richard Perle, Peter W. Rodman, Rumsfeld, William Schneider Jr., Vin Weber, Wolfowitz, R. James Woolsey, and Robert B. Zoellick. The letter was organized as "The Project for a New American Century."

23. Author's interview with Tom Ridge, October 22, 2009.

24. Author's interviews with Robert Kadlec, September 8 and 17, 2009, and John S. Parker, September 21, 2009.

25. Author's exchanges of e-mails with Peter Jahrling, September 16, 2008; author's interviews with John Parker, September 23, 2009; Tommy Thompson, October 6, 2009; and Tom Ridge, October 22, 2009, e-mail response to the author from Michael Kortan, spokesman for FBI director Robert Mueller, November 4, 2010.

26. R. Weiss and D. Eggen, "Additive Made Spores Deadlier; 3 Nations Known to Be Able to Make Sophisticated Coating," *Washington Post*, October 25, 2001.

27. W. J. Broad, "Contradicting Some U.S. Officials, 3 Scientists Call Anthrax Powder High-Grade," *New York Times,* October 25, 2001.

28. "USA Patriot" is an acronym standing for "United and Strengthening America by Providing Appropriate Tools Required to Intercept and Obstruct Terrorism."

29. In an exchange of e-mails with the author on September 16, 2008, and a brief conversation on February 24, 2009, Peter Jahrling conceded that he had spoken in error in the fall of 2001 when he asserted that the anthrax sent to Senator Daschle was treated with bentonite or another additive.

30. Author's interviews with James Burans, April 21, 2009, and Scott Decker, July 27, 2010.

CHAPTER 13: SERIOUS PEOPLE

1. On October 26, 2001, the same day that ABC News aired its exclusive, an article published by *The Wall Street Journal* reported that bentonite might be present in anthrax used in the letter attacks. However, the article was speculative and it stopped short of asserting linkage to Iraq. See J. J. Fialka, D. S. Cloud, and S. Fatsis, "Material in Anthrax May Ease Dispersal—Weapons Experts Examine If Substance Is Additive Used to Boost Potency," *Wall Street Journal,* October 26, 2001.
2. *World News Tonight,* ABC News, October 26, 2001, and *This Week,* ABC News, October 28, 2001.
3. Central Intelligence Agency reports, June 21, 2002, and January 29, 2003; Defense Department Inspector General report, "Review of the Pre-Iraqi War Activities of the Office of the Under Secretary of Defense for Policy," February 9, 2007.
4. *World News Tonight,* ABC News, October 28, 2001.
5. *Good Morning America,* ABC News, October 29, 2001.
6. P. Johnson, "Anthrax Story Pits White House vs. ABC," *USA Today,* October 31, 2001.
7. *World News Tonight,* ABC News, November 1, 2001.
8. Author's interview with Tim Trevan, May 27, 2009.
9. *NewsHour with Jim Lehrer,* PBS, October 17, 2001.
10. Prepared remarks by Richard Spertzel, presented at hearing of the U.S. House International Relations Committee, December 5, 2001.
11. Ibid. See also R. Spertzel, "Iraq's Faux Capitulation," *Wall Street Journal,* September 24, 2002; author's interviews with Richard Spertzel, May 25, 2009, and May 21 and 31, 2010.
12. Author's interview with Richard Spertzel, May 25, 2009; ABC News transcripts, October 26, 28, and 29, and November 1, 2001.
13. Biographical summary of Brian Ross, posted by ABC News, January 2011, http://abcnews.go.com/WNT/brian-ross/story?id=127548.
14. Author's interview with Ari Fleischer, September 4, 2009. Brian Ross, in response to questions from the author about his reports in October 2001 regarding the supposed presence of bentonite or another chemical additive in the anthrax spores that were mailed in the letter attacks, said by e-mail on January 5, 2011: "As is painfully obvious, our sources were very wrong—although at the time they were convinced they were right."
15. *This Week,* ABC News, October 28, 2001.
16. Author's interviews with Thomas Dellafera, April 2010, and other government officials familiar with the anthrax investigation, 2008, 2009, and 2010.
17. L. Allen-Agostini, "A Team Player: Thomas Morris Jr. Was a Model Worker and Avid Bowler," *Washington Post,* October 26, 2001; P. McCombs, "The Man Next Door: Joseph Curseen Jr. Pulled His Community Together," *Washington Post,* October 26, 2001.
18. Author's interviews with government officials involved with the Amerithrax investigation, 2008 and 2009. See also: J. A. Jernigan et al., "Bioterrorism-

Related Inhalational Anthrax: The First 10 Cases Reported in the United States," *Emerging Infectious Diseases,* November–December, 2001.

19. R. Bartley, "Anthrax: The Elephant in the Room," *Wall Street Journal,* October 29, 2001. See also Editorial, "Making the Iraq Case," *Wall Street Journal,* September 5, 2002. It is likely that Robert Bartley's claim about the removal of electrostatic charge from the mailed anthrax was informed by an anthrax-related article published by the *New York Times* on October 25, 2001 (W. J. Broad, "Contradicting Some U.S. Officials, 3 Scientists Call Powder High-Grade"). The article quoted William Patrick, the former Fort Detrick bioweaponeer, as saying that the anthrax sent to Senator Tom Daschle was "electrostatic free" and "appears to have an additive which keeps the spores from clumping." Patrick, during several interviews with the author in 2009 and 2010, said he ultimately changed his mind about the characteristics of the powder, which he never examined. No evidence ever emerged to establish that electrostatic charges with the anthrax were removed. Patrick died of cancer on October 1, 2010; Robert Bartley died on December 10, 2003.

20. *The Early Show,* CBS News, October 18, 2001.

21. *Late Show with David Letterman,* CBS-TV, October 18, 2001.

22. Reuters/Zogby opinion poll, October 25, 2001.

23. Internal chronology of anthrax investigation developments maintained by the FBI.

24. M. Laris and J. Lenhart, "Emerging from the Grip of Anthrax; Va. Mail Handler Reflects on Deadly Struggle and Faces a Changed Life," *Washington Post,* December 6, 2001. See also D. J. Beecher, "Forensic Application of Microbiological Culture Analysis to Identify Mail Intentionally Contaminated with *Bacillus anthracis* Spores," *Applied and Environmental Microbiology,* August 2006.

25. Author's interviews with Robert Kadlec, September 8, 2009, and James Burans, April 21, 2009.

26. Author's interview with James Burans, April 21, 2009.

27. Author's interviews with Dwight Adams, 2009, 2010, and 2011.

28. Author's interviews with Joseph Michael, 2009 and 2010, and contemporaneous documents from the Sandia National Laboratories and the FBI.

29. The Sandia National Laboratories examined anthrax from the letters addressed to the *New York Post* and to Senators Tom Daschle and Patrick Leahy. Due to the scarcity of material retrievable from the letter addressed to Tom Brokaw, the FBI provided no anthrax from it to Sandia.

30. M. Stewart, A. P. Somlyo, A. V. Somlyo, H. Shuman, J. A. Lindsay, and W. G. Murrell, "Distribution of Calcium and Other Elements in Cryosectioned *Bacillus cereus* T Spores, Determined by High-Resolution Scanning Electron Probe X-ray Microanalysis," *Journal of Bacteriology,* July 1980. The article reported an "unexpectedly high concentration of silicon" found inside the spores of *Bacillus cereus,* a close relative of *Bacillus anthracis.*

31. See PR Newswire, "Newsweek Exclusive: Secret New Analysis Suggests Anthrax Attacker May Be a Scientific Whiz, Able to Make 'Weaponized' Form More Sophisticated than Previously Known; Spores in Letter to Sen. Leahy Were Ground to a Microscopic Fineness Not Achieved by U.S. Biological Weapons Experts." *Newsweek* then published its report as a "Periscope" item on April 15, 2002, written by Mark Hosenball, John Barry, and Daniel Klaidman.

32. J. Warrick, "Powder Used in Anthrax Attacks 'Was Not Routine,'" *Washington Post,* April 9, 2002.

33. T. V. Inglesby, T. O'Toole, D. A. Henderson, J. G. Bartlett, M. S. Ascher, E. Eitzen, A. M. Friedlander, J. Gerberding, J. Hauer, J. Hughes, J. McDade, M. T. Osterholm, G. Parker, T. M. Perl, P. K. Russell, and K. Tonat, "Anthrax as a Biological Weapon, 2002: Updated Recommendations for Management," *JAMA,* May 1, 2002.

34. Lead co-author Thomas Inglesby, who after the anthrax attacks became chief operating officer and deputy director of the Center for Biosecurity of the University of Pittsburgh Medical Center in Baltimore, did not respond to e-mails and telephone messages from the author. Nor did Inglesby's lead co-author, Tara O'Toole, who as of 2002 was chief executive officer and director of the Center for Biosecurity of the University of Pittsburgh Medical Center in Baltimore. Four of the sixteen co-authors of the May 1, 2002, *JAMA* article did discuss the matter in interviews for this book. Donald A. Henderson said on June 28, 2010, that the article's reference to "weapons grade" anthrax "treated to reduce clumping" was based on the assertion of a virologist at USAMRIID, Peter Jahrling, who conceded later, in September 2008, that he had spoken in error. Another of the co-authors, Philip Russell, said in an interview on June 6, 2010, that the now disputed claims were propounded by the lead co-authors. Russell, who along with Henderson held a senior position with the U.S. Health and Human Services Department in 2002, said that when the article was written he had not focused on those unsupported claims. Russell said the article was submitted "before the issue [of weaponization] had been examined in any serious detail." Co-author Arthur Friedlander, the longtime Army anthrax researcher, said in an interview on July 16, 2010, that he had nothing to do with the article's claims that the anthrax in the letters was of "weapons grade" and "treated to reduce clumping." Said Friedlander: "I don't know anything about that stuff." Another co-author of the *JAMA* article said that if a basis ever existed for the claims of weapons grade and treated spores, that basis should have been cited in a footnote. This individual spoke on a condition of anonymity with the book's author on June 18, 2010.

35. W. J. Broad and D. Johnston, "A Nation Challenged: Bioterrorism; Report Linking Anthrax and Hijackers Is Investigated," *New York Times,* March 23, 2002.

36. Ibid. See also *CNN Saturday Edition,* March 23, 2002, in which former CIA director R. James Woolsey, one of the earliest proponents of invading Iraq, called the report in that day's *New York Times* "fascinating." Woolsey said the ex post facto diagnosis of cutaneous anthrax in hijacker Ahmad al Haznawi, asserted by researchers Thomas Inglesby and Tara O'Toole, "ties the anthrax attacks to 9/11." The one physician who actually treated Haznawi, Dr. Christos Tsonas, told the author on November 25, 2009, that when he examined the sore on Haznawi's leg, "it was just an infectious ulcer, that's all." In hindsight, Tsonas said that it was not possible to know whether or not it was caused by anthrax. For news coverage that was more skeptical of the memo by Inglesby and O'Toole asserting that one of the September 11 hijackers appeared to have had a cutaneous anthrax infection, see S. Fainaru and C. Connolly, "Memo on Florida Case Roils Anthrax Probe; Experts Debate Theory Hijacker Was Exposed," *Washington Post,* March 29, 2002.

In addition to scouring locations in Florida where September 11 hijacker Ahmad al Haznawi was known to have lived or visited, the FBI sought traces of anthrax within his remains and those of the other three terrorists who hijacked United Airlines Flight 93, which crashed in rural Pennsylvania. According to the author's interviews with investigators, after body parts and bits of tissue were painstakingly recovered from the crash site, investigators were able to assemble partial remains for the four hijackers. On May 15, 2002, FBI lab chief Dwight Adams informed Director Robert Mueller that twenty-two pounds of the hijackers' remains were recovered, according to contemporaneous documents reviewed by the author. At the FBI's lab in Washington, technicians probed the dehydrated materials, including sawing into the foot of one of the hijackers, and sent tissue samples to USAMRIID and the Armed Forces Institute of Pathology. No anthrax was found. The FBI lab was later moved in its entirety from Washington to a facility adjoining a U.S. Marine Corps base in Quantico, Virginia.

37. Congressman Mike Pence's office immediately made public on the Internet his June 11, 2002, letter to Attorney General John Ashcroft, titled, "Congressman Mike Pence Request for Update on FBI Investigation." Pence's unsupported scientific claims about the anthrax used in the attacks were cited favorably in an editorial published on June 13, 2002, by the *Indianapolis Star*. Referring to Pence's letter to Ashcroft, the editorial said the congressman had relayed "the fact" that the anthrax "had been genetically modified to increase its virulence." In fact, tests of the anthrax overseen by the FBI and conducted at USAMRIID and elsewhere found no genetic modification.

38. G. Gugliotta and G. Matsumoto, "FBI's Theory on Anthrax Is Doubted; Attacks Not Likely Work of 1 Person, Experts Say," *Washington Post*, October 28, 2002. In a letter published subsequently by the *Post*, two scientists who had examined electron micrographs of the mailed anthrax challenged the assertion that the material was treated with an additive. The letter writers were Matthew Meselson, a geneticist, and Ken Alibek, a physician who was formerly a top official in the Soviet Union's biological warfare program. See "Anthrax Under the Microscope," *Washington Post*, November 5, 2002.

39. The Sandia National Laboratories promptly informed the FBI of the March 2002 test results showing that the anthrax used for the letter attacks was not treated with silica or any other additive. Bureau officials shared this information immediately with FBI director Robert Mueller and almost as quickly with the White House and elsewhere within the Bush administration, according to present and former government investigators. The FBI relayed the essence of the Sandia results to Senator Leahy on June 6, 2002, by way of a confidential memo. Top staffers of Leahy and Senator Daschle received their first private briefing about the Sandia results on November 5, 2002. An oral briefing of the same information was provided to the two senators on January 9, 2003. Another such briefing was held for the senators' staffers on April 23, 2003. All three briefings were led by the director of the FBI lab, Dwight Adams, according to contemporaneous investigative documents and present and former government officials interviewed by the author in 2008, 2009, and 2010.

40. According to an April 2, 2003, e-mail from FBI agent Ann Todd to five senior bureau officials, including Dwight Adams, Richard Lambert, and Van Harp, Adams briefed Congressman Holt about the findings from the Sandia Na-

tional Laboratories and the general status of the anthrax investigation on April 1, 2003.

41. Author's interviews with Dwight Adams and other present and former government officials familiar with the anthrax investigation, 2009 and 2010.

42. Author's interviews with Tom Ridge, October 22, 2009, and July 23, 2010, and other present and former government officials, 2009 and 2010. The disregarding of the data from Sandia National Laboratories concluding that the anthrax placed in the letter to Senator Daschle was not treated with any additive is apparent in Ridge's own book, published in 2009, about his tenure as the nation's first homeland security advisor and cabinet secretary. In his book, Ridge defined "weaponized" anthrax as material that had been ground finely, its toxicity greatly enhanced by the adding of "other substances." Ridge wrote that the anthrax mailed to Daschle "had been weaponized." See T. Ridge with L. Bloom, *The Test of Our Times* (Thomas Dunne Books, 2009).

43. Author's interviews with Joseph Michael, September 12, 2009, and April 6, May 19, and September 8, 2010.

44. Author's interviews with present and former government officials familiar with the anthrax investigation, 2009 and 2010. A sample of the anthrax addressed to Senator Daschle was sent to the Armed Forces Institute of Pathology for analysis at the request of Peter Jahrling, then a senior scientist at USAMRIID. "This is a matter of national security," Jahrling wrote in a faxed note to the armed forces scientists in late October 2001. On September 25, 2009, Anne Oplinger, a spokeswoman for Jahrling, said that Jahrling declined to confer further with the author regarding the actions he took in the aftermath of the anthrax letter attacks.

45. C. C. Kelly, "Detecting Environmental Terrorism: AFIP's Department of Environmental and Toxicologic Pathology Provides Critical DoD, Homeland Defense Programs," Armed Forces Institute of Pathology quarterly newsletter, October 31, 2002. A spokesman for the institute, Paul Stone, told the author on April 9, 2010, that Florabel Mullick would not respond to questions regarding her analysis of the anthrax. The Armed Forces Institute of Pathology never published in a peer-reviewed scientific journal the results of its analysis of the sample of anthrax that had been addressed to Daschle.

46. Data generated by the Armed Forces Institute of Pathology's examination of anthrax samples from the letter attacks, dated October 25 and 26, 2001, and obtained by the author under the Freedom of Information Act. The Armed Forces Institute concluded that silica, a compound of silicon and oxygen, coated the anthrax spores. The Sandia National Laboratories, however, found that there was no silica on the spore surfaces. Sandia showed that the silicon-containing material was present only in the interior of the spores.

CHAPTER 14: OUR OLD FRIEND SADDAM

1. E-mail from Bruce Ivins to an unidentified colleague at USAMRIID, October 12, 2001. The acronyms "DOD" and "USDA" refer to the Department of Defense and the U.S. Department of Agriculture.

2. Author's interview with Jeffrey Adamovicz, December 7, 2008.

3. E-mail from Bruce Ivins to an unidentified anthrax researcher in Britain, October 13, 2001.

4. E-mail from Bruce Ivins to a colleague, November 23, 2001.

5. E-mail messages from Bruce Ivins to Martin Hugh-Jones, February 7, 2002.

6. FBI summary of November 19, 2001, interview with Bruce Ivins; author's interviews with officials familiar with the anthrax investigation, 2009 and 2010. The FBI found no evidence that Farchaus had anything to do with the anthrax letter attacks.

7. When investigators pressed Bruce Ivins for his basis for suspecting Joseph Farchaus in connection with the letter attacks, Ivins ultimately provided nothing more tangible than his personal dislike of his ex-colleague, saying that Farchaus was "a mean guy who liked to poke people in the chest."

8. The present or former colleagues who Bruce Ivins at various times suggested orally or in e-mails may have perpetrated the anthrax letter attacks included John Ezzell, Joseph Farchaus, Patricia Fellows, Henry Heine, Erik Henchal, Gregory Knudson, and Mara Linscott. Investigators found no evidence that any of them had any role in the attacks. The author spoke with Ezzell, Fellows, Heine, Henchal, and Linscott. Farchaus did not respond to messages left with his lawyer; Knudson did not return a message left with his wife.

9. FBI summaries of interviews with Bruce Ivins, January 23 and 29, 2002.

10. Author's interviews with John Ezzell, 2008, 2009, and 2010. Bruce Ivins, in an interview with the FBI on March 31, 2005, said that he had just recently learned about John Ezzell's work with dry powder anthrax.

11. Justice Department report on the anthrax investigation, "Amerithrax Investigative Summary," issued February 19, 2010.

12. Author's interviews with John Ezzell, 2008, 2009, 2010, and 2011, and sworn statement by Ezzell to Army investigator, May 10, 2002.

13. Other recipients of Bruce Ivins's November 14, 2001, e-mail included his wife, their teenage twins, and several of his classmates from Lebanon High School, among them his mother's favorite, Elaine ("the Brain") Kraus.

14. Author's interview with Scott Stanley, August 10, 2010.

15. Author's interviews with John Ezzell and another scientific colleague of Bruce Ivins, October 27 and 30, 2009. Ivins did submit to a polygraph in early January 2002 and was told by the FBI that he passed. Several years later, however, after the results were submitted to examiners at FBI Headquarters and at the Department of Defense Polygraph Institute, they separately concluded that Ivins displayed "classic" signs of having used "countermeasures" to foil the test, according to the author's interviews with Amerithrax investigators and the Justice Department summary report of the investigation. The summary also suggested that the countermeasures may have been Ivins's use of "a number of psychotropic medications."

16. Author's interview with senior Amerithrax investigators, including FBI agents Lawrence Alexander, Edward Montooth, and Darin Steele, supervising postal inspector Thomas Dellafera, and Assistant U.S. Attorney Kenneth Kohl, March 9, 2010.

17. Author's interviews with John Ezzell, 2008, 2009, and 2010.

18. Author's interviews with John Ezzell, March 30 and May 2, 2009; Edward Montooth, Lawrence Alexander, Darin Steele, Thomas Dellafera, and Kenneth Kohl, March 2010; and Scott Stanley, August 10, 2010.

19. Author's interview with Jeffrey Adamovicz, December 7, 2008; FBI summary of interview with Bruce Ivins, January 29, 2002.

20. Author's interviews with Army Major General Stephen Reeves, 2008, 2009, and 2010, and exchange of e-mails March 4, 2010, with Kathryn Zoon, formerly director of the Food and Drug Administration's Center for Biologics Evaluation and Research.

21. Prepared statement of Secretary Tommy G. Thompson, issued by U.S. Department of Health and Human Services, January 31, 2002.

22. Author's interview with Stephen Reeves, November 21, 2008.

CHAPTER 15: OH MY GOD, I KNOW HIM!

1. Author's interviews with Rita Colwell and Paul Keim, 2009, and Scott Decker, July 27, 2010.

2. Author's interview with Rita Colwell, May 23, 2009.

3. Author's interview with retired FBI agent Bill Godfrey, March 26, 2008.

4. Electronic communication from FBI agent Kenneth J. Williams, based in Phoenix, Arizona, on July 10, 2001.

5. Author's interview with Steven Butler, June 25, 2010; statement of FBI director Robert Mueller on June 18, 2002, to the congressional Joint Intelligence Committee inquiry into the September 11 attacks. See also D. Willman and A. Miller, "Watch List Didn't Get to Airline," *Los Angeles Times*, September 20, 2001.

6. Sworn deposition testimony of Van Harp in connection with Steven Hatfill's privacy lawsuit vs. the Justice Department and the FBI, September 22, 2005; author's interviews with Charles Whistler, January 21 and June 6, 2008, and December 27, 2010. See also S. Eaton, "Ohio FBI Vet in Thick of Terror Probe," (Cleveland) *Plain Dealer*, December 24, 2001, and A. Lengel, "Experience at Work in FBI Anthrax Case; 'Meticulous' Chief of Washington Field Office Looks to Crack the Deadly Scare," *Washington Post*, March 4, 2002.

7. "A Review of Allegations of a Double Standard of Discipline at the FBI," Office of the Inspector General of the United States Department of Justice, November 15, 2002.

8. Sworn deposition testimony of Robert Roth, November 4, 2005, in Steven Hatfill's privacy lawsuit against the Justice Department and the FBI. Van Harp said that his responsibilities related to the aftermath of the September 11 attacks prevented him for several months from being intensively involved in supervising the anthrax investigation. Harp's acknowledgment came in his sworn deposition testimony September 22, 2005, in Hatfill's privacy lawsuit against the Justice Department and the FBI.

9. Author's interview with Nancy Haigwood, May 19, 2009.

10. M. Enserink, "Taking Anthrax's Genetic Fingerprints," *Science*, November 30, 2001.

11. Author's interviews with Paul Keim, 2009, 2010, and 2011, and Amerithrax investigators, including Scott Decker, Scott Stanley, and Rachel Lieber, 2010; summary of investigative information provided by the FBI to the National Academy of Sciences committee that reviewed scientific aspects of the case, December 3, 2010.

12. Author's interviews with John Ezzell, 2008, 2009, and 2010, and with Lawrence Alexander, 2010.

13. Author's interviews with Jeff Adamovicz, December 7, 2008, and John Ezzell, November 18, 2009.

CHAPTER 16: I DIDN'T KEEP RECORDS

1. Separate statements submitted to Army investigation by Bruce Ivins, dated April 18, 2002, May 6, 2002, and May 10, 2002; Ivins's interview with the FBI, March 31, 2005; author's interviews with federal investigators, 2008, 2009, and 2010.

2. Author's interviews with former Army scientists, 2008 and 2009; findings of Army investigator Colonel David Hoover, May 10, 2002.

3. The Justice Department report on the anthrax investigation, "Amerithrax Investigative Summary," issued on February 19, 2010, said that Ivins's success rate with finding presumptive anthrax colonies in "cold" areas of USAMRIID suggested that he "knew where to swab because he knew where he had contaminated the building." Ivins told investigators that his success rate was attributable to his superior technique in swabbing for anthrax.

4. Statements to Army investigation by Bruce Ivins, April and May 2002, and Patricia Fellows, May 6, 2002. Worsham's recollections are also characterized in the Justice Department report on the anthrax investigation, "Amerithrax Investigative Summary," issued on February 19, 2010.

5. Sworn statement to Army investigation by Patricia Worsham, May 6, 2002. Referring to the secretive swabbing and bleaching undertaken in late 2001 by Ivins, Worsham said, "I discounted the importance of his results since he had not considered the issue important . . . enough to confirm the results." Worsham said that Ivins had told her, as of the first week of April 2002, that he first bleached his office and found what "looked like" anthrax "in November or December 2001." Ivins told the Army investigation that he first bleached in December 2001. In a brief interview with the author on September 24, 2009, Patricia Worsham, who was hired at USAMRIID in 1989, continued to defend Bruce Ivins. "You can't work with somebody for twenty years and not get a feel for what they're capable of," she said.

6. Statements to Army investigation by Bruce Ivins, Patricia Worsham, and Gerard Andrews, April and May 2002; author's interviews with Jeffrey Adamovicz, 2008 and 2009, and Gerard Andrews, June 19, 2009.

7. Statements to media by Army spokesman Charles Dasey, reported by the Associated Press and the *Baltimore Sun*, April 20, 2002, by the *Washington Post*, April 25, 2002, and by the *Air Force Times*, May 6, 2002.

8. Army memorandum for record written by Gerard Andrews, encompassing events of April 19–25, 2002.

9. Memorandum to Colonel David Hoover from Army Major General Lester Martinez-Lopez, April 23, 2002.

10. Building 1425 housed both administrative offices and individual hot suites, each dedicated to the study of a specific pathogen.

11. Ibid.; e-mails between David Hoover and Army Colonel Jeffrey Davies, May 5, 2002.

12. Statements to Army investigation by Bruce Ivins, April 18 and May 6, 2002; by Kristie Friend, May 9, 2002; author's interviews with John Ezzell, 2008 and 2009.

13. Statements to Army investigation by Bruce Ivins on April 18 and May 6, 2002.

14. Even a master of anthrax such as Bruce Ivins would have faced great difficulty in containing the spores used to lace the letters. In a peer-reviewed study pub-

lished in August 2006, FBI microbiologist Douglas J. Beecher concluded: "[I]t appears that it is virtually impossible to intentionally place dried spores inside a standard envelope without heavily contaminating its outside surfaces. Even if it were possible to perfectly seal a spore-laden envelope so that no spore could escape from the inside, the outer surface would be so heavily contaminated that spores shed from the surface would present a hazard." See D. J. Beecher, "Forensic Application of Microbiological Culture Analysis to Identify Mail Intentionally Contaminated with *Bacillus anthracis* Spores," *Applied and Environmental Microbiology,* August 2006.

15. Army investigation report, "Anthrax Contamination at USAMRIID," May 2002.

16. Investigators and health officials examined twenty-seven apartments in the Bronx complex where Kathy Nguyen lived and screened a total of 1,710 acquaintances and visitors and patients at the East Side Manhattan hospital where she worked, seeking any sign of anthrax. In addition to the hospital and apartments, environmental samples were collected from area businesses and post offices and the No. 6 Lexington Avenue subway route that Nguyen traveled daily. No anthrax was found. See T. H. Holtz, J. Ackelsberg, J. L. Kool, R. Rosselli, A. Marfin, T. Matte, S. T. Beatrice, M. B. Heller, D. Hewett, L. C. Moskin, M. L. Bunning, M. Layton, and the New York City Anthrax Investigation Working Group, "Isolated Case of Bioterrorism-Related Inhalational Anthrax, New York City, 2001," *Emerging Infectious Diseases,* June 2003.

17. J. Steinhauer, "Hospital Worker's Illness Suggests Widening Threat; Security Tightens over U.S.," *New York Times,* October 31, 2001. The article reported on the case of Kathy Nguyen, who died that day. See also remarks of Dr. Anthony S. Fauci, director of the National Institute of Allergy and Infectious Diseases, a part of the National Institutes of Health, appearing on NBC's *Today* show, October 31, 2001. Fauci said that he was "uncomfortable" with earlier assumptions that a person would have to inhale at least eight thousand spores of anthrax to face the risk of deadly infection.

18. K. S. Griffith, P. Mead, G. L. Armstrong, J. Painter, K. A. Kelley, A. R. Hoffmaster, D. Mayo, D. Barden, R. Ridzon, U. Parashar, E. H. Teshale, J. Williams, S. Noviello, J. F. Perz, E. E. Mast, D. L. Swerdlow, and J. L. Hadler, "Bioterrorism-Related Inhalational Anthrax in an Elderly Woman, Connecticut, 2001," *Emerging Infectious Diseases,* June 2003. See also P. Zielbauer, "Connecticut Detects Anthrax on a Letter Near Victim's Home," *New York Times,* December 1, 2001.

19. Statement to Army investigation by Bruce Ivins, May 6, 2002.

20. Although Bruce Ivins did not warn his junior lab technician, Kristie Friend, that he found what appeared to be anthrax spores on her desk within the office space that they shared, Ivins did convey this information to Patricia Fellows, who was his long-serving technician. Fellows, who also maintained a desk in the office, told an Army investigator that Ivins shared his information with her in December 2001, according to Fellows's sworn statement to the investigator on May 9, 2002.

21. Author's interviews with Darin Steele and Lawrence Alexander, 2010.

22. Author's interview with Jeffrey Adamovicz, January 8, 2009.

23. Author's interview with Gerard Andrews, June 19, 2009.

24. Author's interview with John S. Parker, September 23, 2009.

CHAPTER 17: THEIR SECRET WEAPON

1. Sworn deposition testimony of Robert Roth in connection with Steven Hatfill's privacy lawsuit against the Justice Department and the FBI, November 4, 2005.

2. Author's interviews with current and former federal officials and with Thomas Connolly, 2008 and 2009.

3. Author's interviews with Arnold F. Kaufmann, November 10, 2009; William C. Patrick III, November 28, 2008, and January 9 and November 11, 2009; and Thomas Connolly, 2008 and 2009. William Patrick's report was provided by Science Applications International Corp. to the federal Centers for Disease Control by mid-2001. Patrick analyzed the risks to be expected from an anthrax-laced letter well in advance of the fall 2001 mailings, but the attacks showed him to have been wrong regarding at least two factors. He overestimated the volume of spores that would be needed to kill a person. And he predicted that spores would not aerosolize in a way that endangered broad areas of a building. It turned out that after the anthrax-laced letter addressed to Tom Daschle was opened, on October 15, 2001, spores spread throughout the Hart Senate Office Building.

4. Author's interviews with William Patrick and Thomas Connolly, 2009 and 2010, and Steven Hatfill, June 30, 2010.

5. Sworn deposition testimony of Robert Roth, November 4, 2005, and Brad Garrett, August 17, 2005, in Steven Hatfill's privacy lawsuit against the Justice Department and the FBI; author's interviews with Garrett, 2008 and 2009, and Hatfill, June 30, 2010.

6. *World News Tonight with Peter Jennings*, ABC News, June 25, 2002.

7. Sworn deposition testimony of Robert Roth, November 4, 2005, and Brad Garrett, August 17, 2005, in Steven Hatfill's privacy lawsuit against the Justice Department and the FBI.

8. Author's interview with Amanda Ivins, December 18, 2008.

9. Author's interviews with current and former federal officials, 2008 and 2009; sworn affidavit from FBI agent Mark P. Morin in support of obtaining a warrant to search the residence and other belongings of Steven Hatfill, July 31, 2002; Justice Department report on the anthrax investigation, "Amerithrax Investigative Summary," issued February 19, 2010. The nonlethal simulant that investigators found in Steven Hatfill's apartment was *Bacillus globigii*.

10. Justice Department report on the anthrax investigation, "Amerithrax Investigative Summary," issued on February 19, 2010; author's interviews with current and former federal officials and review of relevant investigative documents, 2008, 2009, and 2010.

11. Author's interviews with present and former government officials familiar with the anthrax investigation, 2009.

12. FBI document prepared for director Robert Mueller's briefing on January 9, 2003, of Senators Tom Daschle and Patrick Leahy.

13. Justice Department report on the anthrax investigation, "Amerithrax Investigative summary," issued February 19, 2010; author's interviews with current and former federal officials and review of relevant investigative documents, 2008, 2009, and 2010.

14. Ibid.; author's interviews with Thomas Connolly, November 11, 2009, and

December 20, 2010, and Steven Hatfill, June 30, 2010. Based on what Connolly and Hatfill told the author in those interviews, the Cipro prescriptions spanned many months and were first used to treat an infection that Hatfill had.

15. Author's interviews with William C. Patrick III, November 28, 2008, and January 9 and November 23, 2009. Patrick told the author on November 23, 2009: "I went to the grand jury in Washington, D.C., and I was asked directly, did I think he did it. And I said I did not."

16. J. Dee, "Expert: Anthrax Suspect ID'd," *Times of Trenton*, February 19, 2002; J. Dee, "Anthrax Expert Stands by Her Claim," *Times of Trenton*, February 21, 2002.

17. The British Broadcasting Corporation report "Anthrax Attacks" was reported from Washington, D.C., by Susan Watts, BBC science editor; the report aired on the BBC's *NewsNight* on March 14, 2002. See http://news.bbc.co.uk/2/hi/audiovideo/programmes/newsnight/archive/1873368.stm.

18. Sworn deposition testimony of Barbara Hatch Rosenberg, July 25, 2006, in Steven Hatfill's defamation lawsuit against Nicholas Kristof and the *New York Times*.

19. N. D. Kristof, "Connecting Deadly Dots," *New York Times,* May 24, 2002.

20. Sworn deposition testimony of Barbara Hatch Rosenberg, July 25, 2006, in Steven Hatfill's defamation lawsuit against Nicholas Kristof and the *New York Times*.

21. N. D. Kristof, "Connecting Deadly Dots."

22. In a written reply on December 30, 2010, to questions from the author, Nicholas Kristof did not address whether he stood behind his statement in a May 24, 2002, column that Steven Hatfill's anthrax vaccinations were "up to date." John W. Huggins, Steven Hatfill's former boss at USAMRIID, testified in Hatfill's defamation lawsuit against Kristof and the *New York Times* that Hatfill did not have a current vaccination against anthrax as of September 1999, when Hatfill last worked there. As for Kristof's statement in the same column that Hatfill "unquestionably had the ability to make first-rate anthrax," Kristof replied: "I believe that it's a matter of public record that Dr. Hatfill's CV lists expertise with wet and dry bacteriological agents, as well as viruses."

23. The use of brackets in Barbara Hatch Rosenberg's statement is cited verbatim from her theory of the anthrax case, which she e-mailed to Nicholas Kristof on June 13, 2002.

24. Author's interviews with Laura Petrou, November 20, 2008, and January 3, 2011, and present and former government officials familiar with the anthrax investigation, 2008 and 2009.

25. Ibid. The June 18, 2002, meeting in Senator Leahy's office, involving the FBI's Van Harp and Barbara Hatch Rosenberg, was described in sworn deposition testimony by Harp, September 22, 2005, and Robert Roth, November 4, 2005, in Steven Hatfill's privacy lawsuit against the Justice Department and the FBI.

26. N. D. Kristof, "Anthrax? The FBI Yawns," *New York Times*, July 2, 2002.

27. Ibid. Nicholas Kristof, in sworn deposition testimony in connection with Hatfill's defamation lawsuit filed against him and the *New York Times,* said on July 13, 2006, that his passage about Hatfill consorting in a hot suite "sur-

rounded only by blushing germs" was based on information he got from Barbara Hatch Rosenberg and a confidential source. Rosenberg, in her sworn testimony on July 25, 2006, said she could not recall having discussed the matter
with Kristof. She termed the anecdote about Hatfill "a well-known fact," but
conceded she had no firsthand knowledge. Thomas Connolly, Hatfill's lawyer,
told the author on December 23, 2010, that the anecdote had "no basis in
fact." Kristof, in a written reply on December 30, 2010, to questions from the
author, did not say whether he stood behind his statement about Hatfill's supposed personal activity in the hot suite.

28. Ibid.; sworn deposition testimony of Barbara Hatch Rosenberg, July 25,
    2006, in Steven Hatfill's defamation lawsuit against Nicholas Kristof and the
    New York Times.
29. N. D. Kristof, "Anthrax? The FBI Yawns."
30. Author's review of sworn deposition testimony from Hatfill's suit against
    Kristof and interviews with present and former government officials familiar
    with the anthrax investigation, 2008 and 2009.
31. The e-mails between Kristof and Rosenberg exchanged on August 4–5, 2002,
    were acknowledged by Rosenberg in her sworn deposition testimony, July 25,
    2006, in Steven Hatfill's defamation lawsuit against Kristof and the *New York
    Times*.
32. In a written reply on December 30, 2010, to questions from the author,
    Nicholas Kristof did not address whether he stood behind his statement in a
    July 2, 2002, column that Steven Hatfill had visited an isolated residence that
    might be among "safe houses operated by American intelligence."
33. N. D. Kristof, "The Anthrax Files," *New York Times,* August 13, 2002.
    Kristof suggested in this column that he had decided to refer for the first time
    to Steven Hatfill by his given name because Hatfill in recent days had spoken
    publicly and "named himself."
    On June 18, 2003, lawyers for Steven Hatfill filed a defamation lawsuit
    against Nicholas Kristof and the *New York Times*. The lawsuit ultimately was
    dismissed in January 2007. The outcome was described by Gilbert Cranberg,
    a University of Iowa emeritus professor and former editorial pages editor of
    the *Des Moines Register*: "Hatfill sued Kristof and the Times for defamation,
    but had nothing to show for his time in court except legal bills. A federal judge
    created a nearly insurmountable hurdle for Hatfill by finding him to be both a
    public official and a public figure. That obligated Hatfill to show that Kristof
    had 'serious doubts' about what he had written. The judge concluded, 'In this
    case . . . there is no evidence to establish that Mr. Kristof knew of the falsity of
    his statements.'" G. Cranberg, "Kristof's Apology to Hatfill," Nieman Watch-
    dog blog, August 29, 2008, http://blog.niemanwatchdog.org/?p=280.
34. Sworn deposition testimony of Robert Roth, given in connection with Hatfill's
    privacy lawsuit against the Justice Department and the FBI, November 4,
    2005.
35. Sworn deposition testimony of Nicholas Kristof in re *Hatfill v. Kristof, the
    New York Times, et al.,* July 13, 2006. In a written reply on December 30,
    2010, to questions from the author, Kristof did not address whether he stood
    behind his statement in a July 2, 2002, column that there was "evidence" that
    the Rhodesian Army wielded anthrax as a weapon against thousands of de-
    fenseless blacks.

36. Ibid.; sworn deposition testimony of Barbara Hatch Rosenberg, July 25, 2006, in Steven Hatfill's defamation lawsuit against Nicholas Kristof and the *New York Times*. On August 17, 2008, *New York Times* public editor Clark Hoyt wrote in his weekly column that "Kristof marshaled the evidence and raised so many questions about Hatfill that he contributed to a cloud of suspicion over the wrong man."

On August 28, 2008, Kristof wrote in his *New York Times* column, "I owe an apology to Dr. Hatfill. In retrospect, I was right to prod the F.B.I. and to urge tighter scrutiny of Fort Detrick, but the job of the news media is supposed to be to afflict the comfortable and comfort the afflicted. Instead, I managed to afflict the afflicted." Kristof did not, however, acknowledge making any factual errors in the 2002 columns he wrote about Hatfill and the anthrax investigation.

Asked whether he stood behind a July 2, 2002, column asserting that Hatfill had given Cipro to people who accompanied him at an "isolated residence," Kristof, in an e-mail to the author on December 30, 2010, suggested that Hatfill had admitted the allegation regarding Cipro. In response to follow-up questions, Kristof said in an e-mail on January 12, 2011, that he was not certain and that the author should check with Hatfill and his lawyers for the details. Thomas Connolly, Hatfill's lead lawyer, noted in interviews with the author that three witnesses who accompanied Hatfill to the residence testified that Hatfill did not offer Cipro to anyone. The three witnesses, George R. Borsari Jr., Karl Klamans, and Tamara McDevitt, were questioned under oath in connection with Hatfill's defamation lawsuit against Kristof and the *New York Times*. Borsari, who owned the residence, located in Virginia's Shenandoah Valley, testified that Hatfill visited during a weekend in October 2001, accompanied by Klamans and McDevitt. According to the sworn testimony, Borsari asked Hatfill over dinner whether, in light of September 11 and the anthrax letter attacks, people should have Cipro on hand. "Steve's answer," Borsari testified on October 23, 2006, "was, 'What would you do with it?' I said, 'Do you know anything about dosages or anything else?' He said, 'You know, if you get anthrax, go to the hospital.' And I said fine. End of conversation."

37. Author's interview with former FBI agent Brad Garrett, February 12, 2009.

38. M. Miller and D. Klaidman, "The Hunt for the Anthrax Killer," *Newsweek,* August 12, 2002.

39. N. D. Kristof, "The Anthrax Files." In a written reply on December 30, 2010, to questions from the author, Nicholas Kristof said that his sources had led him astray regarding the statements in his August 13, 2002, column about specially trained bloodhounds used by the FBI. Without attributing the information to any source or document, Kristof wrote in the column that the bloodhounds, while searching the apartments of Steven Hatfill and his girlfriend, had "responded strongly" to both residences, along with restaurants visited by Hatfill. Kristof also wrote in the column, "The dogs did not respond to other people, apartments or restaurants." In his reply to the author, Kristof said, referring to his sources and the bloodhounds, "I think they just got that one flat wrong."

40. *World News Tonight with Peter Jennings,* "Anthrax Attacks One Suspect, Says FBI," ABC News, October 22, 2002. A notable exception to the booster-

ish media accounts about the bloodhounds was an article published on October 29, 2002, by the *Baltimore Sun*, written by reporter Scott Shane: "FBI's Use of Bloodhounds in Anthrax Probe Disputed."

41. The FBI's Van Harp and Roscoe C. Howard, then the U.S. attorney for Washington, D.C., acknowledged under oath that they confirmed details for *Newsweek* before publication of the magazine's article about the bloodhounds and Steven Hatfill. Sworn deposition testimony of Van Harp, September 22, 2005, and Roscoe Howard, October 17, 2007, in Steven Hatfill's privacy lawsuit against the Justice Department and the FBI.

42. D. Willman, "How Anthrax Case Stalled; Leaks and Senior Officials' Fixation on One Suspect Plagued the FBI Investigation," *Los Angeles Times,* June 29, 2008.

43. Author's interview with Tom Ridge, October 22, 2009.

44. Author's interview with Steven Hatfill, June 30, 2010.

CHAPTER 18: LESS THAN A TEASPOON

1. Interviews in July and August 2009 with Gerald B. Richards, a retired FBI document examiner who studied images of the envelopes and letters used in the anthrax attacks at the request of the author.

2. C. W. Shepard, M. Soriano-Gabarro, E. R. Zell, J. Hayslett, S. Lukacs, S. Goldstein, S. Factor, J. Jones, R. Ridzon, I. Williams, N. Rosenstein, and the CDC Adverse Events Working Group, "Antimicrobial Postexposure Prophylaxis for Anthrax: Adverse Events and Adherence," *Emerging Infectious Diseases,* October 2002. In his 2010 memoir, *Decision Points,* former president George W. Bush said that in the wake of the anthrax letter attacks, both he and Laura "were advised to take Cipro."

3. Report of the General Accountability Office, "Capitol Hill Anthrax Incident," June 2003, http://www.gao.gov/new.items/d03686.pdf.

4. The Supreme Court building closed on the afternoon of Friday, October 26, 2001, and did not reopen until ten days later, on November 5. During the closure the Supreme Court convened to hear oral arguments on three separate days at the E. Barrett Prettyman Courthouse in Washington. On October 29, Chief Justice William Rehnquist opened the first of those sessions by saying it was the first time the Supreme Court had "met outside our building since the building opened in 1935," http://www.supremecourt.gov/orders/journal/jn101 .pdf, page 273.

5. Testimony of Defense Secretary Donald Rumsfeld to the House Armed Services Committee, September 18, 2002, and the Senate Armed Services Committee, September 19, 2002.

6. President George W. Bush, "Address to the Nation on Iraq from Cincinnati, Ohio," October 7, 2002.

7. Author's interviews with former Senate majority leader Tom Daschle, February 23, 2010, and Representative Henry A. Waxman, Democrat from California, December 12, 2008.

8. Senator Tom Harkin's remarks came during the U.S. Senate debate of the Iraq war resolution, October 10, 2002.

9. In his interview with the author on February 23, 2010, Tom Daschle acknowledged the influence of the anthrax letters, and how the attacks affected

passage of the Patriot Act and the later resolution to authorize war. The combination of September 11 and the anthrax attacks, Daschle said, led to a regrettable "rush to judgment on policy." He added, "It didn't take long for the president and others to segue into an Iraqi connection with 9/11. And then the anthrax attacks talked about 'Allah.' There was sort of a religious tone to the message, even though it turned out that there was no religious connection at all. But it was made out to be that, playing into the stereotypes that many of us had. And then the third leg was this notion that there's weapons of mass destruction that can be used against us."

10. Although the resolution won bipartisan support and the votes of a majority of Senate Democrats, most Democrats in the House opposed it. The votes among Democrats were 81 in favor and 126 opposed in the House; 29 in favor and 21 opposed in the Senate.

11. In addition to his rank as an Army general, Colin Powell served as chairman of the Joint Chiefs of Staff from October 1989 through September 1993.

12. For details of Iraq's mythical mobile germ weapons labs, see: B. Drogin, *Curveball* (Random House, 2007).

13. Presentation by Joseph R. Michael, specialist at Sandia National Laboratories; Michael spoke at a conference of the American Society for Microbiology in Baltimore, Maryland, February 24, 2009.

14. Author's interviews with Paul Keim, 2009 and 2010; Keim's presentation at conference of the American Society for Microbiology in Baltimore, Maryland, February 24, 2009.

15. On November 2, 2010, Colin Powell, communicating through an aide, Peggy Cifrino, declined the author's request for an interview regarding matters related to the anthrax letter attacks, including the statements Powell made at the United Nations in February 2003.

16. "USAMRIID Employees Earn Top Civilian Award," *Fort Detrick Standard,* March 19, 2003. Besides Ivins, the other recipients of the award were scientists Louise Pitt, Stephen Little, and Patricia Fellows, who, by the time of the ceremony, had begun work for a private research institute.

17. Address to the nation by President George W. Bush, March 19, 2003.

18. Author's interview with Victor M. Glasberg, August 12, 2009.

19. Author's interviews with Thomas Connolly, 2008, 2009, and 2010, and Steven Hatfill, June 30, 2010.

20. Author's interviews with Thomas Connolly and Mark A. Grannis, August 20, 2009.

21. Author's interviews with officials from the U.S. Senate and the administration of President George W. Bush, 2008 and 2009; sworn deposition testimony of Robert Roth, November 4, 2005, in Steven Hatfill's privacy lawsuit against the Justice Department and the FBI.

22. Author's interviews with Bruce Gebhardt, March 19, 2009, and Richard Lambert, June 25, 2010. FBI director Mueller, in a June 18, 2002, closed-door appearance before a congressional panel investigating the September 11, 2001, attacks, utilized remarks prepared for him by Lambert to deny speculation that the Saudi royal family had bankrolled the hijackings. Lambert said that he accompanied Mueller to Capitol Hill for that and related briefings.

23. FBI document prepared for Director Mueller's briefing on January 9, 2003, of Senators Tom Daschle and Patrick Leahy about the status of the anthrax in-

vestigation; author's interviews with Tom Daschle, February 23 and September 27, 2010.

24. Entry in Red Cross, Frederick County, Maryland, personnel file on Bruce Ivins; author's interview with Peggy Magnanelli, August 8, 2009.

25. E-mail from a Red Cross official to Bruce Ivins on December 13, 2002.

26. K. Leckie, "FBI Searches Catoctin Woods," *Frederick News-Post,* December 13, 2002.

27. Author's interview with Barb Christie, August 10, 2009.

28. Author's interviews with Miriam Fleming, August 18, 2009, and Barb Christie, August 10, 2009. In addition to the Red Cross's support in providing food, water, and shelter for operations in Frederick Municipal Forest, the FBI had recruited other outsiders to assist with aspects of the pond searches. Ivins later told the FBI that he knew nothing about the nature of the search when he volunteered the day before.

29. E-mail from Bruce Ivins to Mara Linscott, December 15, 2001.

30. Author's interview with FBI spokeswoman Debra Weierman, August 27, 2009, along with others familiar with the pond searches, 2008 and 2009; materials prepared by the FBI for Director Robert Mueller's briefing of Attorney General John Ashcroft on March 31, 2003.

31. M. W. Thompson, "New Find Reignites Anthrax Probe," *Washington Post,* May 11, 2003. On March 31, 2003, FBI director Mueller and his designated leader of the investigation, Richard Lambert, had briefed Attorney General Ashcroft regarding details of the pond searches, including the removal of the plastic container. Lambert displayed pictures and said that it might be a "glove box," laboratory equipment that enables a scientist to work safely with dangerous material through hand portals, according to FBI materials prepared for the briefing and the author's interviews with present and former officials familiar with the anthrax investigation, 2009 and 2010.

32. Author's interview with John Ezzell, August 11, 2009.

33. Author's interviews with Henry Heine, Lawrence Alexander, Thomas Dellafera, and John Ezzell, April 2010.

34. S. Shane, "FBI Might Drain Md. Pond as Part of Its Anthrax Probe: Spores Reportedly Found During Dec., Jan. Searches of Waters near Frederick," *Baltimore Sun,* May 12, 2003.

35. CNN, *American Morning,* "Anthrax Investigation," featuring Daryn Kagan and Kelli Arena, May 12, 2003. The preliminary test result cited by CNN referred to a false indication of anthrax on the plastic box retrieved by investigators from the pond, according to contemporaneous investigative documents and the author's interviews with Amerithrax investigators and scientists who examined the data firsthand. They said the invalid result was caused by laboratory contamination.

36. *CBS Evening News,* May 8, 2003.

37. *World News Tonight,* June 9, 2003.

38. D. Willman, "How Anthrax Case Stalled; Leaks and Senior Officials' Fixation on One Suspect Plagued the FBI Investigation," *Los Angeles Times,* June 29, 2008.

39. T. Locy, "Anthrax Investigators Tail Scientist '24/7,'" *USA Today,* May 29, 2003.

40. Author's interview with Brad Garrett, May 27, 2008.
41. Author's interviews with Brad Garrett and Thomas Connolly, 2008 and 2009; sworn deposition testimony of Garret, August 17, 2005, and Robert Roth, November 4, 2005, in Steven Hatfill's privacy lawsuit against the FBI and the Justice Department. Roth died in March 2008 after a brief bout with cancer.
42. Author's interviews with Thomas Connolly, 2008 and 2009.

CHAPTER 19: SOME NEW ANTHRAX VACCINE

1. The $1.5 billion a year for building a dozen or more biocontainment labs has been allocated from the budget of the National Institute of Allergy and Infectious Diseases, headed by Dr. Anthony Fauci. The facilities are named "Regional Centers of Excellence for Biodefense and Emerging Infectious Diseases."
2. D. Willman, "New Anthrax Vaccine Sunk by Lobbying; America's Sole Supplier Faced Oblivion If Its Rival's Product Was Adopted. It Was Time to Call on Its Connections," *Los Angeles Times*, December 2, 2007.
3. Information from 10-K financial report filed by VaxGen with the Securities and Exchange Commission, December 31, 2005. VaxGen began developing the rPA anthrax vaccine in spring 2002 in a collaboration with USAMRIID and Battelle Memorial Institute. In September 2002, VaxGen won the first of the two contracts from the National Institute of Allergy and Infectious Diseases, totaling $101.2 million, to start developing the vaccine. On October 7, 2003, VaxGen obtained exclusive worldwide rights from the Army to develop, manufacture, and sell rPA.
4. E-mail from Bruce Ivins to Nancy Haigwood, October 22, 2003. Ivins was correct in saying that a federal contract "just was awarded" to VaxGen. However, his comment did not mention that the first such award was made to the company more than a year earlier, in September 2002, by the National Institute of Allergy and Infectious Diseases.
5. E-mail response to the author from Caree L. Vander Linden, spokeswoman for USAMRIID, October 23, 2008; author's interviews with Lance K. Gordon, former chief executive officer of VaxGen, September 1 and 7, 2009. See also Form 8-K financial report filed by VaxGen with the Securities and Exchange Commission, December 2, 2003.
6. Remarks of Majority Leader Bill Frist during debate on the floor of the U.S. Senate over whether to pass Project BioShield, May 19, 2004.
7. Author's interviews with Philip Russell, D. A. Henderson, Stewart Simonson, Anthony Fauci, and Kenneth Bernard, 2008 and 2009.
8. D. Willman, "New Anthrax Vaccine Sunk by Lobbying."
9. Written statement from President George W. Bush, issued by the White House on May 19, 2004, the day the Senate was to vote for final passage of Project BioShield.
10. Letter signed by 758 microbiologists to Dr. Elias A. Zerhouni, director of the National Institutes of Health, March 2005; J. Kaiser, "Détente Declared on NIH Biodefense Funding," *Science*, May 13, 2005; e-mail responses to the author from Rutgers professor Richard H. Ebright, a co-author of the letter to Zerhouni, August 26, 2009; author's interview with Zerhouni, September 1, 2009.

11. Press release issued by the U.S. Department of Health and Human Services, Office of the Secretary, November 4, 2004.

12. E-mail response to the author from Caree L. Vander Linden, October 16, 2008; author's interviews with VaxGen executives who spoke on a condition of anonymity, citing the confidentiality of the contract terms regarding patent royalties.

13. In an e-mail on October 30, 2001, Bruce Ivins described the strong support for testing the next-generation anthrax vaccine that was voiced by Lisa Bronson, a deputy undersecretary of defense who worked closely with Deputy Defense Secretary Paul Wolfowitz. Ivins wrote his e-mail as a summary of a meeting he attended one day earlier at the Pentagon regarding the status of the new vaccine. According to the author's interviews on June 22 and 24, 2010, with Anna Johnson-Winegar, the Defense Department official who hosted that meeting, Bronson had bristled when Ivins reported that he and other USAMRIID scientists were being diverted from working on the new vaccine in order to assist the investigation of the anthrax letter attacks. Ivins wrote in his e-mail that Bronson "expressed strong concern that researchers on the anthrax vaccine mission were being pulled away to do work that technicians could do." Ivins added that Bronson pledged to take action to ensure that "there is no 'bottleneck'" in developing the new vaccine. Bronson, who later left the Pentagon to accept a faculty post at the National Defense University, did not respond to e-mail messages from the author.

14. Author's interviews with Lance K. Gordon, September 1 and 10, 2009, and Arthur Friedlander, July 16, 2010.

15. Author's interviews with Heidi Hoffmann, January 14, 2009, and other scientists involved with the next-generation anthrax vaccine worked on by Vax-Gen, Battelle Memorial Institute, and the U.S. Army.

16. E-mail from Bruce Ivins to a supervisor, April 28, 2002.

17. The FBI eventually concluded that a March 2001 shipment of what Bruce Ivins documented as RMR-1029 to a researcher at the University of New Mexico was either from another batch of anthrax or had been prepared in a way that obscured its genetic profile.

CHAPTER 20: WE'VE GOT OUR MAN

1. Sworn deposition testimony of Van Harp, September 22, 2005, in Steven Hatfill's privacy lawsuit against the Justice Department and the FBI; author's interview with Bruce Gebhardt, March 19, 2009.

2. Author's interviews with senior officials from the administration of President George W. Bush, 2009.

3. Author's interview with Bruce Gebhardt, March 19, 2009.

4. Author's interviews with present and former FBI officials, 2008 and 2009; A. G. Theoharis, The FBI: A Comprehensive Reference Guide (Oryx Press, 1999), p. 222.

5. Author's interview with Bruce Gebhardt, August 17, 2009.

6. Sworn deposition testimony of Richard Lambert in Steven Hatfill's privacy lawsuit against the Justice Department and the FBI, August 3, 2005; author's interview with Scott Decker, July 27, 2010.

7. Sworn deposition testimony of Richard Lambert in connection with Steven

Hatfill's civil lawsuit against the Justice Department and the FBI, August 3, 2005; author's interview with Bruce Gebhardt, August 17, 2009.

8. Videotape of sworn deposition testimony of Richard Lambert, August 3, 2005, in Steven Hatfill's privacy lawsuit against the FBI and the Justice Department; sworn deposition testimony of Van Harp, September 22, 2005, in the same lawsuit.

9. Author's interview with Bruce Gebhardt, April 27, 2010.

10. Author's interviews with present and former government officials familiar with the anthrax investigation, 2009 and 2010, and materials prepared by the FBI for Director Mueller's briefing of Senators Daschle and Leahy on January 9, 2003.

11. Author's interview with Tom Daschle, February 23, 2010.

12. Author's interviews with present and former government officials familiar with the anthrax investigation, 2009 and 2010, and materials prepared by FBI inspector Richard Lambert for Director Mueller's briefing of Attorney General Ashcroft on March 31, 2003.

13. Author's interview with Paul Wolfowitz, November 30, 2010. The author's attempts to reach James Comey were unsuccessful.

14. Transcript of hearing regarding murder conviction of Earl Rhoney before Orange County, California, Superior Court Judge Anthony J. Rackauckas Jr., March 10, 1997. See also G. Hernandez, "O.C. Scent-Based Murder Verdict Is Thrown Out," *Los Angeles Times Orange County Edition,* March 11, 1997.

15. G. Hernandez and B. Hayes, "Charges Dropped in Irvine Murder Case," *Los Angeles Times Orange County Edition,* June 23, 1998; B. Rams, "Suspect in Murder Killed in Car Crash," *Orange County Register,* December 3, 2001.

16. Author's interview with Peter Schlueter, October 14, 2009. See also "Jury Awards $1.7 Million in Wrongful Rape Arrest," *Los Angeles Times,* November 4, 2000; C. Franklin, "Judge Sends 'Monster' Rapist to Prison for 1,030 Years Plus 10 Life Terms," City News Service, September 15, 2004.

17. V. Mabrey, "Scent of a Criminal: Use of Tracking Dogs to Pick Up Scents from Crime Scenes May Be Good in Theory, but Some Cases Have Shown It to Be Unreliable as a Major Source of Evidence," *60 Minutes II,* February 17, 1999.

18. Author's interview with Jenifer Smith, August 6, 2009. Smith retired from the FBI in January 2009.

19. Author's interviews with Dwight Adams and other present or former government officials familiar with the anthrax investigation, 2008, 2009, and 2010.

20. Along with Bruce Ivins, Patricia Fellows was one of four co-winners in March 2003 of the Defense Department's Decoration for Exceptional Civilian Service, for having helped BioPort Corp. bring back into production the nation's only FDA-approved anthrax vaccine. Fellows was recognized for the work she did while a staff microbiologist in the Bacteriology Division at USAMRIID.

21. The document revealing that the bloodhounds had, in addition to Steven Hatfill, identified Patricia Fellows, was written by Inspector Richard Lambert to prepare Director Mueller for his personal briefing of Senators Daschle and Leahy on the night of January 9, 2003.

22. Richard Lambert told the author on June 25, 2010, that he had been "prohibited by FBI Headquarters from commenting" on the anthrax investigation.

23. Author's interview with Michael Mason, January 4, 2011.

24. As of August 3, 2005, approximately thirty FBI agents and fifteen postal in-

spectors were assigned to the anthrax investigation, according to the sworn deposition testimony that day of Richard Lambert in Steven Hatfill's privacy lawsuit against the FBI and the Justice Department. As of September 2006, the FBI reported online that more than 9,100 interviews had been conducted during the course of the investigation along with sixty-seven searches. The same posting said that seventeen FBI agents and ten postal inspectors were presently assigned to the case. As of late 2008, the Amerithrax task force had totaled more than ten thousand interviews, executed eighty searches, and expended more than 600,000 investigator hours, according to a Justice Department summary.

25. Author's interviews with Jenifer Smith, August 1 and October 28, 2009.

26. Condoleezza Rice served as national security advisor through President George W. Bush's first term. As of January 26, 2005, and through the balance of Bush's second term, Rice served as secretary of state.

27. Author's interview with Tom Ridge, October 22, 2009.

28. Author's review of internal FBI memoranda regarding the gathering of samples from Kandahar, Afghanistan, and his interviews with Amerithrax investigators, 2008, 2009, and 2010. See also *The 9/11 Commission Report*, Chapter 5, "Al Qaeda Aims at the American Homeland," issued July 22, 2004. According to the 9/11 Commission, al Qaeda's efforts to grow anthrax in Kandahar were led by Yazid Sufaat, who received an undergraduate degree in biology from California State University, Sacramento. In January 2000, Sufaat had hosted at his apartment in Kuala Lumpur, Malaysia, the first operational meeting of the 9/11 hijackers. Sufaat fled Afghanistan in December 2001 and was captured trying to sneak back into Malaysia. See G. Tenet with B. Harlow, *At the Center of the Storm* (HarperCollins, 2007). See also the Justice Department report on the anthrax investigation, "Amerithrax Investigative Summary," issued on February 19, 2010. A review of the investigation by a committee of the National Academy of Sciences termed the data for the Kandahar samples "inconclusive." See *Review of the Scientific Approaches Used During the FBI's Investigation of the 2001 Anthrax Letters* (Washington, D.C.: National Academies Press, 2011).

29. Author's interviews with Dwight Adams, retired FBI laboratory director, and other present and former officials familiar with the anthrax investigation, 2009 and 2010; FBI materials prepared for the March 31, 2003, briefing held in the office of Attorney General Ashcroft.

30. E-mail from Richard Lambert to Dwight Adams, January 28, 2004. In addition to Steven Hatfill's girlfriend, Lambert's e-mail mentioned a second woman whose DNA might match the speck of skin found on the Leahy envelope, using Whole Genome Amplification: Patricia Fellows, who had formerly worked as a microbiologist at USAMRIID. Fellows was among those who had handled the anthrax letter materials on behalf of the FBI. This meant that, even if Fellows's DNA were found on the Leahy envelope, it could be innocently explained by the official work that she had performed.

31. Author's interviews with present and former officials familiar with the role of the former technician Jacqueline A. Blake in accidentally contaminating the Leahy letter from within the FBI laboratory, 2009 and 2010.

32. Author's interview with Thomas Connolly, August 7, 2009.

33. Author's interviews with Thomas Dellafera, April 12, 2010; Gerald Richards,

October 9, 2009, and December 3, 2010; and other present or former government officials familiar with the anthrax investigation, 2009 and 2010.

CHAPTER 21: EYE EXERCISE

1. M. Enserink, "Taking Anthrax's Genetic Fingerprints," *Science,* November 30, 2001; author's interviews with Paul Keim, 2009 and 2010.
2. Comments on February 24, 2009, by Jason D. Bannan, an FBI microbiologist who had supervised the failed efforts to identify the geographic origin of the water used to grow the anthrax used in the letter attacks. Bannan spoke with journalists in Baltimore, Maryland, following a seminar about the anthrax investigation sponsored by the American Society for Microbiology.
3. Author's review of contemporaneous investigative documents, including e-mails discussing the Flight 93 remains that were composed on May 29, 2002, by FBI agent/scientist David Wilson, FBI laboratory director Dwight Adams, and Daniel Levin, chief of staff to FBI director Robert Mueller; author's interviews with Amerithrax investigators and scientists who assisted the investigation, 2009 and 2010.
4. Author's interviews with Paul Keim, 2008, 2009, and 2010, and Jacques Ravel April 24 and May 8, 2009.
5. Author's interviews with Jacques Ravel, April 24 and May 8, 2009.
6. See P. L. Worsham and M. R. Sowers, "Isolation of Asporogenic (spoOA) Protective Antigen-Producing Strain of *Bacillus anthracis,*" *Canadian Journal of Microbiology,* January 1999.
7. The envelope containing the anthrax-laced letter addressed to NBC anchor Tom Brokaw retained very little of that powdery material by the time it was secured by federal investigators. Consequently, fewer experiments were conducted on it than with the anthrax from the other three letters secured by the investigation.
8. Statements by Patricia Worsham on September 24, 2009, to a committee appointed by the National Academy of Sciences to review the scientific approaches used during the FBI's investigation of the 2001 anthrax letter attacks.
9. Author's interviews with federal officials familiar with the anthrax investigation, 2010 and 2011.
10. Author's interviews with Scott Decker, July 27, 2010, and Scott Stanley, August 10, 2010.
11. Ibid.; author's interviews with Jacques Ravel, April 24 and May 8, 2009.
12. Ibid.; author's interviews with Paul Keim, 2009 and 2010.

CHAPTER 22: PLAY IT STRAIGHT

1. Author's interviews with Lawrence Alexander, March 2010.
2. Author's interviews with officials familiar with the anthrax investigation, including retired FBI agents Brad Garrett, October 28, 2008, and February 12, 2009; Bruce Gebhardt, March 19, 2009; and Michael Mason, January 4, 2011.
3. Sworn deposition testimony of Robert Roth in connection with Steven Hatfill's privacy lawsuit against the Justice Department and the FBI, November 4, 2005.

4. Although the e-mails written and received by Bruce Ivins and his colleagues at their U.S. Army addresses were long available to the FBI, the bureau did not begin reading the correspondence until mid- to late 2004, according to the author's interviews with Amerithrax investigators.

5. Author's interviews with members of the Amerithrax task force, including Rachel Carlson Lieber, Kenneth Kohl, Thomas Dellafera, Edward Montooth, and Lawrence Alexander, 2009 and 2010.

6. Amerithrax investigators reviewed documents and conducted interviews worldwide in order to determine that Ames strain anthrax was being used at a total of eighteen facilities—fifteen in the United States and the remainder in Canada, Britain, and Sweden. The investigators used the same methods to conclude that Bruce Ivins had provided samples of RMR-1029, his special mix of Ames anthrax, only to colleagues at USAMRIID and to researchers at the Battelle Memorial Institute.

7. The investigation's discovery of apparent genetic similarities between samples of anthrax derived from Bruce Ivins's batch of RMR-1029 and the attack letters came through the submission of samples from researchers with whom Ivins had shared the material. These researchers were located at both USAMRIID and the Battelle Memorial Institute in Ohio.

8. FBI summaries of interviews with Bruce Ivins on August 13 and December 12, 2003; Justice Department report on the anthrax investigation, "Amerithrax Investigative Summary," issued on February 19, 2010. During the two aforementioned interviews, Ivins's sample from his flask of RMR-1029 anthrax was referred to as "7737" and "7737—Dugway Ames spores—1997."

9. Author's interview on December 9, 2009, with Richard Bricken, whom Bruce Ivins retained as his first criminal defense lawyer.

10. Author's interviews with Jacques Ravel, April 24, 2009, and Paul Keim and Amerithrax investigators, 2008 and 2009.

11. Author's interviews with Jacques Ravel, April 24, 2009, and Scott Decker, July 27, 2010.

12. Author's interview with Richard Bricken, December 9, 2009.

13. Author's interviews with Amerithrax investigators, including Thomas Dellafera and Lawrence Alexander, 2010.

14. Summary of FBI interviews with Bruce Ivins on March 31 and April 1, 2005.

15. Written communications from Bruce Ivins to Richard Bricken, April 8 and 18, 2005; FBI summary of examination on January 13, 2005, of Ivins's computer-related data at USAMRIID.

16. Author's interviews in March 2010 with Lawrence Alexander, Thomas Dellafera, Kenneth Kohl, Edward Montooth, and Darin Steele and other officials familiar with the anthrax investigation, 2008, 2009, and 2010.

17. Author's interviews with Lawrence Alexander and Thomas Dellafera, March 2010. The unaccounted-for quantity of RMR-1029 anthrax also was cited in the Justice Department report on the anthrax investigation, "Amerithrax Investigative Summary," issued on February 19, 2010. Bruce Ivins claimed in interviews with the investigators and in subsequent e-mail messages to acquaintances that the quantity of RMR-1029 unaccounted for from his flask was the result of his difficulty with math. But Ivins's explanation contrasts with examples of his mastery of math as shown both by his role in helping his daughter pass a course at Shepherd College, "Finite Mathematics," and by his own grades, in-

cluding an A in Finite Math at the University of Cincinnati in December 1964. The preceding is attributable to the author's interview with Amanda Ivins, April 16, 2009, and the author's review of Bruce Ivins's college transcript, as represented by Ivins in his application for employment with the U.S. Army.

18. FBI summary of interview with Bruce Ivins on June 9, 2008, when he said that he had thrown away his Kappa Kappa Gamma–related materials in about April 2006. His impetus, Ivins told the investigators, was that he had just turned sixty. According to the author's interviews, Ivins's explanation left open another motive deemed more plausible by many of the investigators: He discarded the items related to the sorority because they might help incriminate him in the anthrax letter attacks.

19. The book, *Broken Pledges, The Deadly Rite of Hazing,* was written by Hank Nuwer and published in 1990 by Longstreet Press.

20. "AFA Takes Wisconsin to Court," *American Family Association Journal,* October 1999, http://www.afajournal.org/archives/23100000166.asp. Under Wisconsin law, the state government social workers had the authority to question the student without the knowledge or consent of his parents. The AFA lawsuit challenged the constitutionality of the law.

21. Author's interviews with Lawrence Alexander, Thomas Dellafera, and Eileen Stevens, 2010.

22. Ivins may have had another book in mind, *The Killer Strain,* by Marilyn Thompson, which spotlighted John Ezzell's early efforts to scientifically assist the investigation. Thompson's book, published by HarperCollins in 2003, provided no financial consideration to Ezzell. See also L. A. Cole, *The Anthrax Letters* (Joseph Henry Press, 2003).

23. Author's interviews with Erik Henchal on April 27, 2010, and with John Ezzell and other former and present government officials, 2008, 2009, and 2010. Beginning in 1992, Henchal served as a virology researcher and later as an administrator at USAMRIID. He was USAMRIID commander from June 2005 to June 2008 and retired from the Army with the rank of colonel.

24. E-mail from Bruce Ivins to Patricia Fellows, June 28, 2005. Paul Kemp, the defense lawyer that Bruce Ivins hired as of May 2007, appeared not to know of his client's earlier allegations about John Ezzell. On November 29, 2010, Kemp told a panel convened in Washington to discuss the anthrax case: "Dr. Ivins felt that Dr. Ezzell was extremely forthright, very straight." Ivins "felt that there was absolutely no hint of anything, wrongdoing, on Dr. Ezzell's part," Kemp said.

25. Author's interviews with Paul Keim, January 5, 2009, and February 10, 2010. Bruce Ivins complained throughout adulthood of pain from a recurrently strained or torn calf muscle. He was not known to suffer any life-threatening disease. In an interview with the FBI on March 31, 2005, Ivins said that he suffered from ulcers and irritable bowel syndrome, conditions he blamed on his internalizing of negative emotions.

26. Author's interviews with Thomas Connolly and conversations with journalists contacted by Hatfill, 2008 and 2009.

27. Author's interviews with William and Virginia Patrick, 2009 and 2010.

28. Sworn deposition testimony of Debra Weierman, June 29, 2005, in Steven Hatfill's privacy lawsuit against the Justice Department and the FBI.

29. Author's interview with Thomas Connolly, August 7, 2009.

30. Sworn deposition testimony of Robert Roth, November 4, 2005, in Steven Hatfill's privacy lawsuit against the Justice Department and the FBI.

31. Sworn deposition testimony of Roscoe C. Howard Jr., October 17, 2007, in Steven Hatfill's privacy lawsuit against the Justice Department and the FBI.

32. Linn Washington, *Black Judges on Justice* (The New Press, 1994); Web site of the U.S. District Court for the District of Columbia, http://www.dcd.uscourts .gov/walton-bio.html.

33. U.S. District Court Judge Reggie B. Walton's remarks from the bench on October 7, 2004, referred to aspects of two articles published earlier that year: Carol D. Leonnig and Allan Lengel, "Judge Delays Lawsuit to Help Anthrax Probe," *Washington Post,* March 30, 2004; A. Lengel, "Anthrax Probers Still Seek Md. Leads; Frederick Remains a Focus of Attention," *Washington Post,* July 18, 2004.

34. Author's interviews with Thomas Connolly, August 7 and November 11, 2009.

35. Author's interviews with Lawrence Alexander, March 2010, and Brad Garrett and other present and former government officials familiar with the investigation, 2008, 2009, and 2010.

36. As of March 2011, Robert Mueller had not responded to the author's long-standing requests for an interview regarding the anthrax investigation.

37. Announcement by FBI National Press Office, "Richard Lambert Jr. Selected to Report as SAC in Knoxville," August 25, 2006.

CHAPTER 23: SOME CHANGES

1. E-mail from Richard Lambert to FBI laboratory director Dwight Adams, January 28, 2004.

2. Author's interview with Kenneth L. Wainstein, who, as an assistant U.S. attorney, prosecuted Percy Barron, February 8, 2010.

3. "NE Man Gets Long Term for Role in Crime Rampage," *Washington Post,* March 1, 1997.

4. Author's interview with Kenneth L. Wainstein, February 8, 2010. Vincent Lisi's investigative work helped a private defense lawyer, Frances D'Antuono, who presented evidence that persuaded a judge to order the release from prison of Steven Dewitt on Christmas Eve 2004. The circumstances surrounding Dewitt's original arrest and conviction were described in more detail by the Mid-Atlantic Innocence Project, http://www.exonerate.org/case-profiles/steven-dewitt/.

5. Author's interviews with Edward Montooth, March and July 2010, and Vincent Lisi, July 2010.

6. Author's interviews with Edward Montooth and Vincent Lisi, March and July 2010, and other Amerithrax investigators, 2008, 2009, and 2010.

7. Author's interviews with Edward Montooth and Lawrence Alexander, March 2010.

8. Author's interviews with officials familiar with the anthrax investigation, 2008, 2009, and 2010; sworn deposition testimony of Richard Lambert, August 3, 2005, in Steven Hatfill's privacy lawsuit against the Justice Department and the FBI.

9. Author's interviews with Edward Montooth, Vincent Lisi, and Scott Decker, 2010 and 2011.

10. Author's interviews with Thomas Connolly, October 28, 2008, and August 7, 2009; Steven Hatfill, June 30, 2010; and Vincent Lisi, July 8, 2010. Connolly, recalling his conversation with the FBI's Vincent Lisi regarding Hatfill's changed status in the investigation, told the author: "I was fucking shocked."

11. D. Willman, "New Anthrax Vaccine Sunk by Lobbying; America's Sole Supplier Faced Oblivion If Its Rival's Product Was Adopted; It Was Time to Call on Its Connections," *Los Angeles Times,* December 2, 2007.

12. E-mail from George Korch to Bruce Ivins, December 17, 2006.

13. E-mail from Bruce Ivins to George Korch, December 17, 2006.

14. Two e-mails from Bruce Ivins to Mara Linscott, January 2007.

15. Author's interviews with Nancy Haigwood, April 19 and May 19, 2009, and Amerithrax investigators, including Lawrence Alexander, Armando Garcia, Daniel Borsuk, Thomas Dellafera, and Edward Montooth, 2010.

16. Henry Heine was one of the seven present or departed colleagues whom Bruce Ivins fingered in connection with the anthrax letter attacks. The FBI found no evidence that Heine or any of the others played any role in the attacks. Heine told the author and four other journalists on April 22, 2010, that he learned of Ivins's accusation against him in real time from the FBI. "I just shrugged my shoulders," Heine said. "I said, 'Okay. Maybe he's trying to put the pressure back on me because he figures I've got bigger shoulders and I can handle it.'"

17. Author's interviews with Amanda Ivins, December 3, 2008, and Henry Heine, Edward Puls, Lawrence Alexander, Rachel Lieber, and Thomas Dellafera, April 2010.

18. E-mails from Bruce Ivins to Nancy Haigwood and others, October 11, 2006; December 5, 15, 20, and 27, 2006; January 17, 2007; March 5, 2007; and May 24, 2007.

19. Author's interviews with Nancy Haigwood, April 19 and May 19, 2009.

20. Author's interviews with Nancy Haigwood, December 4, 2009, and Amerithrax investigators, 2008, 2009, and 2010.

21. Author's interviews with Nancy Haigwood and Carl Scandella, 2009.

CHAPTER 24: GO TO THAT SAMPLE

1. Author's interviews with acquaintances and family of Bruce Ivins, including Amanda Ivins, December 3 and 4, 2008, and Jeffrey Adamovicz, January 8, 2009.

2. FBI summary of interview with Bruce Ivins on February 27, 2007; author's interviews with Lawrence Alexander and Darin Steele, March 2010, and Richard Bricken, December 9, 2009.

3. Author's interviews with Amanda Ivins, 2008 and 2009, and Paul Kemp, January 8, 2010.

4. Author's interviews with Amanda Ivins, December 18, 2008, and January 24, 2011.

5. Web postings made to GreekChat.com by Bruce Ivins, posing as Goldenphoenix, April 16, 18, 27, and 28, 2007; Ivins signed his own name to another tribute to Caitlin Hammaren, posted April 21, 2007, on Legacy.com.

6. E-mail from Bruce Ivins to Nancy Haigwood, April 20, 2007.

7. Wikipedia posting made by Bruce Ivins, writing as jimmyflathead, on July 8, 2007.

8. Author's interview with Paul Kemp, September 25, 2008.

9. Author's interviews with Richard Bricken, December 7 and 9, 2009.

10. Author's interviews with Paul Kemp, 2008 and 2009, and FBI synopsis of the session in which Kemp and another lawyer for Bruce Ivins were allowed to read but not take notes from transcripts of Ivins's two May 2007 appearances before a federal grand jury.

11. E-mail from Bruce Ivins to Mara Linscott, May 23, 2007.

12. Author's interviews with Jacques Ravel, April 24 and May 8, 2009, and Matthew Feinberg, August 11, 2010. Extraction of the DNA that was analyzed by Ravel for the fourth morph was performed for the FBI by the Midwest Research Institute, in Palm Bay, Florida, according to Feinberg.

13. Justice Department report on the anthrax investigation, "Amerithrax Investigative Summary," issued February 19, 2010; author's interviews with Amerithrax investigators and affiliated scientists, 2008, 2009, 2010, and 2011. Of the 1,070 samples of anthrax collected worldwide by Amerithrax and subjected to laboratory testing, 123 yielded inconclusive results. Based on definitive testing of the remaining 947 samples, 8 of them contained the same four morphs that were identified from the anthrax in the letters.

14. Reference Material Receipt Record filled out by hand by Bruce Ivins with relevant notations on May 1 and June 15, 2001, obtained by the author September 2008; author's interviews with Amerithrax investigators, 2008, 2009, and 2010.

15. Author's interviews with Edward Montooth and Vincent Lisi, March and July 2010.

16. Justice Department report on the anthrax investigation, "Amerithrax Investigative Summary," issued on February 19, 2010; author's interviews with Amerithrax investigators, 2010. The FBI's scrutiny of the Battelle Memorial Institute began in 2002 when Agent Charles Whistler questioned more than one hundred scientists at Battelle's headquarters in Columbus, Ohio, according to the author's interviews with Whistler and other investigators.

17. Commercial flights from Columbus, Ohio, nearest to Battelle, and Philadelphia or Newark would require about four hours of flying time. The round-trip drives from either of those destination airports to Princeton and back would take nearly two hours. Considering time spent getting to the first airport, going through security twice, renting a car—and waiting for the return flight—the total elapsed time of such a trip could span from eight to twelve hours or longer.

18. Author's interviews with Amerithrax investigators, 2008, 2009, and 2010. The FBI also concluded that a March 2001 shipment of what Bruce Ivins documented as RMR-1029 to a researcher at the University of New Mexico was either from another batch of anthrax or had been prepared in a way that obscured its genetic profile. Inventory logs maintained by Ivins showed the transfer to the University of New Mexico researcher and a separate shipment to Covance Inc., a company that was conducting tests on animals. A spokeswoman for Covance, Laurene Isip, told the author on September 19, 2008, that the company was neither equipped nor licensed to handle live anthrax. According to the author's interviews with federal investigators, the material sent to Covance was first irradiated, rendering it harmless to humans.

19. Author's interviews with Amerithrax investigators, including Edward Montooth and Lawrence Alexander, 2010 and 2011.

20. E-mail from Bruce Ivins to Mara Linscott, September 12, 2001; author's interviews with Erik Henchal, October 30, 2010, and John Ezzell, 2008, 2009, and 2010.

21. Author's interviews in 2008, 2009, and 2010 with several microbiologists experienced in handling anthrax or other *Bacillus* spores, including John Ezzell, James Burans, and William Patrick. For the material that was mailed, Ivins could have tapped quantities of anthrax spores suspended in liquid that were sitting on his lab shelf and/or freshly grown the spores himself.

22. Summary of FBI interview with Bruce Ivins, January 16, 2008.

23. Summary of FBI interview with Bruce Ivins, February 13, 2008; author's interviews with Amanda Ivins, December 3, 2008, and April 16, 2009. In an e-mail to Mara Linscott on September 7, 2000, Ivins wrote that his sleeping separately from his wife "appears to be a permanent situation (her decision, but it honestly doesn't bother me.)"

24. The Justice Department's final report on the anthrax investigation noted that investigators collected 1,014 "exemplar sets" from "copy machines located inside or near the vicinity of every known biological laboratory that possessed virulent Ames anthrax in 2001" and that no matches were found to three unique copy imperfections discovered on the letters to Senators Daschle and Leahy. These imperfections, called "trash marks," are typically caused by specks of debris on a machine—and routine cleaning would remove such potential evidence. Because it was not until months later that investigators collected an exemplar set from the photocopier at the USAMRIID library, it cannot be eliminated as the site where the messages in the anthrax-laced letters were copied, Agent Lawrence Alexander and Gerald Richards, a retired FBI document examiner, told the author on June 7, 2010. Alexander told the author subsequently that the USAMRIID library photocopier was examined in February 2002, five months after the first letters were postmarked.

25. Justice Department report on the anthrax investigation, "Amerithrax Investigative Summary," issued February 19, 2010; FBI summaries of interviews with Bruce Ivins, including March 31, 2005.

26. Letter from Bruce Ivins to the editor of the *Frederick News-Post,* published August 24, 2006. Although Ivins said in this letter that "Jews are God's chosen," he imparted a sharply different impression of his viewpoint regarding Judaism to some scientific colleagues. When Lesley Russell, then a fellow researcher at the Defense Department's medical research university, once objected to holding exams on Yom Kippur, Ivins startled her with his retort: "Easter was the anniversary of the time your people killed my Lord." Author's interviews with Lesley Russell and Alison O'Brien, July 29, 2009.

27. FBI summary of interview on October 23, 2007, with an acquaintance of Bruce Ivins.

CHAPTER 25: THE REST OF US

1. E-mail from Bruce Ivins to Mara Linscott, September 26, 2001, in which Ivins wrote in part: "I just heard tonight that the Bin Laden terrorists for sure have

anthrax and sarin gas . . . Osama Bin Laden has just decreed death to all Jews and all Americans. But I guess that doesn't mean a lot to the ACLU."

2. E-mail from Bruce Ivins to Mara Linscott, July 6, 2000.

3. The FBI took custody of Ivins's RMR-1029 flask in mid-2004 after it became apparent that he and others at USAMRIID may not have submitted all of the isolates of Ames strain anthrax in their control, as called for in a federal subpoena. It was only after the FBI's outside team of scientists analyzed RMR-1029 independent of Ivins's submitted sample that an apparent match was found between it and the attack material. This ultimately raised serious questions among investigators because the sample of RMR-1029 that Ivins submitted to the investigation on April 10, 2002, did not match.

4. FBI agent Scott Stanley's notes of the instructions voiced by Patricia Worsham at the meeting on March 29, 2002, included a diagram of all scientists sitting at the table with them, including Ivins. However, Stanley's notes were unknown to Agents Lawrence Alexander and Darin Steele when they questioned Ivins on November 1, 2007. Stanley's notes were not relocated until spring 2008, at which point they became a tool in showing that Ivins appeared to have knowingly flouted Worsham's instructions and the terms of the federal subpoena with his submission of a sample of anthrax from his flask of RMR-1029 on April 10, 2002.

5. Author's interview with Scott Stanley, August 10, 2010. See also Justice Department report on the anthrax investigation, "Amerithrax Investigative Summary," issued on February 19, 2010.

6. The federal subpoena requiring scientists at USAMRIID to submit samples of Ames strain anthrax was dated February 15, 2002; it specified: "[I]f the stock is an agar culture, do not use a single colony, but rather use an inoculum taken across multiple colonies."

7. Bruce Ivins's February 27, 2002, submission of a sample from his flask of anthrax inventoried as RMR-1029 was rejected because he used the wrong type of test tubes. The other half of the sample was sent to Paul Keim's lab at Northern Arizona University. Keim stored the test tubes, unexamined, until 2006.

8. Author's interviews with Paul Kemp, September 25, 2008, October 2 and 13, 2008, and December 18, 2009.

9. Unbeknownst to both Bruce Ivins and the FBI, half of the sample of anthrax that Ivins submitted on February 27, 2002, was sent from the FBI's repository at USAMRIID to the lab of Paul Keim, at Northern Arizona University. According to Keim, Ivins's sample had originally been sent to Arizona from USAMRIID by John Ezzell, who was assisting the FBI investigation. According to the author's interviews in 2009 with Ezzell, who at the outset of the investigation established the evidence repository on behalf of the FBI, half of the test tubes constituting the sample actually were discarded by Terry Abshire, Ezzell's lab assistant. The portion of Ivins's sample that remained at USAMRIID had been promptly destroyed because the test tubes used by Ivins did not comply with the federal subpoena of February 15, 2002.

10. FBI summary of interview with Bruce Ivins at USAMRIID on November 1, 2007; author's interviews with Lawrence Alexander, Darin Steele, Edward Montooth, Thomas Dellafera, Kenneth Kohl, and Rachel Lieber, March 2010; John Ezzell and Paul Keim, 2008, 2009, and 2010; and Carl Scandella, March 28 and July 19, 2009.

11. FBI summary of interview with Bruce Ivins as he was driven from USAMRIID to a hotel in Frederick, November 1, 2007; author's interviews with Thomas Dellafera, March 2010, and Scott Stanley, August 10, 2010.

12. Author's interviews with officials familiar with the anthrax investigation, 2008, 2009, and 2010.

13. Federal documents related to the Amerithrax task force's search of Bruce Ivins's office and nearby lab facilities on November 1, 2007. Materials seized were itemized in U.S. District Court on November 9, 2007.

14. Of the potential reward of up to $2.5 million, the FBI and the Justice Department were committing $2 million and ADVO Inc., a direct mail company, was pledging the additional $500,000.

15. Author's interviews with Paul Kemp, 2008 and 2009.

16. Author's interviews with Amanda Ivins, as well as Paul Kemp, Thomas Dellafera, Lawrence Alexander, and other officials familiar with the anthrax investigation, 2008, 2009, and 2010.

17. Bruce Ivins sent the three friendly e-mails to Patricia Fellows on June 7, 2007.

18. Author's interview on June 19, 2009, with C. W. Ivins, who said he learned from Amerithrax investigators that Bruce Ivins had called him a "gun nut."

19. Bruce Ivins's purchases of the three handguns were documented in receipts that investigators found in a search of his house on November 1, 2007. The search also revealed that in February 2006 Ivins completed an application to purchase a fourth handgun.

20. Summary of FBI interview with Bruce Ivins, February 13, 2008.

21. Author's interviews with Amanda Ivins and Paul Kemp, 2008 and 2009.

22. Author's interviews with Paul Kemp and Thomas DeGonia in 2008, and Kemp alone in 2009 and 2010.

23. Author's interview with Kenneth Kohl, September 2, 2010. As of the November 19, 2007, meeting with Bruce Ivins's lawyers, Kohl had been trying to slow the pace of the investigation, wary of moving too far, too soon, with Ivins, as he believed the task force had done earlier with Steven Hatfill. Kohl's position on Ivins had frustrated members of the Amerithrax task force, notably the FBI's Vincent Lisi. It was not until the spring of 2008 that Kohl became convinced of Ivins's guilt, at which point he supported seeking his indictment for the anthrax murders. Kohl told the author that, in his view, he at no point misled either Bruce Ivins or his lawyers about Ivins's evolving status in the investigation. Investigators first told Paul Kemp about the March 29, 2002, meeting and the oral instructions not to "pick" single colonies of anthrax on July 29, 2008, the day that Ivins died.

CHAPTER 26: NOT A SCINTILLA OF EVIDENCE

1. E-mail reply to a question from the author to Edward Montooth on July 19, 2010; author's interviews with Amerithrax investigators, 2010.

2. D. Hofstadter, *Gödel, Escher, Bach: An Eternal Golden Braid* (Basic Books, 1979). The book was awarded the 1980 Pulitzer Prize for general nonfiction.

3. D. B. Searls, "The Linguistics of DNA," *American Scientist Journal*, November–December 1992.

4. Author's interviews with Thomas Dellafera, Kenneth Kohl, Edward Montooth, Rachel Lieber, Lawrence Alexander, and Darin Steele, March 2010.

5. Author's interviews with Lawrence Alexander, March 2010, and Nancy Haigwood, 2009 and 2010.
6. Author's interviews with colleagues of Bruce Ivins and government officials familiar with the anthrax investigation, 2008, 2009, and 2010.
7. Summary of FBI interviews with Bruce Ivins, January 16, 2008; author's interviews with Edward Montooth, Thomas Dellafera, Lawrence Alexander, and Rachel Carlson Lieber, March 2010, and Vincent Lisi, July 8, 2010.
8. Web site posting by Bruce Ivins on February 20, 2007, as cited in a sworn affidavit from U.S. postal inspector Thomas Dellafera in support of obtaining a warrant to search Ivins's house and vehicles, October 31, 2007.
9. Author's interviews with Daniel Borsuk and Armando Garcia, 2010 and 2011. The two investigators found no potential evidence in the basement of what used to be the Ivins family drugstore.
10. Summary of FBI interviews with Bruce Ivins, January 16 and February 13, 2008; author's interviews with Edward Montooth, Thomas Dellafera, Lawrence Alexander, and Rachel Lieber, March 2010, and Montooth and Vincent Lisi, July 2010.
11. Author's interviews with Bill and Ann Hirt, January 30, 2010.
12. E-mail from Bruce Ivins to Ann Hirt, February 2, 2008.
13. D. Willman, "U.S. Attorney's Office Accused of Anthrax Case Leaks; Lawyers for a 'Person of Interest,' Who Was Never Charged in the Deadly 2001 Mailings, Name Three Federal Officials," *Los Angeles Times,* January 12, 2008.
14. Transcript of U.S. District Court proceeding, January 11, 2008.
15. Transcript of U.S. District Court proceeding, February 19, 2008.
16. Author's interviews with Amanda Ivins, 2008 and 2009.

CHAPTER 27: CRAZY BRUCE

1. E-mail from Bruce Ivins to Patricia Fellows, March 11, 2008.
2. E-mail from Bruce Ivins to Patricia Fellows, March 12, 2008.
3. E-mails from Bruce Ivins to Ann and Bill Hirt, March 12, 2008.
4. E-mail from Bruce Ivins to Cheryl Linscott, March 17, 2008.
5. Author's interviews and exchanges of e-mails with USAMRIID spokeswoman Caree L. Vander Linden, September 2008.
6. E-mail from Bruce Ivins to Mara Linscott and Cheryl Linscott, March 19, 2008.
7. Author's interviews with Amanda Ivins, C. W. Ivins, and Paul Kemp, 2008 and 2009; Bruce Ivins's e-mails to Mara Linscott and others, beginning in 2000. When Diane Ivins called for an ambulance on March 19, 2008, she told the dispatcher that she believed her husband had taken too many sleeping pills or Valium, possibly with alcohol, according to an investigative report filed by Frederick police officer Ryan Forrest and a supplemental report by Detective Gene Alston.
8. Author's interviews with Amanda Ivins, 2008 and 2009, and Paul Kemp, January 4, 2010. Although Amanda told the author that her mother said to her more than once that Bruce had tried to kill himself on March 19, 2008, Diane spoke differently that afternoon to Frederick police officer Ryan Forrest. He questioned her inside the house, moments after Bruce Ivins was placed in an ambulance. According to Officer Forrest's report: "I asked Ms. Ivins if she be-

lieved that her husband was attempting to commit suicide and she stated 'no.' Ms. Ivins stated Mr. Ivins had new medication and that she believed he took the wrong one by mistake. . . . I advised Ms. Ivins that I was conducting an investigation and wanted to make sure Mr. Ivins was not attempting to harm himself. Ms. Ivins assured me that her husband would never harm himself." Forrest also wrote that Diane Ivins "was very uncooperative and repeatedly requested that I leave the residence."

9. Inventory of items recovered by the FBI from Bruce Ivins's household trash on the morning of April 22, 2008.
10. Author's interviews with Amanda Ivins, December 3 and 18, 2008.
11. Ibid.

CHAPTER 28: NOT A KILLER AT HEART

1. Author's interviews with Paul Keim, Edward Montooth, Rachel Lieber, and Scott Stanley, 2009, 2010, and 2011.
2. E-mails from Bruce Ivins to Patricia Fellows, March 11 and 12, 2008.
3. Author's interview with Judith McLean, June 7, 2010.
4. E-mails from Bruce Ivins to Mara Linscott, June 27, July 4 and 6, August 12 and 14, 2000, and December 15, 2001; message posted by Bruce Ivins on GreekChat.com under a pseudonym, Prunetacos, September 3, 2006.
5. Transcripted conversation between Bruce Ivins and Patricia Fellows, on June 5, 2008. The conversation was recorded by the FBI and was included in the Justice Department report on the anthrax investigation, "Amerithrax Investigative Summary," issued on February 19, 2010.
6. Author's interviews with Lawrence Alexander, March 11, 2010, and Rachel Lieber, August 27, 2010.
7. One of the e-mail addresses and passwords created by Bruce Ivins was docsnivi54, perhaps borrowed from the name given the "liver stimulant" concocted by his pharmacist grandfather, C. Wilbur Ivins, and proudly touted by Bruce's pharmacist father, Randall Ivins.
8. Author's interviews with Paul Kemp, 2008, 2009, and 2010.
9. If Bruce Ivins had confessed to the anthrax letter attacks during the "off-the-record" session with the investigators on June 9, 2008, the terms of his limited immunity grant may well have allowed prosecutors to use that statement against him if, at trial, Ivins's lawyers proclaimed his innocence.
10. The photocopied anthrax-laced letter addressed to Tom Brokaw and the *New York Post* did not include boldfaced symbols for the other two nucleotides in the DNA sequence of an organism, C for cytosine and G for guanine.
11. FBI summaries of interviews with Bruce Ivins on February 13, 2008, and June 9, 2008; author's interviews with Amerithrax investigators, 2010 and 2011. When Ivins was asked by the FBI on February 13, 2008, which books he had given to Patricia Fellows, he failed to mention *Gödel, Escher, Bach: An Eternal Golden Braid,* but he did cite two others: *Vaccine A,* the 2004 book by Gary Matsumoto regarding anthrax vaccinations administered to U.S. service personnel, and *The Anthrax Letters,* Leonard Cole's 2003 book. Fellows told investigators that Ivins became angry when she informed him that she had not read *Gödel, Escher, Bach;* she said she ignored his demand that she return it.
12. E-mail from Bruce Ivins to Mara Linscott, July 26, 2000.

13. FBI summary of interview with Bruce Ivins on June 9, 2008; author's interviews with government officials familiar with the anthrax investigation, 2010.

14. Author's interviews with Amerithrax task force officials Thomas Dellafera, Kenneth Kohl, Edward Montooth, Rachel Lieber, Lawrence Alexander, and Darin Steele, March 2010.

15. In conversations with the author, both Douglas R. Hofstadter and David B. Searls said that Bruce Ivins may have related the concepts explored in their works to his own realm of microbiology. Hofstadter, who was questioned by the FBI in early 2008, told the author on May 7, 2009, that Ivins might have been "stimulated" by his book, *Gödel, Escher, Bach: An Eternal Golden Braid.* As for the highlighting of the DNA-significant As and Ts in the first anthrax mailing, "It might have felt to him like he was in touch with something cosmic. It's as if he really selected out the As and the Ts." Searls, in an e-mail response to the author on February 17, 2010, said that the search in *Gödel, Escher, Bach* for connections of art and nature to "mindbending logical paradoxes" may have enticed Ivins. "If Ivins was prone to grandiosity or slightly unhinged, this would be a way of associating the 'secrets of the universe' to his own work in microbiology." In a follow-up response to the author on February 24, 2010, Searls said that both *GEB* and his 1992 article, "The Linguistics of DNA," "seek mathematical order in nature, which may have appealed to his religiosity. Both works are related to cryptography, which evidently obsessed him, and specifically to the genetic code, which is a significant part of the government's case. Finally, both works establish a connection between science and more humanistic pursuits."

16. E-mail from Bruce Ivins to unidentified Army recipients, June 10, 2008.

17. The federal investigators were confident they could prove that, contrary to his assertion, Bruce Ivins did receive detailed and timely instructions for submitting samples of anthrax to the FBI repository, including on March 29, 2002, when he was present at the meeting where USAMRIID scientist Patricia Worsham explained the specifics of the instructions while stressing their importance to the investigation, according to notes taken during the session by a participating FBI agent-scientist, Scott Stanley. This was twelve days before Ivins submitted a sample, on April 10, 2002. In his June 9, 2008, interview with the investigators, Ivins said that he was aware of no instructions until he received an e-mail on May 24, 2008, from a USAMRIID colleague, John Ezzell. But the investigators could point to both the March 29, 2002, meeting and a phone call Ivins made to FBI agent Scott Decker on February 27, 2002, informing him that he would submit a sample of anthrax "per subpoena today," according to the agent's notation of the conversation. The subpoena referred to was dated February 15, 2002, and it contained detailed instructions about how the sample was to be prepared.

18. FBI summary of interview with Bruce Ivins, June 9, 2008; Justice Department report on the anthrax investigation, "Amerithrax Investigative Summary," issued on February 19, 2010.

19. Author's interviews with Paul Kemp and Thomas DeGonia and with other lawyers familiar with the anthrax investigation, 2008, 2009, and 2010.

20. Author's interview with C. W. Ivins, June 8, 2009.

21. Author's interviews with Amanda Ivins, December 3 and 4, 2008, and January 8, 2009, and Paul Kemp, September 25, 2008.

22. The author, at the time a reporter for the *Los Angeles Times,* was the stranger who approached Steven Hatfill on the afternoon of June 27, 2008, at the Washington, D.C., intersection of 18th and M Streets, Northwest.

23. D. Willman, "Anthrax Subject Receives Payout," *Los Angeles Times,* June 28, 2008.

24. Author's interview with Steven Hatfill, June 27, 2008.

25. Author's interview with Russell Byrne, November 16, 2008.

26. Author's interviews with Paul Kemp, August 29 and September 25, 2008, and Rachel Lieber, March 20, 2011.

27. Posting by Bruce Ivins, writing as Goldenphoenix, on the Web site GreekChat.com, July 7 and 8, 2008. In his profile as Goldenphoenix, Ivins described his interests as "Lurking, observing," and his occupation, "Preparing potions."

28. Postings by Bruce Ivins, writing as bruceivi, on YouTube, July 2008. See D. Willman, "Ivins Claimed He Knew Who Sent Anthrax," *Los Angeles Times,* September 25, 2008.

29. S. Huff, " 'You Know What We Do to Moles? We Kill Them!' Did Bruce Ivins Troll YouTube?," truecrimereport.com, August 5, 2008; author's interviews with Lawrence Alexander, 2010.

30. Author's interviews with officials familiar with the Amerithrax investigation, 2008 and 2009.

CHAPTER 29: I'M NOT GOING DOWN

1. Author's interviews with Amanda Ivins, December 3, 2008, and Jean Duley, 2010.

2. Author's interviews with Jean Duley, 2010; Duley's sworn testimony at a hearing in Frederick County, Maryland, District Court on July 24, 2008.

3. Sworn affidavit from U.S. postal inspector Charles B. Wickersham in support of obtaining a warrant to search the personal effects of Bruce Ivins, July 12, 2008; author's interviews with Jean Duley and people familiar with her interactions with Bruce Ivins, 2010.

4. Author's interviews with Jean Duley and people familiar with her interactions with Bruce Ivins, 2010 and 2011.

5. Author's interviews with Jean Duley and others who were familiar with Bruce Ivins's visits to Comprehensive Counseling Associates, 2010.

6. Ibid. Ivins's comment about "ghetto" areas of Frederick referred to neighborhoods on the southwest periphery of downtown that are home to African Americans. The late-night walking that he described appeared to be the same activity that was observed by the federal investigators who followed him.

7. E-mail from Bruce Ivins to Mara Linscott, September 21, 2001.

8. Sworn affidavit from U.S. postal inspector Charles Wickersham in support of obtaining a warrant to search the personal effects of Bruce Ivins, July 12, 2008; author's interviews with Jean Duley and people familiar with her interactions with Bruce Ivins, 2010.

9. The three handguns owned by Bruce Ivins that were seized by investigators who searched his house on November 1, 2007, had not been returned to him as of July 9, 2008.

10. Oral remarks from Jean Duley to Frederick police officer Reed Preece on July

10, 2008, as recapped in an investigation report by Detective Gene Alston, September 9, 2008; sworn affidavit from U.S. postal inspector Charles Wickersham in support of obtaining a warrant to search the personal effects of Bruce Ivins, July 12, 2008; sworn testimony of Jean Duley at a hearing in Frederick County, Maryland, District Court, July 24, 2008; FBI summary of investigative information received by agents on the afternoon of July 10, 2008; author's interviews with Jean Duley and people familiar with her interactions with Bruce Ivins, 2010.

11. E-mail to the author from Paul Kemp, January 14, 2010; sworn testimony of Jean Duley at a hearing in Frederick County, Maryland, Circuit Court on July 24, 2008; author's interviews with Jean Duley and people familiar with her interactions with Bruce Ivins, 2010.

12. Author's interviews with Frederick police sergeant Matthew Burns, January 14 and 19, 2010, and Jean Duley, 2010; Duley's sworn testimony at a hearing in Frederick County, Maryland, Circuit Court on July 24, 2008.

13. Author's interviews with Arthur O. Anderson, May 9, June 29, August 8, and September 24, 2008; "memorandum for record" filed on August 7, 2008, by Anderson with USAMRIID regarding his final conversation with Bruce Ivins.

14. Author's interview with Jeffrey Adamovicz, December 7, 2008.

15. Report filed by Reed Preece of the Frederick Police Department, one of the officers who helped apprehend Bruce Ivins at Fort Detrick on July 10, 2008. Preece also rode with Ivins in the ambulance from Fort Detrick to Frederick Memorial Hospital. Preece's report was summarized in an investigative report submitted by Detective Gene Alston on September 9, 2008.

16. Author's interviews on January 14 and 19, 2010, with Frederick police detective Matthew Burns, who was present when Bruce Ivins was apprehended at Fort Detrick on July 10, 2008.

17. Author's interview with Paul Kemp, September 25, 2008.

18. Author's interviews on January 14 and 19, 2010, with Frederick police detective Matthew Burns, who was present when Bruce Ivins was apprehended at Fort Detrick on July 10, 2008.

19. Author's interview with Paul Kemp, September 25, 2008.

20. Verbatim recording of two messages that Bruce Ivins left on Jean Duley's telephone voice mail on July 11, 2008; author's interview on December 28, 2010, with Daniel Borsuk, the FBI agent who made the recordings from Duley's voice mail. The audio messages were posted online by the *Frederick News-Post*.

21. Author's interviews with Jean Duley, Daniel Borsuk, and Armando Garcia, 2010.

22. Author's interviews with Daniel Borsuk and Armando Garcia, 2010 and 2011, and others familiar with the anthrax investigation, 2008, 2009, 2010, and 2011. The order to open Bruce Ivins's psychiatric records to the Amerithrax task force was made after his death and under seal by U.S. District Court Judge Royce C. Lamberth. See also Justice Department report on the anthrax investigation, "Amerithrax Investigative Summary," issued February 19, 2010.

23. Author's interviews with Judith McLean, April 30, 2010, Daniel Borsuk, June 3, 2010, and others familiar with the anthrax investigation, 2010.

24. Author's interview with Lawrence Alexander, May 3, 2010.

25. Inventory of items seized in search of Bruce Ivins's house on July 12, 2008, as sworn to by FBI agent Marlo Arredondo on July 17, 2008.

26. Author's interviews with Amerithrax investigators, 2009 and 2010.

27. Author's interviews with Amanda Ivins, December 3 and 4, 2008, and January 8, 2009.

28. Author's interview with Paul Kemp, September 25, 2008.

29. Voice mail from Rachel Lieber to Paul Keim on August 21, 2008, in which Lieber described her and other officials' efforts to prevent Bruce Ivins from harming himself.

30. Sworn petition signed by Jean Duley on July 24, 2008, in which she provided reasons why she was seeking a judicial peace order in Frederick County, Maryland, barring Bruce Ivins from having any contact with her; author's interviews in 2010 with Jean Duley and people familiar with her interactions with Bruce Ivins.

31. Audiotape recording of Jean Duley's sworn testimony at a hearing presided over by Maryland district judge W. Milnor Roberts and the judge's signed temporary peace order, July 24, 2008. Although Ivins returned to Frederick that same day, police never served him with the peace order.

32. Bruce Ivins's visit to the local Giant Eagle supermarket to buy, among other things, Tylenol PM was verified by information provided to Frederick Police by Diane Ivins and by store records, according to an investigative report compiled by Detective Gene Alston.

33. Author's interview with Frederick County library spokeswoman, Elizabeth Cromwell, September 5, 2008.

34. Sworn affidavit from FBI agent Marlo Arredondo filed with a federal judge in support of obtaining a warrant to search e-mail accounts established by Bruce Ivins, August 7, 2008; author's interviews in 2010 with Amerithrax investigators, who said the Web site Ivins checked from a computer in the Frederick library was anthraxinvestigation.com, maintained by Edward G. Lake.

35. Author's interview with Amanda Ivins, December 3, 2008.

36. At no point did anyone connected with the Amerithrax task force suggest publicly that Bruce Ivins and Mara Linscott were linked romantically. The author found no evidence that the two ever were.

37. Author's interview with Paul Kemp, September 25, 2008.

38. Frederick Police Department summary of interview conducted by Detective Gene Alston with Diane Ivins on August 8, 2008; notes provided to Frederick police from three paramedics, Kalab Edwards, Robert James, and Jonathon Newman, who responded to Diane Ivins's 911 call; hospital notes from Dr. Madusar Raza, who treated Bruce Ivins and spoke with Diane Ivins at Frederick Memorial Hospital on July 27; author's interview with Alston, July 7, 2010. Newman, in his notes summarizing his efforts to revive and transport Bruce Ivins to the hospital, made brief mention of Ivins's past troubles. "Family states only history is psychiatric in nature past suicide attempts."

39. Author's interviews with Detective Gene Alston, July 7, 2010, and Amanda Ivins, January 13, 2011; contemporaneous hospital notes entered by Megan Shinabery, the nurse who on the morning of July 27, 2008, asked Bruce Ivins whether he had tried to kill himself, and by Karen Snyder, a nurse who that afternoon observed the blue-ink handwriting on Ivins's leg.

40. Author's interviews with Amanda Ivins, June 30, 2010, and January 19, 2011,

and Detective Gene Alston, July 5, 2010; contemporaneous notes from Frederick Memorial Hospital staff, as summarized by Alston in his investigation report, September 9, 2008. Detective Alston's report also stated that FBI agents had observed the arrival of emergency responders to the home of Bruce Ivins. Once he was delivered to Frederick Memorial Hospital, agents who were gathered outside asked a Frederick police officer, Douglas E. Stephenson, to report Ivins's condition to them because they did not want to enter the hospital, according to Stephenson's "Incident/Investigation Report" filed later that day, July 27, 2008.

41. Contemporaneous hospital notes gathered by Detective Gene Alston.

42. Information initially provided by hospital personnel stated that Bruce Ivins's blood had high levels of "Tylenol with Codeine," according to an investigative report filed by Frederick police sergeant Bruce DeGrange on August 1, 2008. The police learned later that codeine was not present.

43. Author's interview with Paul Kemp, September 25, 2008. Although it was Rachel Lieber who informed Kemp about the suicide attempt, he noted that Diane Ivins had earlier left him a phone message, which he had not yet reviewed.

44. Author's interviews with Amanda Ivins, December 3, 2008, June 30, 2010, and January 19, 2011; contemporaneous notes from July 29, 2008, of Dr. Myung Hee Nam, as summarized by Detective Gene Alston in his investigation report, September 9, 2008.

45. Contemporaneous notes from Frederick Memorial Hospital staff, as summarized by Detective Gene Alston in his investigation report, September 9, 2008. Alston noted in his report that, based on his and Diane Ivins's examination of the three prescriptions that Bruce Ivins had filled at Giant Eagle on the afternoon of July 24, 2008, only one of those pills, Seroquel, was gone. According to what Diane Ivins told Alston in a tape-recorded interview on August 8, 2008, officers who entered the house the early morning of the suicide attempt briefly searched Bruce Ivins's bedroom and the bathroom where he was found unconscious. Police conducted no other search of the house. The FBI deferred to the local police and took no part in investigating the circumstances of the suicide. An investigator for the state medical examiner's office, Deborah Frye, who responded to the hospital shortly after Ivins's death, had authority to order an autopsy. Frye concluded that there were no suspicious circumstances surrounding the death that merited an autopsy, according to the author's interview on July 2, 2010, with Kimberly Thomas, an investigator with the medical examiner's office in Baltimore. Frye did not respond to telephone messages left for her by the author. Maryland law grants the medical examiner's investigators wide discretion in deciding whether an autopsy should be performed. Alston's report noted that the police failed to secure as evidence the container with remnants of the reddish orange liquid that Ivins apparently drank in the hours before he was found unconscious in the upstairs bathroom. Alston concluded his report: "The only thing this investigation has not uncovered is how the acetaminophen [Tylenol] was introduced into Bruce Ivins body."

46. Bruce Ivins told acquaintances that Sinclair Lewis's *Arrowsmith* was one of two books that inspired him to pursue a career in science. Ivins made this point in an e-mail to Mara Linscott on July 26, 2000.

47. Author's interview with Amanda Ivins, December 4 and 18, 2008.
48. Author's interviews with Amanda Ivins, December 18, 2008, and January 19, 2011.
49. Author's interviews with Amerithrax investigators, 2011.
50. Diane Ivins declined the author's requests to discuss her husband and their years together. Before hanging up her telephone on September 15, 2010, she said, "No thank you. I'm not interested."
51. Author's interview with Richard Murphy, September 10, 2008.
52. Author's interviews with Amanda Ivins, 2009, 2010, and 2011.
53. In an interview with the author on October 2, 2008, Paul Kemp said he saw no basis to question that Bruce Ivins committed suicide, adding: "I have received ten thousand e-mails from every lunatic in America, suggesting it wasn't suicide."
54. Author's interviews in 2010 with five participants in the July 29, 2008, meeting at the U.S. Attorney's Office in Washington, D.C.: Lawrence Alexander, Thomas Dellafera, Rachel Lieber, Edward Montooth, and Vincent Lisi. In an interview with the author on April 8, 2011, Paul Kemp characterized his remark to Lieber as a "false compliment."

EPILOGUE

1. Congressional Research Service and contract details reviewed by the author show that, as of mid-2010, the manufacturer of the only FDA-approved anthrax vaccine, Emergent BioSolutions Inc., formerly BioPort, had been paid about $1.1 billion by the federal government. Emergent BioSolutions' deliveries to the civilian stockpile are in addition to its sales to the U.S. military, which as of late 2007 had totaled more than $300 million. According to Emergent BioSolutions, its anthrax vaccine was administered to 2.4 million U.S. service personnel from 1998 through mid-2010.
2. D. Willman, "Apparent Suicide in Anthrax Case; Bruce E. Ivins, a Scientist Who Helped the FBI Investigate the 2001 Mail Attacks, Was About to Face Charges," *Los Angeles Times,* August 1, 2008.
3. Author's interviews with present and former government officials familiar with the anthrax investigation, 2009 and 2010. The sources told the author that the senior Bush administration appointee who in advance of the August 6, 2008, news conference advised officials not to mention Steven Hatfill's name was Assistant Attorney General for National Security J. Patrick Rowan.
4. Letter from Jeffrey Taylor to Thomas Connolly, August 8, 2008. Taylor wrote that the "evidence led to one man, Dr. Bruce Ivins, and excluded your client as a subject or target of the investigation. As the Department stated publicly on August 6, 2008, we believe that Dr. Ivins, acting alone, committed the anthrax mailings. . . . We have concluded, based on lab access records, witness accounts, and other information, that Dr. Hatfill did not have access to the particular anthrax used in the attacks, and that he was not involved in the anthrax mailings."
5. K. Bohn, "FBI to Examine Computers in Anthrax Probe," CNN, August 7, 2008; S. Hemingway, "FBI Director: Anthrax Killer Acted Alone," *Burlington* (Vermont) *Free Press,* August 8, 2008; author's interview with Sam Hemingway, February 15, 2010.

6. This question was asked at the August 18, 2008, news conference by Gary Matsumoto, the same journalist who helped produce accounts for ABC News in October 2001, the *Washington Post* in October 2002, and *Science* magazine in November 2003 asserting that the anthrax used in the letter attacks may have been treated with an additive.

7. Transcript of FBI-sponsored news conference to discuss scientific underpinnings of the anthrax investigation, August 18, 2008; the event was attended by the author.

8. D. Willman, "Scientist Admits Mistake on Anthrax; He Says He Was Wrong When He Told Officials That Material Used in the 2001 Mailings Had Been Weaponized," *Los Angeles Times,* September 17, 2008; author's exchange of e-mails with Peter Jahrling on the afternoon and evening of September 16, 2008. Jahrling's admission of error came within hours of a House Judiciary Committee hearing at which Representative Jerrold Nadler, Democrat of New York, cited the Armed Forces Institute of Pathology's 2001 examination of the spores as he pressed FBI director Robert Mueller about the anthrax investigation.

9. Transcript of hearing of the Senate Judiciary Committee, September 17, 2008, attended by the author.

10. The FBI's conclusion that the anthrax used in the letter attacks was not artificially enhanced could have come as no surprise to Senator Patrick Leahy as of September 17, 2008, the date of the Judiciary Committee hearing. Indeed, the FBI had briefed him and his staff on this several times over the years. For instance, on June 6, 2002, bureau officials told Leahy in a private memorandum, "Tests concluded on the anthrax recovered from the letters mailed to Senators Daschle and Leahy and the NY Post do not contain added fumed silica. If present, the nanometer sized spherical fumed silica particles would be easily observed in our analysis." (The underlined emphasis is as the words appeared.) The FBI memo, based on the work done at the Sandia National Laboratories, was obtained by the author. On November 5, 2002, January 9, 2003, and April 23, 2003, FBI lab director Dwight Adams personally provided Senators Daschle and Leahy and their senior staffers with details of the Sandia National Laboratories' analysis, which found that the anthrax used for the letter attacks was not treated with silicon or any other additive.

11. Transcript of hearing of the Senate Judiciary Committee, September 17, 2008, attended by the author.

12. D. Willman, "Senators Question FBI's Handling of Anthrax Probe," *Los Angeles Times,* September 18, 2008. Senator Leahy did not respond to the author's additional requests for an interview, expressed via e-mail and telephone in December 2010 to his spokesman, David Carle.

13. Presentation of Joseph Michael of Sandia National Laboratories at a meeting of the National Academy of Sciences' "Committee on the Review of Scientific Approaches Used During the FBI's Investigation of the 2001 *Bacillus anthracis* Mailings," September 25, 2009, attended by the author. The anthrax put into the letters addressed to Tom Brokaw and the *New York Post* also contained trace amounts of a common laboratory contaminant, *Bacillus subtilis,* another spore-forming bacterium. The parent flask of RMR-1029 did not contain this contaminant, nor did the letters addressed to Senators Daschle and Leahy. FBI scientists and outside experts who assisted the bureau told the author that the

Bacillus subtilis found in the New York letters was likely due to the bacterium's common occurrence in the environment. The scientists affiliated with the investigation said that neither the presence of silicon nor the *Bacillus subtilis* affected their conclusion: RMR-1029 was linked by the DNA evidence to the anthrax used for the letter attacks. These issues also were discussed by government and outside scientists who were involved with the investigation, including Jason Bannan, an FBI microbiologist, at a conference of the American Society for Microbiology, in Baltimore, Maryland, February 24, 2009, attended by the author.

14. Robert Mueller announced that he was seeking the review by a committee of the National Academy of Sciences during his appearance before the House Judiciary Committee on September 16, 2008.

15. "The Amerithrax Case: Report of the Expert Behavioral Analysis Panel," August 2010.

16. Author's interviews with Richard O. Spertzel, including on May 21, 2010.

17. Author's interview with Randall J. Larsen, September 19, 2009.

18. The staying power of the unsupported claim made in the May 1, 2002, *JAMA* article by Thomas Inglesby et al. was demonstrated more than a year later: In fall 2003, *Science* magazine published a report that prominently cited the *JAMA* article's statements that the anthrax sent to Senator Tom Daschle was of "weapons grade" and had been "treated to reduce clumping." See G. Matsumoto, "Anthrax Powder: State of the Art? Although the Investigation Seems Focused on the Idea That the Senate Powder Could Have Been 'Homemade,' Some Experts Say That's Improbable," November 28, 2003.

19. Tara O'Toole, the lead co-author with Thomas Inglesby of the May 2002 *JAMA* article, was confirmed by the U.S. Senate in November 2009 to her appointment by President Obama as undersecretary of science and technology within the Department of Homeland Security.

20. Web posting by Meryl Nass on February 21, 2010. See: http://anthraxvaccine .blogspot.com/2010/02/fbi-case-closed-and-ivins-did-it.html. Nass, whose criticisms of the evidence against Bruce Ivins were quoted by outlets such as the *Washington Post,* the Associated Press, and the *Hartford Courant,* said earlier under oath that she believed "a government program" had tried to burn down her house in Freeport, Maine. Nass said a "diagnosis of exclusion" led her to conclude that she was targeted because of talks she gave in 1999 to Air Force pilots in which she disparaged the military's mandatory anthrax vaccine program. Nass's testimony came in a sworn deposition, October 9, 2006, in Steven Hatfill's defamation lawsuit against Nicholas Kristof and the *New York Times.*

21. Web posting by Barry Kissin on February 22, 2010. See http://anthrax vaccine.blogspot.com/2010/02/fbi-case-closed-and-ivins-did-it.html.

22. Comments made by Lew Weinstein to a videographer in Washington, D.C., on November 29, 2010, and posted by Weinstein on his Web site, Case Closed. See http://www.youtube.com/user/americassurvival#p/u/4/4zI69unuq6A.

23. Correspondence delivered to the National Academy of Sciences committee examining scientific aspects of the anthrax investigation and signed by Barbara Hatch Rosenberg, Stuart Jacobsen, and Martin Hugh-Jones, July 22, 2010.

24. For Colin Powell's comments, see G. Kessler, "Powell Says New Data May

Have Affected War Decision," *Washington Post,* February 3, 2004. For the financial cost of the Iraq War, see A. Belasco, "The Cost of Iraq, Afghanistan and Other Global War on Terror Operations Since 9/11," Congressional Research Service, July 16, 2010. For the war deaths of Americans and Iraqis, see H. Fischer, "Iraq Casualties: U.S. Military Forces and Iraqi Civilians, Police, and Security Forces," Congressional Research Service, February 25, 2010; V. B. Grasso, B. Webel, and S. Szymendera, "The Defense Base Act (DBA): The Federally Mandated Workers' Compensation System for Overseas Government Contractors," Congressional Research Service, April 9, 2010. Of the more than 5,000 American deaths in Iraq, about 4,400 were military personnel and the remainder were civilian contractors.

25. Author's interview with Tom Ridge, October 22, 2009. In a memoir, Ridge also said that "many" officials in the Bush administration believed that the anthrax letter attacks were linked to Iraq. See T. Ridge with L. Bloom, *The Test of Our Times* (Thomas Dunne Books, 2009).

26. U.S. Defense Department transcript of phone interview with Paul Wolfowitz conducted by Karen DeYoung of the *Washington Post* on May 28, 2003, http://www.defense.gov/transcripts/transcript.aspx?transcriptid=2676.

27. Author's interview with Paul Wolfowitz, November 30, 2010.

28. Ibid.

29. Testimony of Defense Secretary Donald Rumsfeld to the House Armed Services Committee, September 18, 2002, and the Senate Armed Services Committee, September 19, 2002.

30. G. W. Bush, *Decision Points* (Crown, 2010).

31. Sworn testimony given at a hearing of the U.S. House Energy and Commerce Committee's subcommittee for oversight and investigations, October 4, 2007. Details of the federal government's funding for an exponential increase in specially equipped biocontainment laboratories were provided by Keith Rhodes, chief technologist of the U.S. Government Accountability Office, and two specialists from nonprofit organizations, Edward Hammond of the Sunshine Project, and Alan Pearson of the Center for Arms Control and Nonproliferation. Rhodes, Hammond, and Pearson said that, as of fall 2007, approximately four hundred facilities and fifteen thousand researchers and other lab personnel were handling biological weapons agents. Also, author's interviews with Alan Pearson, 2009, and Edward Hammond, September 1, 2010. Record-keeping ambiguities may explain why the number of such facilities cited later by the Centers for Disease Control is lower. Von Roebuck, a spokesman for the CDC, which licenses the biocontainment labs, told the author on September 3, 2010, that as of that date, 249 BSL-3 labs, 7 BSL-4 labs, and a total of 11,457 scientists were licensed to handle the "select" list of biological agents.

32. Ibid. Level 3 labs are designed for work with organisms that can cause death in humans, such as anthrax, tularemia, and plague. Level 4 labs are for work with pathogens that also cause death but for which there is no known cure.

33. Meeting of the National Science Advisory Board for Biosecurity, "Public Consultation for Personnel Responsibility," Bethesda, Maryland, April 3, 2009.

34. *Hardball with Chris Matthews,* MSNBC, October 17, 2001.

35. In an interview with the author on September 11, 2010, David Franz said that although he believed it was possible that Bruce Ivins was the perpetrator, he

was not convinced of his guilt. Franz cited two reservations: His own lingering suspicion that the anthrax used in the letter attacks may have been artificially treated by a foreign sponsor; and the unproven speculation, promoted in early 2002 by Thomas Inglesby and Tara O'Toole, that one of the September 11 hijackers may have contracted a skin-anthrax infection in mid-2001. Looking forward, Franz said he viewed as "very unlikely" the threat of a wayward insider at any U.S. biodefense research facility.

36. Remarks of P. Frederick Sparling at a meeting of the National Science Advisory Board for Biosecurity's Working Group on Personnel Reliability.
37. "Enhancing Personnel Reliability Among Individuals with Access to Select Agents," report of the National Science Advisory Board for Biosecurity, May 2009.
38. Author's interview with Paul Keim, September 1, 2010.

APPENDIX: THE CASE AGAINST BRUCE IVINS

1. Author's interview with Gerard Andrews, June 19, 2009.
2. J. Warrick, M. W. Thompson, and A. C. Davis, "Scientists Question FBI Probe on Anthrax; Ivins Could Not Have Been Attacker, Some Say," *Washington Post*, August 3, 2008.
3. E-mail from Bruce Ivins to a scientist at the privately owned Battelle Memorial Institute, September 20, 2001.
4. Author's interview with John Ezzell, September 19, 2010.
5. Author's interview with John Ezzell, February 15, 2009. William Patrick, the microbiologist who helped lead the Army's offensive biological weapons program, told the author on January 9, 2009, he was convinced that Bruce Ivins, using equipment at USAMRIID, could have dried the anthrax used for the mailings. "The beauty of anthrax is you can dry it any damn way you want, and not kill the spores," Patrick said.
6. The weight of the anthrax contained in the envelope addressed to Senator Leahy was noted in a document used by the FBI to brief officials from the CIA on April 12, 2002. In multiple interviews with the author, Ezzell recalled that the Leahy anthrax weighed about nine tenths of a gram.
7. Douglas Beecher, the FBI microbiologist, underscored the apparent impossibility of determining precisely how much anthrax was loaded into the letters in a phone conversation on October 22, 2001, with a physician at the Centers for Disease Control. Beecher's contemporaneous notes of that conversation state: "It is not known (nor can it be known) how the spores escaped from the letters, or how much of each powder escaped during processing. Each letter may have differed depending on the integrity of the envelope, the energy imparted during handling, etc."
8. Douglas Beecher described his efforts to grow an anthrax simulant with a high concentration of spores during a presentation at Rutgers University on March 26, 2009. His presentation was titled, "Amerithrax: One FBI Scientist's Account of Forensic Microbiology and Investigating the 2001 Anthrax Attacks." The lab equipment that Beecher used to grow and dry *Bacillus cereus* included an incubator, a centrifuge, and a lyophilizer.
9. Author's interviews with Peter Setlow, April 24, 2008, and May 29, 2010. On

one occasion early in the investigation, in June 2002, Setlow, along with other outside experts, was invited to Washington by the FBI for a consultation regarding the growth and drying of *Bacillus* spores.

10. In interviews with the author, John Ezzell said that "three hundred to four hundred" Petri dishes, or blood agar plates, of anthrax could be grown simultaneously within a single incubator at USAMRIID. Both Ezzell and another microbiologist with experience preparing anthrax, James Burans, told the author during interviews in 2009 and 2010 that it would take a matter of days to grow enough plates of anthrax to yield one gram of finished material.

11. Author's interviews in March and April 2010 with Darin Steele, an FBI scientist and agent who frequently entered and made observations within the laboratory used by Bruce Ivins at USAMRIID. The presence of hundreds of flasks stored in that lab was pointed out in the Justice Department report on the anthrax investigation, "Amerithrax Investigative Summary," released on February 19, 2010.

12. Bruce Ivins's unaccounted-for quantity of RMR-1029 anthrax was cited in the Justice Department report.

13. The lax control of dangerous pathogens at USAMRIID was underscored by an inventory conducted by the Army in early 2009. Officials found more than 9,200 samples in refrigerators and freezers that had not been logged in the institute's database, meaning the materials were stored without documented controls. The unaccounted-for materials included vials containing anthrax, Ebola virus, botulinum toxin, and the bacterium that causes tularemia. See N. Hernandez, "Inventory Uncovers 9,200 More Pathogens; Laboratory Says Security Is Tighter, but Earlier Count Missed Dangerous Vials," *Washington Post,* June 18, 2009; Y. Bhattacharjee, "Discovery of Untracked Pathogen Vials at Army Lab Sparks Concerns," *Science*, June 26, 2009.

14. Prepared remarks by Richard Spertzel, presented at hearing of the House International Relations Committee, December 5, 2001.

15. R. Spertzel, "Bruce Ivins Wasn't the Anthrax Culprit," *Wall Street Journal,* August 5, 2008.

16. Author's interviews with Richard Spertzel, May 25, 2009, and May 21 and 31, 2010.

17. G. Gugliotta and G. Matsumoto, "FBI's Theory on Anthrax Is Doubted; Attacks Not Likely Work of 1 Person, Experts Say," *Washington Post,* October 28, 2002.

18. G. Matsumoto, "Anthrax Powder: State of the Art? Although the Investigation Seems Focused on the Idea That the Senate Powder Could Have Been 'Homemade,' Some Experts Say That's Improbable," *Science*, November 28, 2003.

19. Author's interviews with Joseph Michael and government scientists familiar with the anthrax investigation, 2009 and 2010.

20. D. Shoham and S. M. Jacobsen, "Technical Intelligence in Retrospect: The 2001 Anthrax Letters Powder," *International Journal of Intelligence and Counterintelligence,* March 1, 2007.

21. B. Ross, C. Isham, C. Vlasto, and G. Matsumoto, "Troubling Anthrax Additive Found," ABCNEWS.com, October 26, 2001. In response to written questions from the author, Gary Matsumoto declined on December 22, 2010, to comment on the earlier media accounts that he helped produce.

22. See *Review of the Scientific Approaches Used During the FBI's Investigation of the 2001 Anthrax Letters* (Washington, D.C.: National Academies Press, 2011).

23. Author's interviews with scientists experienced in handling *Bacillus* spores, including Peter Setlow, John Ezzell, Paul Keim, and James Burans, 2008, 2009, and 2010.

24. The research documenting the propensity of anthrax spores to absorb silicon from growth medium was led by Peter Weber, a chemist at the Lawrence Livermore National Laboratory. Weber presented his team's results on September 25, 2009, to the National Academy of Sciences committee that reviewed aspects of the Amerithrax investigation. Other peer-reviewed research has documented the natural presence of silicon in a closely related species of *Bacillus*. See M. Stewart, A. P. Somlyo, A. V. Somlyo, H. Shuman, J. A. Lindsay, and W. G. Murrell, "Distribution of Calcium and Other Elements in Cryosectioned *Bacillus cereus* T Spores, Determined by High-Resolution Scanning Electron Probe X-Ray Microanalysis," *Journal of Bacteriology,* July 1980. The article reported an "unexpectedly high concentration of silicon" found in the spore coat of *Bacillus cereus*. See also R. Hirota, Y. Hata, T. Ishida, and A. Kuroda, "The Silicon Layer Supports Acid Resistance of *Bacillus cereus* Spores," *Journal of Bacteriology,* January 2010. The article reported that silicon was found to exist naturally inside the spores of *Bacillus cereus*.

25. *Review of the Scientific Approaches Used During the FBI's Investigation of the 2001 Anthrax Letters* (Washington, D.C.: National Academies Press, 2011).

26. Author's interviews with Joseph Michael and Dwight Adams, 2009, 2010, and 2011.

27. *Review of the Scientific Approaches Used During the FBI's Investigation of the 2001 Anthrax Letters* (Washington, D.C.: National Academies Press, 2011).

28. Author's interview with Dwight Adams, February 23, 2011. Adams was not contacted by the National Academy's review committee.

29. All four of the signature mutations, or morphs, were found in samples from the letters addressed to the *New York Post* and to Senators Tom Daschle and Patrick Leahy. Because of mishandling of the letter to Tom Brokaw by New York City health officials, not enough anthrax could be retrieved to test for the morphs.

30. *Review of the Scientific Approaches Used During the FBI's Investigation of the 2001 Anthrax Letters* (Washington, D.C.: National Academies Press, 2011).

31. The report by the committee of the National Academy of Sciences praised the FBI's efforts to develop well-validated tests, called assays, but criticized the bureau for not being more "efficient." For example, in its finding 5.6, the committee said, "The development and validation of variant morphotype mutation assays took a long time and slowed the investigation. The committee recognizes that the genomic science used to analyze the forensic markers identified in the colony morphotypes was a large-scale endeavor and required the application of emerging science and technology. Although the committee lauds and supports the effort dedicated to the development of well-validated assays and procedures, looking toward the future, these processes need to be more efficient."

32. See "Criminal Jury Instructions for the District of Columbia," Bar Association of the District of Columbia.

33. Author's interviews with Peter Setlow and Paul Keim, 2009 and 2010.

34. Examples of Bruce Ivins's contempt for tabloids, including the *National Enquirer,* included a letter he wrote to the *Frederick News-Post,* published April 12, 1997, in which he mocked a recent editorial that questioned the safety of manufacturing of anthrax and other biowarfare vaccines at Fort Detrick. Ivins wrote that the editorial used "words that would do a tabloid proud," adding, "What is being proposed is a vaccine production facility, not a lethal biological agent production facility. The only way I can think of being seriously injured by anthrax or plague vaccine is to get plunked on the head by a vial of the stuff." As for the *National Enquirer,* Ivins said in an e-mail on May 21, 1999, to W. Russell Byrne: "I wonder when the National Enquirer will come out with its headlines on 'Guinea Pig Soldiers Get Killer Vaccine'"; and, Ivins wrote in a July 7, 2000, e-mail to Mara Linscott: "I certainly don't want to see any headlines in the National Enquirer, 'PARANOID MAN WORKS WITH DEADLY ANTHRAX.'"

35. The electronic card records at USAMRIID showed that, during nighttime hours from January through July 2001, Bruce Ivins spent a total of 8 hours, 48 minutes in the hot suite, an average of 1¼ hours per month. Starting in mid-August 2001, his hours surged noticeably: In August he logged 11 hours, 15 minutes; in September, 31 hours, 28 minutes; and in October, 16 hours, 13 minutes. In November, Ivins was down to 6 hours, 20 minutes, and in December 2001, 3 hours, 4 minutes.

36. Author's interviews with Amerithrax investigators in 2009 and 2010; Justice Department report on the anthrax investigation, "Amerithrax Investigative Summary," issued on February 19, 2010.

37. The National Academy of Sciences committee that reviewed aspects of the anthrax investigation examined the circumstances surrounding Bruce Ivins's disputed sample, which he submitted on April 10, 2002. The committee concluded that "the evidence is strongly suggestive that the disputed sample was not taken from RMR-1029." The probability of a sample being taken from RMR-1029 but testing negative for all four morphs "might be on the order of 1 percent," the committee said. See *Review of the Scientific Approaches Used During the FBI's Investigation of the 2001 Anthrax Letters.*

38. E-mail from Bruce Ivins to Mara Linscott, September 26, 2001.

39. In e-mails or other statements, Bruce Ivins sought to implicate a total of seven present or former colleagues in the anthrax letter attacks: John Ezzell, Joseph Farchaus, Patricia Fellows, Gregory Knudson, Henry Heine, Erick Henchal, and Mara Linscott. Ivins offered no credible basis for his allegations and the Amerithrax investigation found that none of those named by Ivins had any role in the attacks.

40. "The Amerithrax Case: Report of the Expert Behavioral Analysis Panel," August 2010.

INDEX

ABOUT THE AUTHOR

DAVID WILLMAN is an investigative journalist whose work has prompted major public reforms—including a ban in 2005 of drug company payments to government scientists at the U.S. National Institutes of Health. He was awarded the Pulitzer Prize for investigative reporting in 2001 for articles in the *Los Angeles Times* exposing how unsafe prescription drugs had been approved by the Food and Drug Administration. His reporting led to the withdrawal of Rezulin, an aggressively marketed pill for Type 2 diabetes. Willman's many national honors include the top award bestowed by Investigative Reporters and Editors Inc., and, with colleagues, the George Polk Award. His groundbreaking reporting in 2008 on the investigation of the deadly anthrax mailings was honored by the Scripps Howard Foundation as the year's best Washington-based coverage.